THE GOOD YEARS

Books by Walter Lord

THE GOOD YEARS

DAY OF INFAMY

A NIGHT TO REMEMBER

THE FREMANTLE DIARY

The Good Years

From 1900 to the First World War

BY WALTER LORD

Harper & Brothers, Publishers, New York

Library of Congress catalog card number: 59-10585

For

MARGIE HORNBLOWER

Contents

A thirty-two page section of illustrations will be found following p. 148

These were the Good Years . . .

Good, not because rich men rode in private railroad cars and Society gave magnificent parties. Most people rarely traveled, and many went to no parties at all.

Good, not just because the world was at peace. Millions of so-called "little brown brothers" took violent exception to America's fumbling (if well-intentioned) imperialism.

Good, not even because a shirt cost only 23 cents. The child who often made the shirt got only $3.54 a week.

These years were good because, whatever the trouble, people were sure they could fix it. The solutions differed of course—Theodore Roosevelt had his Square Deal, Carry Nation her hatchet—but everyone at least had a bold plan and could hardly wait to try it.

In this sense, the period could be called the Confident Years, the Buoyant Years, the Spirited Years . . . or perhaps named after some bright, hopeful color, like the Golden Years.

It could be done, but such tags are the invention of pundits, social historians, and professional name coiners. To the many varied people who lived through the era—the men and women who wistfully recall marching for suffrage, rebuilding San Francisco, or cheering wildly for Woodrow Wilson—these were, and still are, the Good Years.

THE GOOD YEARS

1900

A New Year

"There is not a man here who does not feel 400 per cent bigger in 1900 than he did in 1896, bigger intellectually, bigger hopefully, bigger patriotically, bigger in the breast from the fact that he is a citizen of a country that has become a world power for peace, for civilization and for the expansion of its industries and the products of its labor."
—Senator Chauncey Depew

A fine, dry snow powdered the sidewalk as William J. Witt and Anna Waddilove, two young German-Americans, entered Liederkranz Hall in Jersey City and stood before the Reverend Rufus Johnson of Trinity Baptist Church. Dr. Johnson eyed his watch for a few moments, then began reading, and pronounced the Witts man and wife at 12:01 A.M., January 1, 1900. The time was important, for the Witts wanted to be the first couple married in the twentieth century.

They were a year too soon. Actually the new century would not begin until 1901. As the newspapers patiently explained, the first century obviously ended with the year 100, so the nineteenth had to end with the year 1900.

Still the Witts weren't convinced, nor were many other sentimental German-Americans. After all, the Kaiser himself said this was the day, and in Berlin at this very minute thirty-three guns were saluting the new era. Addressing his officers, Wilhelm promised the rebirth of "my Navy," so that in the coming century Germany might win "the place which it has not yet attained."

I

Elsewhere, mathematics prevailed, and the big celebration was postponed for another year. Except for the Witts, Jersey City had an uneventful New Year's Eve. The Metropolitan Wheelmen of Boston bicycled quietly to Newburyport. In St. Louis Mr. and Mrs. Thomas Lawler held a candy pull. In New York financier J. Pierpont Morgan played solitaire in his library. Downtown some merrymakers roamed Wall Street, drowning the Trinity chimes with fishhorns, but most people were satisfied with less. At the 28th District Republican Club, the members sipped hot punch while President Charlie Hecht rendered "When the Swallows Homeward Fly."

Yet the idea would not die that there was something special about moving into 1900. That irrepressible brigade who write letters to the London *Times* fired salvo after salvo, arguing that this was indeed the turn of the century. "If," explained the Reverend Grimley, Rector of Norton, "a bride in her hundredth year were to pass from the altar of my church to the vestry, she would give as her age to be entered in the register 99. Her hundredth year would be labeled 99 until its very close."

In New Orleans, a city endowed with a keen sense of romance, people also felt that 1900 marked a fresh start. A boisterous crowd swarmed along Canal Street, gaily saluting an open carriage of girls at the corner of St. Charles. The girls opened up on them with Roman candles. If this wasn't launching a new century, the police shuddered to think what next year would be like.

The New York *Tribune* sensed it too. "No new century began yesterday. Avoid all delusions on that head," intoned the editor, "but those who had to date anything found that there was a queer sensation in writing '1900,' and they felt that something momentous had happened to the calendar."

So in the end the Kaiser, with his flair for the dramatic, was right. A new century is something that's not measured but felt. And nearly everybody felt that New Year's 1900 was a milestone—a time to relish past accomplishments, a time to thrill to the promise of the future.

The newspapers did plenty of both. The *New York Times* on December 31, 1899, devoted nearly four editorial columns to a review of the Nineteenth Century. It proudly paraded the list of inventions—steam engines, railroads, telegraph, ocean liners, telephones, electric lights, even the cash register. They would pave the way for even greater advances. "We step upon the threshold of 1900 which leads to the new century," concluded the editorial, "facing a still brighter dawn of civilization."

Sunday sermons struck the same note. The Reverend Newell Dwight Hillis could scarcely contain himself: "Laws are becoming more just, rulers humane; music is becoming sweeter and books wiser; homes are happier, and the individual heart becoming at once more just and more gentle."

No wonder hopes were high. From coast to coast, the country had never seen such good times. The Portland *Oregonian* called 1899 "the most prosperous year Oregon has ever known." The Cheyenne *Sun-Leader* agreed: "Never has a year been ushered in with more promise." The Louisville *Courier-Journal:* "Business in Louisville was never better, if as good." The Boston *Herald* perhaps summed it up best with an interesting thought: "If one could not have made money this past year, his case is hopeless."

For a man with a little talent, there seemed no limit. Andrew Carnegie, the gnomelike Scotch steelmaster, saw his annual profits double. Coal operators had the best anthracite year in history. The slump of 1893-95 was all but forgotten—since those dreary days Southern cotton goods were up 92 per cent, manufactured exports 88 per cent, glass output 52 per cent. No one noticed that the glass production record was achieved with the help of a ten-year-old child who had to tie stoppers on three hundred dozen bottles a day.

Even the usually discontented farmers were happy. Kansas barns bulged with a bumper corn crop. The cities and towns of the Midwest enjoyed a fantastic Christmas season. A Minneapolis jeweler figured that on one day during the holiday rush his diamond sales ran at the rate of $2,400 an hour.

Sales were high, but prices were low—just the way the system was meant to work. A Chicago couple furnishing a home could easily get a mahogany parlor table for $3.95 . . . a sofa for $9.98 . . . a brass-trimmed bed for $3. Food wasn't much of a problem with corned beef selling at 8 cents a pound. Clothes were equally reasonable—in Denver turtleneck sweaters were eight cents apiece, felt hats 89 cents, top-quality suits $10.65. Wages might be modest by later standards, but a man from Birmingham, Alabama, could still celebrate New Year's respectably, when six-year-old whiskey cost $3.20—for four quarts.

In Washington President William McKinley contentedly faced his annual New Year's reception, when the whole public could file by for the handshake the President so enjoyed. It was another election year, but there were no worries this time. The informal partnership between business and the Administration had proved itself. William Jennings Bryan, the young Democrat who made Wall Street shiver in '96, seemed as remote as his discredited platform of free silver. McKinley could stand with perfect confidence on the brief, irrefutable slogan "The Full Dinner Pail."

But prosperity was only part of the story. An endless stream of exciting discoveries offered concrete evidence of the abundant life ahead. The new X-ray was revolutionizing surgery. Walter Reed's experiments might end yellow fever. The caterpillar tractor would lighten farm work. The gramophone and Pianola would bring joy to the home. Electricity promised untold wonders—not just light but help on all sorts of household chores; some man had even invented a toaster.

Best of all was the motorcar. Its growth had been phenomenal. On April 1, 1898, an adventuresome soul bought the first American machine ever made specifically for sale. By 1900 some eight thousand cars sputtered about the country. Over one hundred taxis graced the streets of New York; Chicago even had a motor ambulance.

The new invention did pose some problems. "The operator," explained one writer, "must combine the intelligence of the driver with that of the horse." Tires cost $40 apiece. In New York cars had to stay out of Central Park, carry a gong, and keep under nine miles an hour. More fundamental, according to *McClure's* magazine, was the difficulty of finding suitable terminology: "The French, with characteristic readiness in getting settled names for things, have formally adopted the word 'automobile' for the vehicle and 'chauffeur' (stoker) for the driver. But we of the English tongue are slower."

4

All this only added to the intrigue. Still a rich man's toy, anyone could see that the motorcar would someday belong to everybody. Already eighty firms, capitalized at more than $380 million, were banking on it.

Countless miracles, boundless prosperity—they would go on and on —it was that simple. And perhaps this feeling that everything was so simple contributed most of all to the optimism and confidence that greeted the twentieth century. Wealth was simple—small boys grew up on Horatio Alger: if you were good and worked hard, someday you would be rich. Rules were simple—nice people didn't mention sex, and even smoking was questionable. President McKinley once cautioned a photographer, "We must not let the young men of the country see their President smoking." Pleasures too were simple. New Yorkers might rave about the Floradora sextet, but most people made their own amusement. Seymour, Connecticut—a typical small town—had its own orchestra, drama group, German band, and Gilbert and Sullivan troupe.

Government especially was happily simple. In 1900 the Navy Department's budget was $55 million. Sixty years later, a single atomic submarine cost as much. Washington offices were pleasantly informal— one administrative clerk liked to keep a hen by his desk. Kind, portly President McKinley was the most accessible of men. "It is not always necessary, though better, to make an engagement to see the President," wrote White House correspondent Albert Halstead. In launching an abortive drive for the 1900 Democratic nomination, Admiral Dewey blandly explained, "Since studying the subject, I am convinced that the office of the President is not such a very difficult one to fill. . . ."

By the same token the future was simple. The rewards would go to the virtuous. "A certain manly quality in our people," observed commentator John Bates Clark, "gives assurance that we have the personal material out of which a millennium will grow."

And what would this millennium be like? As the new century dawned, wise men gave their prophecies and predictions. Perhaps inspired by Mr. and Mrs. Witt's marital enterprise, Mayor Lawrence Fagan of Hoboken saw a "Greater Jersey City" which would eclipse

New York across the Hudson. Professor John Trowbridge of Harvard envisaged a nation-wide network of trolley car lines, binding the country together. Edward Everett Hale thought that by 1975 people might be shot through a tube from Texas to Georgia. Russell Sage thought millionaires were safe, for "they are the guardians of the public welfare." John Jacob Astor predicted a pedestrian's paradise—transparent sidewalks high above the traffic. Ray Stannard Baker, a crack reporter of the day, saw the traffic problem itself nearing solution: "It is hardly possible to conceive the appearance of a crowded wholesale street in the day of the automotive vehicle. In the first place, it will be almost as quiet as a country lane—all the crash of horses' hoofs and the rumble of steel tires will be gone. And since vehicles will be fewer and shorter than the present truck and span, streets will appear less crowded."

Only a few great men refused to peer into the crystal ball. Thomas Edison explained, "I don't care to play prophet to the twentieth century: it's too large an undertaking." When asked about the mission of the dramatist of the future, George Bernard Shaw acidly replied, "To write plays." The New York *World* regretted that the young Irishman didn't take himself more seriously.

No such reticence from H. G. Wells, who was easily the most prolific prophet around. For six consecutive issues the *North American Review* carried his lively "Anticipations." Later events showed some to be a little visionary: for instance, the Anglo-American republic centered east of Chicago. Others were somewhat myopic: "Probably before 1950 a successful aeroplane will have soared and come home safe and sound." Others were just plain wrong: "I must confess that my imagination, in spite of spurring, refuses to see any sort of submarine doing anything but suffocate its crew and founder at sea." But many of Wells' predictions proved amazingly accurate. He didn't guess the words, but he certainly saw air-conditioned houses . . . detergents . . . suburbia . . thruways . . . "togetherness" . . . do-it-yourself . . . and that idea breathlessly voiced by market researchers some fifty years later, "the vast stretch of country from Washington to Albany will be one big urban area."

Unlike some of the seers, Wells thought there would still be wars. On land, victory would depend on balloon power; on the sea, a light

ironclad equipped with a murderous ram. "Unless I know nothing of
my own blood," he explained, "the English and Americans will fight
to ram."

Here was a revealing observation. It unconsciously gave away the
one belief above all others that obsessed many minds as the twentieth
century began. This was the conviction that the British and American
people were bolder, braver, truer, nobler, brighter, and certainly better
than anyone else in the world. As the New York *Evening Post* pointed
out in its New Year's Day editorial on the Boer War, "Englishmen
have, on the whole, taken their unexpected disasters in South Africa in
manly fashion. One can imagine what would have happened in France
under similar circumstances. . . ."

It naturally followed that the future belonged to the Anglo-American
"race." Together with the Germans, explained Professor John W.
Davis, they were "particularly endowed with the capacity for establish-
ing national states, and are especially called to that work; and therefore
they are intrusted, in the general economy of history, with the mission
of conducting the political civilization of the modern world." Kipling
was less pontifical:

> Take up the White Man's burden—
> Send forth the best ye breed . . .

In taking up the burden this New Year's Day, both Britain and the
United States had more than they bargained for. The British were
getting nowhere with the Boers in South Africa. The Americans were
having little better luck in the Philippines, that trying legacy from the
Spanish-American War. And in each nation many people smirked at
the other's embarrassment. Sober minds tried to put things in proper
perspective. *Harper's Weekly* urged Americans to mourn the British
defeats, "if we have a proper pride of race." Good Englishmen gave
an older brother's advice on the Philippines. "I think," Colonel The
O'Gorman told young Senator Albert Beveridge during a fact-finding
trip to the Far East, "you must do nothing but fight them. When we
are in a row with Orientals, that is the way we do. They do not understand anything else."

Senator Beveridge returned convinced. By now he was intrigued by

7

the opportunities offered by the whole Orient. Here was the market America needed when she could no longer absorb her own production. "And just beyond the Philippines," he reminded the Senate, "are China's illimitable markets. We will not retreat from either."

Secretary of State John Hay had his eyes on China too. This very New Year's morning the papers happily announced that Hay had won all the great foreign powers to his Open Door policy. Under its terms each country gave the others equal trading rights in any "sphere of influence" it enjoyed in China. A happy solution for everybody and especially for America—the last power on the scene and the only one without a sphere of influence.

But more than trade was involved. Entirely apart from the commercial aspect, there was something exciting about the Open Door idea . . . something that caught the nation's imagination. Suddenly expansion was no longer a matter of grabbing territory; it was part of the duty of guarding the weak.

"It would be difficult to do a greater wrong to the people of China than to leave the nation to itself," declared D. Z. Sheffield in the January, 1900, *Atlantic Monthly*. "Here is the substance of the matter: China needs protection and guidance even to the point of wise compulsion."

And there was no doubt who had the responsibility. As Senator Beveridge explained, "God has not been preparing the English-speaking and Teutonic peoples for a thousand years for nothing but vain and idle self-contemplation and self-admiration. No! He has made us the master organizers of the world to establish system where chaos reigned. . . . He has made us adepts in government that we may administer government among savages and senile peoples."

So the American traders, diplomats, soldiers, and missionaries marched off to the Orient—parvenu imperialists but with a sense of lofty mission. And even as they went, success seemed in the air. "There are many signs of times," concluded D. Z. Sheffield, "which assure us that the day is not distant when China will be delivered from its effete civilization and will come under the power of those motives which have their source in the vital truths of the Christian revelation."

1900

The Fumbling Imperialists

"A new day has dawned. Civilization will never loose its hold on Shanghai . . . the gates of Peking will never again be closed against the methods of modern man."

—SENATOR ALBERT J. BEVERIDGE

On the morning of April 1, 1900, six of the Americans to whom civilization was committed lay fogbound on the China Sea. Mrs. Edwin H. Conger, wife of the American minister at Peking, was returning from a visit to the States; with her she brought her daughter Laura and four other ladies whom she wanted to show the wonderful things being done for China.

Naturally the fog was exasperating. The more so since Mrs. Conger —by now rather used to diplomatic prerogatives—could do nothing to hurry along the little Japanese steamer *Negato*. "I have to watch myself," she confided to her diary. "The Captain is running this ship and I must hands off."

Her patience was rewarded. The fog lifted, and on April 3 the *Negato* dropped anchor off Tientsin. Handkerchiefs fluttered as an official launch bobbed alongside. Aboard was Minister Conger himself —GOP wheelhorse . . . Civil War veteran . . . close friend of President McKinley.

Ashore the ladies were whisked to the legation's special train, and

9

then ninety miles inland to Machiapu, the rambling station just outside the walls of Peking. A waiting caravan of carts and sedan chairs carried them through the Yungting gate, and now they were in the crowded outer city, with its bustling shops and markets. Continuing on, they passed through another massive wall and into the newer Tartar City. Within its walls and just ahead lay the mysterious Imperial City, and within that the even more mysterious Forbidden City. It was all like a nest of boxes, but the caravan didn't go any deeper. Just before the Imperial City, it turned into the foreign quarter on Legation Street and drew up at the American compound. Fireworks popped and crackled, celebrating the return of the minister's lady.

In no time Mrs. Conger was back in the daily routine—picnics . . . formal calls . . . stiff dinners at the British Legation, where Queen Victoria's portrait seemed to chaperon the proceedings. Far gayer were Sir Robert Hart's lawn parties. The old gentleman was Chief Inspector of the Imperial Chinese Customs; he had been in China forever and by now had accumulated a private brass band. On a more modest scale were Mrs. Conger's own "Wednesday afternoons," when the Continental set tried to adjust to homelike Iowa hospitality.

It was a compact little world completely isolated from the Chinese. Concentrated in the small area between the Imperial Palace on the north and the great Tartar Wall on the south, the diplomatic community visited back and forth, strolled Legation Street, shopped at Imbeck's, and watched each other endlessly. Was Baron de Pokotilov about to wring another concession for his Russo-Chinese Bank? Were the Germans planning to extend their new sphere of influence beyond Shantung Province? Arriving last on the scene, the Americans played a minor role in this political game, but they lived the same way and were equally interested in the latest mysterious visitors stopping at the Hôtel de Pékin.

Completely engrossed in themselves, no one saw much of the Chinese—just the harassed officials of the Tsungli Yamen, as the Imperial Foreign Office was called. Here the diplomats went to complain, or demand some new concession. Beyond that there was little contact. The legation community shared nothing with the rest of teeming, crowded Peking except the heat, the dust, and the endless stray dogs that all seemed to bite.

This April everything was the same as always—only not quite. Visitors to the trading quarter noticed that the price of knives was soaring. Signs appeared in doorways announcing "Swords made here." People's gardeners and houseboys began to disappear. Soon the legation colony noted a new rudeness on the streets—often the unmistakable phrase "foreign devil" snarled by some passerby. Around the end of April posters blossomed on the walls, partly religious mumbo-jumbo but partly very clear indeed: "The will of Heaven is that the telegraph wires be first cut, then the railways torn up, and then shall the foreign devils be decapitated."

The old China hands understood. The native patriotic society colloquially called Boxers—literally "Fists of Righteous Harmony"— was spreading to Peking from the south, preaching its anti-foreign gospel. And it had fertile soil to grow on. Foreign governments had exacted humiliating territorial concessions. Foreign railroads had thrown thousands of boatmen out of work. Foreign missionaries were interfering with local courts when native Christians were involved. The foreigner also proved a convenient scapegoat to blame for flood, famine, and now the drought that parched the country. Nor did it help when a boy arrested for suspicious behavior confessed that he had been paid by foreigners to poison the wells.

It made no difference that the Americans had no sphere of influence, or that the American missionaries were mostly mild men and women innocuously engaged in teaching school. To the Boxers all foreigners were alike; all were to blame for China's troubles.

And to this the Boxers had an easy answer—kill the foreign devils. For those who feared foreign guns and bullets, they had another answer—the Boxers couldn't be hit. Wear the Boxers sash, carry the yellow paper talisman, learn the cant, follow the ritual, and the true believer would be protected. High priests of the movement were happy to demonstrate; bravely they faced "firing squads," and the doubters were quickly convinced . . . unaware that the shots were blank.

Patriotic Chinese flocked to the Boxer banners, and others not so idealistic joined in the lively hope of plunder. The Chinese imperial government looked on passively, and under the circumstances, this amounted to approval.

Here and there, a few Chinese warned their foreign friends. Around the middle of May Dr. Robert Colter, an American physician in Peking for eighteen years, got the word from a grateful native patient. He passed the news along to the U. S. Legation, but made little impression. Writing the folks at home a few days later, Minister Conger assured them there was no danger. Outside on Legation Street, long carts full of swords and spears began coming in from the outer city.

About the same time, Bishop Favier of the French Cathedral heard from his native converts ("secondary devils"), who were also scheduled for slaughter. On May 19, he urged Minister Pichon to send for troops: "Peking is surrounded on all sides and I beg you will be assured I am well informed."

Sir Claude MacDonald, the British minister, was told about the bishop's appeal but he didn't worry. He had been with the Army in Egypt before turning diplomat, and he knew that these colonial storms blew over. A few blocks away a new Boxer poster proclaimed "An admirable way to destroy foreign buildings."

On May 24, the legation district suddenly stirred. Sedan chairs hurried through the streets converging on the British compound. It was Queen Victoria's birthday, and Sir Claude was celebrating with a state dinner. Afterward, by the light of weird colored lanterns the sixty carefully selected guests sipped champagne on the lawn and danced to the music of Sir Robert Hart's brass band. In the servants' quarters red and black cards mysteriously appeared, warning that those who waited on the foreign devils were also doomed.

By the end of the month the diplomatic families were starting as usual for their summer homes in the nearby western hills. Among the early arrivals were the wife of the American first secretary, Mrs. Herbert Squiers, her three children, two governesses, and an attractive house guest from home, Polly Condit Smith. They had barely settled on the 28th, when they saw huge clouds of smoke rolling up from the Fengtai railway junction just below.

In Peking a breathless, dusty messenger clattered up Legation Street, shouting that the Boxers were burning Fengtai station and its sheds. Worse still, they were besieging the Belgian engineers and their families at Chang Hsin Tien some sixteen miles away. The ministers frantically compared notes, not knowing what to do.

Others moved faster. M. Auguste Chamot, Swiss proprietor of the Hôtel de Pékin, recruited a rescue team that saved the Belgians. Dr. George Ernest Morrison, resourceful correspondent of the London *Times,* forgot about his deadline . . . rushed to the hills where he knew the Squiers family were stranded. An hour later Squiers himself borrowed a Cossack from the Russian Legation and dashed off to join them. The little group huddled all night in the flickering light of the Fengtai flames, then slipped back to Peking in the morning.

But it was no longer safe anywhere. In Peking itself, the Boxers were now burning the little trolleys that creaked along the foot of the outer wall. Again Dr. Morrison set out for the scene. He was an incurable wanderer—once he was even court physician to the Sultan of Wazar —but he had never seen anything like this. A howling mob tried to tear him apart. He turned and ran back to the Legation District.

Fortunately, help was coming. The ministers had finally demanded more guards, and the relief train arrived from Tientsin in the last fading daylight of May 31. It unloaded detachments of American, British, Russian, French, Italian, and Japanese marines—340 men altogether. (Some Germans and Austrians would come later.) They had been scraped together on the spur of the moment—so hastily that the Americans came in winter uniform and the Russians forgot their cannon. But they were there. And as they marched toward the Legation District, the Chinese mobs fell back silent. The British consular students knew it was just what the beggars needed; they rushed to greet their men, singing "Soldiers of the Queen."

That was all it took. In a day or so life was normal again. At the Peking Club, the members once more sipped their ices, or complained about Count von Soden, the young German military attaché who played vile tennis and worse billiards.

While Peking relaxed, the provinces blazed in violence. At Yungching two young English missionaries, Harry Norman and Charles Robinson, were seized and beheaded on June 1. At Paoting-fu, thirty-two more missionaries were trapped. The Reverend Horace Tracy Pitkin—a stern, lantern-jawed man of God from Philadelphia—sold his life dearly, firing at the Boxers until his ammunition ran out. More often the doomed missionaries were gentle to the end. "Thank heaven we drove them off without killing any," was one of the last entries in the Reverend Herbert Dixon's diary. When Mrs. Arnold Lovitt of the American Baptist Mission was seized at Taiyuan-fu, she told her captor, "We have done you no harm, but only sought you good, why do you treat us so?" The Boxer carefully removed her glasses before beheading her.

Minister Conger seemed paralyzed. When asked for a military escort to help rescue the American Board Mission at nearby Tungchow, he regretfully explained that he must not risk his marines. The Reverend W. S. Ament sighed, went to Tungchow alone and saved the people himself. In their exasperation, the American missionaries cabled President McKinley direct on June 8. It was a courteous message, appealing for help and pointing out that the Chinese government's policy was "double-faced."

Would the Imperial Telegraph Service forward such an outspoken message? Certainly. Only one change was required: the hyphen must be erased and "double faced" charged as two words.

In a way the incident symbolized the whole struggle. The simple gullibility of the West; the polite, impenetrable ambiguity of Peking officialdom. To the foreigners, this sort of behavior was one more example of Chinese hypocrisy. Actually it was often indecision. The aged, rouge-smeared Empress Dowager sat isolated in her pink palace, pulled this way and that. The court intrigue was incredibly complex —there was even a false eunuch. The vain old woman was generally influenced by the last person who saw her, and Prince Tuan—father of the heir apparent and foe of everything foreign—usually managed to be that. But not always. Sometimes it was pleasant Prince Ching, who thought railways might even help China; sometimes it was crusty General Jung Lu, who knew what a Krupp gun could do. It was all so difficult for an ex-Iowa congressman to fathom.

Then on June 9 the drift became crystal clear. The Boxers burned the grandstand at the race course—the foreign colony's own center of social intrigue. Four young British consular students could hardly believe such villainy was possible. Riding out to investigate, they were mobbed by swarms of Boxers chanting, "Kill! Kill! Kill!" They barely made it back to safety.

Chinese government troops watched with interest from the walls. They took no active part, but their banners bore the legend "Exterminate the foreigner." Rumor spread that soldiers and Boxers together would turn on the legations that night. Nothing happened, but Sir Claude MacDonald had now seen enough. He wired Tientsin for heavy reinforcements. The reply was encouraging—Admiral Seymour would leave at once with nine hundred men.

All next day the legations waited. No one knew that the railway was destroyed. Nor could anyone check; the wires were now out. On June 11 the Japanese Chancellor Sugiyama set out for the station, hoping to pick up some news. He had just passed Yungting gate when some Chinese soldiers appeared, yanked him from his cart, and hacked him to pieces.

Back at the American Legation Minister Conger sat at his roll-top desk, pondering what to do. In the drawing room—a wonderful hodge-podge of Ming vases, Morris chairs and calendars pasted on lacquered walls—Mrs. Conger filled in her diary: "If men think he should do more for them and say unkind things, he does not let it hurt him, and replies kindly but firmly."

Baron von Ketteler, the German minister, believed in action. Years before, when he was military attaché, his blue eyes and handsome mustache made him quite the most dashing blade in Peking. Since then he had served in Washington, married an American heiress, and generally settled down. But he still had a low boiling point, and he reached it on the morning of June 13. Down Legation Street, before his very eyes, came a pony cart carrying a Boxer in full regalia—ribbons, white tunic, red sash, everything. None had ventured so close before, and this man was even sharpening his sword on his boots. The baron personally yanked him off the cart and thrashed him with the heavy cane he liked to carry.

The example was ignored. That afternoon bands of Boxers broke into the outer city and began burning churches. The diplomats did nothing, but once again the Swiss hotelkeeper Auguste Chamot rose to the occasion. He and his young American wife (a McCarthy from San Francisco) rushed to the blazing South Cathedral, brought back a padre and twenty-five nuns.

The fires continued: Asbury Church . . . the blind asylum . . . Sir Robert Hart's customs buildings. When Watson's drugstore went up on the 16th, explosive chemicals sprayed flames all over the trading quarter. Soon they spread to the huge pagoda atop the Chien gate, a famous Peking landmark. The foreign colony gasped to think that a people could do such a thing to their own most cherished possessions. In the Imperial City the Empress Dowager watched grimly from a little hill to the west of the Southern Lake.

The crisis came June 19. That afternoon the Tsungli Yamen delivered eleven red envelopes to the eleven legations. Inside each a polite letter on ruled rice paper explained that relations were broken; the ministers and their staffs must leave within twenty-four hours—specifically, by 4:00 P.M. the following day.

Minister Conger rushed from the American compound, joined his colleagues at the Spanish Legation. Here they sat around, excitedly arguing what to do. To leave would be perilous; to stay would violate all protocol. Finally, it was decided to leave, but to ask for more time. To work out the details, they urged the Yamen to receive them at 9:00 A.M. next morning.

News always spread fast in Peking, but never faster than now. At the American Legation, Polly Condit Smith debated how to fill the single small bag she would be allowed to take—a warm coat or six fresh blouses?

At the American Methodist compound a mile to the east, the missionaries faced a far grimmer problem. Some seven hundred native Christians had come to the place for protection. Evacuation would mean leaving them behind—to certain death. Nor would it help for

16

the missionaries to stay with them; that would draw the Boxers' attention all the more quickly.

In the small hours of the night the missionary leaders penned a desperate plea to Minister Conger: "For the sake of these, your fellow Christians, we ask you to delay your departure by every pretext possible. . . . We appeal to you in the name of Humanity and Christianity not to abandon them. . . ."

Conger was unimpressed. The Legation staff began rounding up ponies and carts for the flight. The missionaries assembled their frightened Chinese schoolgirls . . . broke the news . . . gave them money and told them to scatter when the time came to leave. It was as difficult to say as it must have been for the girls to understand. Men like the Reverend Frank Gamewell had devoted their lives to spreading the ideals of Christ. No matter how hard they tried to justify their departure, they couldn't help wondering whether this was really the Christian thing to do.

On the morning of June 20 the ministers reassembled at 9:00 but the Yamen hadn't answered their request for an audience. The consensus was to wait a little longer. Baron von Ketteler announced he would go anyhow. They said it was dangerous. He replied nothing would happen; he would go unarmed. They pointed out that the Yamen might not meet. He replied he could wait—he was taking along a book and a box of good cigars.

So he set out in his sedan chair, accompanied only by his secretary Heinrich Cordes and a few outriders to lend a little prestige. They had just passed the Arch of Honor on Hata Men Street when a Chinese soldier, with peacock feathers in his hat, stepped out from the curb. He pushed a rifle through the window of the Baron's chair and pulled the trigger.

Minutes later Herr Cordes, wounded and exhausted, staggered into the Methodist compound, where the missionaries were still trying to prepare the schoolgirls to shift for themselves. He shouted that von Ketteler had been assassinated, then collapsed from loss of blood. Runners sped to the legation with the awful news.

Now flight was out of the question. It would simply lead to more massacres. All groups were ordered to the British compound to stand siege until help could come. Again the question arose about saving the Chinese Christians. Again Minister Conger said no: there simply wasn't room. His colleagues seemed to agree. This was too much for Dr. Morrison, the stalwart *Times* correspondent: "I should be ashamed to call myself a white man if I could not make a place for these Chinese Christians."

No answer. So Morrison did something about it himself. With the help of Professor Huberty James, a knowledgeable teacher at Peking University, he wangled the use of Prince Su's palace, or fu, next to the British Legation. The prince wouldn't be using it, and (who knew?) the loan might be a good investment if the allies held out. The argument worked, and now there was room for everyone. "Come at once within the Legation lines," Conger hastily wrote the Methodists; then the wonderful words they could hardly believe: "And bring your Chinese with you."

The missionaries had only twenty minutes to get ready. Just enough to grab the first thing in sight—one lady settled on a hot-water bottle. Then off on the long trek to the Legation district—71 missionaries, wives and children . . . 124 native schoolgirls, strangely lamb-faced . . . 700 Chinese converts staggering under rolls of bedding . . . 4 stretcher bearers carrying the wounded Herr Cordes . . . 20 U.S. Marine guards, tramping along in the sleepless way of men who had seen too much duty.

Reaching the Legation district, the party split. The natives turned off into Prince Su's fu, where 2,000 Catholic converts had already gathered. The missionaries halted briefly at the U.S. Legation; then continued on as arranged, to the British compound.

Here they would be comparatively safe, for Her Majesty's Legation formed the heart of a good defensive position. To the north was the Hanlin Library; its walls were thick and no one thought the Chinese would wreck its centuries of culture. To the east (across the Imperial Drainage Canal that ran through the whole position) lay Prince Su's fu —now strongly held by Japanese marines. The southern front was the great Tartar Wall, forty feet thick. American and German marines held a three-hundred-yard segment along the top; and the U.S. detachment seemed in good hands under Captain Jack Myers, a resourceful Georgian who boasted perhaps the best set of whiskers in Marine history. The west side seemed weaker, but the imperial carriage park at least offered an excellent field of fire.

The whole perimeter measured about a mile and a half in circumference. It included most of the legations ... various foreign banks and stores ... the club ... M. Chamot's beloved Hôtel de Pékin. With luck they could hang on here for a week or so; everything else would have to be sacrificed.

That anyhow was the plan as the Methodists poured into the British compound about noon on June 20. They were the last to arrive, rounding out perhaps the most cosmopolitan garrison in history. Besides the diplomats of eleven different lands, here were scholars, travelers, churchmen, financiers, and statesmen. M. Pokotilov, the mysterious Russian banker, stood muttering to himself, clutching his famous black brief case. Sir Robert Hart seemed lost in thought—perhaps contemplating the wreck of forty years' service in the Chinese government. Dr. W. A. P. Martin, seventy-one-year-old president of the Imperial University, huddled with Dr. Arthur Smith, whose *Chinese Characteristics* was the outstanding book in a field they all now confessed they didn't understand.

Minister Conger's party made a group in themselves. Mrs. Conger, warmhearted but a bit eccentric, was telling people that the whole trouble lay in their minds. Nevertheless, her daughter Laura remained wildly upset and her friend Mrs. Woodward clearly longed to be back in Chicago.

On a lower official level but feeling far superior socially, the Squiers party watched the Congers with tolerant amusement. The first secretary was immensely stylish in the new, clean-cut Arrow collar man fashion—a complete break with the bearded legions of the nineties. He loved books, ceramics, and fine food. The Squierses lacked essentials like everyone else, but it turned out they had enough champagne for every meal.

The American diplomats and their families were all assigned to the doctor's quarters, as Sir Claude struggled to sort out his 414 unexpected guests. This was something he could do with astuteness. The difficult French and Russians got houses to themselves. The Germans and Japanese shared the students' quarters—they seemed to get along well together. The Royal Marines got the fives court. The American missionaries jammed the chapel; the overflow ended up in the loft, floundering among bowling pins, lantern slides and relics from the Diamond Jubilee.

In Sir Claude's own residence the smoking room became a bachelors' quarters; the ballroom a ladies' dormitory. Dr. Morrison and the Hong Kong and Shanghai Bank shared an open pavilion—all the more crowded because the doctor installed his reference library. Another pavilion served the guests of the Hôtel de Pékin. M. Chamot and his American bride stayed behind in the hotel itself, where they ground flour and ran a sort of catering service for discriminating refugees.

Food was in fact the big problem for everyone. Counting the natives in the fu, there were more than 3,000 people to feed. Yet only the American Methodists had collected any stores and these were abandoned at the mission. Some 150 ponies were quickly rounded up—mostly left over from the spring race meeting. Then a few mules and even a cow.

Several nearby shops were also well stocked, but the ministers weren't sure of their authority. This didn't bother Herbert Squiers. In his army days, his scorn for red tape had been the despair of his superiors. Now it came in handy.

As the Chinese deadline approached on the afternoon of June 20, Squiers swept into action. Aided by his fifteen-year-old son Fargo, he collected everything in sight—some sheep he ran across near the British compound . . . eight thousand bushels of wheat at the Broad Prosperity Grain Shop . . . tons of rice stored near the Imperial Drainage Canal. The Chinese kept their shops open and accepted with smiles the informal requisition slips. But around 3:00 the shutters rattled down; little strips of red paper signifying Happiness appeared on the slats; and the proprietors simply vanished.

At 4.00 P.M. sharp a Chinese rifle cracked somewhere north of the

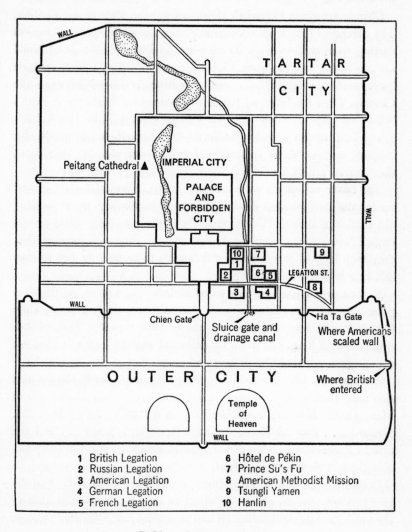

WALL

TARTAR
CITY

WALL

Peitang Cathedral ▲ IMPERIAL CITY

PALACE
AND
FORBIDDEN
CITY

10	7		9
1			
2	6	5	LEGATION ST.
3		4	8

WALL

Chien Gate

Sluice gate and
drainage canal

Ha Ta Gate
Where Americans
scaled wall

OUTER CITY

Where British
entered

Temple
of
Heaven

WALL

1	British Legation	6	Hôtel de Pékin
2	Russian Legation	7	Prince Su's Fu
3	American Legation	8	American Methodist Mission
4	German Legation	9	Tsungli Yamen
5	French Legation	10	Hanlin

Peking, Summer of 1900

French Legation. A French sentry fell shot through the head. The siege was on.

Chinese trumpets brayed in chorus as gunfire erupted on all sides. The defenders caught an occasional glimpse of black-turbaned figures darting from wall to wall. These were no Boxer rabble, but trained soldiers with European guns: General Tung Fu-hsiang's fierce Khansu braves—ten thousand Mohammedan cutthroats feared by even the Chinese. Then the Imperial Bannermen joined in, then Prince Tuan's "Glorified Tigers," then Jung Lu's huge Peking Field Force. Each group had its own garish uniform—the Khansu artillerymen, for instance, sported violet embroidered jackets—but despite their dress, they proved tough, cautious fighters remarkably hard to hit.

The Boxer volunteers were an easier target. Hordes of them moved up for the long-awaited day of reckoning. Screaming curses, waving old flintlocks, muzzle-loaders, spears, tridents, anything—little groups dashed forward in plain sight. If they still felt they were invulnerable, they soon learned otherwise. It didn't seem to matter. As fast as they fell, new believers took their place.

No one ever knew just how many Chinese there were. As the days passed, the estimate climbed from 80,000 to 100,000 to 360,000. Certainly it seemed that way, but of course the number was less. Perhaps Admiral Kempff was close when he estimated 20,000 Chinese troops, not counting the thousands of Boxers and rioters that joined the attack.

Against them was an official force of 450 legation guards. On the plus side they were generally tough and resourceful—men like Gunner's Mate Joseph Mitchell, a mechanically gifted sailor from the U.S.S. *Newark* . . . Colonel Shiba, the little Japanese dynamo . . . and the cynical Baron von Rahden of the Russian detachment, who was probably the best shot in the Far East.

But they were so few. Forty-three of the men had already been detailed to help Bishop Favier, holding out in the Peitang Cathedral to the north, and the remaining 407 had poor guns and little ammunition. The Austrians' machine gun and the Americans' Colt automatic looked useful, but the Italian one-pounder was a museum piece, and the British Nordenfeldt, 1887 model, had a cute trick of jamming every fourth round.

In this crisis, the foreign colony's cosmopolitan complexion proved a great asset. There were, it turned out, a good many accomplished military men present. The polished Captain Labrousse of the French Infanterie de Marine had been passing through, on his way from Tongking to Paris by way of Siberia. Nigel Oliphant of the Imperial Chinese Bank once served in the Scots Greys. That chap Vroublevsky, in town to brush up on his Chinese, was actually a lieutenant in the Ninth Eastern Siberian Rifles. In all, some seventy-five refugees turned out to have military talent and were gratefully added to the defense force.

Still, they were few enough, and it seemed a sickening waste when Professor Huberty James was captured at the very start. He had been checking Prince Su's fu and was returning by the unguarded north bridge over the Imperial Drainage Canal. A little risky, but James loved the Chinese and just couldn't believe they would harm a European. So they caught him easily and hustled him off into the dusk. Two days later his head was displayed in a cage over Tung Hua Gate.

As darkness ended this first day, some of the besieged were mildly startled to see the Italian Minister Marchese di Selvago Raggi sauntering about in evening dress. Most of them were too miserable to care. The night was stifling . . . every child wanted a drink of water . . . the people sprawled on mats and tables seemed to take up far more room than they did in the day. They were apparently arranged just to be tripped over. Outside Chinese bullets criss-crossed the sky, clipping branches from the trees in the hot courtyard.

June 21 was complete confusion. Nothing accomplished; no one in charge. Toward evening Captain Thomann, skipper of the Austrian cruiser *Zenta,* assumed command by virtue of seniority and a vile temper. The results were almost fatal. On the morning of the 22nd Thomann suddenly ordered everybody back for a last stand in the British Legation. The various marine detachments tumbled in, abandoning the French Legation, the Tartar Wall, all the strong points. There was no Chinese attack at the time, and the order seemed idiotic.

The sheer folly of it all blasted the general apathy. It dawned on the ministers that they weren't bound by the seniority rules of the Austrian Navy. They fired Thomann and appointed their host, Sir Claude MacDonald. It was a fortunate choice. Whatever his capacity as a diplomat, Sir Claude was trained in the "hollow square" tradition and this crisis was made for him. He rushed the men back to their posts before the astonished Chinese had time to move in.

The next step was to erect some defenses. A difficult problem, for no one, including Sir Claude, knew anything about fortifications. He and the others were gentlemen trained to fight in the open, not build barricades. The solution came from a most unlikely source. It seemed that the Methodist missionary Dr. Gamewell had planned some excellent defenses for their abandoned compound. Could he, Sir Claude inquired, help here? He certainly could. The Reverend Frank Dunlop Gamewell was no ordinary missionary. Raised in a mechanically-minded family—his father invented a fire alarm system—he had gone to both Rensselaer Poly and Cornell Engineering School. He knew everything about construction.

This remarkable find was too good to waste. Sir Claude put Dr. Gamewell in complete charge of the legation's defenses. He could ignore the whole jerry-built command chain of colonial colonels, gentlemen strategists and obstructive veterans of the American Civil War. From this point on, the defense took a new turn.

Pedaling furiously about on his bicycle, Gamewell seemed everywhere at once. Now he was building a blockhouse by the main gate on the east, now a bombproof for the hospital to the south. The Chinese were beginning to use artillery; this meant stronger earthworks on the north—a seven-foot wall should do. Rumors of Chinese mining on the west—the counter mines should be twelve to fourteen feet deep. And at night his head swam with figures that had nothing to do with missionary work: a Mauser bullet would penetrate one-quarter inch of brick, a Krupp shell fifty-four inches. A thoroughly professional engineer was at work.

Sandbags were needed everywhere, and the women sewed with a vengeance. Caught in the surging spirit, Lady MacDonald donated the legation curtains, sheets, table linen. When these were gone, someone raided Prince Su's palace, and bags appeared made of costly Ningpo silks and tapestry. A nearby clothing store was searched, and one man found a suit he had ordered but never picked up. He put it on, brought the rest of the stock back for more sandbags.

In the midst of the sewing, a dilemma arose. A sentry announced that the bags were too small—he wouldn't risk his neck behind protection like that. When the ladies made them larger, a marine complained they now broke too easily.

As usual, it was Dr. Gamewell who resolved the problem. Cycling up from nowhere (he always appeared magically just when you needed him), he jotted down some figures and told the women, "No matter who tells you to do different, follow these measurements." Then with a polite "good morning" he vanished as swiftly as he had arrived.

Gunfire pounded the new defenses till 11:30 A.M. on June 23, when all fell strangely silent. Suddenly smoke spiraled up from the great Hanlin Library, just north of the legation. Again the enemy had done the unexpected. Until this moment it was assumed that the north was secure, since the Chinese wouldn't endanger their greatest library. Now they were burning it, trusting the flames would spread to the legation.

The alarm bell on Jubilee Tower clanged wildly. All ages raced to the danger spot. While sharpshooters gave covering fire, volunteers dashed into the Hanlin property and hacked at the burning walls, trying to clear away the sections nearest the legation. Bucket brigades formed to help check the flames. Madame Pichon, wife of the French minister, toiled next to a coolie. Mrs. Conger's party of ladies worked as a team. The resourceful Lady MacDonald supplied them with basins, kettles, pans, finally dozens of chamber pots with which the legation was amazingly well supplied.

The battle looked hopeless. The flames roared skyward, feeding on the Hanlin's priceless collection of scrolls and documents. In the compound, children beat at the embers that showered down. On a rockery high in the Forbidden City the Empress Dowager watched with interest, while her current favorite General Tung Fu-hsiang purred assurances that the end was near for the foreign devils.

Perhaps it was a change in wind . . . or the courage that can keep men trying when logic says all is lost. In any case, twilight found the Hanlin in ashes, but the British Legation still intact.

The 24th was the first Sunday under siege, and someone hesitantly asked the Reverend Gamewell, "Are you going to stop?"

"The most worshipful thing," he answered, "the divinest thing to do today is to stretch every nerve to protect these women and children."

Just as well, for it turned out to be a harrowing day. To the north and east, the Chinese battered at Prince Su's fu, and the Japanese barely hung on. To the south, the Russian Bank was blown up and the American compound almost captured. On top of the broad Tartar Wall, hordes of Chinese prepared to sweep the German and American marines off the vital segment bordering the Legation District. If that went, enemy guns would command the whole position. Somehow the marines kept the Chinese off balance until this barricade could be strengthened. The British Legation itself was attacked from the west. Again, the fires . . . again, the clanging alarm bell . . . again, the bucket brigades. This time they faced an added hazard; the Chinese were now so close they lobbed hot bricks over the legation wall. The emergency hospital in the Chancellery filled faster.

They struggled on. June 25, their first horsemeat . . . one of Sir Claude's racing ponies. June 26, U.S. Marine Sergeant Fanning died fighting on the Tartar Wall—neither the first nor the last to go, but he had a jaunty touch that would be missed. June 27, the William Moores had a baby; Dr. Martin, who had a healthy streak of ham, told them to call the child "Siege" because it ought to be raised.

There was a trace of the Old Breed in them all. The Squierses solemnly discussed vintage wines. Miss Cecile Payen, one of Mrs. Conger's guests, pulled out her water colors and began sketching. An English Customs Volunteer sat under fire in the fu, teaching a Japanese marine tick-tack-toe. The militarily inept formed a company of irregulars called "Thornhill's Roughs." They armed themselves with anything left over—one had a *fusil de chasse* decorated with a picture of the Grand Prix.

All the time, their plight grew more serious. And the Chinese always excelled at the tactics that were most nerve-racking—clusters of flaming arrows, sky rockets, hot bricks that showered down from nowhere. Occasionally Boxer fanatics dashed up to the walls carrying bamboo poles with kerosene-soaked rags tied to the end. Usually they were stopped, but sometimes flames mushroomed skyward. The Imperial troops proved poor artillerymen but excellent at using their pet "gingals"—huge two-man guns, sometimes ten feet long, which were aimed like rifles. The shooting, the yelling, the blare of trumpets never seemed to end.

At night the women were especially terrified. Dr. Gamewell understood perfectly, and no matter how busy he was, he always had time to give them a word of encouragement. Standing bashfully outside Lady MacDonald's ballroom, where some of the Methodist ladies were quartered, he would call into the dark, "It's all right—it's never as bad as it sounds."

Welcome words, but as night after night passed with no let up—as day after day the casualties mounted—the besieged began to wonder. How long would they be able to last?

Up to this point, there had been no doubt. They could last until relief came. Admiral Seymour should arrive any day, and in fact, every night the men watching the southern horizon saw hopeful signs. On June 26, the Japanese thought they saw their army's rockets. On June 30, a German officer thought he saw a German naval searchlight. Sir Claude knew the man was wrong: it was clearly a British light. Next morning he posted the following announcement on the community bulletin board by the Jubilee Tower: "This morning at about two o'clock I saw the searchlight of Her Majesty's ship *Terrible*. I recognized it as the searchlight of that ship because it has a very characteristic searchlight."

But the days passed and nobody came. Worse, the messengers that were lowered over the Tartar Wall to make contact just disappeared. Why didn't they carry out their mission and come back as instructed? Where was Seymour anyhow? What was the matter with everybody?

July 2 brought one of those near-disasters that can make men forget all about self-pity. The Chinese almost drove the Americans off their segment of the Tartar Wall. Enemy barricades went up within twenty-five feet of the Marines, pinning them down completely. Something had to be done right away, or the wall—and everything else—would be lost.

Just before dawn on the 3rd, Captain Jack Myers assembled a small force behind the threatened position. Around him crouched his fourteen American Marines, fifteen Russians, and twenty-six British. A few yards away the Chinese barricade loomed black and ominous in the early-morning light. It was a dramatic situation—made for a man like Myers. He leaned toward amateur theatricals and only recently had courted serious trouble with a satire on the Kaiser.

Now he worked his men up to fever pitch. He told them that the Chinese position must be taken . . . that the odds were against them . . . but the life of every woman and child depended on their success. Young Oliphant of the British volunteers thought the whole performance was a bit overdone, but most of the men were tremendously moved. When Myers ended with a shout to charge, they swept forward with a yell, completely routing the surprised Chinese. Two marines were killed in the charge, and Captain Myers tripped over a spear, wounding his knee. He would be out of action indefinitely, but the day was saved.

The victory really made the Fourth of July for the American colony. Previously there had been some rather pointed remarks that the famous U.S. Marines seemed strangely cautious. Now the legation staff proudly celebrated the day with little flags in their lapels. Minister Conger showed everyone the framed copy of the Declaration of Independence that hung in his office—a bullet had pierced the lines that criticized George III. It was quite a conversation piece. Mrs. Conger meanwhile slipped quietly to the little plot where six marines now lay buried. Gently she covered the graves with a silk American flag.

It was a day to think of home—especially for the bereaved Baroness von Ketteler. A lot had happened since she was plain Maud Ledyard, daughter of the president of the Michigan Central Railroad. She had married the titled aristocrat, traveled over the world, faithfully followed the success formula for a wealthy American girl—and what a bleak future now. Miles from home, her husband killed, her own life in danger, no one to turn to except the unbearably correct German Legation staff. In the gray hours of dawn she would stand at her window, pale and grief-stricken. Once she turned and caught the arm of Mrs. Frank Gamewell, who happened to be passing. "I am so alone," she said.

Another time the baroness stopped Mrs. Conger. "No title, no position, no money can help us here," she sighed; "these things mock us." Even Sir Claude might have agreed the day a Chinese cannon ball crashed into the legation's state dining room, grazing the Queen's portrait.

To maintain some pretense of return fire, the defenders desperately kept shifting their four guns. In a single week the Italian one-pounder was used at the British stables, the Tartar Wall, the legation library, the fu, the Hanlin earthwork, the fu again, the stables again, and finally the main gate.

Then came the happy discovery of an old Chinese gun barrel, 1860 vintage, lying in a blacksmith shop within the lines. It was immediately appropriated by Gunner's Mate Mitchell, the inventive American sailor. He took a Welshman named Thomas into his confidence, and together they built a whole new cannon. It turned out to be a remarkable mongrel—Chinese barrel, Italian carriage, Russian ammunition, British and American crew. Sensing symbolic implications, the English christened it "The International Gun." The earthier Americans called it "Old Betsy" and sometimes just "the old crock." Whatever the name, its performance was eye-opening. When formally christened on July 8, the first cannon ball went through three walls. True, it wasn't very accurate, the recoil was terrific, and it always looked as if it might explode. But its devastating roar made up for everything, and Mitchell was the hero of the hour.

He was in for still greater glory. On July 12 Chinese troops in the Hanlin moved up so close that they leaned their banner against the British Legation wall. This piece of impudence was too much for Mitchell. He leaned over the wall and hooked the flag. A Chinese

29

soldier grabbed the other end, and for a few moments all firing stopped while both sides watched a monumental tug of war. With his free hand, Mitchell slung fistfuls of dirt at the Chinese, who finally had to let go. The red and black banner was torn to shreds, but Mitchell happily clutched it when he plunged back into the compound.

Through it all, the children of the American missionaries held their own tugs of war, built their own little forts, played their own games of "Boxer"—oblivious of the peril around them. One of the group, Carrington Goodrich, still remembers side-stepping a real cannon ball that bounded into some game of make-believe.

There were endless close calls—none more frightening than the time Polly Condit Smith sat near the tennis court, trying to cheer up the Baroness von Ketteler. A sniper's bullet whistled by, and Miss Condit Smith dived for the ground, trying to pull the Baroness after her. But the heartbroken widow refused to budge, and a hail of bullets clipped the trees and grass around her. She was still rooted—trying to die—when a customs volunteer rushed to the scene and carried her to safety.

It must have made an exciting story at the Squiers breakfast table the following morning, where the more sophisticated liked to relax a minute before facing the day's ordeal. Besides Polly Condit Smith, the guests usually included Dr. Morrison of the *Times,* the charming Captain Strouts of the British guard, and more recently Dr. Frank Gamewell. He, however, rarely joined in the conversation. He simply sat for a moment, gulping coffee and listening to the others. Then he was off on his bicycle again, pedaling to some new danger point.

By mid-July this was most likely to be the French legation. For some days the defenders there had heard ominous clicks and taps in the ground beneath them. Then, just after 6 P.M. on the 13th, a tremendous blast seared the fading twilight. Flames and smoke shot into the air; bricks and sandbags rained down on the defenders. The mine blew two men to bits, wounded several others. Professor Destalon, a volunteer from the Imperial University, was buried in the debris, then released unhurt by a second blast. The French marines grimly dug into the ruins, somehow managed to hold the position.

Next there was trouble again on the Tartar Wall. Captain Newt H. Hall, the U.S. Marine who had taken over from the wounded Jack Myers, found the enemy fire getting constantly heavier. When Herbert Squiers ordered him to move his barricades even closer to the Chinese, he just couldn't see it. And when Minister Conger supported Squiers, he still couldn't see it. They were indeed a strange pair of military superiors: even an affectionate biographer confessed that Conger's Civil War record was undistinguished, while Squiers had spent fourteen years as a second lieutenant. Perhaps a clever talker like Myers could have side-tracked their strategy, but Hall was the stolid, tactless type and he plainly showed his contempt.

Squiers finally climbed the wall on July 15 and showed Hall exactly where he wanted the new barricade. That night Hall reconnoitered the place, but ended up keeping his men further back at their old position. Other men were later posted at the new spot, and it didn't help Hall in the months to come when it turned out that Squiers and Conger, the dabbling amateurs, had been right. The advanced position could indeed be held and helped the defense immensely.

So many of the bold spirits, the best men, were now gone. On the 15th Henry Warren, a bright young consular student, was killed in the fu. Early on the 16th Henry Fischer, one of the finest American Marines, fell on the Tartar Wall. It was a heartbroken group that gathered that morning at the Squierses' for breakfast. Morrison and Strouts briefly picked at their food, then went to help out in the fu.

It was about 8:30 when they were both brought back—Morrison badly hit, Strouts mortally wounded. The dying captain held out a limp, white hand to Polly Condit Smith. She could only think of that same hand, firm and vigorous, reaching for a cup of coffee just an hour ago.

A gloomy drizzle fell as they buried Strouts and Warren late that afternoon. Most of the legation colony stood at the graveside, when a most unexpected development interrupted the service. A messenger burst through the crowd and handed Minister Conger a letter. The mourners quickly forgot the funeral as they recognized the familiar red envelope used by the Yamen. They crowded around Conger, who ripped out a cable in State Department code. Translated, the message said simply, "Communicate tydings bearer."

It was clearly authentic. No one else had access to the code. (And good cryptanalysis lay in the future.) But who sent the message? When was it sent? Who was "bearer"? And assuming it originated in Washington, how did it come?

Actually, the message came through Wu Ting Fang, the Chinese minister to Washington. Totally isolated from the archaic capital that supplied his credentials, Wu was working on his own for peace. He had no friends—no bloc of sympathetic powers, no support from "world opinion"—he was completely alone. Nevertheless he achieved a miracle. Specifically, he persuaded the State Department to send the cable and the Yamen to deliver it.

At the moment, Conger knew none of this, only that it was genuine. He worked up a brief answer in the same code, outlining the situation and the urgent need for help. Perhaps his reply would never be forwarded, but he had nothing to lose. There was no sign of the Seymour relief force or that any of the earlier appeals had gone through. This at least meant another chance.

It also meant that at least some Chinese might be interested in talking peace. There had been signs of this before. As early as June 25 a board had appeared on the canal bridge suggesting a cease-fire; at the time it seemed like a ruse. Then on July 14 a letter signed "Prince Ching and Others" arrived, requesting that the ministers and their families move to the Yamen where they would be protected until they could be sent home. Nobody had any intention of leaving the fortified legations, but the message did indicate divided councils at the Imperial Palace. Another friendly letter and now the cable for Mr. Conger seemed further evidence. The ministers cautiously suggested that if the Chinese were in earnest, a cease-fire would be the best way to show it.

"Now that there is mutual agreement that there is to be no more fighting," replied Prince Ching and Others, "there may be peace and quiet." With that, a rickety, uneasy truce began on July 17.

The Chinese proved as baffling as ever. They abducted M. Pelliot, a Frenchman from Tongking, but he later returned smiling, having had tea with General Jung Lu. Several cartloads of melons arrived from Prince Ching and Others. Another shipment came with the Empress Dowager's compliments—followed by a message apologizing that they had been delivered to the wrong address. Chinese soldiers conducted a lively black market first in eggs, then in ammunition.

Information was also for sale, at not too reasonable rates. But the purveyors knew just what the customers wanted, and a steady stream of glowing reports poured in, describing brilliant Allied victories, the relief force steadily approaching, the Chinese and Boxers hopelessly routed. The besieged, who had long given up on Admiral Seymour, once more scanned the southern horizon . . . once again imagined they saw searchlights and rockets in the sky.

They had their first word from the outside on July 18. A messenger sent out by the Japanese at the end of June returned to report that a mixed relief force of thirteen thousand would leave Tientsin on July 20. It was cheering to know that help was really coming, depressing to learn that nothing had happened for a month.

The days dragged by, then another messenger on July 28. It was a fifteen-year-old native Sunday-school student the American missionaries had lowered from the Tartar Wall on July 4. Disguised as a beggar, he made it safely to Tientsin; now he was back with a letter for Sir Claude from the British consul. It couldn't have been more discouraging. As of July 22, the relief force hadn't even been organized. "There are plenty of troops on the way," the message vaguely concluded, "if you can keep yourselves in food."

But that was just the problem. Food was running out. Could they last long enough for these apathetic rescuers? The Committee on Food Supply—by now there was a committee for everything—took stock on August 1. They figured there was enough to give each person one pound of wheat and one-third pound of rice a day for nine days. Or five weeks, if they cut out the 2,750 native Christians in the fu—and as conditions grew worse that thought occurred to surprisingly many.

Hunger could do strange things. One evening as Polly Condit Smith strolled beside the Dutch Minister Herr Knobel, they suddenly heard a hen clucking. It clearly belonged to a nearby family of Russians, but that didn't faze Knobel. He quickly pounced on it, and with the bird loudly squawking under his coat, the diplomat and the lady raced away through the dark, like any pair of thieves.

On August 7, they all went on half rations. Worse, there was no milk left for the children. And conditions in the fu were now appalling. No one quite stooped to cutting off the converts, but they certainly didn't get an equal share. The children died faster, and many of the adults could only crawl. Leaves were stripped from the trees, cats ruthlessly hunted down, and the kindly Reverend Martin found himself telling Miss Payen that the Chinese liked to eat dogs anyhow.

To cheer themselves up, the American missionaries tried some hymns one night on the steps of the Jubilee Tower. Next a few numbers like "Tramp, Tramp, Tramp, the Boys Are Marching." Then, in honor of some French marines, a rather shaky "Marseillaise." It became a regular occasion after that, with each country singing its own songs. The Russians offered the added attraction of Madame Pokotilov, wife of the head of the Russo-Chinese Bank. She had been a diva at the St. Petersburg Opera House, and one evening let go with such a rousing interpretation of the Jewel Song from *Faust* that the Chinese fired a volley in her general direction.

The truce was often broken and had collapsed altogether by August 9. A new Shansi regiment took over the attack. They had the latest repeating rifles and swore to finish the foreigners off, "leaving neither fowl nor dog." They swept through the Mongol market on the west, wavered before a blazing return fire, and finally fell back among the ruined huts and shanties.

Word came on the tenth that the relief force was at last under way. It had left Tientsin on August 4, and a message from the commander, General Gaselee, said cheerfully, "Keep up your spirits." More practical was the succinct letter that also arrived from the leader of the Japanese contingent, General Fukushima, who explained that the relief force would approach from the east and ended with the all-important words: "Probable date of arrival at Peking August 13 or 14."

It was the message they had been waiting, praying, and fighting for, but ironically the defenders had little time to celebrate. They were now too hard pressed. The Chinese seemed determined to crush the legations before help arrived.

The nerves of the besieged wore thin. Some of the American missionaries began squabbling—for a while no Methodist would pull the punka while the Congregationalists ate. Several of Mrs. Conger's ladies lost their temper when a squad of dog-tired U.S. Marines didn't stand up and salute them. (Captain Myers had taught them to do it so nicely, and this Captain Hall said they needed to rest.) The ladies took their complaint to the minister, who made a mental note of the incident.

Now it was Monday, August 13. That evening the Chinese attacked as never before. Tough old Gunner's Mate Mitchell feverishly worked "Betsy"—and then suddenly fell, his arm shattered. The Reverend Gamewell dashed from station to station, shoring up the shredding defenses, all the time gulping the coffee he drank to keep going. In the fu, the Japanese and Italians reeled backward. Colonel Shiba had his men bang pots and pans to make his force seem larger—somehow they hung on. In the Mongol market, the Shansi regiments again stormed the west wall of the British Legation. As the bell on Jubilee Tower clanged for a general attack, the tired men and women rushed once more to the stations. Even Sir Claude dashed to the wall—and just as well, for a Krupp shell ripped into his dressing room.

A few yards away the Chinese officers were urging on their men: "Don't be afraid, don't be afraid—we can get through!" But they couldn't. The regiments melted. The men drifted back. About 2:15 A.M. the firing fell off.

Rising above it, a new sound was heard—a faint rumble far to the east. Soon it was louder, and reflected light occasionally danced and flickered along the horizon. Much closer, a machine gun began hammering. The defenders could hardly believe it was true.

"They're coming!" a sentry yelled, bursting into Dr. Martin's quarters.

"Get up, get up! Listen to the guns! The troops have come!" cried Señor de Cologan, the Spanish minister, rushing down the cluttered men's corridor in Sir Claude's residence.

"They are really here," Dr. Gamewell told the missionary ladies sprawled on the floor of the ballroom.

Out of the buildings they poured, happily listening to the gunfire that rolled louder and louder from the east. The ladies at the church served coffee and cocoa—they could be free with it now. The gentlemen began betting on the exact time the relief force would arrive. They were still in little groups, talking, laughing, always listening, long after the sun rose.

During the morning Captain Hall watched shells falling on the Tung Pien gate, where troops were clearly trying to smash their way through. From a distance, it looked like slow going, and Hall scoffed at one of the customs volunteers, who thought he saw foreign troops in the outer city. But it was true. While the Japanese, Russians, and Americans battered at other gates, the British had broken through the almost undefended Sha K'ou gate to the southeast. Now they were cautiously moving toward the huge Tartar Wall.

They knew just where to go, for the American segment of the wall was marked by flags. More important, they knew what to do when they got there, for a message from Sir Claude had told them about the little-known sluice gate of the Imperial Drainage Canal. The main gates in the wall were all held by the Chinese, but the sluice gate was in the American segment. Once through, they could follow the canal straight to the British Legation.

The 7th Rajputs burst past the rotten wooden gate about 2:30 P.M.— the first unit in. Up the nearly dry canal they raced, sliding in the mud, tripping over each other, scrambling to be first at the legation. The defenders heard them and rushed to the canal bank to meet them. The two groups swept into each other's arms, hugged and danced and cried together. Sir Claude tried to lead a cheer, but his voice choked.

It was a supremely rewarding moment, but one of the defenders missed it completely. As the relief force swarmed over the legation tennis court, the Reverend Frank Gamewell was on the north barricade, still hard at work arranging his sandbags, planning his loopholes, bolstering his defenses—a thorough professional to the end.

To the south, more troops were pouring in: the First Sikhs . . .

the 24th Punjabs . . . the First Bengal Lancers . . . the Royal Welsh Fusiliers. Then General Gaselee himself, gallantly embracing Mrs. Squiers and Polly Condit Smith. ("Thank God, men, here are two women alive!") It all seemed right out of Kipling.

The arrival of the American troops was less romantic. They spent a desperate morning, pinned down by fire from the outer city wall. Finally, musician Calvin P. Titus cleared the way by leading a scaling party up the bare face of the wall—an incredible feat ultimately rewarded by the Congressional Medal of Honor.

Once the wall was cleared, the 14th Infantry pushed on into the outer city, but even now the men found the going slow. It was 4:30 by the time General Chaffee finally approached the sluice gate. Prancing ahead of his men on a charger, he looked curiously like a toy soldier.

From the top of the Tartar Wall an American marine called down to the general: "You're just in time. We need you in our business."

Letting this one pass, Chaffee asked, "Where can we get in?"

"Through the canal," the marine shouted back. "The British did it two hours ago."

Actually, there was no need to feel left out. For the winner there's always enough glory for all, and Chaffee's reception was as wild as the British. For the rest of the day everyone simply traded congratulations and compared experiences. The besieged learned how the Boxers had thrown back Admiral Seymour in June; how the allies had fought for weeks to hold Tientsin itself. They apparently owed much of their success to fortifications designed by a young engineer named Herbert Hoover.

The relief force listened with awe to the epic of the siege, and indeed it was something to be proud of. For 55 days some 480 men had held off at least 20,000. The casualty figures alone showed their peril and bravery: 234 men—49 per cent of the defense force—were killed and wounded.

In the general rejoicing, the besieged briefly forgave the combination of timidity, jealousy, and red tape that delayed Gaselee's force an extra month. For their part, the rescuers forgot the myopia in Peking that lulled and misled them right up to the siege. That night they wanted only to wallow in victory, and at the battered Hôtel de Pékin M. Chamot sensed the mood perfectly. Like the good innkeeper he was, he magically produced champagne for everybody.

Next day General Gaselee's men began mopping up. They relieved the isolated Peitang Cathedral, where Bishop Favier had successfully held out. They chased the Empress Dowager, but that crafty old lady eluded them easily, disappearing to the north as they came in from the south. They broke into the Imperial City, then into the palace and the Forbidden City itself, but no one important was there. They fanned out over the country, executed a few Boxers, pulled down some walls, but all the Chinese who mattered were gone. And finally they looted —homes, shops, temples, palaces. Boxer or not, it made little difference. When one Pekinese implored an American soldier to write a notice that would keep out looters, the soldier gladly complied: "USA boys —plenty of whiskey and tobacco in here."

The months that followed were spent by the diplomats in negotiations with the defeated Empress Dowager; by the soldiers in endless reviews, trooping of the colors, and pleasant afternoons taking pictures of one another in the sacred Forbidden City.

The rest of the world shared in their joy. During the dark days of June and July, Peking had been given up for lost, and it was only natural to feel exhilarated now.

The way the great powers co-operated was especially heartening. It seemed to point toward a new era, when countries would forget their rivalries and join together on great projects. Only the tired, weary Viennese couldn't see it. As early as September 3 the Austrian papers predicted that now the danger was over, the clashes would start anew.

Above all, the victory reaffirmed people's faith in the natural supremacy of the Occidental. "History has repeated itself," exulted the London *Times*. "Once more a small segment of the civilized world, cut off and surrounded by an Asiatic horde, has exhibited those high moral qualities the lack of which renders mere numbers powerless." It was all the more intoxicating because there had been some doubts: during July the *New York Times* had announced with surprise, "CHINESE CAN SHOOT STRAIGHT." But now the stars were back on their course.

How did the Japanese fit into this concept? Very easily. Everyone called them "plucky," and they were treated as a phenomenon totally apart from the whole system of racial relationships. The correspondents managed to convey the impression that the Japanese were just like little people.

To the Americans and British, of course, Western supremacy really meant Anglo-American supremacy. "From the first," wrote Dr. Arthur Smith, one of the besieged scholars, "there was a marked contrast between the Anglo-Saxons and many of the Continentals, who for the most part sat at ease on their shady verandahs, chatting, smoking cigarettes and sipping wine; while their more energetic comrades threw off their coats, plunging into the whirl of work and the tug of toil with the joy of battle inherited from ancestors who lived a millennium and a half ago." (This was a little difficult to reconcile with the casualty figures: American and British 50, Continental Europeans 145.)

For America there was a final, special satisfaction. It went together with winning the 1900 Olympics and J. Pierpont Morgan's ventures into international finance. It was the thrill of being an equal partner in the world's triumphs and problems; it was the pride of having arrived.

So the anti-imperialists were routed. They dwindled to a few sweet ladies like Isabel Strong, who worried about the first bar opening in Samoa; or to a few old curmudgeons like Richard Crocker, who complained about "the fashion of shooting everybody who doesn't speak English." In the 1900 presidential election William Jennings Bryan, running against imperialism, couldn't even carry his own state, city, or precinct.

Right-thinking men believed that "assimilation"—everyone agreed that imperialism was an ugly word—was an economic opportunity, a moral duty, God's will, and clearly the virile thing to do. As Princeton's young Woodrow Wilson observed, expansion was "the natural and wholesome impulse which comes with a consciousness of matured strength."

President McKinley, that kindest of men, believed there was even more to expansion than that—it was the least we could do for less fortunate peoples. On the question of annexing the Philippines, he had prayed to God for guidance, and it came to him in the night: "There was nothing left to do but to take them all and to educate the Filipinos and uplift and Christianize them and by God's grace to do the very best we could by them as our fellowmen for whom Christ also died."

So it was with a sense of moral obligation—almost as one owing a debt to his Maker—that McKinley undertook his domestic travels as leader of a new America.

1901

A Good Man's Death

"Now look, that damned cowboy is President of the United States!"
—SENATOR MARK HANNA

Early in the evening of Wednesday, September 4, 1901, a special train glided into Buffalo, New York, bringing President McKinley, apostle of America's new world role, on a most appropriate mission. He was coming to honor the Pan-American Exposition, a lavish international fair designed to dramatize the Western Hemisphere community and, perhaps, make a little money on the side.

The President had only one worry. Mrs. McKinley, a chronic invalid, had been in even poorer health than usual this summer. He had already postponed the Buffalo trip once and spent most of August with her at their simple home in Canton, Ohio. Now at last she seemed better, and he happily brought her along to the exposition, hoping the change would be restful. The crash of a twenty-one-gun salute shattered a car window as the train stopped, and Mrs. McKinley briefly fainted.

It never would have occurred to William McKinley to berate the green artillery lieutenant who fired the salute too close to the train. No one was gentler or more understanding than the President. And this was the real reason for his immense popularity. Again and again some politician would charge into his office, bitterly spouting a grievance. Then came the warm smile, the pat on the shoulder, the soft

41

"My dear fellow, I am most anxious to oblige you, but . . . " Nearly always the visitor left beaming, his anger melted, and wearing a red carnation from the President's desk.

Big business, of course, liked him too. The chief disciples of *laissez-faire* couldn't help taking to a President who said, "Prices are fixed with a mathematical precision by supply and demand." But he was no mere tool of The Interests. Rather, he seemed to sense how the wind blew and intuitively went that way too. He never fawned on his sponsor and friend, the industrialist Mark Hanna; it was Hanna who worshiped him.

But his greatest strength lay with ordinary people—the small merchants, clerks, farmers, and mechanics who still formed the backbone of the electorate. He was one of them, worked hard at it, and they loved him for it. They eagerly consumed his homey rhetoric, published under titles like *McKinley Truths, McKinley Masterpieces,* and *Bits of Wisdom, or Daily Thoughts.*

In return, the President had an encouraging word for everybody. For the Chicago Bricklayers and Stone Masons, representing organized labor: "With education and integrity, every pathway of fame and favor is open to all of you." For the colored people of Alabama, who still looked wistfully to the Republican party for better days: "Cultivate good homes, make them pure and sweet, elevate them, and other good things will follow." For the white people of the South, proudly sensitive of the role played by Confederate veterans in the war with Spain: "Everybody is talking about General Wheeler, one of the bravest of the brave; but I want to speak of that sweet little daughter who followed him to Santiago and ministered to the sick soldiers at Montauk."

To show that he meant what he said—and that he was really the same as everybody else—the President liked nothing better than to shake hands. He never seemed to miss a chance and could work at a rate of fifty a minute. The secret was the McKinley grip. As the line approached from the left, he seized each extended hand . . . gave it a quick downward jerk . . . then a hard pull sideways, sending the astonished greeter spinning off to the right. Everyone who passed got an automatic "Glad to see you" and an equally automatic but magnificent smile. Occasionally McKinley appeared about to crumble, but at the last instant someone always came by who gave him new life— perhaps a Civil War comrade or a lady with a baby. However mechanical, the ritual was immensely popular; it seemed wonderful that this was a country where anybody could walk right up and shake hands with the President.

That was what worried George B. Cortelyou, McKinley's crisply efficient secretary. It was impossible to check on the people who streamed by, and anything might happen. Cortelyou was especially alarmed when he learned that the Buffalo trip would include one of these handshaking affairs on September 6. Unfamiliar surroundings . . . thousands of people flowing through the grounds—he couldn't see it. Quietly he canceled the project. Somehow McKinley learned, gently admonished his misguided assistant, and rescheduled the reception. Just before they left Canton, Cortelyou again tried to get the President to call it off.

"Why should I? No one would want to hurt me."

Cortelyou tried using a little arithmetic: with 100,000 people at the fair, McKinley couldn't possibly greet more than a few in the allotted ten minutes. Why, people would be disappointed, perhaps even offended.

"Well, they'll know I tried, anyhow."

Cortelyou sighed, added a third Secret Service man to the usual pair, and wired Director-General Buchanan to do his best to protect the Chief Executive. With nothing more to be done, he boarded the presidential special. Now at last they were there, and the saluting cannon that shattered the windows showed that at least some sort of guard was already on hand.

The presidential party shakily descended into the arms of a beaming reception committee. The McKinleys were taken in tow by their host, John G. Milburn, the distinguished Buffalo attorney who was president of the Exposition. A few moments later the official party, flanked by fifty cavalrymen, clopped up to the Milburn house on Delaware Avenue, a somber pile of Victorian brick brightened by a big American flag draped clumsily but affectionately over the front door.

September 5 was President's Day—an occasion eagerly awaited by the exposition management, which had so far suffered through a long year of meager gate receipts. They were not disappointed. It was a beautiful morning, and fifty thousand people swarmed around the speaker's stand on the Esplanade. President McKinley's address was appropriate and predictable—a salute to expositions, a ringing call for ships, the Isthmian canal, anything that might appeal to Latin America. It also contained one interesting passage that, for the President, marked a deviation. He came out for limited reciprocity. McKinley had always been a high-tariff man, and the London press thought the statement significant. The American papers, however, buried it on the inside pages, and the Buffalo *Express* went so far as to assure its readers that the reciprocity paragraph meant almost nothing.

Whatever the significance, the exposition crowd didn't care. They had come to see the man who was one of them. As he finished, they broke through the police lines and surged around his carriage. McKinley couldn't resist the temptation, and fifteen minutes of handshaking followed.

A red-haired man held up a little boy, and the President gave the special smile he always saved for children. Joe, one of the natives from Tobin's Hawaiian Village, also got a hearty greeting. The islands had recently been annexed, and this was a good way to show how welcome they were.

Lost in the throng was a twenty-eight-year-old Polish-American, who watched the proceedings with acute distaste. Leon Czolgosz thought "it wasn't right for any one man to get so much ceremony." He just couldn't stand the sight of all those people "saluting him, bowing to him, paying homage to him." He fingered more determinedly than ever the .32-caliber nickel-plated Iver-Johnson revolver he carried in his pocket.

He was still brooding, hating, waiting for a chance to do the thing he wanted, when the President's carriage moved off at 11:30 A.M. for the military review at the stadium. Czolgosz spent the rest of the day moping, while McKinley busily toured the various national buildings, meeting the commissioners . . . greeting honored guests . . . offering gracious platitudes about the exposition.

This was easy to do, for the Pan-American was one of the most imaginative of the great fairs that were currently the rage. "Timekeepers of progress," President McKinley called them, and he was right. They gave a buoyant, confident people the perfect opportunity to savor past triumphs and gape at the new inventions that promised an even brighter future.

At Buffalo, visitors strolled through a wonderland of Spanish architecture, designed to emphasize the Latin American angle. But the maze of coral arcades, pastel missions and gilt-trimmed belfries had local embellishments never seen south of the border. Statuary was everywhere, and it was difficult to decode the symbolism even with the aid of an official program. In the group representing "The Despotic Age," for instance, several ladies being dragged behind a chariot stood for "the ideals of humanity." At the far end of the exposition—and omitted from President McKinley's tour—was the Midway, with all the innocent pleasures that seemed so exciting: the captive balloon . . . the ostrich farm . . . the new Cineograph . . . the cyclorama of the Johnstown Flood . . . that naughty señorita Chaquita.

At night the exposition was even more spectacular, for the buildings were studded with thousands of light bulbs. Until now, no one had tried using electricity for display lighting, and the visitors couldn't get over it—especially the 405-foot Electric Tower that twinkled with 35,000 bulbs. It was a stunning effect and good business too, for the electricity came from Niagara Falls and all agreed there could be no better advertisement.

The lights blazed brighter than ever as President's Day drew to a close. For a final treat, the management put on a mammoth show of Pain's Fireworks. The climax sent the crowd home tingling with the glory of living at a time like this. A breathtaking display called "Our Empire" filled the sky with stars and rockets, representing Cuba, Puerto Rico, the Philippines. As the last fireballs floated lazily down, President and Mrs. McKinley excused themselves, explaining they must retire early, for tomorrow would also be a big day.

A full schedule, but the sort McKinley liked best. The formalities of President's Day were over. On September 6 he could relax. A visit to Niagara in the morning, a chance to enjoy the falls with Mrs. McKinley —they had always meant to go there. Then lunch with the local political men and back to the exposition in time for the public reception that Cortelyou had so foolishly wanted to cancel.

By eight o'clock they were all on their way to Lewiston for the trolley ride up the gorge. For this carefree day in the hot summer sun, the President wore a black frock coat, white vest, morning trousers, stiff shirt, starched collar, and a top hat. Somehow he never wilted, and as usual had a nice word for everybody. When he spied his friend Judge Loran Lewis standing with some grandchildren by the car tracks, he stepped off the gorge trolley and shook hands all around— half a century later the grandchildren still remembered vividly that kind, smiling face.

When the party reached the International Bridge around noon, the President faced a delicate problem. One of the best views was from the Canadian side, but no President had ever left United States soil. McKinley gingerly made his way almost to the middle of the bridge, took in the sights, and successfully returned without leaving the country.

After a cold buffet lunch at the International Hotel, they visited the powerhouse. Its humming generators and dynamos were the pride of an age just discovering the limitless possibilities of electricity. The President was properly interested and especially seemed to enjoy shaking hands with young Addison Barker, the powerhouse elevator boy.

Now it was time to return to Buffalo for the public reception at the Temple of Music. As the special train of four Pullmans slowly moved off, Mayor Butler and the city fathers of Niagara Falls stood proudly on the station platform. They had at least done their share in giving the President an unforgettable day.

Another visitor to the falls that morning was young Czolgosz, still bitter and smoldering. After reading about the official tour in his morning paper, Czolgosz pocketed his revolver . . . treated himself to a barbershop shave . . . and caught the next Niagara trolley. But he never ran across the President and soon returned to Buffalo. By now he had a better plan anyhow.

The reception at the Temple of Music was scheduled for 4:00 P.M., so there was a half hour to kill when the Presidential Special pulled into the exposition grounds at 3:30. Mrs. McKinley was worn out; she retired to the Milburn house for the day. The President was escorted to the Mission Building for wafers and chocolate. As he relaxed to the strains of the Guatemalan Mirambon quartet, a member of the committee paid his respects: "I'm glad to see you back in Buffalo, Mr. President."

"Yes," smiled McKinley, "and I don't know whether I'll ever be able to get away."

At the Temple of Music, Grand Marshal Louis L. Babcock wound up his preparations for the President's appearance. He had a difficult job, for the temple was designed more for concerts than for greeting the public. It was a gaudy, squarish building, mostly cream-colored but with generous splashes of red and gold. The panels in the gilded octagonal dome were blue-green in honor of Niagara's waters. Statues, busts, plaques, tablets were sprinkled everywhere. In *World's Work,* Walter Hines Page guardedly wrote that "its excessive ornamentation and coloring give offense to those whose only measure of beauty is the rigid classical measure." In *Cosmopolitan,* Robert Grant was more outspoken: "That bilious-looking edifice."

The auditorium itself was equally garish, but poorly equipped, except for the largest pipe organ in the United States. The usual stage took up one end; the floor was flat and filled with hard, plain folding chairs. There was little to work with, but Babcock displayed mild imagination in fixing the place up. The chairs were pushed back to make an aisle about ten feet wide, which ran from the east door to the center of the hall, then turned at right angles and continued on to the south door. The backs of the chairs formed the sides of the aisle; they were draped in blue bunting as an extra touch. The crowd would enter from the east and leave by the south. The President would stand at the angle where the aisle turned. To dress the spot up a bit, Babcock borrowed some palms from the stage. Then two large potted bay

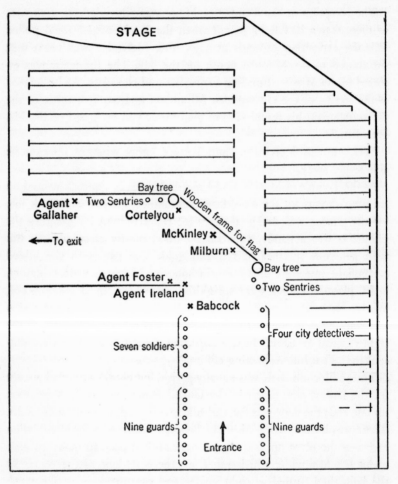

4:07 P.M. *at the Temple of Music in Buffalo. Based on sketch by Louis L. Babcock six days later.*

trees. For a backdrop he hung an American flag on a wooden frame.

Something still was lacking. Suddenly the thought dawned that it would "look nice" to have some soldiers standing around. A call to Captain Wiser of the 73rd Coast Artillery produced ten men and a corporal. Babcock stationed two of them at each end of his little bower. The rest were put across the aisle, so they would face the President. He placed them every yard or so, stretching eastward toward the entrance, until he ran out of men. The eighteen exposition guards would have to fill in the rest of the way. They were posted in two rows, so the people would pass between them. Almost at the last minute it occurred to Babcock that his little force could be more than decorative—he ordered them to keep the line moving and see that no "disorderly character" went by the President.

Now it was almost 4:00. Organist William Gomph was tuning up. The soldiers stood silent and expectant. Mounting cheers outside told that the President was approaching. Mr. Babcock gave a last glance around . . . and went forth to meet his distinguished guest.

President McKinley had a pleasant word for the Grand Marshal, as he stepped from his Victoria, followed by the ever-present Cortelyou and his host Mr. Milburn. The group swept into the temple. The President grasped the arrangements at a glance, instinctively took his place between the two bay trees. Cortelyou stood on his right. Milburn was on his left, to handle any necessary introductions. Four city detectives lined up still further to the left, while another hovered in the rear. Secret Service men Foster and Ireland stationed themselves directly across the aisle, facing their chief. A third, Gallaher, stood to the south. Everyone was in his place; the President nodded to Babcock, "Let them come."

Organist Gomph pealed out a Bach sonata, the east door flew open, and the people poured in. Down the aisle they came, at first two or three abreast but quickly funneled into single file by the guards and soldiers. As they reached the President, he gave them the invariable smile, the downward pump, the sideways pull . . . and off they spun to the south exit.

Even so, the pace wasn't fast enough. Babcock got word to move the crowd more quickly; he opened another door. Then a second complaint; he opened still another door. Then a third complaint; this time he had his men prod the people along. Now they streamed by at a forty-five-a-minute clip. The President seemed satisfied. The guards and soldiers marveled that any man could shake hands so fast; they found it hard just to watch people at this rate.

As the line moved along, handkerchiefs appeared here and there. It was a hot day . . . the kind that makes a person want to mop his brow before meeting the President of the United States. McKinley himself was immaculate. He belonged to that rare species of portly men who always look cool, whatever the temperature.

Five or six minutes had passed, and Cortelyou signaled that it was almost time to end the reception. He pulled out his watch. When he raised his hand, Babcock was to close the doors.

The line still flowed, unaware of this bit of stage-managing. An Italian with a heavy mustache went by. Then an old man who got a courteous bow. Next a woman with her little girl; the child hung back a second in front of the President, then ran laughing after her mother. Next a young man in a dark gray suit, flannel shirt and string tie. It was Leon Czolgosz.

His blue eyes were expressionless; his round, boyish face blankly innocent. His right hand was wrapped in a white handkerchief, as though injured, and held against his side. His left was extended instead. The President reached for it, but the two never clasped. Instead, Czolgosz brushed McKinley's arm aside, raised his "bandaged" right hand, and virtually pressed it against the President's vest.

Two muffled shots came in quick succession at 4:07 P.M. Across the aisle Edward Rice of the Ceremonies Committee had a fleeting glimpse of "something white pushed over to the President." Private Francis O'Brien, four feet to McKinley's left, saw smoke coming from a man's hand. Grand Marshal Babcock, walking over to close the east door and end the reception, whirled around in time to see the President deathly pale but standing straight and unsupported. A thin veil of smoke was fading away.

For a breathless instant McKinley and Czolgosz studied each

other . . . the President with hurt surprise, Czolgosz with vacant disinterest. Then a swarm of soldiers and Secret Service men hurled themselves on the young Pole and down they all went together in a writhing, tumbling heap.

President McKinley swayed into the arms of Mr. Milburn and Detective Geary of the Buffalo police. Someone ripped down the blue bunting and pulled around a bank of folding chairs. They led the President over. He sagged down heavily, gasping, "Cortelyou!" The secretary, of course, was already there and when he bent down to the wounded man McKinley said, "Cortelyou. My wife, be careful about her. Don't let her know."

By now, Committeeman Rice was at the east entrance trying to stop the flow of people into the temple. "Close the door and clear the aisle!" he shouted over and over. Guards cursed and shoved and wrestled the crowd out of the building.

The soldiers had no time for that. They piled on the heap of men that still clawed and rolled about the floor. Secret Service Agent Gallaher tore Czolgosz' smoking handkerchief away, tried to get the revolver. An artilleryman saw his hands on it, thought he was the assassin, and jumped on top of him. James Parker, a colored waiter who had been just behind Czolgosz in the line, saw this pair struggling and piled on them. The revolver clattered loose and Private O'Brien— now on the bottom of the heap—managed to grasp it and stick it in his pocket.

It was an odd battle, for Czolgosz put up no resistance whatsoever. At last, the men untangled themselves. The soldiers struggled to their feet, grimly hanging on to their prisoner. Secret Service Agent Foster, in a rage of frustration, punched Czolgosz on the nose and down they went all over again.

Slumped in his chair, McKinley looked up at the scuffle. Even at a time like this, he couldn't bear to see anyone hurt. "Go easy with him, boys," the President pleaded.

Order slowly returned. Czolgosz was dragged out of the auditorium into a small office near the stage. The President seemed a little better; some color returned to his face. Then he felt under his shirt and glanced at his blood-tipped fingers. He almost fainted. When Cortelyou asked how he felt, he thickly replied, "This wound hurts very much."

Outside the temple the news spread like fire. A loud restless throng surged against the barred doors. A few important people talked their way in. Señor Aspiroz, the Mexican ambassador, asked the President if he was wounded and McKinley patiently replied that he was. When Mr. Buchanan, director-general of the exposition, rushed up it was the President who offered the apology: "I'm so sorry this should have happened here."

An automobile ambulance (pride of the Pan-American's Medical Department) clanged up. The crowd fell silent and then cried in anguish at the sight of the President's stretcher. A few moments later, he was at the little stucco hospital on the exposition grounds. As they carried him into the building at 4:18 P.M., he turned thoughtfully to Cortelyou. "It must," he sighed, "have been some poor misguided fellow."

No one else was as charitable. At the Temple of Music, the artillerymen still pounded Czolgosz as he lay panting on a table in the little office. Outside, voices cried, "Lynch him!" The more purposeful got a rope.

Grand Marshal Babcock quickly recruited more soldiers. They had no ammunition but they looked impressive as they formed a double line at the south entrance. A closed carriage drew up and Czolgosz was hustled into it. Half a dozen police jumped aboard and the driver lashed his horses into a run.

Most of the crowd had been misled by a patrol wagon at the east door. Now they saw their mistake and with a howl of anger set out after the prisoner's carriage. It whirled across the Esplanade, across the Triumphal Causeway, with hundreds in wild pursuit. They were fast catching up as it shot by the Lincoln Parkway gate. But there some fast-thinking guards managed to slam the gates shut, locking the mob in the exposition grounds. The carriage continued safely to police headquarters; the crowd turned toward the stucco hospital.

Here they stood hushed and uncertain. Hope soared or fell, depending on the rumors that rippled through their ranks. The first definite word came at 4:30—the President might live. People hugged one another and silently waved their hats. Carriages and electrics began to roll up, bringing doctors from all over town.

Inside the hospital President McKinley watched them arrive with something less than enthusiasm. "Be careful of the doctors," he had whispered to Cortelyou in the ambulance. "I leave all that to you."

Cortelyou didn't know what to do. He was a stranger in Buffalo; the names of the medical men meant nothing to him. Dr. P. M. Rixey, Surgeon General of the Navy and the President's family physician, might have helped, but he had gone home with Mrs. McKinley. In desperation Cortelyou turned to Mr. Milburn: "You know all these men. When the right one arrives, tell me."

Dr. Herman Mynter, the first well-known surgeon on hand, was by now examining President McKinley. One shot had luckily glanced off a button and done no damage at all; it was found lying loose in the President's underwear. The other was obviously a bad stomach wound, demanding an operation.

But Mynter wasn't picked to perform it . . . nor was Dr. Eugene Wasdin of the Marine Hospital Service . . . nor Dr. Edward Lee of St. Louis, who bustled in as a volunteer. Then at 5:07—exactly one hour after the shooting—a small, gray-bearded man arrived. It was Dr. Matthew Mann, a distinguished gynecologist but certainly not known for any experience in gunshot wounds. "That," whispered Mr. Milburn, "is the man for the operation."

Next problem: Should they operate immediately? There was one good reason to wait. A call had been sent for Dr. Roswell Park, the Exposition's Medical Director and President of the American Society of Surgeons. He was in Niagara Falls but would arrive by seven o'clock. It might be worth the delay to have such an outstanding specialist's advice. On the other hand, both Mann and Mynter were anxious to get going.

All turned to Cortelyou to decide. He consulted several bystanders, including Melville Hanna, the Senator's brother, whose chief qualification seemed to be that he had undergone three operations himself. They all urged speed, so Cortelyou told Dr. Mann to go ahead.

As the President softly murmured his prayers, Dr. Wasdin administered ether at 5:20 and the surgeons plunged into their task. Perhaps it was the serious nature of the wound; perhaps the importance of the patient; perhaps, as some later suggested, it was a subconscious desire to finish before the distinguished Dr. Park could share in the glory. Whatever the reason, rarely have surgeons worked with such frenzied haste. No one took the time to put on caps or gauze. The best instruments went unused. Nobody bothered with a clean excision of the bullet track. In his excitement Dr. Mann petulantly rapped Dr. Mynter's fingers when he felt the other man was too much in the way.

As they worked the nature of the wound became clearer. The bullet had gone straight through the front wall and out the rear wall of the stomach, disappearing somewhere in the President's ample back. They probed a little but never found it. Nor did they notice that the pancreas and kidney were also damaged. Perhaps it was the poor lighting.

Dr. Mann finally decided that the safest course was to close the wound, sew up the President and trust that the bullet would remain harmlessly lodged in the President's back muscles. Dr. Mynter argued that they ought to drain the wound first; admittedly none of them could do posterior draining, but even anterior draining alone would reduce the danger of infection.

They were still arguing when Dr. Park arrived. Dr. Rixey, another late-comer, immediately cornered him: "You are the only man here that I know anything about and I want you to take charge of the case." Park begged off: "Right now it wouldn't be fair to Dr. Mann."

Then they asked his opinion on draining the wound. Again he begged off: "Dr. Mann would know best." Park then turned his attention toward preparing the Milburn home for the President's recuperation. So there was no drainage, and the wound was sewed up while one of the nation's top surgeons busied himself with housekeeping arrangements.

It had been a curious afternoon at the Milburn house. Upstairs all was calm. Mrs. McKinley lay napping, tired from her trip to the falls. Servants tiptoed about, trying not to disturb her. Downstairs, suppressed excitement. Electricians were installing auxiliary lines . . . messengers were carrying in medical supplies . . . Mrs. Milburn and the President's three nieces huddled in a corner, wide-eyed and frightened. Director-General Buchanan struggled to discourage visitors and stem the phone calls that now poured in. Above all, he wanted to hide the news from the President's wife until Dr. Rixey returned from the hospital.

Mrs. McKinley awoke about 5:30 and began to crochet. That was what she always did when the President was away. Altogether, she estimated she had crocheted some four thousand pairs of slippers. But this was no indication of presidential neglect—there was never a more loving husband.

The shadows lengthened . . . twilight . . . dusk. Still the same silence in the halls; only the murmur of voices somewhere downstairs. The President had promised to be home by 6:00; he should be back soon. But to her surprise Mrs. McKinley discovered it was nearly 7:00. Suddenly she began to worry.

An open carriage drove up; Dr. Rixey hurried into the house. As soon as she saw him, Mrs. McKinley knew that something was wrong: "Where is Mr. McKinley; why doesn't he come?"

"I have some bad news for you, Mrs. McKinley. . . ."

They were all amazed how well she took it. Shaken certainly, but no hysterics, no fainting, no Victorian decline. She said she must go to him; they told her gently that wasn't necessary, he was coming to her.

Up Delaware Avenue rolled a small cortege—the automobile ambulance, an escort of soldiers and police, two Secret Service men trailing behind on bicycles. The surgeons' work was done. President McKinley, still under ether, was at last returning to the Milburn home.

Back at the deserted hospital there were few signs that anything unusual had happened. A Secret Service man carefully folded a crumpled frock coat, a powder-burned vest and trousers. The pockets held $1.80 in change . . . a pencil . . . a few cards . . . some keys . . . three cigars . . . a silver nugget . . . three small pearl-handled penknives . . . an American-made watch . . . a worn black wallet. There was not a single clue that the owner of these odds and ends was the President of the United States.

Across town, the pockets of another man yielded pretty much the same sort of thing: $1.54 in change . . . a pencil . . . a card . . . a letter acknowledging dues to a benevolent association . . . and (for an odd divergence) a rubber nipple. This was all the police had to start with in their examination of Leon Czolgosz.

They put him in the sweatbox, but he proved more responsive to reasonable questioning. At first he claimed he was "Fred C. Nieman" but soon admitted his real name. He said he was an anarchist and had no accomplices. He signed his only written statement—a twenty-five-word masterpiece of compression: "I killed President McKinley because I done my duty. I didn't believe one man should have so much service and another man should have none."

Later he elaborated: "I don't believe in a Republican form of government and I don't believe we should have any rulers. . . . I don't believe in voting. . . . I don't believe in marriage; I believe in free love." It turned out he had once been a wire mill worker in Cleveland with strong radical views. He had quit work in 1898 and spent the next two years brooding on the family farm, often reading the anarchist paper *Free Society*. He liked to listen to local anarchists, also to the fire-eating Emma Goldman. He gradually concluded that "it would be a good thing to kill the President and to have no rulers. . . . I heard quite a lot of people talk like that."

In July, 1901, he got the family to buy out his share in the farm. He used the money to come to Buffalo. At the moment he was still drifting, for McKinley's visit hadn't yet been announced. But when it was, he knew just what to do. He took a room over John Nowak's saloon on Broadway . . . bought his .32-caliber Iver-Johnson on Main Street, and bided his time for the right moment.

He was well up in the line at the Temple of Music. The pistol was in his right hip pocket; he didn't pull it out and wrap it in his white cotton handkerchief until he entered the building. He hadn't practiced, but he had no trouble. Everything was in his favor: the crowd . . . the other handkerchiefs around . . . the speed of the line propelled along by the famous McKinley handshake.

Now it was late that night. Czolgosz was back in his cell, and the

President lay resting easily in the large rear room on the second floor of the Milburn house. Dr. Park had laid the groundwork well—a surgical bed, countless pans and basins, a large brass electric fan that droned through the still September night. Nurses were already there, an orderly on the way. The doctors themselves had become a committee, sworn to maintain a united front. They began to issue the neat, precise, optimistic bulletins that would be so familiar in the days ahead. Outside, police lines kept the crowd far away, and the Milburn residence was a picture of quiet and order.

The rest of the nation was in tumult. On Wall Street a reporter told J. Pierpont Morgan just as he was leaving for the weekend. "What!" cried the great financier; then he drifted back to his office, sighing, "Sad, sad."

At Paterson, New Jersey—considered the nation's radical center—even the anarchists were stunned. "We have often discussed President McKinley at our meetings," explained editor Pedro Esteve, "and the general opinion always was that he was a good, broad-minded man who would not hurt us."

In the quiet New England twilight, a fisherman learned from a man shouting on the shore of Darling Lake, Massachusetts. Utterly shocked, old Grover Cleveland rowed in to get the details.

In neighboring Vermont, Vice President Theodore Roosevelt heard while attending a fish and game club outing at Isle La Motte. "My God!" he exclaimed, clapping both hands to his head.

But the man most affected—even more than Roosevelt—was Senator Mark Hanna, the President's friend, adviser, and worshipful admirer. "It can't be possible," he sobbed, and he begged the reporter to phone him all the bulletins as fast as they arrived.

They weren't much help. This was journalism's most competitive, most irresponsible period. If a reporter couldn't get the facts, he made them up. It was better than getting scooped by somebody else's paper. The bigger the story, the worse the temptation.

At Buffalo imagination ran riot, starting with the President's first words after the shooting. There was the pious version: "May God forgive him." And the courtly version: "How could you, sir?" And the heroic version, in which Cortelyou dramatically cried, "But you are wounded!" and the President smiled back, "No, I think not." Reports on later developments were no more reliable.

To get the truth, the only solution was to go to Buffalo. So Cabinet, family and friends came racing through the night, riding those little two- and three-car special trains that important men of the day liked to use when they were in a hurry. Secretary of War Elihu Root was first to appear Saturday morning; the others weren't far behind. Vice President Roosevelt's train arrived at 1:02 P.M. and a small crowd let out a cheer of greeting. Roosevelt sternly silenced them. His strong sense of propriety and even stronger sense of politics knew it was no time for that. But somehow he couldn't help being colorful. He managed a dark suit and black tie, but cocked on his head was a gray slouch hat that inevitably reminded people of the Rough Riders.

However, the real center of attraction proved to be Senator Hanna. He got the biggest headlines, and more space than any Cabinet member. In fact, it was Hanna the papers went to when they wanted to know whether the Cabinet was doing anything important.

And it was Hanna who set the new tone of optimism. The medical bulletins might mean little, but no one could mistake his cheerful face. "When a man like that says I will not die," bubbled the Senator, "the Old Man himself cannot knock him out." And people knew he must be right—he was always on the inside of everything.

So September 7 was a day of hope, as were the days that followed. On the 9th, Hanna called the situation "just glorious" and went back to Cleveland; Roosevelt rejoined his family at Lake Tahawus in the Adirondacks. On September 10 the President had his most comfortable night; on the 11th he asked for a cigar. On the morning of September 12 Dr. Charles McBurney—an outstanding abdominal specialist brought from New York for consultation—returned to Manhattan, glowing with praise for the President's doctors: "This is the climax of human skill. You have reached the supreme limit of science. No greater victory has ever been won. If this wound had been inflicted on a European sovereign, he would surely have died. I congratulate you."

That afternoon the roof fell in. Earlier McKinley had received his first solid food, a little toast. Now it became clear that he couldn't digest it; in fact, his stomach wasn't functioning at all. Liberal doses of castor oil followed, and by evening the President lay weak and exhausted. Heart stimulants failed, and shortly after 2:30 A.M. the doctors sent for the family and friends.

In the pre-dawn darkness of September 13, a neighbor named Perkins stood shouting up at the windows of Mark Hanna's house in Cleveland. The Senator's telephone didn't answer, and Mr. Perkins had been recruited to go over and rouse him. A sleepy response from somewhere upstairs . . . a shocked gasp . . . then windows lighting up all over the house. By 5:24 A.M. Hanna was on his way to Buffalo by special train.

During the morning McKinley smilingly assured the doctors that he hadn't lost heart, but that afternoon he quietly whispered to Dr. Rixey that it was almost over. He was unconscious most of the time now, but once as the doctors administered oxygen he looked up and murmured, "What's the use?"

Secretary Cortelyou brought in Mrs. McKinley around eight o'clock. She sat down by the President's side, her face near his. He put one arm around her, smiled, but didn't speak. Finally she was led away crying. From time to time various members of the Cabinet entered to pay their respects, but McKinley no longer recognized them. An ashen Senator Hanna limped to the bedside and called, "Mr. President!" Getting no response, he begged, "William, William." But no answer ever came.

Occasionally, McKinley murmured a few disconnected lines from "Nearer My God to Thee," once or twice some phrase from a prayer. The press polished this into an eloquent farewell: "Good-bye, all. It is God's will. His will, not ours, be done." Later evidence suggests he was not so articulate, but there is no doubt that such were his thoughts. Dr. Park, who watched the President throughout his illness, was amazed that any man could be so gentle, long after it couldn't possibly be a pose.

"Up to this time," the doctor recalled years afterward, "I'd never really believed that a man could be a good Christian and a good politician."

President McKinley was never conscious after 7:40. Occasionally he clutched Dr. Rixey's forefinger, almost as a baby might do. Once he sighed, "Oh, dear." At 2:15 A.M. Dr. Rixey, who had been listening to the faintly beating heart, straightened up and announced quietly, "The President is dead."

Blissfully unaware of the crisis, Vice President Roosevelt had spent September 13 climbing Mount Marcy, one of the more challenging peaks in the Adirondacks. On the way down, the party paused at a shelf several hundred feet below the top. Drinking in the beauty of the late afternoon, Roosevelt noticed a guide hurrying up the trail from below. He felt at once that it was bad news.

"The President's condition has greatly changed for the worse," ran the wire from Cortelyou. The nearest phone was at the Tahawus Club, ten miles away; the party headed there immediately. On the way, they met a runner with another message: "Come at once." They panted into the Tahawus Club in a roaring thunderstorm. More messages—McKinley was dying.

Someone hitched up a buckboard. At 5:45 P.M. Roosevelt and the driver set off alone on the forty-mile trip to North Creek, where a locomotive was waiting. Through the dark, foggy night the hack raced. Down twisting mountain roads that were often little more than muddy trails. Three times they reined to a stop while Roosevelt and the driver changed horses. Then off again, bouncing along the rocks . . . sliding in the mud . . . clattering down the mountainside as fast as they could go.

Dawn was just breaking when the mud-splattered wagon rattled up to the North Creek station. Roosevelt jumped down and learned from his secretary, William Loeb, that McKinley had died. By the dim light of a kerosene lamp he glanced at the telegram saying that he was now President of the United States. Then he swung aboard the special car, and Locomotive 363—the best the D & H had—pulled out on the first leg of the long run to Buffalo.

They reached the grieving city at 1:34 P.M. Roosevelt, wearing a top hat, which Loeb had miraculously procured in the Adirondacks, entered a carriage with his host, lawyer Ansley Wilcox. As they started off, Buffalo policeman Anthony J. Gavin thrust his head into the carriage window. "Mr. Roosevelt," he asked, "will you shake hands with me?"

Lost in sadness and the seriousness of the hour, the new President absently glanced up, then brightened: "Why, hello, Tony. I'm glad to see you." There is no record indicating how, when, or where the two had met before, but it was the first clue to an astonishing range of presidential acquaintances that would soon fascinate the country.

All that lay in the future. Right now, no one even knew how to swear in the new President. Secretary of War Elihu Root racked his brains trying to remember how it was done when Garfield died. Finally Louis Babcock was dispatched to the city library to check the old press accounts. "The easiest way to study law," explained Root, who had perhaps the best legal mind in the country, "is to get it out of a newspaper."

Shortly after three o'clock the Cabinet and a few selected guests gathered in the somber library of the Ansley Wilcox home. Roosevelt, who had just returned from calling on Mrs. McKinley, stood in a large bay window, tapping his heel on the highly-polished floor. Secretary Root—the senior Cabinet member present—stepped forward, and the two men faced each other. The rest crowded closer in a small semi-circle.

Quiet fell over the room. A stray bird perched on the window ledge, chirping and fluttering. Roosevelt half turned to looked at it, then quickly back to Root. The Secretary started to speak, but his voice choked with tears. At last he managed to ask Roosevelt to take the oath. A moment's pause while the two conferred in whispers. On Root's advice, Roosevelt then declared he was ready and added emphatically: "It shall be my aim to continue absolutely unbroken the policy of President McKinley for the peace and prosperity and honor of our beloved country."

Roosevelt held his right arm straight up in the air—like an eager schoolboy—while Judge John R. Hazel administered the oath. In repeating the words, his high-pitched voice at first seemed nervous. By the end it rang loud and strong. Chauncey Depew, a keen observer of such matters, felt that the final "And I so swear" sounded like a salvo of artillery.

The ceremony was all over, when late that afternoon a carriage rolled up to the Wilcox house. From it emerged a pathetic figure—gray, worn, completely crushed. Senator Hanna knew he was through, but there remained the little niceties of politics. He limped up the path, as to a surrender ceremony. Long before he reached the door, President Roosevelt was bounding down the steps, hands stretched to meet him. It was a typically warm gesture, but the shattered man needed time before he could again appreciate this sort of thing. Right now he could only say brokenly, "Mr. President. I wish you success and a prosperous administration. I trust you will command me if I can be of any service."

"Now FOR CZOLGOSZ!" thundered the Buffalo *Express,* and the tone was no accident. The wheels of justice moved into high gear. Czolgosz was indicted on Monday, September 16 . . . the trial set for the following week . . . and a quick verdict was promised by the press: "There is not a freeholder in Erie County who would not glory in the opportunity to send the assassin to his death."

An unexpected hitch arose when Judge Loran Lewis and Judge Robert Titus, the court-appointed defense attorneys, showed signs of refusing the case. The Buffalo *Courier* urged them not to worry . . . their duty would consist "simply of seeing that the prisoner is tried according to the prescribed forms of law, not to our mind, of an effort to save him." Nevertheless, on the morning of September 21, two days before the trial would open, Judge Titus still hadn't seen his client: "I have not, nor will I. I don't care to see him."

But Governor Odell brought pressure, the lawyers relented, and the trial began on schedule, September 23. As promised, justice was swift. There were no defense witnesses, no effort by the accused to help himself—he didn't believe in courts anyway. The jury found him guilty the following day, and the defense filed no appeal. One month later Leon F. Czolgosz was electrocuted in Auburn Prison, still explaining, "I killed the President because he was the enemy of the good people, the good working people."

But the good people wanted none of this talk. Ruthlessly they hunted down the "anarchists," who included almost anybody with an unkind word for the late President. Carry Nation was mobbed in Rochester, New York—she had called McKinley a friend of the brewers. Twenty-five families were run out of Guffey's Hollow, Pennsylvania, for "anarchistic tendencies." Emma Goldman, mentioned by Czolgosz, was arrested and held in a Chicago jail, although no evidence ever turned up linking her or any other accomplices to the crime. The witch hunt continued for weeks, fed by dark rumors of anarchist celebrations in a Pennsylvania ravine . . . in a Kansas coal mine.

Far milder comment was aimed at the broken-hearted detectives who had guarded the President. Badgered and cornered, Secret Serviceman Ireland recalled an "Italian" who had delayed the line just before the shooting—then denied the whole story. He vaguely spoke of the many people who greeted the President wearing bandages. He stressed Czolgosz' innocent face. He lamely concluded, "I guess we were all dazed."

The doctors had their critics too. Attention centered on the toast they had given McKinley just before his relapse—everyone knew toast was "scratchy." Actually the toast played no role at all. The autopsy showed that the President's stomach, pancreas, and kidney were riddled with gangrene caused by the wound.

Overshadowing all was the universal grief. Crowds gathered at every crossroads to watch the funeral train pass on its sad journey to Washington and later to Canton. While children put pennies on the track, their elders stood hushed and bareheaded. Taking their cue from the deathbed accounts, all joined together in "Nearer My God to Thee" as the crepe-draped Pullman *Pacific* lumbered by.

Throughout the nation all traffic, work, everything came to a stop for five minutes when the President was buried at Canton on September 19. In Britain, for the first time in history the columns of the London *Times* were bordered in black for a foreign chief of state. At the crowded memorial service in Westminster Abbey, Canon Duckworth said that the late President's passing was "an unspeakable loss not only to his own country but to ourselves and, indeed, the whole world."

Eulogies flowed from the most unlikely places. William Jennings

Bryan—certainly at the opposite end of the political universe—called McKinley a "genius." The Pan-American speech, buried in the papers at the time of its delivery, was unearthed and labeled one of the great addresses of all time. For a while it became a standard shorthand exercise.

The clergy especially were carried away. The Reverend R. B. Hall of New York told his congregation, "The great trio of Presidents will henceforth be Washington, Lincoln, and McKinley." The Reverend Dr. Manchester went further: the late President was "even more deeply imbedded and enshrined in the hearts of the people than Lincoln." Dr. E. P. Ingersoll had to go back to Alfred the Great for adequate comparison. The Reverend Charles E. Benedict of Brooklyn produced the ultimate: "William McKinley stands before our gaze today as one of the greatest characters that the world has ever produced."

Along with praise for the departed came prayers for the living. The Reverend David Gregg asked, "Can Roosevelt carry the republic?" He concluded that whatever the answer, the nation could carry Roosevelt. "Let us tell him this," he enthused, "let us tell him we will carry him."

There were those who thought it might be necessary. They agreed Roosevelt was brave, but after all he was only forty-three. And a very young forty-three at that. They recalled only too well the Harvard dude, the theatrical young man in the Badlands, the bragging hunter, the flamboyant "Teddy" who hijacked a transport to get his Rough Riders to Cuba. "GROWTH IN CHARACTER" ran the headline of a biographical sketch in the Buffalo *Express,* but the very wording had an uneasy ring.

Others took a somewhat different but far dimmer view. They recalled the battle for civil service reform . . . the crusading New York police commissioner . . . the Governor who fired the corrupt insurance officials, who successfully fought for the franchise tax, who wouldn't bow to the state political boss. That in fact was what led to the jam they were now in. Boss Tom Platt had finally rid himself of Roosevelt by engineering him into the traditional dead end, the Vice Presidency. At the time it seemed almost a good joke, although Mark Hanna didn't think so. "Don't any of you realize," he had cried, "that there's only one life between that madman and the Presidency?"

Now it had happened. Hanna was still crushed, but others detected hopeful signs that perhaps Roosevelt had settled down. Wall Street was immensely reassured by his touching little speech at the Wilcox house, promising to continue McKinley's policies for the peace, prosperity, and honor of the country. It was also good to hear that he would keep McKinley's Cabinet intact. And several weeks later a letter to Hanna assured the Senator, "I shall go slow." With an almost audible sigh of relief, John W. MacKay of the Commercial Cable Company concluded, "He knows just what we want and will do his best to shape things accordingly. . . . I believe his policy will be conservative and wise—and always for the best interests of business and the country."

But signs soon appeared that at least some things were changing. The White House had been the essence of back porch tranquillity with the childless McKinleys in residence. Now visitors stepped over the Roosevelt children sliding down the stairs on tin trays; or perhaps recoiled as small boys popped out of the large vases in the East Room.

The visitors themselves differed greatly from the friendly politicians that filled the halls in the old days. Now the brittle Henry Adams and the bulging John L. Sullivan seemed to have equal access. Luncheon might find the old Maine guide Bill Sewell and the scholarly British ambassador Lord Bryce sitting together listening to John Fox, Jr., sing his folk songs.

There was nothing sedentary about this new household. One of McKinley's innumerable "official biographers" primly observed, "The President is not a sportsman. Hunting or fishing have no charms for him. The Cabinet officers and even Justices of the Supreme Court have been known to play golf or tennis; no President has ever done so." That was all over. With enormous zest Roosevelt matched holds with jujitsu experts . . . drafted a "Tennis Cabinet" . . . and led squads of perspiring diplomats on long point-to-point walks through Rock Creek Park.

The hours alone were so different. The McKinley working day began at a leisurely 10:00 A.M., stopped at 4:00 for a drive and a nap; in the evening he might spend an hour with Cortelyou, but that was all. Roosevelt was at his desk by 8:30 A.M., and his fascinating mixture of work and play continued till he went to bed that night. No wonder John Hay, the hold-over Secretary of State, wrote that he might leave whenever Roosevelt wanted, "or when I collapse."

There was, as the Brooklyn *Eagle* termed it, "a new velocity of administration." And it left in its wake little incidents that couldn't possibly have happened in the old days. Three weeks after taking over, Roosevelt appointed a new federal judge in Alabama. It was news to Mark Hanna, who had always been consulted on such things. The Senator wrote, asking why such haste. Roosevelt's courteous reply explained why he wanted to decide the matter quickly—and left no doubt where he felt the power of decision lay.

A month later Hanna took up his pen again. He had studied the draft of Roosevelt's first message to Congress; he wondered whether there might be too much emphasis on corporation control. The President sent a soothing reply the following day, but when the message appeared in December, the very first recommendation called for new controls.

And so the changes multiplied. Small matters, but nonetheless important. For this was something far deeper than a reshuffling of personalities. A whole new philosophy of life was bursting into focus.

1902

Big Stick, Big Business

"If we have done anything wrong, send your man to my man and they can fix it up."

—J. PIERPONT MORGAN to President Roosevelt

No sense of change stirred the air as J. Pierpont Morgan sat down to dine on the evening of February 19, 1902, at his brownstone house in New York. There were the usual guests—favored associates from Morgan's great banking house—and the usual conversation, for the day had been pleasantly uneventful. The market closed high; the Morgan-financed U.S. Steel Corporation was running smoothly; and now a new merger, the Northern Securities Company, was well under way. This "holding company" controlled the once-competing Northern Pacific and Great Northern railroads. It would dominate the entire Northwest, and perhaps later the whole country. There seemed no limit to the possibilities.

The telephone rang. The call was urgent, and Mr. Morgan excused himself. A newspaperman was on the line with a bulletin from Washington. It was a laconic announcement by Attorney General Philander C. Knox: he had been ordered by the President to proceed against the Northern Securities Company for violating the Sherman Antitrust Act—the federal law forbidding combinations "in restraint of trade or commerce."

Morgan returned to the table looking amazed, appalled, but most of all hurt. He should have been warned, he told his guests. He should have had a chance to fix things up, or at least dissolve the combination voluntarily. To attack him this way was all wrong. Worse, it was ungentlemanly. After all, Roosevelt came from their own class.

Some of the guests just couldn't believe the news. When a reporter called at the house later, Morgan's partner Charles Steele sputtered, "A great surprise . . . no such action was expected . . . we are wholly in the dark." And he hopefully concluded, "I am inclined to doubt the report."

No wonder. The Sherman Antitrust Act had long been a dead letter. When the American Sugar Refining Company had cornered 98 per cent of the industry's output in 1895, the Supreme Court failed to see anything illegal. The law, explained the court, applied to commerce, not production or the simple exchange of stock certificates. There were those who couldn't see the difference, but it never bothered old Attorney General Olney: "You will observe," he wrote placidly, "that the government has been defeated on the trust question. I always supposed it would be, and have taken the responsibility of not prosecuting under a law I believe to be no good."

Behind this benign attitude lay a deeper reason why the gentlemen at the Morgan house were so shocked by Roosevelt's action. Traditionally America was the land of *laissez-faire*. Men of energy should be free to build their factories and railroads, compete with each other any way they liked. The best would win out, and the nation would be the gainer. The wealth that flowed to the victors was their just reward and carried the blessing of a Higher Power. "God gave me my money," explained John D. Rockefeller.

The "trusts" or combinations that followed were the natural outgrowth of this philosophy. Men saw that competition was often wasteful; great savings could be achieved by joining to cut overhead and end duplication. Others saw that they could sometimes make more by combining to raise prices, instead of competing to lower them. The Sherman Act was meant to stop this, but the Supreme Court took care of that. Now it was clear sailing. When the wire nail "trust" was organized in 1895, nails cost $1.20 a keg; a year later the price was $2.55.

With a little imagination a man could make money in more subtle ways. The trusts were usually formed by exchanging stock in the participating firms for stock in the new combination—often on highly inflated terms. When Consolidated Steel & Wire merged with several other companies to form American Steel & Wire, every $100 share of Consolidated was exchanged for $350 in American's stock. When American became part of a still larger combination, the shares were again exchanged—this time for $490 in stock. Finally, when even this giant was absorbed by Morgan's new U.S. Steel Corporation, the shares were exchanged for a third time. The lucky owners now got $564.37 in U.S. Steel stock. In this way those on the "inside" made over 450 per cent profit. To materialize, it required only unloading the "watered stock" on somebody else.

The little group at the top saw nothing wrong with any of this. To corner a market, to juggle prices, to manipulate stocks, to subsidize a Senator were all part of the game. Part of what boss Tom Platt of New York called, "the right of a man to run his own business in his own way, with due respect of course to the Ten Commandments and the Penal Code."

These men were not naturally callous. They had no evil intent. But they had lost touch. The vastness of their operations, the complexity of their corporate structures kept them far from their employees and the people they served. Isolated in their stone châteaux, their yachts, their private Pullmans, they had no chance to see how their schemes affected others. Sociologist E. A. Ross summed it up well at the time: "There's nothing like distance to disinfect dividends."

So they were surprised and indignant—and painfully arrogant—at any hint of interference. "It's none of the public's business what I do," snorted financier George Baker. "I owe the public nothing!" echoed Pierpont Morgan.

Of all these proud leaders, certainly the most spectacular were the railroad men of the West. And this was only natural. These were the days before highways, airplanes, and effective regulations. The man who ran the railroad controlled the destiny of shippers, buyers, farmers, cities, and states.

The result was distasteful but inevitable. "When the master of one of the great Western lines travels towards the Pacific in his palace car," Lord Bryce observed with awe, "his journey is like a royal progress. Governors of States and Territories bow before him; legislatures receive him in solemn session; cities seek to propitiate him."

At the turn of the century two of these potentates—Edward H. Harriman and James J. Hill—were locked in deadly combat. Harriman, whose mousy look hid the fiercest ambition on Wall Street, was a stockbroker turned railroad man. He had brilliantly revamped the defunct Union Pacific system, running from Omaha to the Coast. Hill, a rough, shaggy little giant of volcanic temper, had built the Great Northern and dominated the neighboring Northern Pacific. These lines ran parallel but to the north of the Union Pacific, from St. Paul and Duluth to Puget Sound. Neither Hill nor Harriman had an outlet in Chicago. But the well-heeled Chicago, Burlington & Quincy had . . . plus connections with the South and access to the rich Iowa market. The battle began when both men tried to pluck this plum.

Hill fired the first shot. After a halfhearted try in 1897, he made a serious effort to capture the line in 1899. This time he was backed by Morgan, who had taken a shine to Hill during the Northern Pacific reorganization. From now on, Wall Street's great autocrat would back the rough-and-tumble railroad man in all his ventures. But even the House of Morgan couldn't pry the Burlington loose from its thousands of small stockholders. They knew a good thing when they had it.

Now it was Harriman's turn. Hill's attempt suggested that far more than Chicago and a few new markets were at stake. The Burlington in unfriendly hands would be a serious threat to the Union Pacific. So all through the spring and summer of 1900 Harriman courted the Burlington's thrifty share owners. He had no better luck, although he was backed by Morgan's great rival, the investment firm of Kuhn, Loeb & Company.

By January, 1901, Hill was ready for another try. Now he too saw the danger of the Burlington in unfriendly hands and he too talked less about Chicago, Southern connections, and Iowa crops. These goals were replaced by the far greater incentive of stealing the march on his old antagonist.

Hill and Morgan were willing to pay more now, and at last the Burlington owners succumbed to temptation. The negotiations were concluded—perhaps openly, as Hill claimed; perhaps secretly, as Harriman insisted. In any case, these things get around, and late in March Harriman paid a little call on Hill. He brought with him Jacob Schiff of Kuhn, Loeb. Schiff was an unusually sensitive man for this life, philanthropic and deeply religious. Often it seemed that he just couldn't swallow Wall Street any longer, but in the end he always managed to suppress his feelings.

Delicately Schiff asked whether the rumors were true—was Hill trying to get control of the Burlington? Nonsense, came the answer. Hill wasn't remotely interested in the stock; he didn't have any intention of controlling the property.

But in a few days there could no longer be any doubt about it. So they had another meeting, and when Schiff asked why he had been misled, Hill explained that there were some things you just had to do. Harriman filled the awkward pause with an offer: he would like to put up a third for an equivalent interest in the Burlington purchase. He didn't say so at the moment, but he thought that this would at least give him a chance to sit on the board and keep an eye on things. Hill was emphatically not interested.

"Very well," said Harriman, "this is a hostile act and you must take the consequences." A significant remark, in the light of what later happened. At the time, Hill simply shrugged it off. By now he had the Burlington in his pocket. The meeting adjourned.

It was true that the Burlington was won. But Hill and Morgan had used the big Northern Pacific as a vehicle to carry the purchase. In this line they had operating control, but not an actual majority of the stock. This gave Harriman his opening. He would get the Burlington by capturing the Northern Pacific itself. He would swallow the line that had swallowed the line he wanted.

It was such brazen buccaneering that Schiff felt compelled to write a "conscience" letter to Hill on April 8. He stressed his friendship "wherever our business interests may place us." He expressed his hope "that nothing has come between us."

For anyone who knew Schiff, the letter was as good a tip as Harriman's blunt threat, but the buoyant Hill didn't worry. He knew that the Northern Pacific was capitalized on 800,000 shares of common stock and 750,000 of preferred with voting rights . . . together worth $155 million. Neither he nor Morgan could imagine anybody scraping together the $78 million necessary to steal it from them. Nor did they realize how vast Harriman's resources were—or that he would mortgage anything he owned to get more. With the situation apparently under control, Hill went back to the West Coast and Morgan sailed to France to enjoy the sun at Aix-les-Bains.

Quietly, very quietly, Harriman and Schiff began buying Northern Pacific stock on the open market. A little here, a little there, never too much at once. By April 15 they had collected 150,000 shares of common and 100,000 of preferred. Despite their efforts at secrecy, the market began to edge up with this lively demand—101 on April 22 . . . 109 on the 27th . . . 119 on the 29th. The conspirators held their breath.

They needn't have worried. The market was riding a fabulous boom. Besides, Northern Pacific had just taken over the Burlington in a brilliant stroke—it ought to go up. The Morgan forces slept on. In fact, feeling that Northern Pacific was now absurdly overpriced, they decided to shear a few lambs. A trusted Morgan associate sold 35,000 shares to someone who apparently didn't know much about the security market. The Northern Pacific itself sold an additional 13,000 from its own reserves. Then the Morgans sold 10,000 more. All of it dropped into Harriman's lap.

In Seattle James J. Hill was puzzled. He was a railroad man, not a Wall Street tycoon. He left those problems to Morgan. But he did read the papers and by the end of April he was far less complacent than his Eastern friends. Over 500,000 shares of Northern Pacific traded in three days. Surely the general public wasn't that excited about buying a piece of America's future. Clearly something was up. The place to be was New York.

He moved the way an empire builder should—fast and by special train. The Great Northern coupled up his big, varnished private car; the superintendent of the Western Division himself gave the engineer his instructions: "The road is yours to St. Paul."

They rocketed off. The tracks were cleared ahead, and the special streaked across the West on the fastest run ever made to the Mississippi —a change at St. Paul ... again at Chicago ... and into New York just before noon on Friday, May 3.

Charging downtown, Hill headed not for the friendly Morgan bank —there was nothing delicate about his approach to problems—but straight for the William Street offices of Kuhn, Loeb & Company. This was the enemy citadel; here he would find the root of the trouble. What, he asked Jacob Schiff, were they all up to?

The impeccable Schiff fairly purred assurances. Kuhn, Loeb was indeed buying up Northern Pacific on Harriman's orders. But there was nothing to fear. They only wanted a fair share in the Burlington management. Since Hill had turned him down, this was the only way to get it. Certainly no interest in Northern Pacific. In fact, they hoped Hill would stay and run it for them.

It was enough to enrage a far milder man than Hill, but somehow he held his temper. He still couldn't believe there was serious danger. He boasted that he and Morgan held at least 350,000 shares of Northern Pacific and he didn't see how anybody could buy enough stock on the open market to outgun them.

"That may be," replied Schiff placidly, "but we've got a lot of it."

There was no point in further arguing. Hill stalked out, muttering, "I'm safe. I still don't believe it can be done."

But he must have had his qualms. That evening he again called on Schiff, this time at his home. Now Hill adopted a new approach. He too was reassuring—the Burlington wouldn't dream of hurting Harriman. And he was reasonable—something could be worked out to give Harriman a say in its affairs. And, of course, he was occasionally his old tough self—call off the raid or go down in ruin. Schiff listened patiently, courteously ... and didn't budge an inch.

Schiff, in fact, was now convinced that the battle had been won.

73

Harriman had 420,000 of the 750,000 preferred shares, 370,000 of the 800,000 common. Still a minority of the common but certainly a majority of both, and all the stock had voting rights. True, the preferred could be retired next January, but the company would be reorganized in time to prevent that. So better let well enough alone. The price was already too high, and there was no point in making Hill even angrier. Schiff went to bed that night planning to do no more buying.

Harriman wasn't so confident. Maybe the preferred stock could be retired before he could name the new management. Schiff and the lawyers thought this was impossible, but they could be wrong. If so, he would end up with a lot of useless preferred, a minority of common, and the Hill-Morgan crowd still in control. Better buy another 40,000 shares of common, just to be sure.

There was only one hitch. The strain of this immense secret raid had been too much. Now Harriman was sick with excitement. On Saturday, May 4, he just couldn't pull himself out of bed. The phone would have to do. He called Kuhn, Loeb, told Mr. Heinsheimer, one of the partners, to buy 40,000 more Northern Pacific common. Heinsheimer said, "All right," and Harriman sank back satisfied. Now at last he could relax.

But the order never went through. Wall Street too has chains of command, and at Kuhn, Loeb no one dared to make such a purchase without clearing at the top. This took time, for Schiff couldn't be located. When finally reached, he had to act quickly. The market closed early on Saturday and there was no chance to consult Harriman. Still confident, he decided against the order.

It proved one of those turning points that men like to debate. If Harriman had been well enough to go to Kuhn, Loeb, he might have personally rammed his order through. Or if Schiff had been at the office, Harriman's phone call might have been enough. As it was, the market closed at noon with Harriman 40,000 shares short of certain control.

Fate played no such tricks at the nearby offices of J. P. Morgan & Company. Hill barged in early, now convinced that Schiff wasn't bluffing. Clearly they had all been caught. Morgan holdings of

Northern Pacific common were down to 260,000 shares. Yet this was their only hope. If they could control the common, all they had to do was delay any reorganization of the company until January. If they could do that, they could retire the preferred and remain in control.

They quickly cabled Morgan for authority to buy 150,000 more shares of common. This would fatten their holdings to 410,000—a bare majority, but enough.

The walls of the Grand Hotel at Aix-les-Bains must have shaken with the old man's rage when he read the message. How could they have been such fools? Well, there would be time for discipline later. Right now, he shot back his approval.

Morgan men sped over the floor when the market opened on Monday, May 6. They were everywhere, buying all the Northern Pacific in sight. The price soared—114 . . . 118 . . . 121 . . . 127½.

As the stock rose, gamblers and speculators moved in. They had no idea who was buying Northern Pacific, but they did know it was overpriced. It must be heading for a fall. They began selling short—that is, selling Northern Pacific stock they didn't own, hoping to pick it up later at a lower price before delivery was due. If the stock was still high at that time, they felt they could always borrow enough to meet their commitments until the price came down. And it was bound to fall within a few hours.

But Tuesday morning Northern Pacific was still climbing—127½ . . . 133 . . . 140 . . . 143¼. Again, the short sellers moved in. This time they were sure it had to fall, and when it did the killing would be bigger than ever. If, for instance, a man sold 5,000 shares at 140 and the stock dropped to 120 by delivery time, he would clear $100,000 just like that.

By noon some "shorts" were in trouble. The stock was still rising, and yesterday's sales were now due for delivery. Then, when they tried to borrow enough shares to cover themselves, they discovered there was little Northern Pacific to be had. And that at outrageous loan rates.

They didn't know it at the time, but the explanation was a matter of simple arithmetic. When trading began Monday, the combined Morgan and Harriman interests already held 630,000 of the 800,000 shares of

Northern Pacific common. This left only 170,000 shares that could be bought. But on Monday and Tuesday 539,000 were "sold."

Most of this stock just didn't exist. By Tuesday night Morgan's men had collected 124,000 shares, leaving only 46,000 to meet the large commitments made by the gamblers and speculators. Most of the remaining shares were in socks, mattresses, and safe deposit boxes all over the country. The few blocks still on the market were held by smiling figures who offered to lend them at 15 per cent interest, or sell them at perhaps 17 points above closing price. The speculators weren't that desperate—yet.

Sometimes a man could learn more at the Waldorf bar than he could on the Street. That evening, as the weary speculators compared notes in the taproom, the truth dawned at last. Northern Pacific had been cornered. Who had all the stock was still a mystery—some said it was a Vanderbilt raid. In any case, the "shorts" were trapped—they had to buy any stock left at astronomical prices, or fail to deliver and go broke.

A Hill-Morgan spokesman was vaguely sympathetic: "It is a very unpleasant episode in high finance." Over at the Hotel Netherland old James J. Hill wasn't even that consoling. He said he knew nothing about the whole affair: "I have not bought a share of Northern Pacific in six months. I'm president of the Great Northern, you know, and I'm not interested in Northern Pacific. I don't know anything about Mr. Morgan's relations to the road—we are two separate individuals."

On Wednesday the 8th, Northern Pacific continued to soar: 155 . . . 161 . . . 173 . . . 180. Harriman and Morgan had finished their buying; now the "shorts" were to blame. Frantically they bid against each other, trying to get enough Northern Pacific to cover their commitments. Usually there was none for sale, and then followed the desperate effort to borrow some. When one tough operator lent 1,000 shares at 35 per cent, there were gasps of disapproval. An hour later it looked like a bargain—the rate was up to 85 per cent.

To raise the money, the harassed "shorts" began unloading their other holdings. Soon everything but Northern Pacific was heading down: Steel off 7 points . . . Union Pacific 8½ . . . Copper 12. And so the market drew to a chaotic close—Northern Pacific leveling off around 160, everything else plunging down.

The drinks were stronger than usual that night at the Waldorf. Excited crowds of men surged from the café to the bar to the billiard room and back again. Many didn't bother to dress . . . something almost unheard-of at the time. Big plungers like James R. Keane and John W. ("Bet-You-a-Million") Gates sat at their favorite tables, while lesser lights hovered around, hoping for some sort of tip or advice that might save them. But the big men had little to say and perhaps the soundest observation of the night came from dry, sardonic Jefferson M. Levy, who knew a thing or two about Morgan & Company: "It looks like the little boys commenced something while the big boy was away."

It was now obvious who the contending forces were, but at the Hotel Netherland, Mr. Hill still enjoyed his little game of possum. Asked if he was struggling for control of the Northern Pacific, he carefully explained, "My dear sir, we never had control, we don't want control, and under the law we could not have control." Then, looking the *Herald* reporter squarely in the eye, he declared, "Really, I have had no more to do with this than the man in the moon."

Thursday, May 9, dawned wet and gray. Long before opening time a restless crowd milled around the doors of the Produce Exchange, where the stock market met while its own new building was under construction. The flag drooped at half mast for some departed financier, making the damp day even more depressing.

The doors opened and news began trickling out. It couldn't have been worse. Northern Pacific opened at 170, then shot up to 200 . . . 320 . . . 650. The "shorts" were frantic—willing to do anything to get enough stock to stave off bankruptcy. J. S. Bache & Company even chartered a special train to bring down 500 shares that had turned up in Albany.

All other holdings went down the drain, and the rest of the market crashed. American Tobacco down 21 points; Missouri Pacific 33; Leather Preferred 17. Standard Oil had opened at 800, tumbled to 650 by midmorning. To kill the rumor that broker A. A. Housman had died of shock, friends persuaded him to go downtown and walk around.

Outside the Exchange, a well-dressed lady emerged from a hansom cab. Leaning on the arm of a colored butler she made her way to the door and asked for the latest on Steel Preferred. They told her it was down to 83, and she instantly burst into tears: "God help me, I am ruined!" She stumbled back to the cab, little knowing that the worst was yet to come. Before the day's end, Steel sagged to 69.

The hideous climax came just before noon. The firm of Street & Norton sold some poor soul 300 shares of Northern Pacific common at 1000. "Boys," cried partner Ed Norton, "I am more sorry than I can tell you, but I can't help it."

"It is just like crucifying one's friends," piously added Hartwig Baruch, another of the gentlemen on top.

It couldn't go on. Hundreds of "shorts" were insolvent, with no hope of ever paying off. Thousands of innocent stockholders had lost their entire savings as other shares crashed. The whole market was as big a shambles as the littered floor of the building itself. At noon Kuhn, Loeb and Morgan & Company announced a truce. They agreed not to require any deliveries that day. Another agreement quickly followed—the "shorts" would be allowed to settle at $150 a share. Relieved and exhausted, Wall Street began pulling itself together.

The leading contestants took it rather jovially. Harriman had been stricken with appendicitis during the crisis and on coming out of ether asked for a phone. Not to call his family, but to tease Hill: "I just wanted to tell you the operation's over and I'm perfectly all right!"

Hill himself ambled into the Kuhn, Loeb offices a few days later but found Schiff out. Strolling over to Felix Warburg's desk, he asked, "How is Schiff?"

"Not very happy."

"He takes things too seriously," laughed Hill.

Schiff was indeed feeling contrite. While Harriman and Hill shrugged it all off, he carefully penned some more of his "conscience" letters. One, of course, went to Morgan, "caring much as I do for your respect and opinion." Another to Hill confessed, "It made me unhappier than I can tell you to find myself for the first time in fifteen years in a position where you and I could not go together arm in arm. . . ."

If Schiff was uncomfortable, the country as a whole was downright indignant. It had been scared out of its wits. True, the stocks quickly bounced back, but millions of small investors had been endangered by two huge combinations ruthlessly battling against each other. This certainly wasn't the way the system was meant to work. The future held boundless promise, but that assumed the nation's financial giants were, as they claimed, devoted custodians of the national wealth. It surely didn't hold true if they went around, as the *Times* put it, "like cowboys on a spree, shooting wildly at each other in entire disregard of the safety of the bystanders."

Perhaps both sides felt a little guilty—more likely they were simply appalled at the cost of battle. In any case, they quickly called off the fight. It still wasn't clear who controlled the Northern Pacific, but rather than go to some law court, they reached an amicable understanding at the Metropolitan Club. On May 31 they agreed that Morgan, who had a majority of the common stock, would name a new board of directors. Harriman, who had a majority of common and preferred together, would be given places on it. The preferred would be retired, insuring Morgan-Hill control, but Harriman would be protected.

To put the treaty on a permanent basis, the Northern Securities Company was launched on November 12, 1901. Technically, it was a holding company, taking the stock of the Great Northern and Northern Pacific railroads and giving its own in return. Actually, it did far more than that. It let everybody sleep at night. Harriman got three seats on the new board, which would end the nightmare of a Hill-controlled Burlington creeping into his territory. Hill and Morgan got a railroad combination so large that no one could ever steal it out from under them. It was capitalized at $400 million. Some $122 million was "water," but still it was stock. It would take $200 million worth of shares to seize control. Not even Harriman could pull that off. Nothing could hurt them now.

It never dawned on any of them that the government might interfere. After all, Roosevelt had promised to follow McKinley's footsteps. Yet his record suggested little sympathy for many business practices. As early as 1894 he had written that bankers and railroad kings needed "sound chastisement." And during his governorship of New York, boss Tom Platt frankly told him that he was reputed to be "a little loose" on the trust question.

His first message to Congress had been another storm warning. It clearly stated that the old antitrust laws were "no longer sufficient." On the other hand, he also stressed the benefits that big business gave the nation. To many, the net effect was soothing. As "Mr. Dooley," humorist Finley Peter Dunne's fictional saloonkeeper, put it: "Th' trusts are heejus monsthers built up be th' inlightened intherprise iv th' men that have done so much to advance progress in our beloved counthry."

And for that matter, the President was not against trusts. He was simply against "bad" trusts. He was not opposed to great wealth— just the "malefactors of great wealth." Roosevelt tended to see all questions as moral issues—good or bad—and business was no exception. If he felt a trust was charging fair prices and giving good service, let it live. If it was restraining trade and jacking up rates, then it was evil and should be stopped. As he later explained, "Draw the line on conduct and not on size."

The difficulty was that Roosevelt, and Roosevelt alone, would decide who was good and who was bad. His duty, he declared, was to "stand with every one while he was right, and to stand against him when he went wrong." But how to know whether you were "right" or "wrong"?

There were certain clues which the Morgans and Harrimans— preconvinced they were right—couldn't hope to see. Roosevelt, for instance, scorned "the men who seek gain not by genuine work but by gambling." In other words, speculators, financial manipulators, and almost anyone on Wall Street. Their wealth was tainted and "wrong." He also detested arrogance and contempt for authority. It didn't help James J. Hill when he cynically pointed out that under the law he couldn't take over the Northern Pacific—and then ended up with it anyway.

So the Northern Securities Company was ripe for attack, and the President began laying his plans. Early in 1902 he secretly asked Attorney General Knox for his opinion. Knox felt the merger was illegal and that he could win the case in court. Roosevelt told him to go ahead.

No other official was consulted. The news that stunned Morgan's dinner guests on February 19 was as big a surprise to the Cabinet. Secretary of War Root, in fact, was quite put out. Roosevelt admired Root immensely but felt the Secretary was too close to Wall Street to take any chances on this matter. After all, nothing else had ever been kept secret from the Street.

It was this element of surprise—as much as the attack itself—that made stocks tumble the following day. Until now, whenever the government planned to do anything affecting business, it had the courtesy to let Wall Street know in advance. Suddenly, the lines of communication were down.

The first reaction was fury at Roosevelt. "Disturber of the rights of vested interests!" was probably the politest comment. The *Herald* decided that the President was "probably the most abused man in the world for the day." Out in St. Paul, James J. Hill declared he was in the fight to stay and he darkly promised that those who opposed him would regret ever doing so.

Anger gradually gave way to cockiness. "We may give the Department of Justice something to do!" a Northern Pacific director remarked cheerfully. The legal mind, in fact, was already at work. One downtown lawyer explained that the "Northern Securities Company was not a trust but a repository." Another figured that if the worst came to the worst, the company could be reorganized in Britain and remain completely immune. All agreed that the President had been poorly advised by Knox, who was dubbed "that country lawyer from Pennsylvania."

Still, Pierpont Morgan hated the thought of a lawsuit. It was bound to disturb the market. Besides, it was all wrong to be hauled up in court like some common thief. This sort of thing should be settled quietly, in a paneled room. Something could always be worked out between two equals.

On Sunday, February 23, Morgan visited the White House and had a long talk with the President and Attorney General Knox. He was still hurt, he said, that Washington had given him no warning of the suit.

"But that is just what we did not want to do," Roosevelt remarked.

"If we have done anything wrong," persisted Morgan, "send your man to my man and they can fix it up."

"That can't be done."

At this point, Knox broke in to explain, "We don't want to fix it up; we want to stop it."

Ignoring him, Mr. Morgan turned back to the President, "Are you going to attack my other interests, the Steel Trust and the others?"

"Certainly not," Roosevelt said, "unless we find out that they have done something that we regard as wrong."

There was no point in further discussion. Morgan left, so bitter that he composed a violent letter to the President—happily never mailed. The Attorney General pressed the case, and two years later emerged the winner. By a 5-4 vote, the Supreme Court reversed its decision in the Knight case . . . held that the Northern Securities Company was in violation of the Sherman Antitrust Act . . . and ordered the company dissolved.

But it was not the decision that mattered; it was the mere act of filing the suit. The public was enchanted. It had come to accept the idea that business was all-powerful. The moral fervor of Roosevelt's denial was a thrilling, tingling change. And, humanly enough, almost everyone enjoyed the discomfort of the great magnates. "Wall Street," observed the Detroit *Free Press,* "is paralyzed at the thought that a President of the United States would sink so low as to try to enforce the law."

It was done not blatantly, not arrogantly, and almost always balanced by a kind word for business—or a stern word for reformers—but it was done. To describe his technique, Roosevelt used a quotation that gave birth to one of the great phrases of the period. "I have always been fond," he said, "of the West African proverb, 'Speak softly and carry a big stick, you will go far.'"

So the Big Stick was brandished—and government took on a new dimension. The Chief Executive was no longer a decorative by-stander. He seemed in the middle of everything, swatting the "bad," defending the "good." People might not always agree with him, but they couldn't deny he was there. And like him or not, they had to admit he was everybody's President.

So people naturally turned toward Roosevelt in the fall of 1902 when a great anthracite coal strike gripped the country. The trouble had been brewing a long time. Conditions in the mines were appalling. Average earnings ran $560 a year for the miners, far less for loaders, dumpers and other workers. The hours were hideous—hoisting engineers worked twelve-hour shifts seven days a week. And there was always the company store. At the Markle Coal Company, twelve-year-old Andrew Chippie's forty cents a day was regularly credited against a debt left by his father, killed four years before in a mine accident.

To the men's cause came a dark, moody young man named John Mitchell, leader of the United Mine Workers. In contrast to the rabble-rousing organizer people expected, Mitchell was shy, quiet, and dreadfully earnest. His invariable dark suit and big black necktie gave him an almost priestlike appearance. There was an air of Lincolnesque romance about him that drew the miners by the thousands. In March, 1902, he felt strong enough to ask for more pay, shorter hours, a uniform method of weighing coal, and above all union recognition.

The operators would have none of it. They were mostly Eastern railroads serving the big anthracite regions. A closely knit group, they saw eye-to-eye with each other perfectly and would be a hard nut to crack. And they were all the more determined because they felt they had already been talked into one unnecessary raise. During the 1900 campaign Mark Hanna had persuaded them to grant a 10 per cent increase to lubricate McKinley's election, and now it was cemented into the wage structure. They were damned if they would do it again.

Mitchell suggested a mediation committee composed of men like Archbishop Ireland and Bishop Potter. The operators declined. "Anthracite mining is a business," explained President George Baer of the Reading Railroad, "and not a religious, sentimental or academic proposition."

On May 12 some 140,000 miners walked out and the strike was on. As the weeks dragged by, the tension grew. The strike fund ran low, and although the workers had been coached against violence, stones began flying. Behind the scenes, efforts continued to get the two sides together. Mitchell was always willing but the operators were adamant. Their obstinacy exasperated even conservatives like Mark Hanna, who was now worried about the effect on the fall election. Morgan was drafted to try his hand—he had a certain amount of influence with any railroad man anywhere. But it didn't work here. George Baer wouldn't yield an inch.

He had no doubt about his position. It was bestowed from Above. "The rights and interests of the laboring man," he wrote Mr. W. F. Clark of Wilkes-Barre, "will be protected and cared for—not by the labor agitators, but by the Christian men to whom God in his infinite wisdom has given the control of the property interests of this country...."

The crisp September air brought matters to a crisis. These were the days before gas, oil, and electric heating. Nearly everyone depended on anthracite. It was nearly all gone now, with a heatless fall and winter in prospect. The few remaining carloads soared in price—from $5 . . . to $14 . . . to $20 a ton. Enterprising residents of Rochester, New York, began chopping down the city's telegraph poles. Riots broke out in Passaic, New Jersey. Schools and plants began closing all over the country.

The White House had never tried to settle a strike before (although it had broken a few), but that didn't stop Roosevelt now. Nor did the injured leg he had recently suffered when a trolley hit his carriage near Pittsfield, Massachusetts. That was a close one—the man next to him killed—but Roosevelt thrived on physical challenge, and now he whirled about in a wheel chair, imperiling his personal staff. Telegrams went out to Mitchell and the operators asking them to meet him in Washington on October 3. They would gather at 22 Jackson Place, where Roosevelt was temporarily staying while the White House was remodeled.

"I can't imagine what idea he may have that will change my determination," remarked one of the operators as he swung aboard the special train that took them in a group to the capital. They spent the night in their Pullmans and the following morning they moved in a procession of glistening carriages to Jackson Place. Mitchell and his aides arrived somewhat more modestly—by streetcar.

Roosevelt, wearing a gray dressing gown, explained that he represented the third party to the dispute—the public. He stressed that he had no legal right or duty to call them together but appealed to their patriotism to end the strike. Mitchell requested the President to appoint a commission—he would go along with whatever it said. Before the operators could comment, Roosevelt asked everybody to retire until after lunch to ponder his words. The operators' carriages headed back to the railroad yard.

For the next few hours the private Pullmans must have trembled with fury, for when the operators reassembled at Jackson Place they outdid each other in angry statements. Mr. Baer, who by now had earned a deathless reputation as their chief spokesman, thundered: "The duty of the hour is not to waste time negotiating with the fomenters of this anarchy and insolent defiance of law, but to do as was done in the War of the Rebellion, restore the majesty of law, the only guardian of a free people, and to re-establish order and peace at any cost."

The others talked the same way, and Mr. Truesdale of the Lackawanna Railroad came up with an unexpected argument. He pointed out that he had a lot of children in his mines and it was positively dangerous for their young minds to be in contact with radicals like John Mitchell.

They stormed out, Baer snarling, "We object to being called here to meet a criminal, even by the President of the United States." It was all in the point of view. Roosevelt later observed that Mitchell was the only man in the room who behaved like a gentleman—including himself.

"Well, I've tried and failed," the President glumly wrote Hanna that night. The strike dragged on. Violence spread. Some ten thousand National Guardsmen moved in. A soldier shot a miner at Shenandoah; strikers wrecked two trains near Wilkes-Barre, blew up a bridge leading to the Slattery Colliery at Tuscarora. Roosevelt arranged to have Governor Stone request federal troops, then ordered General J. M.

Scofield to stand by. At the President's signal he was to take over and run the mines.

Before this drastic moment arrived, Secretary of War Elihu Root's sharp legal mind saw the way out. From years of corporate practice, he felt that fear of losing face was now the chief stumbling block. If it could be made to appear that the operators were dealing with their own men and not with John Mitchell, something might be worked out. With Roosevelt's blessing he hurried to New York and spent a day with Pierpont Morgan on the banker's yacht *Corsair*.

Their plan called for an impartial commission appointed by the President. It would decide "all questions at issue between the respective companies and their own employees, whether they belonged to a union or not." Actually this was what Mitchell had suggested in Washington but it was far more palatable coming from Root. Also, the proposal was carefully phrased so that the commission didn't appear to be mediating between the operators and the union.

Morgan applied a little pressure and the operators accepted the plan. But they specified that the commission should include a businessman who knew the industry, a mining engineer, a judge from eastern Pennsylvania, an Army or Navy officer, and a man of prominence eminent as a sociologist. There was no union man on the list.

Through the night of October 15 Roosevelt, Root, and two Morgan partners—George Perkins and Robert Bacon—sat in the temporary White House trying to get the operators to add a union representative. There were endless relayed phone conversations: Roosevelt to Bacon to Morgan to Baer and back again. But the net result was always the same—nothing doing. Around midnight the President suddenly realized that the operators were objecting not to a union man but to anybody specifically described as one. A certain ostrichlike quality made them amenable to the appointment of a union man, provided he was called something else. Roosevelt quickly appointed the Grand Chief of the Order of Railway Conductors as the "eminent sociologist" and everyone was happy.

The strike ended and the commission went to work. Months later it granted most of the union's demands. But that was an anticlimax.

What excited people was Roosevelt's role in engineering the settlement. Nothing like it had ever happened before. He gave government new stature merely by bringing the parties to Washington. And by saying that he was representing the third party in the dispute—the public—he sowed the seed of an exciting new idea. Instead of being passive spectators, the people themselves had an active part to play in shaping the better world to come.

Here was a great revelation. It had occurred to few before. Where evil was known to exist, people either accepted it as part of the game or felt there was nothing they could do anyhow. Roosevelt changed all that. Scholars would later complain that his ideas were naïve and oversimplified, that he knew nothing about economics, that he never offered any genuine, carefully developed program. He did something infinitely more important—he awoke the nation's conscience.

All sorts of crusaders suddenly marched forth on a vast unco-ordinated reform movement. Most of them were not sour, or against the capitalist system. They were all for it. They simply wanted to root out the evils that threatened it—to save it—to make it even better.

One group fought for new regulations. Gifford Pinchot of Pennsylvania began his battle for conservation. Senator David Elkins of West Virginia sponsored a law against freight rebates. Roosevelt himself pushed through a Bureau of Corporations, empowered to investigate big interstate companies. Business bitterly protested. "Just as bad as need be," was the way John Archibald of Standard Oil quaintly phrased his objections. But the President was adamant. "If you do not let us do this," he warned Pierpont Morgan at a Gridiron dinner, "those who come after us will rise and bring you to ruin!"

Other reformers had a different attack. The trouble, they felt, was that the country had grown too big—the people had lost their old voice in affairs. Laws should be passed to restore it . . . to recreate the town-meeting approach to problems. Then the abuses would vanish; the electorate, if assured control, was bound to look after its own interests. In short, the ills of democracy could best be cured by more democracy.

The specific remedies were simple. "Initiative" would let people

87

pass legislation on their own, free from crude political influence; "referendum" would let them throw the bad laws out—Oregon adopted both in 1902. "Recall" would let the voters fire the public servants who turned sour. "Direct primaries" would take nominations out of smoke-filled hotel rooms, giving the choice back to the voters themselves. Wisconsin introduced this in 1903, spurred on by her new reform Governor Bob La Follette. Hopes ran high: Minnesota's Senator Washburn called direct primaries "the greatest political proposition ever introduced into American politics."

At the city level the same spirit prevailed. A host of reform mayors appeared on the scene. In Cleveland, roly-poly Mayor Tom Johnson battled the traction interests for a municipally-owned streetcar system—that would give the city back to its citizens. In Toledo Mayor "Golden Rule" Jones ran on the platform that gave him his nickname. The "interests" all fought him, but he was elected and re-elected. "Everybody is against me but the people," he boasted and the Golden Rule marched on.

The reforms that filled the air were almost always political in character. There was little interest in economic or social legislation. Workmen's compensation, wage and hour laws, old-age security held little appeal. Make the climate right, people felt, and the workers could bargain for their own protection—they didn't need any paternal government to do it for them.

But when it came to welfare work, the reformers were everywhere. In Chicago Jane Addams, a perky, well-bred spinster, was quickly discovered. She had established a social settlement called Hull House in 1889, but for years people regarded her as a harmless zealot. Now volunteers came from all over the country to study her efforts to provide medical help, family guidance, protection for widows, in short, anything that might win a better life for the poor.

Others turned to prohibition as the key to a finer world ahead. It was not just the goal of a few religious groups or eccentrics like Carry Nation. Thousands of people saw a very real connection between the liquor industry and the corrupt local governments they were trying to reform. One way to clean house was to kill the saloon. For many of the "drys" it was a personal sacrifice, but they were happy to make it for the good of everybody.

A little simple perhaps, but all the panaceas were simple. Do this one thing—take this one step—and any problem, whatever it was, could be solved. This was clearly the mood when a group of distinguished Americans met at Tuskegee, Alabama, in 1902 to consider the Negro problem. Under the benign leadership of Booker T. Washington, the conference declared that the future of the colored race depended on such steps as "keeping out of large cities, prompt and willing payment of all taxes, keeping out of court, avoiding all forms of extravagance. . . ."

In the thrill of reform, most Americans turned unexpectedly against some of the imperial ventures that seemed so intoxicating just two years before. The casualty lists and a certain disillusionment over yesterday's "little brown brother" had something to do with it. "I have never met a more unlovable people," wrote *Harper's* Philippine correspondent. But it went deeper than that. Suddenly it seemed all wrong to be bullying other people. A great outcry went up against General Funston when he "unsportingly" trapped the Filipino guerrilla leader Aguinaldo. And later, in a pang of conscience, Washington returned half of the $24 million indemnity levied on Peking after the Boxer Rebellion. Far better to use it to send Chinese students to the United States—that was the way an enlightened nation should behave.

Popular writers and commentators quickly took up the new spirit of reform. Edwin Markham's poem "The Man with the Hoe"—a touching tribute to the downtrodden—enjoyed a great vogue. In the October, 1902, issue of *McClure's,* young Lincoln Steffens wrote "Tweed Days in St. Louis"—the first of an immensely popular series he called "The Shame of the Cities." In the November issue, Ida Tarbell—a stern schoolmarm of a reporter—began her shattering exposure of the Standard Oil Company's ruthless climb to dominance. Other writers fell in line—Thomas Lawson took apart the Amalgamated Copper Company . . . Burton Hendrick the life insurance business . . . Charles Edward Russell the beef trust.

The reading public eagerly consumed these behind-the-scenes tales of evils they had always suspected. The great magazines happily shoveled them up. The articles grew more and more lurid, until President Roosevelt—originally a great supporter of the trend—got fed up and said the writers were "Muckrakers." It proved another example of the President's felicitous gift for coining a phrase.

Like the other reformers, most of the Muckrakers had nothing against the system. They too were only trying to save it. When an occasional exception like Socialist Upton Sinclair came along, no one really understood what he was trying to say. Sinclair's book *The Jungle* was meant to attack not just the evils of the Chicago stockyards but the whole capitalist system. He hoped it would turn more to Socialism, but the net effect was the Pure Food and Drug Act. He tried to win men's hearts, he complained, but only reached their stomachs.

It had to be so. In 1902 the nation's basic optimism was stronger than ever. America was still the land of limitless possibilities—these bright new reforms simply made sure it would stay that way. And all the while, daily life remained superbly uncomplicated. The President's own son went unattended to public school. Young people were thrilled by the new game Ping-Pong. Their elders earnestly debated such questions as whether a Mormon could legally be elected a U.S. Senator. And everybody, young and old, sang "In the Good Old Summertime," the new song that conveyed so well their peace and contentment.

1903

"The Whopper Flying Machine"

"The example of the bird does not prove that man can fly. Imagine the proud possessor of an aeroplane darting through the air. It is his speed alone that sustains him. How is he ever going to stop?"

—SIMON NEWCOMB

With the whole nation absorbed in the drama of "bear" raids and cornered shorts, it was quite natural for the co-proprietor of a small bicycle business to use Wall Street terminology in writing a cheerful postcard to his shop mechanic.

"Flying machine market has been very unsteady the past two days," scribbled Orville Wright at Kitty Hawk, North Carolina, on October 20, 1903. The card, addressed to Charlie Taylor back home in Dayton, Ohio, continued: "Opened yesterday morning at about 208 (100% means even chances of success) but by noon had dropped to 110. These fluctuations would have produced a panic, I think, in Wall Street, but in this quiet place it only put us to thinking and figuring a little."

Orville and his brother Wilbur had been "thinking and figuring" about flying machines for a long time now. In 1899 they had built a big box kite incorporating some of their theories. Its most novel feature was a method of warping the wings to get lateral balance. It flew beautifully.

In 1900 they took the next step—a man-carrying glider. To test it, they picked Kitty Hawk, which offered a steady wind, wide-open beaches, and plenty of privacy. Here they tinkered with the machine for five weeks, but it wasn't until the last day that they dared go up in it. It too flew beautifully.

In 1901 they were back in Kitty Hawk with a bigger glider. Now their flights were bolder and longer—280 . . . 300 . . . 335 feet. Clearly they were getting quite good—that much was obvious to anyone who took the trouble to watch.

But few did. The taciturn people of Kitty Hawk had their own problems to worry about. They knew, of course, that the Wrights were experimenting at Kill Devil Hills, four miles down the beach, but it was a mighty long walk. And when you got there, often there was no flying to see. Young Elijah Baum marveled at the way the brothers would sometimes sit for hours, just studying the buzzards, hawks, and gulls that wheeled overhead.

The Wrights fully reciprocated the natives' indifference. Even in this isolated community they lived a world apart. They visited little, kept mostly to themselves—talking, watching the birds, or puttering with their glider. Fifteen-year-old Truxton Midgett, who delivered a lot of their supplies, was especially impressed by the close way they worked together. He had a brother of his own, and he knew how hard this could be.

Without realizing it, Midgett had put his finger on the most remarkable quality about the Wrights. They were not only inseparable as brothers, but their very minds seemed to complement each other. They would bat a problem back and forth for hours, until almost invariably a solution appeared—the joint product of two brains working in perfect harmony. And so they passed the summer of 1901, returning again to Dayton late in August.

Just about the time they arrived home, the September, 1901, issue of *McClure's* appeared with an article exploding the myth of the flying machine. Professor Simon Newcomb, the distinguished astronomer, compared it to squaring the circle. It was one of those things we would never be able to do. And in the December, 1901, *North American Review,* Admiral George W. Melville pointed out that no one had even laid the necessary groundwork: "Where, even to this hour, are we to look for the germ of the successful flying machine? Where is the preparation today?"

At this moment in Dayton, the Wrights were testing over two hundred different wing surfaces. By using a specially-built wind tunnel, they learned that a wing's front edge shouldn't be too sharp ... that deeply cambered wings were inefficient ... that narrow wings had relatively more lifting power. Most important, they discovered that all previous air pressure tables were hopelessly inaccurate. Page after page they jotted new figures, spelling out exactly what pressure would support different surfaces at different speeds and angles.

In 1902 they returned again to Kill Devil Hills with a new glider based on the wind tunnel data. It proved the best yet—could soar even better than the hawks. For still greater stability, they added a tail ... then a movable rudder. With these improvements they broke all gliding records—622½ feet the week before they went back to Dayton that October.

The next step was a motor. On December 3, 1902, they wrote to ten manufacturers, seeking a 180-pound gasoline engine that could develop 8 h.p. No luck, so they built their own. Next, a propeller. It turned out that marine experience was no use at all. The approach was completely hit-or-miss; if one didn't work, shipbuilders simply tried another. But in the air this could obviously have fatal results. So again, the Wrights built their own. Now for better uprights. Once more, tests showed past theories were invalid. Once more, the Wrights designed their own.

By September, 1903, they were back at Kill Devil Hills, slowly assembling the flyer. They had come a long way since 1900, but the big biplane still looked pretty much like a box kite. A spider web of struts and wires held the forty-foot wings in place. The pilot lay on a "cradle" amidship, working with his hips the wires that warped the wings. In front was a horizontal elevator; in the rear a vertical tail with the new movable rudder. The engine nestled ominously alongside the pilot. It drove the two pusher-propellers by means of a clanking chain drive that reminded people of the builders' background in the bicycle business. The whole affair weighed an impressive 605 pounds without pilot. No wonder the Wrights proudly nicknamed it the "whopper flying machine."

As they quietly worked away, Simon Newcomb delivered another blast at the whole idea of mechanical flight. Writing in the October 22 issue of the *Independent,* the professor was especially concerned with the aeronaut's problem of landing safely: "How shall he reach the ground without destroying his delicate machinery? I do not think the most imaginative inventor has yet even put on paper a demonstrative, successful way of meeting this difficulty."

The following morning the Wrights were putting the finishing touches on their landing skids.

Still, they were far from being ready. All through October and November they made endless adjustments. They mounted the engine. They trussed the wires. They tested the method of starting. They measured the air pressure on the front elevator.

And one day they learned that another man had just failed to fly. Professor Samuel P. Langley, Secretary of the Smithsonian Institution, tried to launch his plane from a barge in the Potomac, but it flopped into the river before the eyes of a derisive press. The news did not discourage the Wrights—they just studied all the data they could get on Langley's attempt.

The Wrights had their own troubles too. They broke a propeller shaft . . . sent to Dayton for another . . . broke that . . . had to dig up still another. This time Orville himself rushed to Dayton, picked up some strong steel rods, was back in Kitty Hawk by December 11.

December 14, and at last they were ready. First, a few minor repairs in the morning. Then a final check on the launching device. This was a sixty-foot monorail made by laying four fifteen-foot planks end to end. The flying machine sat on a dolly which rolled down the track. After picking up enough speed, the pilot theoretically tilted the wings and took off. Crude, but Langley had spent $50,000 for his starting equipment, while this cost only $4.

The Wrights' device had the added virtue of being portable. On a windy day they could lay the track on the level beach and take off from there. On a calm day, like this one, they could take it to Big Hill, or one of the other nearby dunes, and lay it on the slope for extra speed.

Of course, all this required manpower, and assistance came from an unexpected source. The men at the Kill Devil Life Saving Station, about a mile away, liked to watch the Wrights in their spare time and volunteered to pitch in whenever called.

The signal came at 1:30 P.M., fluttering from the side of the Wrights' shed. As promised, the men drifted over—Tom Beacham, John Daniels, Bill Dough, Bob Westcott, "Uncle Benny" O'Neil. Then two small boys and a dog turned up, drawn by the little gathering on the barren sands.

Through the bright afternoon sunlight the procession marched toward Big Hill, about a quarter-mile away. To move the flyer more easily, they put it on the track. As they pushed it along, they would pick up the last rail section and re-lay it ahead, over and over again.

Now they were on the hill, pondering the inevitable question: who should have what Wilbur called "first whack"? The Wrights solved the problem in characteristic fashion—they tossed for it. Wilbur won and lay down at the controls, the way a child goes sledding. A moment later the motor roared into action. The two small boys jumped with fright, grabbed their dog, and fled from the scene.

Down the track the flyer rolled, Orville dashing alongside, trying to balance the wing tip. Wilbur pulled at the wires, and in his excitement pulled too hard. The plane shot up at a 20° angle, stalled, and fell back to the ground.

Anybody else would have been discouraged. But not the Wrights. They knew exactly what went wrong. More important, they knew what went right. The motor, the controls, the launching device all worked perfectly. Next time the machine was bound to fly. That evening Wilbur wrote his father and sister Katherine, "There is now no question of final success." Next morning he followed up with a wire: ". . . Success assured. Keep quiet."

Why so secret? The answer seems to lie in the complex personalities of the Wrights themselves. In a way they were visionaries, but they also

95

had a sharp eye for patent rights. They wanted recognition, but they also had a small-town suspicion of big-city newsmen. They were confident of success, but they dreaded the taunts if anything went wrong.

The 15th and 16th were spent quietly, making further adjustments. By the second night all was ready for another try.

Thursday, December 17, dawned cold and cloudy. A strong wind blew from the north at twenty to twenty-five miles an hour. A thin glaze of ice coated the puddles about the camp. A poor day, but the Wrights were anxious to get on with it.

At 10:00 A.M. the men at the life-saving station saw the signal. Another try would be made. Those who were free dropped over—John Daniels, Bill Dough, and Adam Etheridge. Then W. C. Brinkley of Manteo turned up; he was another of the local residents who had begun to take an interest in the Wrights. Finally, came Johnny Moore, a carefree, seventeen-year-old who lived about three miles down the beach. He was the Tom Sawyer type, although certainly a little old for the role.

Soon they were again hauling the plane to the starting point. But now the job was easy, for there was no need to use the hill on a windy day like this. The track was simply laid on level sand about one hundred feet from the Wrights' shed. Here the men placed the machine on the dolly, which rested as before on the monorail. Orville set up a camera and pointed it at the spot where he expected the plane to take off. He told John Daniels to press the button just after it left the ground—of course, it was going to fly.

The motor sputtered, then roared. The chain drive clanked away and the two pusher-propellers whirled around. The flyer trembled all over.

It was Orville's turn now, and at 10:35 A.M. he lay down in the cradle amidships. He too looked like a boy out sledding, but in another sense he looked like a misplaced businessman. As always, he wore a starched collar, tie, and dark suit. Wilbur, dressed the same way, took his stand by the right wing, to help balance the machine as it started on its way. Near his feet lay a shovel . . . a can of nails . . . a hammer sticking in it. Not very spectacular equipment, but somehow symbolic of two mechanically gifted men who didn't pretend to be scientific geniuses.

Orville released the wire that anchored the machine to the end of the monorail. Slowly—then faster—it lumbered down the track into the teeth of the wind. Wilbur ran alongside, holding the forward upright of the right wing. John Daniels put his finger on the camera button.

About forty feet down the track Orville jerked the front elevator wires. Up . . . up it rose, bobbing and wobbling through the air ten feet above the ground. It stayed up only twelve seconds, it went only 120 feet—but it certainly flew.

There couldn't have been less excitement. Wilbur and Orville knew it would work all along. The five spectators were pleased but not especially surprised. They had watched the Wrights gliding for three years—this seemed pretty much the same, except that this time the machine had a motor.

They hauled it back to the starting point and prepared for another flight. First, though, they had to warm up. Everyone pushed into the Wrights' little shack and crowded around the faithful carbide-can stove. Overhead were the "patent" beds, looking a little like Pullman upper berths. Along the unpainted walls were cans of food, pots, plates, and the bread pan which Orville used to bake rolls. It didn't look like the sort of place to solve the eternal problem of flight.

Nor was the conversation now about flying. Looking under the plain wooden table, Johnny Moore spied a bucket of eggs—more eggs in one place than he had seen before in his life. The people of the Outer Banks scratched along as best they could; when they did any feasting at all, it was invariably fish. This then was amazing.

He asked one of the life-saving crew where they all came from. The man reminded Johnny of a scrawny hen that was flapping around just outside the shack. "Well," he explained, "that chicken lays eight to ten eggs a day." Now here was something interesting. Moore bolted out to study the hen.

Convulsed with laughter they all trooped out to the machine again. Now it was Wilbur's turn. At 11:20 A.M. he took off, and again the plane bobbed along about ten feet above the ground. This time it went about 175 feet before slamming down into the sand. At 11:40 Orville tried again and got 200 feet.

It was exactly noon when Wilbur took off on the fourth flight. Again the flyer bounced along uncertainly for 100 feet or so. But now he understood the controls better. Even more important, he had the intuitive sense of balance that could only come from four years' experience flying gliders above the sands of Kitty Hawk. He knew just what to do and the machine responded perfectly. Two hundred . . . 300 . . . 600 . . . 852 feet it flew before an unexpected gust finally brought it down. It had been in the air for 59 seconds.

That afternoon the Wrights turned to the pleasant task of informing the world of their triumph—but it seemed that the world wasn't interested. A wire telling their father to "inform press" produced nothing even in their home-town paper, the Dayton *Journal*. Some editors agreed with Simon Newcomb—a flying machine was impossible. Others confused airplanes with airships. Everyone knew that the great Santos-Dumont could keep his dirigible up an hour, make it circle the Eiffel Tower, do all sorts of things. Unless an aviator could match this, there was no story.

Only Editor Keville Glennan of the Norfolk *Virginian-Pilot* really understood. He had first heard of the Wrights in 1902, while covering a shipwreck on the Carolina coast. He instinctively realized it would be a great story if they ever got off the ground. Through a leak in the local telegraph office, Glennan now learned it had happened. He bannered the news across his front page.

But attempts at the *Virginian-Pilot* to sell the story elsewhere fell flat—only five papers bought the item and gingerly ran it the following day. When others finally picked it up later, the news proved quite a challenge to the city desk. No one knew quite how to handle the Wrights' achievement. The New York *Tribune* solved the problem in the neatest fashion. It carried the item on the sports page—just underneath the account of a sandlot football game in Brooklyn.

That seemed the best place, even after the new invention was better understood. Many of the most ardent enthusiasts thought of it only as a piece of sporting equipment. As late as 1907, a speaker at the International Aeronautical Congress thought that at best the flying machine might someday prove "useful in explorations of otherwise inaccessible places, such as mountain tops, swamps, or densely wooded regions."

All agreed it had little commercial future. The Wrights didn't think anyone would fly at night. And most authorities felt no one would ever build a machine large enough to carry a payload. Even in 1911, aviation expert W. B. Kaempffert believed that the invention would probably remain "a racing machine for gilded youth." Mr. Kaempffert also felt that the machine had little use in war: "that wholesale destruction of life and property which would seem obviously to follow from the mere existence of military flying-machines, freighted with bombs and grenades, is not to be looked for."

The reason? Kaempffert went back to a homely analogy: Every small boy knew how hard it was to drop a snowball on someone from a third-story window. Well, it would be all the more difficult to hit anything from a machine flying thirty-five miles an hour.

The Wrights themselves thought that their invention would be a great force for peace. Through aerial reconnaissance each side could learn what the other was doing and wouldn't dare start anything itself. Their friend Octave Chanute agreed. Writing them in 1905, he even went a step further. He thought that the invention "will make more for peace in the hands of the British than in our own, for its existence will soon become known in a general way, and the knowledge will deter embroilments."

If so, Chanute had cause for hope. In 1904 the Wrights didn't go to Kitty Hawk, flew instead from Torrance Huffman's pasture near Dayton. By October they had made over fifty flights without attracting their neighbors, much less anybody in Washington. Then one day a letter unexpectedly arrived from Lieutenant Colonel J. E. Capper of the Royal Aircraft Factory at Aldershot. He would like very much to meet them.

The colonel and his wife proved charming guests. He knew a good deal about the Wrights. In fact, that was why he was here. Would the Wrights care to propose terms toward supplying their machine to His Majesty's Government?

The Wrights said they would think it over, and in January, 1905, wrote a letter still marking time. Eight days later they launched a serious campaign to interest Washington. For a long while they got nowhere. Twice, in fact, they received from the War Department virtually the same form letter of refusal.

Ultimately, there was the appropriate, happy ending. The British negotiations fell through; Washington saw the light. But not until 1907—after the Wrights had enjoyed nearly four years of successful flying.

It wasn't that Americans were oblivious of progress. They were enchanted when they understood. But the inventions that carried real meaning—that made life so exciting—were the simple things. A steady stream of them poured out these days . . . touching one and all, enriching the life of everyone: the safety razor, the "perpetual pencil," the subway, the long-distance telephone that now reached from New York to Omaha. With wonders like these, there seemed no end to the possibilities. Nobody even blinked at the advertisement for "Best-Light," a mysterious method that gave six times more light than electricity and cost only two cents a week.

The home especially seemed to take on new attractiveness from these inventions that "really counted." For the first time plumbing was coming into its own. "The luxury and pleasure of a shower bath," declared the Standard Sanitary ad, "is a revelation to those not already acquainted with its charming delights."

Entertainment too broadened in scope and meaning. There was, of course, the new Victor Talking Machine that played disks instead of the usual cylinders. But what especially intrigued people was the Kinetoscope, or Vitagraph—it had a dozen names—that projected moving pictures on a screen. It had been the tag end of vaudeville shows since the late '90s, but now it was suddenly coming into its own. First, little theatres, and now in 1903 a film with a plot—*The Life of an American Fireman*—that instantly promised a whole new field of diversion.

The automobile also was drawing closer to daily reality. It was even getting reliable. In the late summer of 1903, as the Wrights prepared their power-flyer, the whole nation cheered E. T. Fetch and M. C.

Krarup, the dauntless pair who made the first coast-to-coast auto trip. They drove their Packard "Pacific" from San Francisco to New York in fifty-two days, but the press assured the public that, despite this fast time, they had many difficulties along the way. One stretch, according to *Popular Mechanics,* "made the autoists think they had certainly strolled beyond the domains of human aggression. An indefatigable perseverance and determination, however, successfully steered them out of this unearthly region." It turned out that the editor was referring to Utah.

Next year a whole caravan of autos painfully crawled in the opposite direction. This time, however, they were not going cross-continent. They were heading for the great Louisiana Purchase Exposition in St. Louis, Missouri.

"Meet Me in St. Louis, Louis" the Pianolas tinkled, and it seemed the whole country obeyed the command. The theme of the show was the world's progress since the Chicago Fair of 1893, and crowds surged into the Machinery Building to watch the latest developments—even a paper-box factory in full operation.

As an up-to-the minute touch, the management offered free hydrogen to any visiting aeronauts, but again, what delighted most people were the exciting discoveries that made for a fuller life—the new electrical hearing aids, or the demonstrations of "house cleaning done by pneumatic process without removing the carpets." This one was destined to be known as the vacuum cleaner.

Visitors to St. Louis long remembered the mechanical wonders that filled the Fair, but they remembered even longer the fun they had. At the Buffalo Exposition the Electric Tower had dominated the show, preaching the miracle of electricity. At St. Louis, the symbol to most people was nothing so educational—instead, it was the huge Ferris wheel that rose 250 feet in the air. It lazily revolved the whole summer long, leaving its thousands of passengers pleasantly giddy from the sheer wonder of it all.

Nearby sprawled "The Pike," that most fabulous of midways. Besides the usual Streets of Cairo, Streets of Seville, and other "educational" concessions, it occasionally promised such startling innovations as a beauty contest. Sadly the Reverend Thomas B. Gregory clucked his disapproval: "No truly refined girl would submit to such a thing. The bare thought of it would drive her mad."

For the innocent, there were seventy-five miles of walks and paths, festooned by nothing more offensive than the symbolic statuary that always graced such shows. "That is a particularly fine Diana," cried President Theodore Roosevelt the day he inspected the fair. And no one in the official party had the heart to tell him that it happened to be Apollo.

By now everybody loved this side of Teddy anyhow. Wall Street might rant about his "unsettling influence." Reformers might complain that his bark was worse than his bite. But almost everybody enjoyed the flashing teeth and glasses . . . the sweeping opinions . . . the scrapes and tangles . . . the way he threw himself into everything.

He had such enthusiasm, such boundless interest in any subject. At the height of the anthracite coal crisis, he took time out to write Herbert Putnam at the Harvard Library for "histories or articles on the early Mediterranean races . . . or a good translation of Niebuhr and Momsen or the best modern history of Mesopotamia. Is there a good history of Poland?" And the night he was thrashing out the final settlement with Pierpont Morgan, he also wrote Kermit at Groton: "Who plays opposite you at end? Do you find you can get down well under the ball to tackle the fullback? How are you tackling?"

His exuberance suited the national mood exactly. And it was this rather than any clear-cut economic or political policy (he still had none, except what was "right") that built up such a huge following when he ran again in 1904. He stood for everything the nation was, while his Democratic opponent—stuffy, gray Judge Alton B. Parker—seemed everything the nation was not. Roosevelt buried the judge under the largest landslide in history, and victory bonfires burned throughout the land.

The following afternoon Wilbur and Orville Wright dragged their "whopper flying machine" out of its weather-beaten shed in the Huffman pasture near Dayton. Wilbur climbed aboard and took off on a three-mile flight that lasted over five minutes. It was their longest to date, and flown specifically in honor of what they called "the phenomenal political victory."

As usual they drew no headlines. But in the end this was perhaps inevitable. For the Wrights remained simple, unostentatious mechanics. Basically, they were still the proprietors of a small-town bicycle shop— they never pretended to be anything else. And the activities of such men, however talented, enjoyed little popular interest. These were the days before the emergence of the scientist and inventor—or even the sport and movie star—as a public personality. For the vicarious glamour that enriches drab lives, people turned invariably to the dazzling world of Society and fashion.

1905

The Golden Circus

"A man who has a million dollars is as well off as if he were rich."
—John Jacob Astor

New inventions, glittering fairs, the excitement of a country bursting at the seams held little appeal for a courteous, reserved New Englander whom everyone assumed to be French—Louis Sherry of St. Albans, Vermont. As New York's favorite caterer and restaurateur, Sherry naturally leaned toward preserving the Established Order. And Society responded—they all came to his handsome restaurant on Fifth Avenue or engaged him to handle the sparkling parties that filled their leisure.

Sherry's big leather-bound order book suggested that the 1905 season would be one of his busiest. It began auspiciously with Mrs. Astor's ball, to which some 450 guests (not Ward McAllister's Four Hundred) dutifully reported on the evening of January 9. They came at 11:00, arriving from heavy, richly served dinners all over town—a centerpiece of 3,000 roses graced the Harry Lehrs' table at the St. Regis. Already buried under ten courses, the Lehrs' 100 guests now embarked on a nine-course midnight supper at Mrs. Astor's—terrapin, fish, canvasback duck, *pâté de foie gras* and so on.

With this foundation, they had to dance a cotillion. But perhaps Mrs. Astor's favors made it all worth while—everyone got Directoire canes, paper weights, leather pen wipers, rubber-bulb automobile horns, gold

104

pencil cases, china figurines, whips, jardinieres, and leather letter cases.

When it was over, the guests sat down for another supper—more terrapin and four other courses. By now there were only fifty survivors. Possibly Ward McAllister was right after all—there were only "the Four Hundred" and they had gone home, leaving only the social climbers to battle on to the end. More likely, most of the guests were just worn out.

For this was the era of massive entertainment. Night after night the rich and fashionable vied with one another in achieving the spectacular. Two weeks after Mrs. Astor's ball, James Stillman installed an artificial waterfall in his dining room for a dinner dance. On another occasion Rudolf Guggenheimer stocked the Waldorf's Myrtle Room with nightingales borrowed from the zoo. The Cornelius Vanderbilts imported the first act from the Broadway musical *The Wild Rose,* complete with cast and scenery, for an "at-home" during one of Newport's famous tennis weeks.

In the competitive whirl, some hosts simply turned to the bizarre. Cornelius K. G. Billings marked the completion of his $200,000 stable by giving a Horseback Dinner at Sherry's. Livery stable nags were brought by freight elevator to the grand ballroom. The honored guests mounted them and dined in the saddle from precariously balanced trays. The dinner was served by waiters disguised as grooms, while grooms (perhaps disguised as waiters) hovered in the rear to clean up any mess.

At Newport, society was invited to a formal dinner to meet a new arrival, Prince del Drago of Corsica. The "prince" turned out to be a monkey in full evening dress—the joint inspiration of Mrs. Stuyvesant Fish and her personal jester, Harry Lehr. The dinner went on, and as the monkey sipped his champagne, all agreed it was one of Mrs. Fish's cleverest ideas yet.

In the search for something new, the fashionable naturally turned to fancy-dress balls. While Newport amused itself with the exotic ("come-as-one-of-your-servants"), New York went for the lavish, and even the outlandish. In 1904, Mr. Lloyd Warren gave a Far Eastern masquerade that almost touched the high-water mark set by the Bradley-Martin ball of the '90s. At Mr. Warren's dance the guests were told to come in

Oriental costume. Some were a little vague on their geography—a good many Turks, Egyptians and Greeks showed up—but it was still a brilliant spectacle.

As the gay 1905 season got under way, invitations went out for another fancy-dress ball. The host was a dark, sensitive, twenty-eight-year-old New Yorker named James Hazen Hyde. Like Louis Sherry, he had little interest in mechanical contraptions like flying machines. His tastes ran to eighteenth-century coaching, *faisan piqué Louis XV,* 1830 beaver hats, royal purple ascots, embroidered French dressing gowns. And in the winter of 1905, he could afford them all.

His father, Henry B. Hyde, had made a vast fortune in the insurance business. Feeling that most of the companies lacked imagination, the elder Hyde formed the Equitable Life Assurance Society in 1859. He began with little more than a large sign and a box of cigars for the customers he hoped would come, but the very first day he wrote $100,500 in policies. From this promising start he built the Equitable into a mammoth organization of 600,000 policyholders and $400 million in assets. The company became an obsession—it was more than a business, it was a hobby, a monument, a cherished possession.

Originally he hoped to leave this prize to his first son, Henry B., Jr., but the lad died at the age of ten. So he transferred his attention to the younger James Hazen. With loving care he trained the boy, taught him to be proud of the Equitable . . . to think of it as his own.

There was only one trouble. Young James Hazen Hyde was not what is normally called the business type. His tastes ran more to literature, music, good food, fine living. Early in his teens he visited France and fell in love with the country. Not with the gaiety of Paris—or the attractions other boys smirked about—but with the exquisite culture of French civilization. He loved the salons, the poets, the theatre and ballet. In his enthusiasm he soon adopted French clothes, mannerisms, even what he considered to be a French appearance.

He grew a sharp-pointed little Henry IV beard, combed his thick black hair in a wavy pompadour, affected tight-fitting black frock suits. His spats, gloves and waistcoats lent generous splashes of color to the ensemble. Usually he capped it off with an immaculately ironed silk hat—not in the jaunty Edwardian style, but with the brim flat and turned down. It reminded unsophisticated people of the hats traditionally worn by French villains on the stage.

This was the young man who suddenly inherited controlling interest in the Equitable, when his father died of overwork in 1899. At the time James Hazen Hyde was only twenty-three—just one year out of Harvard. Realizing this, the old man had arranged for James Alexander —a loyal long-time official of Equitable—to serve as president and trustee for the boy until he reached thirty. Still, it was a pretty sharp transition. As first vice president, Hyde found himself with an annual salary of $100,000 and the prospect of limitless power.

It was enough to turn the head of anybody his age, and Hyde was perhaps more vulnerable than others. He already had extravagant tastes, and he was quite impressionable. Seeing this innocent young sentry guarding the Equitable's $400 million, the sharper denizens of Wall Street swooped in with all kinds of flattering proposals.

They made him director of forty-six companies, including nineteen banks and fourteen railroads. They let him in on all sorts of promotions and schemes. They persuaded him, in return, to deposit the Equitable's money in their banks, to invest the Equitable's funds in their ventures. And they showed him how that could earn him a little extra. For instance, the Oregon Short line, on which Hyde served as director, sold $1,250,000 in bonds to "James H. Hyde and Associates" at 96, which in turn sold the bonds to Equitable at 97—clearing a $25,044 profit in five days.

Hyde's problem was not getting but spending his money. And it was that way with most of the rich. These were the days before taxes and high living costs. Nor were there any brakes on the desire to spend. No recent depression left a lingering fear that conspicuous wealth might be in poor taste. No carefully trained sense of propriety curbed the natural inclination of rich people to act that way. There were exceptions of course—take those quiet Rockefellers—but they were few. For the most part, the privileged poured their money into projects that amused or interested them, while the not-so-privileged watched the splash.

And it was quite a splash. William K. Vanderbilt's palace on Long Island boasted a garage for one hundred motorcars. His brother George used more men on his North Carolina estate than the Department of Agriculture had for the entire country. Pierpont Morgan spent over a million dollars in one year for old scrolls and tapestries. William Fahnestock decorated the trees around his Newport "cottage" with artificial fruit made of fourteen-carat gold. Mrs. John Jacob Astor enjoyed a two-ton bathtub cut from a solid block of marble. The O. H. P. Belmonts treated their horses at Newport to pure linen sheets embroidered with the family crest. Running out of ideas, financier Thomas Lawson paid $30,000 to have a carnation named after his wife.

James Hazen Hyde's tastes weren't as sumptuous, but in his way he was more eye-catching. He loved, for instance, coaching and was perhaps the country's best four-in-hand whip. Clattering along New York's avenues, he cut quite a sight, sporting a fawn-colored driving coat with large pearl buttons. On these occasions he discarded his shiny topper for a tall fuzzy beaver, but this made him no less conspicuous.

At one point Hyde established a regular stage run from Holland House to the front of George Gould's estate at Lakewood, New Jersey, seventy-eight miles away. To make the trip more attractive, he had a little inn at New Brunswick done over in the style of Olde Englande. Here the paying passengers could descend for an appropriate luncheon. Not exactly profitable but certainly spectacular.

His taste in entertaining ran along similar lines. He loved the cosmopolitan, the flashy, any occasion that could be considered part of the good life. He undoubtedly enjoyed taking Alice Roosevelt to the Horse Show in 1904—she was as worldly as they came. And it must have been pleasant to be seen with the President's daughter.

Not that there weren't less public occasions. For instance, the sophisticated little suppers he sometimes gave in his stables at Bay Shore. The French writer Jules Hurst vividly recalled one "where ladies donned old postillion hats or bull fighters' bonnets and blew hunting horns while everybody danced the cake walk."

Best of all, however, were the big parties. Who could forget his 1902 dinner for Ambassador Cambon of France? It cost the Equitable

$12,600, but it was a brilliant affair—everybody came—and any young man couldn't help but enjoy being the center of so much attention.

Perhaps that triumph was in the back of his mind as he labored over plans for his 1905 masquerade. Ostensibly it would honor his niece, Annah Ripley, but she was rarely mentioned in the notices that appeared in the Society columns. It seems more likely that he just wanted to make a magnificent gesture.

The ball's motif was almost inevitable: the Court of Louis XV. As a special attraction—these days you had to give your guests more than just a party—he would import Madame Gabrielle Réjane, the current toast of Paris. She agreed to appear in a *commedietta* written especially for the occasion. He then recruited his friend Whitney Warren, an architect trained at the Beaux Arts, to convert Sherry's into a reasonable replica of Versailles.

New York Society began preparing for the great day—"le Mardi 31 Janvière 1905," according to the programme—with the varied emotions people have always approached costume parties. Mrs. George Gould went all-out, happily choosing the role of Marie Leczinska, the wife of Louis XV. She ordered a glittering ensemble of satin and pearls, trailing a long train of green velvet lined with ermine and embroidered with gold and emeralds. On the other hand, Mrs. F. Egerton Webb couldn't be bothered and felt she could get by with a powdered wig.

A few of the men self-consciously ordered court costumes; a good many more rummaged through trunks in the attic. Major Creighton Webb found an old toreador suit—not exactly right, but it would do. Georges A. Glaenzer salvaged the sheets of a Bedouin; it looked suspiciously like one of the costumes at Lloyd Warren's party last year. Most took the easy way out, settled for hunting pinks or the evening dress of their coaching club. History does not record how one of the young extra men, Franklin D. Roosevelt, solved the problem.

Starting at 10:30 that Tuesday evening, a steady stream of carriages and electrics rolled up to Sherry's. The young host had ordered all to be there by eleven o'clock, and even Mrs. Stuyvesant Fish managed to shepherd her small dinner party of sixty to the restaurant on time. Straight to the third-floor ballroom they trooped. Before entering, a moment's pause to pay their *devoirs* to the splendid young man who made it all possible. Looking at him in his uniform of the New York Coaching Club—coat of myrtle green, black satin knee breeches, black silk stockings, and assorted medals—the insurance business seemed very, very far away.

Now to the ballroom and a breathtaking sight: Whitney Warren had gone wild with roses. Bushes, arbors, trellises, vines—every way a rose could grow. A latticework of roses crossed the south side of the room, screening both wings of the stage that had been built for the evening's performance. Rosebushes banked the ballroom floor itself. Rose trellises covered the galleries overlooking the room. Just like a real *loge grillée,* the savants said. From here reporters could watch the party without the guests having to look at them.

Promptly at eleven, conductor Nahan Franko tapped his baton, and the room swelled with the beautiful music of the Metropolitan Opera House's forty-piece orchestra. Eight of the season's debutantes advanced uncertainly to the center of the floor. There they were joined by eight equally uncertain young swains. The girls were dressed *à la Carmargo* (with baskets of roses, garlands of roses, wreaths of rosebuds) and the young men were predictably clad as Pierrots. Together they struggled through a gavotte. "Hearty applause was their reward."

Next, with unintentional cruelty, the ballet corps of the Metropolitan Opera showed how it should be done. Mlle. Enrichetta Varasi whirled gracefully through an intricate eighteenth-century figure, assisted by Herr Conreid's finest dancers.

Now it was almost midnight. A hum of excitement filled the room. Then, through the west portal, came four court lackeys carrying a *vernis Martin* sedan chair. Midway across the room they gently lowered it and out stepped Madame Réjane herself to the shrill delight of the 350 guests. She was, of course, dressed in the eighteenth-century fashion, but she was wise enough not to outdo any of the Society matrons.

A gracious greeting from the host . . . a few final adjustments . . . and the rose-tinted curtain went up. The *commedietta* turned out to be a little French bedroom farce called *Entre deux Portes,* written by Dario Nicodemi especially for the occasion. The plot involved a couple who tried to make each other jealous by staging separate flirtations in their neighboring bedrooms. The final curtain found all misunderstandings forgotten and the lovers locked in each other's arms.

This rickety vehicle was handled with tolerant skill by Madame Réjane and her company. A generous critic called the plot "ingenious" and all agreed that at least the scenery was wonderful. It had been imported from Paris by Mr. Hyde especially for the evening. The *Metropolitan Magazine* later called this "a very wise precaution when one remembers the rattle-trap settings to which Réjane treated her American audiences this season."

A blast of bugles followed the show and Hyde led his guests down to the supper room on the second floor. Here they found that Whitney Warren had again outdone himself. The room had been turned into a Versailles garden. Overhead was a rich canopy, under foot a rolling lawn. Along the sides were trellises, marble statues, even running fountains.

And, of course, there were more roses than ever. They lined the walls. They rambled over the gilt latticework. They bloomed on the trees that sheltered the sixty tables. And through them all peeped thousands of colored light bulbs, making the rosy vista even rosier.

A bell tinkled. The diners fell silent, and Madame Réjane arose from her gilded chair at the host's right. Charmingly she recited a little poem called "Apropos." It turned out to be another creative effort written just for the evening and dwelt, fittingly enough, on Franco-American friendship. After this salute to the *entente cordiale,* the guests plunged into *consommé Voltaire.*

The dawdlers were still sipping their Pol Roger '89 when the music began again upstairs. Now it was dancing for everyone. As the glittering couples swirled about, the twinkling lights were easily eclipsed by Mrs. Fish's turquoises, Mrs. Belmont's *parure* of emeralds, and especially by Mrs. Potter Palmer's diamond tiara, diamond dog collar, and diamond breastplates.

At three o'clock everybody came downstairs again for another supper. After the guests had their fill of bouillon, sausages, ham, and chicken, the survivors mounted to the ballroom for more dancing.

Wistfully looking on from the sidelines was Mrs. Clarence Mackay. She had so burdened herself with props and equipment that she was completely immobilized. In a moment of excess ambition, she had decided to come as the eighteenth-century actress Adrienne Lecouvreur playing her great role of Phèdre. Now she found herself equipped with a scepter, tangled in folds of silver cloth and turquoise, and trailing a train so long that it had to be carried by two little Negro boys in pink brocade. When she managed to move at all, they trudged wearily after her most of the night.

Dawn found Mrs. Mackay still holding out, but with train unhooked and pages gone. In the debris of torn vines and withered rose petals, she joined Mrs. Joseph Widener in thanking an ever-radiant James Hazen Hyde.

"You have given us a most delightful eighteenth-century dinner, but I think the time is ripe for a little twentieth-century breakfast," hinted Mrs. Widener.

It seemed a fine idea, and Hyde gallantly asked what she would like.

"Fishballs!" said Mrs. Widener, and for those who heard it, her earthy response broke the spell of Versailles for good.

The ball was over. Madame Réjane lay exhausted, unable to appear at the benefit for St. Mary's Hospital Wednesday afternoon. Society showed greater recuperative powers. The diamond-studded Mrs. Potter Palmer got to the same benefit, wearing a toque of golden grapes. Thursday she was still going strong at a charity ball at the Waldorf— this time clad in white gauze with straps of bronze spangles.

The press dutifully reported every detail. Its attitude toward the ball was favorable, even envious. The New York *World* especially approved the invitation list. The paper pointed out that this was more than just another gathering of the Four Hundred: the guests included names from the opera and stage. On February 5, the *World*'s Society editor paid Hyde another compliment: "Unlike many of those who do Society, he is serious and an excellent man of business."

At the Equitable there was some difference of opinion. Old James Alexander had long been upset by Hyde's deals and associates; he considered them reckless and irresponsible. The young man's social life somehow confirmed his worst suspicions. And now this ball: it was the last straw. Bitter dissension racked the firm: Hyde and his imaginative friends like E. H. Harriman on one side; Alexander and old-line management on the other.

On February 9 one of the Alexander faction demanded that Hyde resign, arguing among other points that he had put on a cancan at the ball. (Ironically, no one would have shuddered more than Hyde if such a breach of decorum had occurred.)

At another meeting the Hyde clique grew so excited that at one point Harriman was literally speechless. For a few seconds all he could do was yelp, "Wow! Wow! Wow!" This caused Judge William Cohen, one of the opposition, to remark coldly: "Mr. Harriman, that is one aspect of the situation which had quite escaped my attention."

Such blazing dissension soon reached the *World*. Publisher Joseph Pulitzer quickly forgot his Society editor's little paeans to the imaginative host who was also "serious and an excellent man of business." He smelt a far hotter story.

By mid-February all New York was lapping up the *World*'s exposé of "High Life Insurance" at the Equitable. On February 19 the paper's Sunday supplement printed stolen pictures of guests at the ball. And in the merciless lens of photographer Byron's camera, the impression was devastating. There was no suggestion of an evening of old-world culture; only shot after shot of bewigged lackeys, foppish young men, and spoiled-looking girls, their powdered hair lumped clumsily above their bland, patched faces.

Looking at them, it was easy to believe the rumors of scandalous goings-on. And the denials only focused greater attention on the stories. When one flustered Hyde spokesman announced that the ladies' costumes were not "diaphanous," eager readers raced for their dictionaries. Estimates on the cost of the ball soared from $75,000 . . . to $100,000 . . . to $200,000. Whatever it was, the *World* darkly (though mistakenly) hinted that the Equitable policyholders were the real hosts.

Matters came to a head March 31. The Equitable's contending factions met face to face at the offices of the Superintendent of Insurance. Alexander "trembled with rage and indignation." He demanded that

Hyde agree at once to a mutualization plan that in effect would end his control of the company. The alternative: Alexander would go to the Attorney General and demand a public investigation. Hyde, described as "almost wild with anger," had overnight to think it over.

The following morning at ten o'clock, a brightly polished hansom set out from the Hyde residence on East Fortieth Street. On either side of the horse's bridle, a rosette of artificial violets nestled in a frame of green leaves. The coachman, splendid in tan livery, wore a bouquet of violets in his buttonhole. The young gentleman inside sported no violets but did wear a royal purple cravat. In this way James Hazen Hyde drove downtown for what amounted to an abdication ceremony —he agreed to the mutualization plan.

Now to get him out completely, the *World* stepped up its din. It found elevator men who recalled that Hyde wouldn't say good morning to them. It interviewed Bay Shore merchants who said, or were persuaded to say, "He's a little too Frenchified for us plain people." It printed a dandified picture of H. Rogers Winthrop, the inexperienced thirty-year-old whom Hyde appointed financial manager of the Equitable. It joyfully reported the appalling analogy offered by a loyal adherent: this inept soul explained that Hyde's activities were really no different from those pursued by a successful champagne salesman.

No one could stand this sort of drumfire. Hyde soon resigned. By then there had been so many charges and countercharges that the state investigated the whole insurance business. From September 6 to December 30, 1905, the Armstrong Committee's bright young counsel Charles Evans Hughes patiently chipped at the facts. He discovered how interlocking directorates worked—George W. Perkins of Morgan & Company sold George W. Perkins of New York Life $8 million worth of shaky International Mercantile Marine bonds floated by Morgan & Company. He discovered what politics could do—Mutual spent thousands on a mysterious "House of Mirth" located conveniently near the Albany legislature. He discovered that the very symbols of virtue can be tainted—old James Alexander, Equitable's shining knight, had played around with a few syndicates himself. (He also had six relatives on the payroll.) The following year, new regulations reformed the whole business.

To many, the most interesting result came sooner. On December 28 —two days before the investigation closed—James Hazen Hyde boarded the French liner *La Lorraine*. "I wish to deny emphatically that I am going to live abroad," he told the reporters who saw him off. But thirty-five years passed before the period's most gilded youth—finally driven by the Nazis from his beloved France—quietly returned to his native land.

The pratfalls of the privileged gave ordinary people a steady diet of excitement. They loved watching Charlie Schwab squirm, when the president of U.S. Steel was discovered gambling at Monte Carlo. They lapped up stories of fantastic poker games on the Atlantic—it was said one millionaire lost $90,000 in a friendly session on the *Kaiser Wilhelm II*. They savored the antics of Harry Thaw, who wrecked cafés and rode a horse up the steps of the Union League Club.

The very week of the Equitable crisis, young Thaw married the lovely show girl Evelyn Nesbit. Everyone wondered whether this new responsibility would quiet him down. The question was answered a year later on the roof of Madison Square Garden. It was the opening night of the musical *Mamzelle Champagne*. Thaw was there with his wife, as was the country's leading architect, Stanford White. While a sextet called the "Big Six" sang "I Could Love a Million Girls," Thaw slipped away from his table, walked over to White, and shot him dead.

"You deserve this. You have ruined my wife!" he cried, and at the trial that followed, the public hung on the lurid details. There was little sympathy for Thaw, who eventually got off by pleading insanity, but enormous interest in the stories of high jinks in high places. The murdered White seemed almost a stage roué—a wicked hide-out, a velvet swing to allure innocent girls, the inevitable glass of drugged champagne.

Nor were the vagaries of the rich just something to watch. Sometimes they affected people directly. Especially in the growing number of cases where automobiles were concerned. The "bubble"—as everybody called it—was still considered a rich man's toy, and he certainly treated it that way.

Alfred G. Vanderbilt made a sport of eluding New York policemen in his big red touring car. One day in 1905 he dashed past patrolman

Hanlon going eighteen miles an hour. This, of course, was well above the ten-miles-an-hour speed limit. Hanlon gave pursuit on a bicycle. He scored a rare triumph by nabbing Vanderbilt when the millionaire bogged down in a Harlem mudhole.

About the same time Pierpont Morgan's coupé struck a Mrs. Mary Socco on Park Row . . . and drove on downtown without bothering to stop. Police eventually caught up with the driver but Mrs. Socco withdrew her complaint, according to the *World,* "when she learned of the wealth of the occupant in the coupé." On another occasion Mrs. Stuyvesant Fish managed to run down the same Negro three times with her electric. Incredibly the man emerged unhurt and ran off. There was no question of legal redress. He was only too happy to escape.

When local authorities tried to establish some sort of order, the automobilists quickly bristled. The Duke of Manchester, visiting New York with his bride, was politely indignant to find he couldn't have a driver's license for the asking. "A duke who is fit to be trusted with an American wife," he complained, "is certainly fit to be trusted with a 'bubble' in New York, provided he knows how to run it."

He missed the point. It was not a question of ability, but behavior. And the only thing more lethal than one automobilist was a collection of them. This was immediately apparent when the first Vanderbilt Cup Race was staged in 1904. The world's best cars and drivers competed over a course that ran through the quiet lanes and hamlets of Long Island. There were thrills galore, and word quickly spread that this was something to see.

When the second race was staged in 1905, Society went en masse to the scene. Starting time was set at 6:00 A.M., and the morning star still shone as the long line of autos and carriages crept toward the shaky grandstand on Jericho Turnpike. In the first gray light of dawn, the elite stood nervously around, listening to the motors warm up, watching blue fire spout from the exhausts.

The scene reminded some of early-morning hunt meets, others of a Roman chariot race. In any case, they had never known anything quite like it—which was obvious from their dress. Mrs. Tiffany Belmont chose tweed; Mrs. Oliver Harriman dripped pearls. Miss Catherine Cameron's Gainsborough hat seemed better suited to a Buckingham Palace lawn party. Perhaps the most remarkable sight was Mrs. Reginald Brooks, who blended together a Persian veil, Panama hat, and Scotch knockabout suit.

The gentlemen too were uncertain. Most wore riding clothes, as though going to a hunt, but Herman B. Duryea wore a splendid gray cutaway, gloves and mauve tie. Only W. K. Vanderbilt, Jr., seemed sure what to do—he wore a black satin Norfolk jacket, black leather trousers, and thoroughly professional-looking automobile goggles.

As the twenty cars roared off on the twenty-eight-mile course, the fashionable cheered and waved. Pietro Lancia, the daredevil Italian driver, stood up in his big Fiat and saluted them back. The race was ten laps—with not much to look at in between—so most of the time the spectators gossiped, or gaped at the Duchess of Marlborough's box, or nibbled at sandwiches supplied by enterprising farmers at Delmonico prices. All agreed that the local people were outrageous—charging as much as $50 for a parking space near the course.

And yet there was something to be said on their side. The racers roared through Jericho, Brookville, Greenvale, Lakeville, other towns at over sixty-five miles an hour. The dashing American Foxhall Keene clipped off a telegraph pole. Louis Chevrolet broke an axle and veered into a ploughed field, scattering fans and farmers alike. Joe Tracy, the plucky American who finished third, conceded that he saw "some dogs lying on the track near Mineola." Auguste Hemery, the Frenchman who ultimately won, coolly calculated, "Someday a dozen people will be killed if means are not found for keeping American courses free." The emotional Lancia was more complaining: "Thousands . . . all in the way."

It spelled a grave problem to Woodrow Wilson, the president of Princeton. Several months later he declared, "Nothing has spread socialistic feeling in this country more than the use of the automobile. . . . To the countryman they are a picture of arrogance of wealth, with all its independence and carelessness."

Wilson was right about autos but wrong about people. Except for a small, smoldering minority, Americans felt no resentment toward the little world of Privilege that lived this special life. Far from turning "socialistic," some were frankly envious. Four days after the Hyde Ball, Katy Cogan and Sophia Peterson—a pair of impressionable Harlem teenagers—were so overwhelmed by the press accounts that they ran away from home. Their avowed purpose: "not to return until they had gained a place in Society." A generation later, girls might run off to Hollywood, or to become "models," but at this time the epitome of glamour was the Social Register.

On a slightly more dignified scale, the same sort of thing was going on all over the country. Everywhere the newly-rich were battering at the gates of local Society—the best fruit of success they could imagine. Charles Dana Gibson depicted these climbers in searing cartoons. Frederick Townsend Martin was more philosophical: "I remember very well the first great march of the suddenly rich upon the social capitals of the nation. Very distinctly it comes back to me with what a shock the fact came home to the sons and daughters of what was pleased to call itself the aristocracy of America that here marched an army better provisioned, better armed with wealth, than any other army that had ever assaulted the citadels of Society."

Most people were less ambitious. They didn't expect to make Society, but they didn't feel downtrodden either. On the contrary, they were content to sit back and enjoy the show. The average American has always enjoyed watching conspicuous spenders in action, and until the discovery of TV, screen and sports stars, Society filled the role. The press realized this and served what amounted to a minute-by-minute account of fashionable doings.

So in 1905 it was front-page news when, during Robert Goelet's dinner at Sherry's, Miss Laura Swann's hat caught on fire . . . or when a group of stately Boston ladies abandoned side saddle . . . or when Yale and Princeton played football that November in New Haven.

For football was another Society monopoly. True, all sorts of schools played it, but the only ones that counted were Yale, Harvard, and Princeton. They won the headlines, dominated the All-American teams, and provided a steady flow of heroes—usually bandaged and limping—who had an enthusiastic national following. The Saturday of the 1905 Yale-Princeton game, the New York *Tribune* bothered to mention only one game west of the Hudson—those interesting Carlisle Indians were playing the University of Cincinnati.

But all eyes watched the fashionable converge on New Haven. They rolled north in fifty special parlor cars, their needs recorded in page after page of Louis Sherry's order book. *Gumbo passé* led off the seven courses served in Captain R. B. McAlpin's car . . . *huîtres à la Camile* for Mr. McCall . . . *croquettes exquise* for E. S. Auchincloss. The best Sherry waiters went along to serve the Krug '98 and Apollinaris water for the ladies.

That afternoon Yale routed Princeton 23 to 4, and as the private cars lumbered back to New York, the Sherry waiters were again on the job. In Car No. 2126 the Auchincloss party enjoyed post-game refreshments that might seem strange to a later generation—they had sandwiches, tea, and lady fingers.

Crowds jammed Grand Central as the specials pulled in, apparently content just to gape at the people who had been on the scene. Accounts of the game filled the front page Sunday, and everyone suffered with Captain Cooney of Princeton, who was so shattered by the disaster that he couldn't face the press.

No doubt about it, Society put on a wonderful show—whether football, parties, regattas, or automobiling. Everyone was entertained, and no one seemed bitter. Let Professor Wilson shake his head, most people went along with the New York *Tribune*'s salute to the end of 1905: "Never did a year close with a better record—never did a new year dawn with prospect brighter—Good times go marching on!"

1906

The Town That Refused to Die

> *"From the Ferries to Van Ness you're a Godforsaken mess,*
> *But the damndest finest ruins—nothin' more or nothin' less."*
>   —LAWRENCE W. HARRIS, from his poem
>   "The Damndest Finest Ruins"

Society never glittered more brightly than at San Francisco's Grand Opera House on the evening of April 17, 1906. Mrs. James Flood was bathed in diamonds and pearls. Mrs. Frederick Kohl couldn't outdo her, but she achieved extra effect by carrying a single American Beauty rose. Other bejeweled ladies vied for attention with varying degrees of success.

The occasion was one of the rare visits paid by the Metropolitan Opera Company—a moment of high civic triumph for the richest, gayest, loveliest, most cosmopolitan city in all the West. This was not the opening night—that had been the evening before—but it offered something far more exciting: Enrico Caruso as Don José in *Carmen*. His golden voice was never better. As the final curtain fell, the old theatre rocked with cheers, and the *Call*'s reporter Laura Bride Powers sighed in rapture, "It was sublime!"

By midnight the post-opera suppers were in full swing. San Francisco loved any excuse for a party, and Caruso's superb performance amply served the purpose. The great man himself held court in the

Palace Hotel bar, joyously sipping ponies of brandy. In the nearby Ladies' Grill a young San Francisco couple, Mr. and Mrs. Sidney Ehrman, sat with other members of the cast. Ehrman was the Metropolitan's local attorney, and an avid opera fan. He enjoyed these late suppers, especially when baritone Antonio Scotti presided over one of his famous poker sessions. Then the ladies were packed off, and the gentlemen often lingered till dawn. But tonight Scotti was nowhere to be seen, and the Ehrmans went home around 2:30 A.M.

For others the evening was still young. At the Oyster Loaf, a small all-night café, actor John Barrymore sadly surveyed the depleted state of his finances. He was due to sail for Australia at noon with William Collier's road company of *The Dictator,* and he longed for one last fling. But he was already overdrawn on his salary, and the best his companion, music critic Ashton Stevens, could produce was a single silver dollar. Sometime before three o'clock they left, Barrymore drifting over to the new St. Francis Hotel. He was half-inclined to touch Collier for another loan. Then he thought better of it, wandered off into the night. Legend has turned the remainder of his evening into an amorous one. Actually it was quite innocent—he spent the hours between 3:00 and 5:00 at a friend's house, halfheartedly examining a collection of Chinese glass.

A young city fireman named Rudy Schubert spent a far more eventful night. A three-alarm blaze swept the Central California Canneries warehouse on Bay Street, and Schubert's outfit, Engine Company No. 38, was in the thick of it. They didn't get back to the engine house on Bush Street until nearly 3:00 A.M. Schubert climbed upstairs, kicked off his boots, threw himself down on the bed. He hoped nothing more would happen tonight.

Two blocks away the horses kicked and stamped at a livery stable on Post Street. James Hopper, a reporter on the *Call,* passed by on his way home from work. Hearing a shrill neigh, he asked a stablehand what seemed to be the matter. "Restless tonight," the man answered without much interest, "I don't know why."

The city was quieter now. Here and there someone banged at a piano, and lights still burned at the Poodle Dog on Bush Street . . . in

Chinatown . . . along famed Barbary Coast. San Francisco never went completely to bed, but this was the best it could do. A brief hush between the noises of night and those of the day.

Yet, Caruso couldn't sleep. No performer was ever more ebullient, but even he sometimes felt the strain. Last night's *Carmen* was a triumph, but it left him keyed-up and nervous. Now he tossed fretfully in his luxurious sixth-floor suite at the Palace. Somewhere a clock struck 4:00.

Forty miles to the north, novelist Jack London's wife Charmian woke up with a start. She couldn't imagine why. All was quiet at their country place near Sonoma, and it was only a few minutes before 5:00. She curled up, trying to get back to sleep.

Back in the city, dawn was breaking. Herbert Alwee, a real-estate man living on fashionable Nob Hill, got up in the semi-dark. He had to go to Oakland and catch the train for a business trip east. Just after 5:00 A.M. he boarded a cable car on Clay Street and rattled off toward the ferries. There were only eight passengers on the car at this unearthly hour. As it clanked by Portsmouth Square, they sat moodily silent in the first soft light of morning. It was too early to care, but Wednesday, the 18th of April, was clearly going to be a lovely day.

At Third and Market streets three other men also drank in the new dawn. They had just put in a long night on the *Examiner* and were now waiting to take the trolley home. The first sunlight filtered through the early-morning mist, lighting up the top of the stately Call Building. As they waited, someone embarked on a long funny story. Recalling it later, none of those present could remember how it ended.

Several blocks away another newsman, William G. Zeigler, was likewise heading home. He had been all night at the Press Club. Now, turning down Powell Street, he stopped for a light at a corner cigar stand. He reached for the open lamp that hung down on a cord. He didn't know it, but the time happened to be—by the Lick Observatory —exactly 5:12:12 A.M.

The lamp swung wildly toward him. Zeigler grabbed, missed, fell against the counter. For an instant, he thought that the cord hadn't swayed, that he himself was just a little unsteady. Then there was no doubt. Glass showered down. The top of the Columbia Theater crashed in a shower of dust and plaster. The cornice of the James Flood Building swung out over the street. For a harrowing second it hovered over him, then swung back in line.

On the Clay Street cable car, Mr. Alwee landed in the lap of another passenger already lying on the floor. The three *Examiner* men at the trolley stop fell to the street in a heap. Caruso hung onto his bed for dear life. Barrymore, who had never gone back to his hotel, listened to a cascade of flying Ming glass. Charmian London watched the treetops through her window, as they thrashed and swayed in the dawn.

It was simply incredible. Cracks yawned in the streets. Water geysered into the air from a hundred ruptured mains. Trolley tracks writhed and buckled. The whole earth ripped and heaved—"like a man shakes a rug" . . . "like a dog shakes a rat" . . . everyone had his favorite description. It was worse in the soft, filled land south of Market Street, but it was bad everywhere.

The big and the small crashed together. The Valencia Street Hotel collapsed in a splintered heap—its four wooden floors telescoping into one. A falling telegraph pole sliced a milk wagon in two on Mission Street. An avalanche of bricks buried Patrolman Max Fenner, affectionately known as "the Terrible Swede," at Mason and Ellis. Some 520 cemetery monuments toppled, all falling east or slightly north of east.

Uptown, a marble statue of "The Diving Girl" (the quintessence of Victorian modesty) crumbled on the lawn of 1801 Van Ness Avenue. Downtown, the whole City Hall tumbled in ruins. Tall "stone" columns crashed to the ground—and turned out to be hollow iron, loosely filled with bricks and clay. Huge slabs of masonry clattered off the walls, leaving the dome a gaunt bird cage silhouetted against the morning sky. More than the girders were exposed—the whole corrupt mess of Mayor Eugene Schmitz's administration lay bare for all to see.

The noise had a little of everything—milk cans rolling down Mission Street . . . cattle bellowing near the waterfront . . . glass, plaster, chimneys, china falling everywhere. And over it all, the sound of the earthquake itself—a long, grinding rumble. To philosopher William James, lying in his bed at nearby Stanford University, it went from *crescendo* to *fortior* to *fortissimo*. To the more professional ear of Metropolitan conductor Alfred Hertz, it had "an uncanny *mezzo forte* effect, something comparable to the *mezzo forte* roll on a cymbal or gong."

In the uproar, Mrs. Gustavus Browne thought for a moment that a volcano had erupted, for ashes from her bedroom fireplace choked the air. Young Dr. René Bine at first thought he was dreaming and waited to wake up. But most people sensed the truth immediately—earthquakes were an old story in California. Even something to boast about, as long as they stayed within bounds. "I hope they'll treat you to a little bit of an earthquake while you're there," Harvard's Professor Bakewell told William James when he left for Stanford. "It's a pity you shouldn't have that local experience."

Now as he lay in his swaying room, James thought to himself with a curious sense of fulfillment, "Here's Bakewell's earthquake after all." He was anything but scared. On the contrary, he felt strangely elated. The philosopher in him was delighted that such an abstract idea as "earthquake" could assume such overwhelmingly concrete form. "*Go it,*" he cried to himself, "and go it *stronger!*"

Later he thought a lot about this reaction. He talked to others, decided that hardly anyone was afraid while the shaking lasted. But he was wrong. Many San Franciscans were understandably terrified. As William Zeigler clung to the cigar stand on Powell Street, two customers burst from a basement restaurant at his feet. Both fell to their knees . . . one man praying, the other asking how to pray. Zeigler himself reeled into Market Street, shook hands with a man he had refused to speak to for ten years.

After forty-eight seconds the shaking died . . . then a final teeth-jarring convulsion . . . then nothing more except occasional aftershakes. An eerie silence fell over the city. The air was thick with dust and smoke, but the only sound was an occasional brick or piece of glass falling like spent rain. Once again, the earth had shifted along the age-old San Andreas Fault. Once again it had settled back in repose. The earthquake was over.

No fire bell ever sounded—the alarm system was wrecked—but the men at Engine Company No. 38 knew they would be needed. Rudy Schubert helped hitch up the horses, piled on the truck, and they clanged off to Chief Dennis Sullivan's headquarters at Bush and Kearney. He would tell them what to do.

They found the place in chaos. The chimney of the California Hotel next door had crashed through the chief's roof, sliced through three floors, and buried the apparatus. Worse, Sullivan himself, trying to reach his wife, had fallen through the hole. Now he lay fatally injured, completely out of action.

The men from No. 38 stood helplessly for a few seconds, freed a horse whose hoof was caught in the door sill, then quickly pulled themselves together. They set off to look for a fire.

They had no trouble finding one. Thick columns of smoke already spiraled up from a dozen different places. Overturned lamps and stoves—plus plenty of kindling wood—had given the fires a good start.

Guided by the smoke, No. 38 raced down Market Street . . . pulled up at Main, three blocks from the ferries. A brisk fire was burning on the south side of Market. The men hooked up the hose, wrenched open the hydrant. Water spurted out . . . then mud . . . then nothing. They moved to the next hydrant—with the same result. After trying three more, they realized that the mains had snapped, that San Francisco was largely without water.

No one else suspected yet. And at the Palace it was just as well. The guests were excited enough. Never did opera stars behave more like opera stars. Caruso was beside himself. Somehow his valet Martino managed to get him into some clothes, and soon he was rushing down the sixth-floor corridor. Spying Antonio Scotti, he bellowed "Totonno!" but didn't halt his flight. He next encountered Alfred Hertz in the lobby. "Alfredo!" he sobbed. He rushed up to the great conductor . . . hysterically hugged him . . . announced it was the end of the world . . . and continued on to the street.

Other members of the company joined him—Hertz, a topcoat thrown over his pajamas . . . Louise Homer, wearing her husband's trousers . . . Josephine Jacoby, barefoot in her nightgown.

They soon grew chilly, standing outside in the early sunlight. Some of the singers returned to the lobby, where the Palace management—always up to any situation—served hot coffee. Alfred Hertz had a better idea. Recruiting his first cellist, he visited a saloon across the street. There they downed a full quart of whiskey. Normally, Hertz thought it would have knocked him out. This morning he didn't even feel it.

The less resourceful lingered in the street. Dr. Ernest Fleming, a guest at the hotel from Southern California, noticed two women standing nearby. One turned to the other: "What wouldn't I give to be back in Los Angeles!" This struck such a sympathetic chord that the doctor offered his coat to the ladies. All the time he kept one eye on the blaze farther down Market Street, but it seemed to him that the Fire Department had turned it.

Brigadier General Frederick F. Funston knew better. The acting commander of the Army's Pacific Division had been jolted from his bed like everyone else. He rushed from his house on Nob Hill, hurried down California Street to check on the damage. Now he stood at the corner of Sansome, watching Engine Company 38's hopeless battle against the flames. He decided to call out the Army. He had no orders —not even a request for troops—but Funston wasn't the type to worry about that. A tough little soldier of fortune, he had never been one of the mold. He was an embarrassment in polite Army post society but the perfect man for keeping order in a burning city.

Alternately running and walking, he hastened up Nob Hill to the Army stable on Pine Street. It was more than a mile, and when he arrived he could scarcely stand. Gasping for breath, he scribbled the orders that would set the troops in motion.

Nothing more to be done at the moment, so he walked to the crest of Nob Hill for a look at the city. San Francisco's hills are breathtakingly steep, and from this distance there were few signs of damage. Occasional toppled chimneys, the naked dome of the City Hall, little else. But no one could miss the thick black smoke that rose from the whole area south of Market Street. There was no wind, and the columns rolled straight up into the sky.

What impressed Funston the most was the silence. No bells or sirens

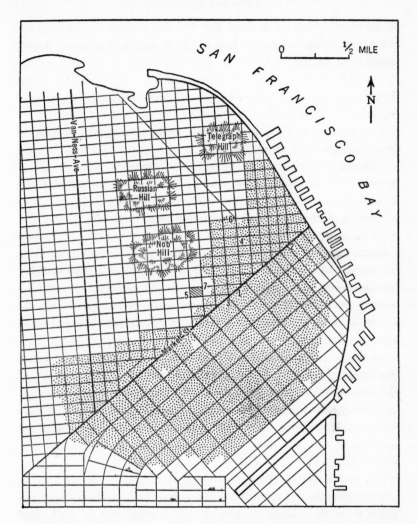

FIRST DAY. (1) 5:13 A.M. . . . *Caruso jolted from bed at the Palace Hotel.*
(2) 5:30 . . . *Fireman Rudy Schubert finds there's no water.* (3) 11:00
. . . *Call Building goes.* (4) 2:30 P.M. . . . *Engine Co. 38 tries blasting.*
(5) 4:00 . . . *John Barrymore naps at the St. Francis Hotel.* (6) 5:00 . . .
A. P. Giannini saves the Bank of Italy's cash. (7) Midnight . . . *Jack
London watches the flames sweep toward Union Square.*

or crash of falling walls from the city. No excited shouts from the crowds watching with him. There was little talking, and that in hushed tones.

It was different close up. In the shambles south of Market, no one had time to stand back in awe of it all. As the flames spread, men waged a desperate battle to rescue people trapped in the debris . . . to get the injured to safety . . . to save their belongings . . . to hold the fire off just a little bit longer.

Without water, it was hard to do much. The crew of Engine No. 38 scoured the nighborhood for cisterns and roof tanks, but the task seemed impossible. Yet they had to try—the muffled calls for help from a hundred piles of tangled wreckage told them that.

At the telescoped Valencia Street Hotel, fifty volunteers pried at the timbers, trying to reach eighty men buried somewhere underneath. At Thirteenth and Valencia, more volunteers tugged at a mass of debris pinning down an old man and woman. At the splintered Brunswick— another of the shabby rooming houses south of Market—it was too late to do anything. The place was now an inferno; the defeated rescue team stood a block away, pale and helpless.

As the fire approached the Grand Opera House on Mission Street, Metropolitan manager Ernest Goerlitz remained optimistic. After all, the place was "fire-proof." For a while he even toyed with preparations for the day's matinee, *The Marriage of Figaro*. When it finally dawned on him that the term "fire-proof" never contemplated quite this situation, there was only time to save a few violins. By 8:15 flames were licking the roof.

Now there was also danger north of Market Street. A big blaze in the financial district approached the Postal Telegraph Building, just across from the Palace. Only one line still worked, but the staff stayed on. Once, however, there was a break in the service. It occurred just after some unknown clerk tapped out the following message: "I'm going to get out of office, as we have had a little shake every few minutes, and it's me for the simple life."

The guests at the Palace felt much the same way. Fire was approaching from two directions. It was high time to leave. Alfred Hertz dashed back to his room for some hasty packing. Perhaps it was his speed, perhaps his state of mind, perhaps the quart of whiskey—in any case, when he reappeared, he was wearing a brown coat, gray vest, and black evening trousers. He left behind his watch and pocketbook, but did remember to bring an empty cologne bottle.

He also took the time to knock on the door of Fred Rullman, a Metropolitan ticket agent. Hertz hadn't noticed Rullman on the street and wondered if he had been hurt. "Who's there?" was the sleepy response to the knock. Rullman almost certainly had the honor of being the last person to wake up in San Francisco that morning.

Back on the street, the Palace guests straggled up to Union Square, several blocks further away from the flames. Its two acres of greenery—and comparative safety—had attracted hundreds. Here and there individuals stuck out in the crowd—an old gentleman examining the inscription on the Dewey Monument through glasses that had no lenses . . . a man in pink pajamas, pink bathrobe, with pink blanket, strolling barefoot on the gravel. Photographer Arnold Genthe wandered about in riding habit; John Barrymore was still in evening dress. Producer William Collier, sporting a flowered dressing gown, spied his young star and called out cheerfully, "Go West, young man, and blow up with the country!"

Barrymore eventually sauntered over to the Bohemian Club, downed some brandy, brought back another glass for one of the Metropolitan singers. Part of the company had been staying at the thirteen-story St. Francis, which bordered the square, and now they were having an emotional reunion with the Palace contingent. Rossi kept pounding Caruso on the back, wailing that the great tenor had lost his voice. Only Pol Plançon seemed in complete control of himself. He stood calmly erect, immaculate in top hat and frock suit. He had, however, neglected to dye his beard—which he did every morning—and it was now a bright green.

Caruso, who wore a towel around his neck and brandished an autographed picture of Teddy Roosevelt, soon announced that he was going back to the Palace for his trunks. Antonio Scotti was horrified and begged him not to. Caruso gave him a look of majestic contempt and stalked off, the faithful Martino trailing behind. They got the trunks out, all right, but in the course of it Caruso tumbled into one more adventure—a fist fight with one of the Palace's Chinese house-boys.

Such battles were the exception. Most people were amazingly calm. By 8:00 A.M. most of General Funston's seventeen hundred regulars were patrolling the town, but the explanation lies deeper. There was a spirit of selfless dedication in the air that had nothing to do with bayonets.

Even Mayor Schmitz seemed to feel it. He had been orchestra leader at the Columbia Theater—a fiddle-playing nonentity whose election was a triumph of crooked politics. Everyone knew that he was Abe Ruef's man, that the two of them divided the swag. No one expected Schmitz to show any strength, much the less now. But he surprised them all. He rose magnificently to the occasion, full of leadership and the ability to take swift, decisive action. Quickly he told the troops and police to kill any looters . . . he stopped the sale of liquor . . . he ordered all gas and electricity turned off . . . he warned the people to stay indoors at night . . . he sent a tug to Pinole for dynamite to fight the fire . . . he organized a Committee of Fifty, rallying the most important citizens (and some of his bitterest enemies) to help him.

This spirit was no monopoly of the prominent. Shy, retiring people who had never thrown their weight around were suddenly doing the most remarkable things. Miss Sarah Fry, for years a quiet Salvation Army sister, lifted a chair high above her head . . . sent it crashing through the glass door of a locked drugstore . . . helped herself to medical supplies for the injured. Gentle Dr. René Bine coolly com-mandeered an auto at pistol point to get to the hospital and lend his help. The Christian Millers' chauffeur Charles took the family car, organized a shuttle service to evacuate the wounded and homeless.

Watching them all, an interesting idea occurred to William James, who had come in from Stanford to check on some friends. He decided that "just as in every thousand human beings there will be statistically so many artists, so many athletes, so many thinkers, and so many potentially good soldiers, so there will be so many potential organizers in times of emergency." These "natural ordermakers," he concluded, would take care of everything—no one else need to worry. Banking on this philosophy, he happily spent the day gathering impressions and munching ZuZu gingersnaps as they city blazed on.

Even the best "natural ordermakers" couldn't do much without water. By 8:00 there were more than fifty separate fires, slowly merging together. By 9:00 the Opera House was a total loss; by 9:30 the Emporium, largest department store west of Chicago, lay smoking in ruins.

The firemen retreated slowly, trying wherever possible to hold the line at Market Street. It was one of the widest in the world—if there was any chance, it ought to be here. Engine Company No. 38 dug in at the Palace. The hotel staff were fighting the flames with the building's own water supply. But they were too enthusiastic. Rudy Schubert still shakes his head, recalling how they squandered it on flying embers and cinders that made no difference. Eventually they ran out and were as helpless as everyone else.

By 10:00 a blaze farther uptown was creeping toward the ruins of the City Hall. That didn't matter, but most of the injured had been collected in the nearby Mechanics Pavilion. Doctors, police, volunteers began moving them out.

The fire outguessed everybody. Its size and scope were simply beyond comprehension. Men who felt they were taking the wisest of precautions discovered again and again that they had really done nothing at all. At more than one bank, merchants were still putting their records in the vault, while the worried bank was moving its own records out. Countless householders took their furniture to friends' homes where it would be "safe"—only to see it burn up there instead. Residents who filled tubs and basins with water prided themselves on their foresight—as if it would do any good.

And of course there were those who went along as usual. At A. P. Giannini's flourishing Bank of Italy, assistant cashier Armando Pedrini opened for business at 9:00. When the boss didn't turn up, he decided to carry on as if nothing had happened. So all morning long he ran a normal banking operation, oblivious of the peril outside.

On Telegraph Hill another San Franciscan showed greater awareness. Six-year-old William Murray—son of a fireman and himself destined to become the city's fire chief—had been given a little fire wagon by the men in his father's engine company. Seeing the grownups unable to cope with the flames, young William decided to help. He coasted down the hill on his "apparatus." At the water front he ran into a group of men trying to save some files from a warehouse. They quickly expropriated the wagon, and William never saw it again.

Wagons, carts, baby carriages—anything on wheels would do. The great retreat was on. From mid-morning Wednesday, an endless tide of people crawled ahead of the flames toward the hills, the parks, the open squares. San Francisco was a cosmopolitan city, and there was never a more cosmopolitan crowd—a Japanese bearing a portrait of the Emperor . . . a little girl with a blind puppy . . . an old woman carrying a parrot that kept squawking, "Hurry! Hurry! Hurry!"

A thin, tired Italian woman struggled up Telegraph Hill, pushing and pulling a sewing machine on casters. The drawer kept falling out, spilling the brightly colored spools on the sidewalk. Others would stop and pick them up—people were never more kind to each other— and she would go on a few steps. Then it would happen all over again. Somehow she just couldn't manage it.

The opera stars too were on the move. Caruso re-emerged from the Palace with three trunks, while Scotti searched for some kind of wagon. They had decided to go to their friend Arthur Bachman's house near Alta Plaza. He was Sidney Ehrman's brother-in-law and another devoted opera goer—he would certainly take them in.

Scotti finally found a teamster who demanded $300 for the two-mile trip. Never mind—anything to get away. They piled the trunks on the wagon, climbed on top, and creaked off to safety.

Three other members of the company had it easier. A big touring car rolled into Union Square, carrying Dr. Harry Tevis of Nob Hill and his house guest, singer Emma Eames. They quickly scooped up Marcella Sembrich, Andreas Dipple and Pol Plançon (complete with green beard). The machine then chugged back up the hill to Tevis' mansion. Here they sat on the steps wrapped in steamer rugs, watching the distant flames, snugly convinced that their troubles were over.

But even they must have gasped when the Call Building went. This was San Francisco's skyscraper—an eighteen-story affair crowned with an ornate dome full of sculptured curlicues and portholes. The fire had been nudging closer for some time—gnawing at the Winchester Hotel to the south, then the *Call*'s editorial offices in a flimsy wooden building next door.

Shouts for help, and at 11:00 the firemen at the Palace moved up Market Street to see what they could do. Once more Rudy Schubert found himself wrestling with a hydrant that refused to produce. As he and his mates looked on, a flicker of light glimmered on the fourth floor . . . smoke gushed out of the portholes far above . . . and the next instant windows were popping all over the building. The men on Market Street fled in a shower of falling glass. In the space of a few short seconds, the city's tallest building had been turned into a chimney, with flames billowing up through the dome and on into the sky. The firemen were as helpless as a frail-looking lady watching from Nob Hill, who simply sighed over and over, "It is so terrible."

But the worst news of all came from the Hayes Valley district. This was on the north side of Market Street, far to the west of the fires downtown. Just before noon, a lady living at the corner of Hayes and Gough thought a cup of tea might soothe her frayed nerves. She lit her stove, forgetting that the quake had shaken down the chimney. In minutes, the roof . . . the house . . . the block was on fire. Assistant Chief Pat Shaughnessy went to the scene, but it was too late. The Market Street line was broken. The fire now covered four square blocks and was sweeping east toward the emergency hospital established in the Mechanics Pavilion.

The doctors and nurses rushed to evacuate the injured. In their haste, they paid little attention to a row of bodies lying in a corner. One of them was Willis Hammond, a hardware drummer, who had been buried in the collapse of the Golden West Hotel. It turned out that he was not dead at all—only stunned—and now in the uproar he came to, jumped up and fled with the rest.

About 12:30 the big Pavilion went up in a flash. The blaze roared on east, around and behind the outflanked firemen.

Mayor Schmitz decided it was high time for dynamite. Perhaps blowing up a few buildings might check the flames. Early in the afternoon he found Acting Chief John Dougherty and urged him to try it. Dougherty was skeptical. Like most firemen, he felt it only turned buildings into kindling wood and made a hotter fire. Still, he had no better idea; he would see what happened.

It was not a happy experiment. Chief Sullivan, the only man who understood explosives, lay in the hospital. The soldiers from the Presidio tried their hand; usually they blew up buildings too close to the flames to do any good. Artillery Lieutenant Charles Pulis grew tired of waiting for one charge to go off . . . he went closer to investigate . . . blew himself up with the building. Rudy Schubert helped set off some black powder on California Street, only succeeded in setting another fire.

Through all the explosions that ripped the town, John Barrymore lay napping in his room at the St. Francis. It had been a long night for him—a worse morning—and now he was determined to rest.

Lying there he missed the sight that broke San Francisco's heart— the end of the old Palace Hotel. During the morning the city's beloved "caravansary" lived a charmed life. First, thanks to its own reservoir, later to pure luck. But by three o'clock both water and luck had run out. It burst into flames—everywhere at once—according to most spectators. Fire raged through the famed Palm Court, poured out the broad bay windows. For a long while an immense American flag continued to wave from the top of the roof. Then a final surge of flame and it too was gone.

It was late afternoon before Barrymore arose. With all that excitement outside—and the stronger smell of things burning—he just couldn't sleep any longer. He looked out to find the fire much, much closer. He dressed, this time in tweeds, and set off for the house of some friends on Van Ness Avenue.

Plenty of others were headed that way. Van Ness ran through the heart of San Francisco's new, wealthy residential district, and its wide expanse never looked more inviting. Many refugees weren't content to stop there. They had already been forced to move several times; they would take no more chances. Pushing and dragging their trunks, they headed for the "Panhandle" . . . The Presidio . . . Twin Peaks . . . the farther the better. Metropolitan stars Campanari and Rossi discovered each other deep in Golden Gate Park; it was almost like Stanley and Livingstone.

In the midst of the retreat crawled two shabby fruit wagons, property of L. Scatena & Company. The Italians who urged on the horses looked like any other refugees; the orange crates in back even more commonplace. But $80,000 in gold lay hidden under the fruit. A. P. Giannini was saving the Bank of Italy's cash. He had reached town around noon, decided to leave just before 5:00, and now was heading for his house in San Mateo. The rescued gold—secreted in Giannini's living-room fireplace—was destined to help rebuild San Francisco . . . and launch one of America's most fabulous banking careers.

Giannini had abandoned his bank just in time. By 5:15 it was gone, and the flames moved on Portsmouth Square. Here was the Hall of Justice, headquarters for the Mayor's Committee of Fifty. It had been picked precisely because it seemed so safe—now it was going too. The Committee marched off to the Fairmont Hotel on Nob Hill, where they *knew* nothing could happen.

The newspapermen were more realistic. At 7:00 P.M. the *Chronicle* and *Call* men held a joint meeting in the editorial offices of the *Evening Bulletin*. It was dark now, and there was of course no electricity. Outside, the streets—once so silent—echoed with the roar of flames, the boom of dynamite, the harsh scraping of trunks dragged along the sidewalk. Inside, the men thoughtfully studied each other in the flickering glow of the fire. The talk was low and serious. As the session ended, word was passed to the *Chronicle* staff: "The men of the *Chronicle* will meet in the Chronicle Building tomorrow at one o'clock, if there is any *Chronicle*." Then to the *Call* staff: "The men of the *Call* will meet at the Fairmont tomorrow at one o'clock, if there is any tomorrow."

By 8:00 the *Chronicle* men, at least, were no longer left in doubt. James Hopper watched the Crocker Building next door begin to burn. The fire took hold in the most leisurely way—a window shade here, another there—it seemed almost insolent in its deliberation. But in half an hour the place was a furnace, and the Chronicle Building was soon lost too.

This new fire spread westward . . . eating its way through the shopping district, directly toward Union Square. It was completely unopposed. No water, no dynamite, no manpower, nothing. Jack London, who had arrived from Sonoma to take in the drama, was fascinated that any surrender could be so complete. As late as 9:00, soldiers and watchmen patrolled the district. By 1:00 they all were gone. The stores and hotels and theatres were still there—no damage at all—but utterly abandoned. Ashes sifted softly down on the dark deserted buildings, blanketing the silent streets. Several blocks away two cavalrymen sat outlined against the flames, the last rear guard of a retreating army.

The fire was almost at Union Square now. As it fastened on the famed Bohemian Club, an ancient retainer named Omar sat motionless on the front steps. He finally left, but not until he had made it abundantly clear that desertion was not for him.

In the square itself a man was still trying to get a load of trunks to safety. They were piled on a wagon—but there were no horses. He offered $1,000 for a team—but there were no takers.

By 1:30 three sides of the square were ablaze; by 2:00 the fourth side—including the wagon—was burning. The tall St. Francis flared brightly—helped along by John Barrymore's crumpled dress suit and a $20,000 wardrobe left behind by Mme. Sembrich.

The flames next swirled into Chinatown, giving rewrite men all over the nation a matchless opportunity. "I saw hundreds of crazed yellow men flee," ran one eye-witness account. "In their arms they bore their opium pipes. Beside them ran baggy-trousered women. Far beneath the street levels were many others. Women who never saw the day from their darkened prisons and their blinking jailors were caught like rats in a huge trap. The secrets of these burrows will never be known."

Actually, no group was better behaved than the city's Chinese. And there never was a day when racial barriers were less conspicuous. Like most San Franciscans, they saved their quota of worthless bird cages; they made their way to the parks and beaches; they shared with others the little they had.

136

If there was any difference, they had more water. By 1:00 A.M. Engine Company 38 had retreated to Chinatown, and to the men's surprise, they got a good steady stream from a cistern at Pine and Powell. It was their first break since the fire began. The battle went pretty well for a while, but shortly before dawn it was the same old story. The hose coughed, sputtered, went completely dry.

It had been a discouraging night for everyone. As Sidney Ehrman watched the burning city from Alta Plaza, Caruso stood gloomily nearby. Suddenly he tried a few notes. They couldn't have satisfied him, for he burst into tears, sobbing, "Ho perduto la voce!" Then he wandered off into the darkness. The Arthur Bachmans did their best to comfort him, but he was disconsolate. He flatly refused to sleep in the house, ending up under a tree in the yard.

At that he was better off than Alfred Hertz. The Metropolitan conductor made his bed in an abandoned trolley, standing near the zoo. After a restless night, he was awakened at dawn by the roaring of lions and tigers. He had no idea where he was but feared the worst. Hazy in his knowledge of California geography, he wondered whether, on top of everything else, he had strayed into "the jungle."

Sembrich and Eames were little more comfortable. All Wednesday they felt happily safe at the Tevis mansion on Nob Hill, but the doctor was worrying. He knew what a strong breeze from the south might do. When the *Chronicle* went, he broke the news to his charges—they would have to leave. The singers were upset, but Tevis reassured them: even if he lost everything, he would stick with them. They all went to North Beach, and while the ladies lay drenched with dew on the ground, Tevis sat quietly beside them.

Night began to fade, and the pink glow to the east promised that Thursday, the 19th, would be another beautiful day. But Tevis had his eyes on a different glow—an angry orange smear across the southern sky. That wind from the south was blowing now, and the flames were sweeping straight up Nob Hill.

So it was going too—the splashy summit where California's early millionaires had flaunted their wealth with huge, arrogant palaces. Few of the builders were still alive—and most of the widows didn't care—but the Hill stood for power and position. Many San Franciscans were more awed by its doom than by the loss of any office building downtown.

Around 4:30 A.M. soldiers entered the closed Huntington mansion, began moving out some of the paintings. At the towering Hopkins Institute—once Mark Hopkins' conception of home—Lieutenant C. C. McMillan had no men handy, but he recruited Barbary Coast idlers (some say at gunpoint) to help carry out the museum's art collection. The bleary drifters made an odd but appealing sight as they puffed and sweated under their burdens of enduring beauty.

Down the street Will Crocker's butler Head was at work too. He piled California Street high with Renoirs, Monets, Flemish tapestries, and finally Jean François Millet's masterpiece, "Man with the Hoe."

Just below the crest of the hill, Jack and Charmian London rested on the steps of a more modest house. About 5:15 the owner appeared, turned his key in the lock, and on sudden impulse asked them in. He said his name was Perine, explaining, "Yesterday morning I was worth $600,000. This morning this house is all I have left. It will go in fifteen minutes."

His tone was cheerful—almost matter-of-fact—as he showed them around: "That is my wife's collection of china. This rug upon which we stand is a present. It cost fifteen hundred dollars. Try that piano. Listen to its tone. There are few like it. There are no horses. The flames will be here in fifteen minutes."

His feelings broke through only once. That was when Charmian did try the piano. Quickly he raised his hand in a gesture that begged her to stop.

Mr. Perine overestimated the speed of the fire. It took much longer than fifteen minutes to reach Nob Hill. But the result was the same —all the houses burned. Almost the last to go was the handsome wooden mansion of Dr. Harry Tevis. There would have been time to get a good deal out, but there was no one around to do it. True to his promise, the doctor loyally remained with his frightened *prima donnas*.

The unfinished, dazzling white Fairmont Hotel, rising above the very crest of the hill, caught around 11:00 A.M. As it went, the Com-

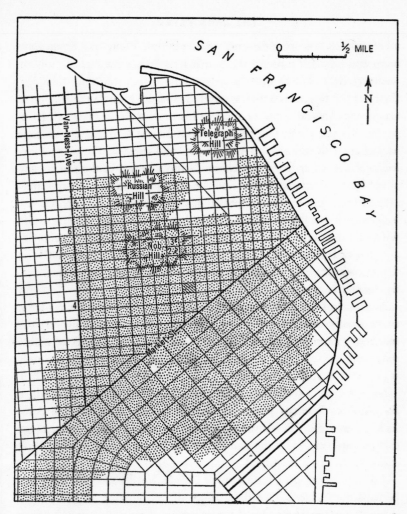

SECOND DAY. *(1) 1:00 A.M. . . . Engine Co. 38 retreats to Chinatown. (2) 4:30 . . . Barbary Coast drifters help save paintings at the Mark Hopkins Institute. (3) 11:00 . . . Fairmont Hotel goes. (4) Noon . . . A brave man saves St. Mary's Cathedral. (5) 3:00 P.M. . . . General Funston does some blasting. (6) 5:00 . . . Rudy Schubert fights the flames crossing Van Ness Avenue. (7) 5:30 . . . Franklin Lane finds a working hydrant in the nick of time.*

mittee of Fifty—so confident only the evening before—packed up once more and left, this time for the North End Police Station.

Others were pulling out altogether. Late in the morning Adolphus Busch of the St. Louis brewing family managed to circle the fire, catch the ferry to Oakland and take off in his private Pullman. The Metropolitan company had no private car, but Ernest Goerlitz did manage to wangle a launch. Word was passed, and most of the singers collected at the water front. Somehow Caruso was lost in the shuffle, and as the launch prepared to shove off the great tenor still hadn't appeared.

Suddenly there was a commotion at the entrance to the pier. Caruso had arrived, but the troops weren't letting him through. Shouts, wails, wild gesticulations. Then the singer had an inspiration. Producing his autographed picture of Teddy Roosevelt, he pointed dramatically to the inscription. The troops waved him through, and he jumped into the launch in triumph.

At Oakland the party swarmed aboard the Overland Limited—they could hardly wait to get going. Baritone Campanari, however, did pause long enough to give a brief interview. It proved a classic of understatement. Asked what he thought about the earthquake, he simply replied, "It is such a change."

By now others were long since gone: Barrymore to some friends at Burlingame; William James on the last wobbly train to Palo Alto; Jack London back to his ranch, vowing he would "never write about this for anybody." (By the end of the day he was frantically trying to make his *Collier's* deadline.)

Among the escapees, businessman George Kessler of New York was perhaps the luckiest. Two days before the earthquake he had bought a motor car for $3,500. Now the purchase came in handy. He filled the car with his friends, spun past Golden Gate Park and on to the country.

Curiously, most of the refugees resented his kind. In 1906 the automobile was still an expensive gadget. Using one to get out was almost taking unfair advantage—doing something that others couldn't do—a poor way to behave in this most democratic of catastrophes.

The press was full of hostile (and unauthenticated) stories about motorcars: L. E. Ryter saw a pet dog on the seat of an auto which wouldn't pick up a wounded man . . . a party of automobiling dudes were thrown out and made to do honest work . . . a man in a gasoline runabout rammed some poor people. Frank Searight, a contemporary journalist, told this harrowing tale:

Down the street came a great automobile. It was occupied by two society women who had recovered from the shock, if they had not slept through it. They were out to see the sights—the awful, heartrending sights—and their chauffeur was bowling them along at a fairly rapid rate of speed on the only open street near Market. It was heartless, cruel, inhuman, unnatural, fiendish—for they laughed as they came through the lines of suffering mortals and between the rows of wounded and dying.

But there was a happy ending: Uncle Sam's boys turned the Society women out and seized the car for relief work.

Thursday noon, no one had time to think very much about automobiles, evacuees, or anything except the fire itself. Nob Hill gone, it now rolled westward through blocks of wooden houses and flats toward Van Ness Avenue—the last big barrier left. Stop it here, and the Western Addition could be saved. Lose Van Ness, and all was gone.

Acting Chief Dougherty stationed his men for a final stand. Once again Rudy Schubert and the weary crew of No. 38 dug in to face the approaching flames; once again the odds seemed overwhelmingly against them. In some ways the situation was even worse than earlier, for much of the equipment was now damaged or scattered. No. 38, for instance, found itself trying to cover an eleven-block front—from Washington to Eddy. On the other hand, the street was wide, and occasionally there was water. Dougherty had managed to run hoses from the Bay for more than a mile up the avenue.

The men took their places—an embattled band awaiting the enemy assault. At the water front, fireboats, tugs and thirty steam fire engines pumped brine to strategic points. Reinforcements from Oakland, Alameda, Sacramento joined the tired defenders. Soldiers and marines waited with more powder and gun cotton. Volunteers stood by with brooms, soaked blankets, potato sacks to beat out the sparks and embers.

From his bedroom window on the west side of Van Ness, traction magnate James Stetson watched the approaching fire through field glasses. Just ahead flew a curious vanguard—scores of pigeons flapping wildly about in search of safety.

About 12:00 it hit Van Ness near O'Farrell. A blast of flame shot across the avenue toward the high steeple of Saint Mary's Cathedral. The spire began smoldering. As the crowd watched, a tiny figure climbed to the top and beat at the blaze with a coat or wet sack. He finally got it out. Legend has it that the hero was the Reverend Charles Ramm. Less sentimental witnesses say it was no athletic padre but one of Admiral McCalla's sailors.

At 2:30 P.M. the fire almost crossed again, three blocks to the north. By 3:00 General Funston's men were backfiring the whole east side of Van Ness from Bush to Washington. By deliberately burning buildings in the path of the blaze, they hoped to leave it nothing to feed on. But the fire licked across anyhow, and once more firemen, soldiers and volunteers flailed at the little flames springing up on the west side of the street.

The battle seemed lost to General Funston. He grimly wired Washington, FIRE CROSSED VAN NESS AVENUE TO THE WEST AT 3:30 P.M. ALMOST CERTAIN NOW THAT ENTIRE CITY WILL BE DESTROYED. He was wrong, but it was close. At one point there was only one hose working, manned not by professional firemen but by a young lawyer named Timothy Fitzpatrick and a few others of equal amateur standing. Somehow they held the flames at bay.

Farther up Van Ness, soldiers pounded James Stetson's front door: "Get out of this house!"

"But this is my house and I have a right to stay here if I choose!"

"Get out damn quick and make no talk about it either!"

There was no use arguing. At 4:45 Stetson retreated a block west, where he waited to see whether his house would burn up or blow up. It could be either. Soldiers were now ranging up and down the avenue, setting off charges on both sides of the street. As usual, the dynamiting was sloppy. The buildings collapsed into piles of scattered debris that offered fresh fuel for the flames.

There were, however, a few neat jobs. Mostly the handiwork of a very unlikely demolitions man—Franklin K. Lane, a prominent Democrat recently named to the Interstate Commerce Commission. Watching from Russian Hill, he was sure dynamite would help if properly applied. He confided these thoughts to a contractor named Anderson, who knew a good deal about blasting. The two teamed up, found some explosives, selected an attractive target.

"How do you want this house to fall?" asked Anderson, the authority.

"Send her straight up," Lane airily replied. When all was ready, he touched the detonator wires. The house rose twenty feet intact, then vanished into dust and splinters. Lane was utterly fascinated. "It looked," he recalled, "like a scene in a fairy book."

At six o'clock they were still at it, when word came that the fire had definitely crossed at Sacramento. Lane dropped his blasting experiments, rushed to the scene. A few buildings were burning, but they were going slowly. He was sure that just a little water would turn the tide. The hydrants were supposed to be dead; but somewhere, he felt, there must be one that still worked. He sold this idea to a fireman, and together they began making the rounds. They were on their seventh hydrant when it happened—a full, steady gush of water.

Surprised and delighted—for his theory certainly had no scientific basis—Lane rounded up pumpers, hoses, and men to work them. Engine Company No. 38 never fought harder—Rudy Schubert found himself even tearing at burning shingles with his bare hands. The water held, and once again, by the narrowest of margins, the west side of Van Ness Avenue was saved.

Noting that his house was still standing, James Stetson decided to slip back in. The troops were busy elsewhere, so there was no one to stop him. With hat down and collar up—like a man on a winter's day —he ran through a blizzard of sparks to his front door. Once inside, he spent the rest of the evening mobilizing a pathetic arsenal of pots, buckets, basins, and mops.

They were never needed. At 3:00 A.M. the wind suddenly shifted. Strong gusts began blowing from the west, turning the fire toward the north and the east all along Van Ness. Feeling the cool breeze on their aching necks and tired, soaked shoulders, the weary firemen suddenly realized that the fight was won.

Worn out by the struggle, Rudy Schubert got permission to look for his wife. Their new home must have gone the night before, but he felt she was probably safe with a brother at Coast Guard headquarters. She was, but Schubert didn't find out till the following day. On his way to the Presidio, he blacked out from exhaustion and fell unconscious to the street.

The victory on Van Ness had its price. Men had been shifted from other stations, and the fire now swept northeast into what remained of the "old" city—Russian Hill and its modest, comfortable homes . . . North Beach, teeming with Italians . . . Telegraph Hill with its jumble of picturesque shanties and broken-down houses.

All Friday the 20th the fishermen, the laborers, the clerks, the small householders who filled these sections struggled to save the little they had. Usually they lost, but sometimes they gallantly won. Toby Irwin, a tough little prizefighter, organized a team that saved a whole block of houses on Telegraph Hill. He had them all sweating—Tim O'Brien, who worked in the warehouse down the hill . . . his brother Joe, who had a job in the lumber yard . . . Herman, the grocery clerk. As they battled away with mops and blankets, an old Irishwoman whom none of them knew caught the enthusiasm and labored up and down the hill with buckets of water. When that was gone, some Italian broke out a barrel of Chianti, and they used that too. It was the perfect demonstration of William James' theory about "natural ordermakers."

There was something more mystical about the drama that unfolded at 1654 Taylor Street, an old shingled house near the top of Russian Hill. The owner was Eli T. Sheppard, once U.S. consul at Tientsin, later international law adviser to the Japanese government. He had prospered through the years and eventually added a wing to the place, which he rented to E. A. Dakin, an ardent G.A.R. man. Mr. Dakin dabbled in business, but his real love was flags. He had them all—the jack of the *Oregon*, the launch flag of Dewey's *Olympia*, and so on. They filled a whole room in the house.

Wednesday morning the Sheppards and Dakins were shaken out of bed with the rest of San Francisco. During the day Mrs. Sheppard filled the bathtubs and washbasins, while her husband bought dozens of siphon bottles filled with seltzer water—it was all he could get. Mr. Dakin raised his largest American flag in honor of the occasion.

The Sheppards left early Thursday; but the Dakins hung on until evening. Then soldiers and police ordered them out. As a final gesture, Dakin went to the roof . . . dipped his big flag three times in salute . . . lashed it to the masthead . . . and sadly left.

A squad of soldiers near the hill watched this ritual with interest. As Dakin said later, "They seemed to think about it." When the fire crept up the hill Friday morning, they suddenly acted. There was no thought-out plan—certainly no orders—just an irresistible impulse to save the house with the flag.

The men swarmed over the smoldering porch, ripping out the posts and railing. They climbed to the roof and used the Sheppards' siphon bottles on the sparks that landed. They slammed mud and sand at the fires just starting under the eaves. And when they were through, they had saved the house with the flag—the only building left standing on the east side of Taylor Street for nearly two miles.

By dusk on Friday it was all over. The fire had been cornered at the foot of Telegraph Hill, where the tugs and fireboats could drown it in endless streams of water. Rudy Schubert, rested and revived, slowly made his way in that direction. He would miss the final moment—when the last flames were put out in the grain warehouse between Sansome and Battery—but he felt satisfied already. He now knew his wife was safe . . . Engine 38 was in good shape . . . the fire was under control. As he walked along, a man standing in a doorway spied his helmet and called, "Hey, fireman, have a beer!" And why not? This was the time to start living again. He downed one—and then two—of the best hookers he ever had in his life.

Slowly the people filed back to see what was left. And it was very little. The U.S. Mint still stood; Superintendent Leach's men had barricaded themselves behind steel shutters and fought off the fire all Wednesday. The gloriously Bohemian Montgomery Block and the Hotaling Whisky warehouse also survived, both sheltered by the thick walls of the Appraisers Office. A few other buildings remained here and there. But 490 blocks were in ruins, 25,000 buildings in ashes, 225,000 people homeless, over 450 lives lost.

Those were the cold statistics. More important, the San Francisco that everyone knew was gone. Not just a big city, but a gracious, care-free, immensely appealing pattern of life. The natives of course adored it, but visitors too fell in love with its beauty and sophistication. San Francisco, they said, knew how to live—now suddenly it was shaken to pieces and burned to the ground.

At the same time, it must be admitted that not everyone regretted the loss. "It was the wrath of God for the wickedness of the city," declared Mrs. Jessie Rudisill of Denver, who had been there and should know. "Why, they tell me there is nothing in Paris, nothing anywhere to equal the depravity of San Francisco. It was God's judgment, this earthquake. I believe it. I believe it."

The irrepressible San Franciscans had a ready answer for this sort of analysis. In the words of Charles K. Field:

> If as some say, God spanked the town
> For being over-frisky,
> Why did He burn the churches down
> And save Hotaling's Whisky?

They had little time for post-mortems anyhow: the clean-up job alone was staggering. General Funston's men impressed anyone they could catch—California's Secretary of State worked alongside some millhands. One conspicuous shirker who nevertheless wrote home a glowing account of his labor was John Barrymore. Asked whether to believe it, Barrymore's uncle, John Drew, replied: "Every word. It took an act of God to get him out of bed and the United States Army to put him to work."

Wild stories spread about scores of looters shot and hanged in the ruins. Actually the regulars killed no one, trigger-happy militiamen only two. Self-appointed vigilantes shot a third man, who turned out to be H. C. Tilden, a prominent citizen carrying out important relief work at the time.

Nobody seemed to care; by now everyone was too busy rebuilding. The first orders went out for construction steel while the fire was still burning. The City of Paris store sent its department heads east to buy

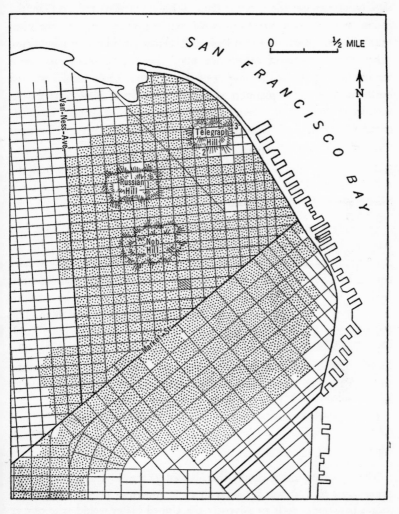

THIRD DAY. *(1) Morning . . . Soldiers save the house with the flag. (2) Afternoon . . . Toby Irwin saves a block of buildings. (3) Night . . . the fire dies.*

completely new stock at once. On April 22, A. P. Giannini wrote his depositors, announcing that the Bank of Italy was ready to lend them the money to build back. San Francisco's own insurance company, the Fireman's Fund, cheerfully (or at least so it seemed) paid off on its policies.

An electric spirit of resurgence filled the air. People forgot their sentimental regrets at the passing of the old; they could hardly wait to build the new. City planners sketched furiously at blueprints for "a metropolis finer than Paris." Sensing the mood, a young crockery merchant named Jack Dohrmann excitedly wrote his father in Europe:

> The inconveniences of living, great as they may seem, dwindle away into insignificance behind that new spirit, which, like a Phoenix rising from the flames, seems to have entered into the mind and soul of each one for a greater and better San Francisco than ever.

The nation rushed to help. Washington appropriated $2,500,000. Los Angeles bakers contributed free bread—25,000 loaves a day. John D. Rockefeller gave $100,000. Sarah Bernhardt raised $15,000 at a special benefit in Chicago, a city which already knew something about fires. James J. Jeffries, the heavyweight champion, raised money by auctioning oranges at $20 apiece—and he dared anybody not to buy them. The Philadelphia Athletics gave $639.39—their share of one day's gate. E. H. Harriman's railroads gave $200,000, but cash was not enough. The little banker considered the earthquake a personal challenge and rushed to San Francisco himself. He plunged into relief work with the energy he normally reserved for a raid on an enemy railroad.

Foreign nations wanted to help too, but Theodore Roosevelt declined with thanks. Speaking for the President, General Stewart L. Woodford explained the decision:

> The President meant simply that, bowed as the American people were under their load, it was his wish that the American people show to the world that under such an adversity the United States would take care of its own; and, spurred on by the indomitable courage which this people have always exhibited under stress of distracting calamity, set up their flag and build a new city, even though the earth shook beneath its foundations.

It was not the decision of a country with an inferiority complex. On the contrary, Americans were never more proud of themselves.

In Houston, Texas, little "1900" arrived via that clever novelty, the automobile, to start the new century off on a fitting note of progress.

Peking 6 July. 1910.

We are here surrounded by Chinese troops who have fired upon us continuously since the 20 June. without any effort being made on part of chinese Govt to stop them At present we hold the following le...

Courtesy of The Rev. M. Gardner Tewksb...

The march of Western civilization took a brief detour in China, when the Boxers tried to exterminate the "foreign devils." Besieged in Peking, British Minister Sir Claude MacDonald scribbled frantically for help (above), but relief first came from a most unlikely source—the Reverend Frank Gamewell and his "Fighting Parsons" (below). Dr. Gamewell, second from left, built the fortifications that enabled the foreigners to hold out.

Courtesy of The Rev. M. Gardner Tewksb...

Additional help came from Gunner's Mate Joseph Mitchell, U.S.N., who built this picturesque cannon. Called the "International," it had a Chinese barrel, Italian carriage, Russian ammunition, British and American crew.

More professional assistance was provided by the U.S. Marines, who held a key position on the Tartar Wall. The goggles were general issue.

President William M
Kinley liked to sha
hands with anyone, and
Buffalo on September
1901, he paid the pri
Here the *Leslie's Wee*
staff artist accurately
picts the exact mome
when anarchist Le
Czolgosz shot and fata
wounded the President

Next day, Vice President Theodore Roosevelt burst on the scene. Surrounded by reporters, he declared this was no time for an interview. A week later McKinley was dead and Roosevelt was President.

Great Northern Railway

Brown Brothers

On Wall Street jungle law still prevailed, as E. H. Harriman (left) almost captured the Northern Pacific Railway from James J. Hill (right). In the end they decided it was cheaper to combine—and discovered to their surprise that Roosevelt took the antitrust law seriously.

The Age of Aviation dawned when the Wright brothers made their first flight at Kitty Hawk in December, 1903. Curiously, few people were interested. Even when the Wrights made this twelve-mile flight in Dayton two years later, the only spectator was Mr. Huffman, who owned the pasture where they practiced.

The Wright brothers scorned the goggl and flying togs affected by other ear aeronauts. Except for the derbies, this how they looked when they flew—a pa of unpretentious small businessmen ordinary suits.

Culver Service

Far more exciting to most people was this huge Ferris wheel at the St. Louis Fair in 1904. Here was something anyone could appreciate, and the whole nation sang "Meet me in St. Louis, Louis."

Name _Mrs. Astor_ _450_ Persons.

8½ 5 th Ave.

Monday
Date _January 9 th 1905_   Time _Midnight_

Menu

Consommé Moluske
(Clam Broth with Chicken Bouillon)

Terrapin

Suprême de Poussins Courcel

Canard Cannanbects

Hunting   Gelée

Pâté de foie   Pois en Croute

Salade Oriental? M ^r Henry.

Mousse au foie gras

Fraises fondantes   Marron glacé.

Petits fours   Bonbons.

Pay de labras   Mandarins Glacé   Cerises fondantes
Supper for Musicians
{Menus}   Café
60 Waiters
Complete Service
Tables. Chairs
Lemonade
4 Maids
4 Valets
Ladies. Guests coat Racks
Wine Man, futs, Ice, Salt
Sauterne Punch
Claret
12 Musicians

Courtesy of Sherry, Inc.

The period was one long party for Society, with the fashionable restaurateur Louis Sherry usually in close attendance. His catering instructions for Mrs. Astor's ball in 1905 indicated 450 guests—not the legendary "400."

Name Stanford White   6 *Persons.* **211**

Thursday
Date February 23/1905.   Time 11 P.M.

Menu

Consommé de Volaille
en Tasse

Céleri — Amandes

Terrapin Maryland.

Poussins Rôti
Salade Céleri . Pineapple Remoulade

Glace Fantaisie

Gâteaux

Café

Consommé froid
Champagne
Beer
Apollinaris
Rye . Scotch
Menthe
Brandy
1 — 3 Light Candelabras

Courtesy of Sherry, Inc.

Sherry was equally adept at handling small intimate parties, such as this little supper for six at Stanford White's apartment in the tower of Madison Square Garden. These little midnight affairs were the subject of much speculation, but Sherry was the soul of discretion, and here the only suggestive note is the call for candelabra.

California Palace of the Legion of Honor

At 5:13 A.M., April 18, 1906, the ground reeled under San Francisco. Within hours the whole city was burning. That afternoon two pretty, smiling girls posed for their picture on Russian Hill, completely oblivious of the blazing business district in the background.

rico Caruso, in town
th the Metropolitan
era Company, drew
s sketch of himself
tching the fire. Actu-
y he was far more dis-
ught than he looks and
ore he would never
ne back again. He was
man of his word—he
ver did.

But the native San Franciscans faced the disaster with unquenchable spirit. Even
before the fire was out, they started to rebuild. And soon the city's beloved cable
cars were running again—jammed with bustling, derbied men full of exciting
plans for the future.

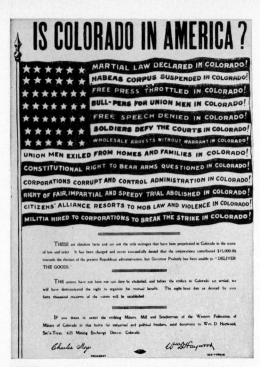

The drive for a better, fuller life took a ...lent turn in the Rocky Mountains, wh... miners and operators waged undeclared ... on each other. The tough union leader ... Haywood listed the miners' grievances ... this striking handbill. He was promp... arrested for defacing the flag.

Haywood was in far deeper trouble when tried in 1907 for murdering ex-Governor Steunenberg of Idaho, one of the miners' enemies. Clarence Darrow appeared for the defense and overlooked nothing. Noting Haywood's little daughter draped around her father's neck, spectator Ethel Barrymore observed that Darrow "had all the props."

HIGH LIFE INSURANCE.

THE REAL HOST ?

EQUITABLE POLICY HOLDER

Society played on. For the most part, the public enjoyed the show, but James Hazen Hyde's fabulous costume ball went too far. The New York *World* hinted darkly that young Mr. Hyde's insurance business had footed the bill. Untrue, but the resulting uproar ultimately led Hyde to leave the country and take up an expatriate's life abroad.

Financial panic seized the country in October, 1907. Everybody was caught—the fashionable at the closed Knickerbocker Trust Company on New York's Fifth Avenue (above) . . . the poor at the equally closed Italian Bank on the Lower East Side (below). Similar scenes unfolded in other cities and towns all over the United States.

J. Pierpont Morgan took complete charge of the country's economy. The President, the Secretary of the Treasury, the other bankers, everybody deferred to him. In two weeks he had saved the banks, restored the nation's confidence, and good times rolled on again.

America on the world stage: In 1908 the Great White Fleet circled the globe, "always ready at the drop of a hat for either a fight or a frolic." Just as ambitious on a smaller scale was the automobile race from New York to Paris. The American Thomas Flyer (shown momentarily bogged down in Siberia) took the $25,000 grand prize.

But the country's proudest international achievement was building the Panama Canal. Here Theodore Roosevelt inspects the diggings. For a man who often wore a Rough Rider's hat on formal occasions, it was perhaps inevitable that he would wear a linen suit on a steam shovel.

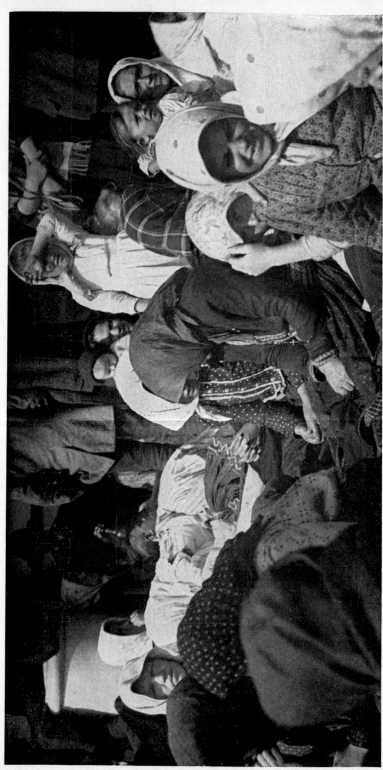

It was a period of extremes, as suggested by two contrasting crowds. Above is the packed deck of an immigrant ship en route to the land of opportunity. On the right-hand page is the 1902 Yale-Princeton

oly. The moment is Chadwick's run, which won the game for Old Eli. For his exploit, Chadwick was chosen All-American, along with six of his Yale teammates, two Harvards and a Princeton man.

April 6, 1909: Robert E. Peary reaches the North Pole. The flags he later planted reflect perfectly the leader's blend of patriotism and gruff sentimentality: Navy League, D.K.E. Fraternity, Polar Flag provided by Mrs. Peary, D.A.R. Peace Flag and Red Cross Flag.

Returning to civilization, Peary was appalled to find Dr. Frederick A. Cook claiming he had reached the Pole first. Peary bitterly attacked Cook's story, and the country had to decide between the modest doctor, shown wreathed in the garland of a conqueror, and the austere commander, here posing fiercely in his arctic furs. The nation chose Peary.

Anglo-American amity reached a new high in 1910 when ex-President Roosevelt represented the United States at Edward VII's funeral. Roosevelt was the only mourner not in military or diplomatic uniform (the State Department prescribed ordinary white tie and tails), but he seemed every bit as impressive as the nine glittering monarchs with whom he marched.

fresh batch of inter-
~~national~~ marriages fur-
~~further~~ cemented bonds with
~~the~~ Old World. In the
~~most~~ spectacular of these
~~matches~~, Lord Decies was
~~the~~ traditional titled Eng-
~~lishman~~, Vivien Gould
~~the~~ traditional American
~~heiress~~. In due course a
~~daughter~~ was born, pre-
~~senting~~ the opportunity
~~for~~ this stylish christening.

The cosmopolites' life revolved around "Seasons." London in May ... Marienbad
in August ... the Riviera in winter. Usually they also fitted in Newport, where
this fashionable trio shows how to dress for the beach.

In 1910, votes for women made a good joke for a magazine cover. An unknown
wit defined a suffragette as "one who has ceased to be a lady and not yet become
a gentleman."

In 1912, women voters were no longer a laughing matter. Some 500,000 New Yorkers cheered the great suffrage parade on Fifth Avenue, and the press gallantly declared that the marchers were all charmingly feminine.

A 37

Underwood & Un

The 1912 Dem
Convention took pl
Baltimore's Fifth
ment Armory. A
brief prayer for calm
beration, it took
stormy days and fo
tumultuous ballot
nominate the "scho
ter" Woodrow Wil

While the conventic
tle raged, Wilson
quietly at Sea Girt
Jersey, with his
and devoted sec
Joseph Tumulty (c
When, at a low po
his fortunes, a coff
vertisement arrived
morning mail, Wils
lightedly announced
company is ce
prompt in its serv

Underwood & Underwo

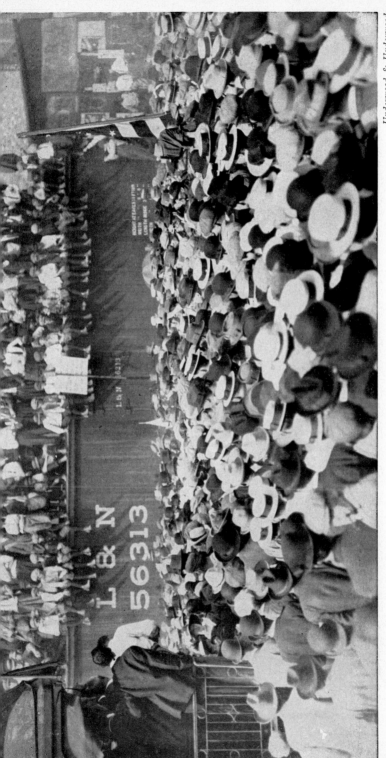

In the campaign that followed, Wilson proved a marvelous stump speaker. On one occasion, saluting the crowd perched on some boxcars, he began, "Ladies and gentlemen in the boxes . . ."

In 1913 the progressive movement was at flood tide, but here and there odd bits of the past remained. It was perfectly legal for mill-owner Frederick B. Gordon (above) to work small children sixty hours a week. He even considered it often a matter of "charity."

objects of "charity"
bout their appointed
. When one little
vorker was asked
he didn't play more,
nswer was simple: "I
t know how."

On June 28, 1914, in faraway Bosnia the Archduke Franz Ferdinand of Austria (above) emerged from the Sarajevo Town Hall, climbed into his motorcar, and moments later was shot to death. Within five weeks all Europe was at war, and British Tommies (below) were on their way to face the Kaiser's armies in Belgium.

In America it all seemed very far away. It was a hot lazy August on the Jersey shore, and few of these bathers realized that their world too had been drastically changed by that distant shot.

Form 1040.

INCOME TAX.

List No. ....

File No. ....

THE PENALTY
FOR FAILURE TO HAVE THIS RETURN IN
THE HANDS OF THE COLLECTOR OF
INTERNAL REVENUE ON OR BEFORE
MARCH 1 IS $20 TO $1,000.
(SEE INSTRUCTIONS ON PAGE 4.)

.... District of ....

Assessment List ....

Date received ....

Page .... Line ....

UNITED STATES INTERNAL REVENUE.

RETURN OF ANNUAL NET INCOME OF INDIVIDUALS.

(As provided by Act of Congress, approved October 3, 1913.)

RETURN OF NET INCOME RECEIVED OR ACCRUED DURING THE YEAR ENDED DECEMBER 31, 191....

(FOR THE YEAR 1913, FROM MARCH 1, TO DECEMBER 31.)

Filed by (or for) .... of ....

(Full name of Individual.) (Street and No.)

in the City, Town, or Post Office of .... State of ....

(Fill in pages 2 and 3 before making entries below.)

1. GROSS INCOME (see page 2, line 12) .... $

2. GENERAL DEDUCTIONS (see page 3, line 7) .... $

3. NET INCOME .... $

Deductions and exemptions allowed in computing income subject to the normal tax of 1 per cent.

4. Dividends and net earnings received or accrued, of corporations, etc., subject to like tax. (See page 2, line 11) .... $

5. Amount of income on which the normal tax has been deducted and withheld at the source. (See page 2, line 9, column A)..

6. Specific exemption of $3,000 or $4,000, as the case may be. (See Instructions 3 and 19) ....

Total deductions and exemptions. (Items 4, 5, and 6) .... $

7. TAXABLE INCOME on which the normal tax of 1 per cent is to be calculated. (See Instruction 3). $

8. When the net income shown above on line 3 exceeds $20,000, the additional tax thereon must be calculated as per schedule below

			INCOME.		TAX.	
1 per cent on amount over $20,000 and not exceeding $50,000....			$		$	
2 " " 50,000 " " 75,000....						
3 " " 75,000 " " 100,000....						
4 " " 100,000 " " 250,000....						
5 " " 250,000 " " 500,000....						
6 " " 500,000						
Total additional or super tax					$	
Total normal tax (1 per cent of amount entered on line 7)....					$	
Total tax liability....					$	

Internal Revenue Service, Treasury Departm

Anyone who escaped the impact of war almost certainly found his life altered by
a new form that arrived in the mail—the first income-tax blank. A married man
making $20,000 in 1913 discovered that he owed Washington all of $160. "From
a cloud no bigger than a man's hand . . ."

George M. Cohan caught the national mood perfectly when in 1906 he composed his stirring, heart-thumping "It's a Grand Old Flag."

There seemed nothing that the nation couldn't do. American medicine had at last conquered the scourge of yellow fever. On the international front, President Roosevelt won the Nobel Peace Prize for his role in ending the Russian-Japanese War. In Panama American engineers moved whole mountains, as they labored to achieve the age-old dream of an Isthmian canal.

True, there was some question about the political background. The revolution that severed Panama from Colombia smacked strongly of U.S. intervention. But after all, people decided, America knew what was best for everybody. Anyhow, it wasn't a case of just bullying the little fellow. If Theodore Roosevelt called the Colombian government "foolish and homicidal corruptionists," he also called Czar Nicholas II of all the Russias "a preposterous little creature."

America was confident and felt it had a right to be. It had earned its place in the sun abroad. It was plunging ahead at home. True, all too many people still labored in darkly dangerous mines, dreary mills and even filthier sweatshops—and every year thousands of new immigrants were dumped into the city slums—but all that would be changed. Settlement work was in full swing, and clean government seemed at last in sight. In 1906 alone, the Pure Food and Drug Act and the Hepburn Act, curbing railroad abuses, were added to the string of reforms.

In this climate no one looked on San Francisco as a symbol of disaster —it was a clarion call . . . an opportunity to show what Americans could do. The moral was not the destruction of the wicked, but the indestructibility of the good. Speaking for the clergy, the Reverend Samuel Fallows saw it clearly:

No earthquake upheaval can shake the determined will of the unconquerable American to recover from disaster. It will simply serve to make him more rock-rooted and firm in his purpose to pluck victory from defeat. No fiery blasts can burn up the asbestos of his unconsumable energy. No disaster, however seemingly overwhelming, can daunt his faith or dim his hope, or prevent his progress.

1907

Trial of a Union Man

"Habeas Corpus be damned; we'll give 'em Post Mortems!"
—ADJUTANT SHERMAN BELL of Colorado

Noting the wave of national sympathy for San Francisco, Chicago writer Richard Linthicum declared, "The American people, despite their differences on a multiplicity of subjects, are at heart one people."

Perhaps, but there remained a great many differences—ugly facts that refused to go away. Honest, upright cotton-mill owners were paying their doffers only $251 a year. While Henry Clay Frick enjoyed his private pipe organ, half the nation's steelworkers earned less than eighteen cents an hour. George Baer might modestly explain that he held his property under the stewardship of God, but many of the coal miners weren't so blessed. Old James Gallagher, for instance, was virtually a serf to that industrial legend, the company store—he worked for one seventeen-year stretch without ever drawing a cent of cash pay.

And when miner Henry Coll showed union sympathies, he was promptly evicted from his company-owned home along with his sick wife, four children, and hundred-year-old mother. The public murmured at this one, but the company indignantly announced that it couldn't be held responsible: Coll's wife didn't die until three weeks later.

No one industry—or any one section—was to blame. These jarring, discordant notes might occur anywhere. And when they did, there was often a day of retribution—harsh, bitter, and sometimes totally unexpected.

Certainly there was no sign that anything unusual might occur on December 30, 1905, in the little sheep-ranching center of Caldwell, Idaho. The day began especially quietly for big, friendly ex-Governor Frank Steunenberg, the town's leading citizen. He was president of the Caldwell Bank, part owner of the local *Tribune,* and the leading sheepman in the area, but this was Saturday and Steunenberg was on the point of becoming a Seventh Day Adventist. So instead of going to work, he joined his family in the hymn "I Need Thee Every Hour" and spent the morning at home.

A soft snow was falling when he left the house that afternoon to take a medical examination for life insurance. Dr. Isham pronounced him fit, and Steunenberg strolled over to the Saratoga Hotel to sign the policy. Then he joined a group of the boys in the lobby. The Saratoga was more than Caldwell's best hotel, it was practically a club where the town's businessmen gathered to drink and talk at the end of the day. Steunenberg was no drinker, but he loved to sit around discussing politics.

He himself, of course, was politically through. His star faded in 1899 when, as Governor, he used strong measures to end the labor trouble in the Coeur d'Alene mining district. After the men—striking for union recognition in the lead, zinc, and silver diggings—blew up the Bunker Hill and Sullivan smelter, Steunenberg lost no time. He called in federal troops, slapped the miners into bull pens, and instituted a permit system which kept a man from working unless he quit the union. Perhaps necessary to restore order, but certainly political suicide. Steunenberg retired the following year and reconciled himself to a pleasant private life in Caldwell.

Now as he chatted with his friends in the Saratoga, it must have all seemed for the best. The ugly business six years ago lay completely forgotten. No more hatred, no more bitter threats by the Western Federation of Miners. In Caldwell the only criticism ever leveled at the Governor was on sartorial grounds—he never wore a necktie and refused to say why. Little matter, it somehow made him even more likable.

As usual at 6:16 P.M.—you could set your watch by him—Steunenberg rose and started for home. It was clearing now, and occasional stars flecked the winter sky as he walked along the quiet, snow-packed street. Halfway there he passed a stranger hurrying in the opposite direction—a stocky man who slowed to a casual pace as he drew opposite the Governor, then hurried on again into the night.

Steunenberg paid no attention, continued toward home. He could already see the big frame house, the friendly lights in the kitchen where Mrs. Steunenberg was putting the final touches on dinner. Reaching the neat wood and woven wire fence that marked off his yard, the Governor went around to the side gate. He pulled it open, went in, turned to close it carefully behind him.

A blinding flash, a shattering blast ripped the night. Six miles away a farmer wondered what the roar was. All over Caldwell people ran into their yards, asking one another what had happened. In his house across the street from the Steunenbergs, Mr. C. F. Wayne dodged flying cups and saucers as his wife cried, "Earthquake!"

Wayne rushed outside, shouted over to the Steunenbergs to find out if everything was all right.

"Come here, quick!"

He found the Governor lying near the splintered gate, Mrs. Steunenberg standing beside him. As Wayne bent over the crumpled form, a weak voice begged, "Send for Mama."

Others soon hurried up, and they tenderly carried him into the house. They placed him on a bed, where he seemed calmly rational. "I can't live," he once said quietly; then a little later, "Turn me over on my side and let my legs hang over the edge of the bed." No one had the heart to tell him that his legs were torn to shreds.

He died thirty minutes later, obviously the victim of a bomb. But who did it? At the Saratoga, half the lobby crowd dashed to the scene to play detective; the less active retired to the bar, where they could debate the question with greater perspective.

About the only person at the Saratoga who seemed totally unruffled was a stocky man who had been in town a good deal the past four months. T. S. Hogan, he said his name was, and he had various reasons for being in Caldwell—he was trying to buy sheep . . . he was purchasing land for a friend . . . he was looking for a place to settle himself. Most of the time he hung around the Saratoga bar, sitting in on the poker game that never seemed to stop. He didn't work, but he always had money.

Hogan had been out when the explosion blasted even the staunchest regulars from the bar. But he walked in, slightly breathless, a few moments later. Not mentioning the blast, he ordered a shot, downed it with steady hand, and helped the bartender tie up a small parcel. He seemed awfully good with his fingers.

Soon he wandered into dinner but only picked at his food. The waitress couldn't help noticing. Then back to the lobby, where he exhibited supreme unconcern in the midst of the general excitement.

All sorts of people were dashing about. Sheriff Nichols threw a cordon around town, blocking every road of escape. Governor Frank Gooding arrived by special train from Boise, bringing two carloads of deputies, prominent citizens, and political hangers-on. One of the arrivals was a shrewd mining man named Joe Hutchinson, and while the others talked and argued, he slipped off to the Steunenberg house and examined the ground near the shattered gate. There he found bits of plaster of Paris . . . also some fish line apparently used to touch off the bomb. This evidence should be useful if a suspect turned up.

And some people felt they had a hot one already. Late Saturday night W. S. Dee told his friend Henry Griffith that it must be "that man Hogan at the Saratoga." Others began saying so too. At first for no special reason—just a small town's suspicion of an idle stranger. But then they recalled how Hogan used to examine the Steunenberg house with field glasses . . . how he would ask about the Governor's whereabouts.

Sunday morning Mr. Griffith asked his friend Sheriff Harvey Brown from Oregon to take a look at Hogan. Brown immediately recognized him—he was no sheep buyer; he was a miner. Brown remembered him well as a union boss at Bourne.

This was enough for Joe Hutchinson. Wangling a pass key, he searched Room 19, where Hogan stopped at the Saratoga. The chamber pot yielded some fish line; it matched the piece found at the Steunenberg gate. Also bits of plaster of Paris—just like that at the murder scene. In Hogan's suitcase Brown found a fishing reel without any line . . . a New Year's card addressed to Charles Moyer, president of the miners' federation . . . a baggage check for a trunk at the station.

The trunk's contents weren't quite in keeping with the interests of a man buying sheep or real estate: nippers for cutting fuses . . . burglar tools . . . a set of disguises. Most interesting of all were papers indicating that Hogan was also known as Harry Orchard. That was the name of the suspect wanted for a 1904 bombing outrage at Independence, Colorado.

They arrested him on New Year's Day, 1906, and he soon admitted that he was indeed Harry Orchard. But that was all. Why was he in Caldwell? Just looking around. The plaster of Paris in his room? For making loaded dice. The field glasses? "I looked around town with them."

They showed him a couple of intercepted communications. One was an unsigned letter from Denver, dated the day of the bombing, saying that "it" (presumably money) had already been forwarded. The other was a wire from Fred Miller, the miners' lawyer in Spokane. Although Orchard hadn't requested legal help, it said Miller was on his way. The prisoner couldn't have been less interested.

They were still nowhere on January 10 when a stout, elderly gentleman checked into the Idan-ha Hotel in nearby Boise. His gold-rimmed glasses, sweeping mustache and blackhorn cane suggested a sweet old professor, but he was something quite different. For this was James McParland, manager of the Pinkerton's Western Division and the greatest detective in America. He had cracked the murderous Molly Maguires in the Pennsylvania coal fields; now the State of Idaho was turning him loose on this case.

From the start McParland felt sure that Orchard was just a tool. The real murderers were the "inner circle" of the Western Federation of Miners, taking their revenge for 1899. For more than ten years there

had been almost open war between the union and the mine owners—
this was the climax.

As yet he had no evidence, nor any reason to suppose that an "inner
circle" existed. But the Molly Maguires had one, and this was clearly
the same sort of business. The job then was to get Orchard to tell all.
Not just confess the Steunenberg murder, but turn state's evidence so
that the whole conspiracy would be exposed and the "inner circle"
punished.

McParland's first step was to have Orchard transferred from Caldwell's cheerful jail to the fortresslike state penitentiary at Boise. Next,
a week in solitary to soften him up. Then, on the afternoon of January
22, the great detective went out to have a little chat.

There were no introductions. Warden Whitney gave them his office
and discreetly withdrew. McParland began talking. Softly, soothingly
he explained the advantages of playing ball with the prosecution.

"You speak your piece very well," broke in Orchard after twenty-
five minutes, "but I don't know what you are getting at. I have committed no crime. Talk about acting square with the state! I never
heard tell of a man who did but didn't afterward pay the penalty."

McParland told of cases where state witnesses went entirely free . . .
Kelly the Bum, for instance, in the Molly Maguire case. Orchard, who
had a thorough knowledge of famous crimes, said that one was different: "Old McParland had it all fixed and he saw to it that whatever
promises he made were kept."

This was a perfect opening. McParland modestly admitted who he
was, then explained why he liked to intercede in such cases: he just
hated to see a mere tool be punished while the true guilty parties escaped . . . and this happened to be Orchard's predicament. In fact, he
pointed out, Orchard now had no friends at all—not even his lawyers.
Their real client was the "inner circle," and their job was to hold him
in line, let him think he'd get off if he kept quiet—right up to the
moment when the hangman silenced him forever.

Orchard still insisted he was innocent, but when McParland left
nearly three hours later, he asked the detective to visit him again.

McParland obligingly returned on January 25. Again he lamented

Orchard's fate—just a tool, while the real murderers went scot-free. It was especially sad, for a man of his intelligence and reasoning power, as his forehead would indicate, had the ability of doing so much good.

"If I could only depend on you," blurted Orchard, "make a thorough confidant of you, I could tell you some things that would surprise you." McParland talked on . . . softly, soothingly as ever.

Orchard listened for a while, then spoke again . . . this time very, very carefully: "Let us suppose a case for the sake of argument. I will now say to you I am guilty of the crime as charged. Now, you understand this is not a confession, but for argument's sake."

McParland understood. Orchard then launched a rather searching inquiry as to what his chances really were. McParland made no promises but declared that if Orchard told all, he was sure the State would "see that you are properly taken care of afterwards." Nor was there any need to fear the pressure of public opinion—the people of Idaho would regard him as a "savior." Take the case of Kelly the Bum. When he turned state's evidence, a grateful populace not only set him free but gave him $1,000 to leave the country.

That seemed to clinch the practical side of the question. Now McParland turned deftly to the moral issue. Did Orchard believe in God? Yes, he thought he did. How about a hereafter? Yes again. Well, why hang and face the hereafter uncleansed of his sins?

"My God," said Orchard, "if I could only place confidence in you. I want to talk." Then he thought better of it, and there was nothing more doing that afternoon.

But the following day—after a night of earnest, fumbling prayer— he was ready. At first to McParland alone, later with the prison clerk taking notes, Harry Orchard poured out his story. It ran on and on— for three days and 135 pages.

He said that, as a young miner, he had planted the lifter charge that wrecked the Bunker Hill and Sullivan smelter in 1899. He said he fixed the bomb that killed two supervisors in Cripple Creek in 1903 . . . that he shot the mine owners' trouble-shooter Lyle Gregory in 1904 . . . that he blew up the depot at Independence, Colorado, killing fourteen non-union scabs. He said he went to San Francisco and bombed Fred

Bradley, manager of the Bunker Hill and Sullivan mine. He said he plotted hard if ineffectually to murder three of Colorado's leading citizens—Governor Peabody, Judge William Gabbert, and Justice Luther Goddard of the State Supreme Court. He said that in the course of these attempts he did get Merritt W. Walley, an innocent bystander who stepped on the bomb meant for Judge Gabbert. And finally, of course, he said he did indeed plant the fatal bomb at the Steunenberg gate.

More important, he said he did all these things (except the 1899 job) as a professional service for the Western Federation of Miners. He said that some of the jobs were specifically ordered by Big Bill Haywood, the federation's snarling, dynamic secretary-treasurer . . . that all had the blessing of quiet, secretive Charles Moyer, the union's president . . . that much of his modest success was due to training received from George Pettibone, a merry Denver shopkeeper who advised the union as a sort of hobby. It was Pettibone—playfully known as "the Devil" because of his interest in fireworks—who taught him how to make a really good bomb. He said that in return for his work, the "inner circle" (by now Orchard could toss around the phrase as easily as McParland) had paid him some $4,000 in fees.

What to make of Harry Orchard and his confession? Certainly McParland wasn't sold on the man himself—he didn't reciprocate the emotional attachment felt by Orchard, who now called the detective a "father." He was "using" the prisoner and privately admitted it. On the other hand, he did think that Orchard was a "true penitent." Yet he just couldn't be sure: "I must be very careful in writing letters to him because you can't tell what might happen." Perhaps the best clue lies in a revealing list of code names used by McParland in referring to various people in the case. Most of the names were black or white— Pinkerton was "Justice" . . . Governor Gooding "Lion" . . . Haywood "Viper"—but the enigmatic Harry Orchard was firmly labeled "Possum."

Whatever his misgivings about Orchard the man, McParland was only too willing to believe the confession. He had entered the case already convinced that a union "inner circle" was behind the crime;

now Orchard's story confirmed his theory. He lapped up every lurid detail (could the "Possum" have been feeding him what he wanted to hear?), and his imagination took off from there. He feared that union "anarchists" would try to poison Orchard . . . that they would "colonize" the area to load any jury . . . that they would storm the jail. "I have unearthed," he wrote Justice Goddard, "the bloodiest crowd of anarchists that ever existed."

It was a feeling shared by Governor Gooding and the state authorities. They too were convinced from the start that the federation was guilty . . . that the leaders were anarchists anyhow . . . that they would stop at nothing in their war against the mining interests of the West. After all, look what had happened in the past few years. The union had pulled innumerable strikes, blown up mines, wrecked trains, burned homes, beaten and murdered nonstriking workers, shown utter contempt for law and order.

There was only one way to deal with men like these—fight fire with fire. That was why Steunenberg had been driven to use his bull pens, why the permit system was launched, why union men and their families sometimes had to be run out of town. By the same token, any means would be justified in bringing Haywood, Moyer, and Pettibone —the real assassins—to trial for the punishment they deserved.

The difficulty was that all three men were in Colorado. They would never come voluntarily to Boise; they couldn't be extradited unless they were fugitives from Idaho justice. And legally, they weren't fugitives unless actually in Idaho at the time Steunenberg was killed. But, of course, they weren't in Idaho—they were going about their daily business in Denver.

Fortunately for the prosecution, the Colorado officials shared Idaho's feelings about the miners' federation. It wasn't difficult to work out an amicable understanding. Relying on the legal fiction that all conspirators to an offense are considered present at the scene of the crime, the Idaho authorities swore that Haywood, Moyer, and Pettibone were all in Caldwell on December 30. This was enough for Governor Muckey McDonald of Colorado. He promptly signed warrants for the men's arrest on Thursday, February 15.

Still, it was necessary to act very, very quietly—let no word of Orchard's confession or the extradition plans leak out. If Haywood, Moyer, and Pettibone once sensed what was up, they might go into hiding. With all the miners in Colorado protecting them, they'd never be found. And, of course, there was always the danger of *habeas corpus*. Through that inconvenient procedure—designed to protect citizens from arbitrary arrest—the men might be released even after they were seized, giving them another chance to disappear.

Again it proved possible for the congenial authorities of Idaho and Colorado to work something out. Instead of arresting the men when the warrants were issued, they decided to wait until Saturday night. By that time the courts would be closed for the weekend, and it would be easy to get the prisoners to Idaho before Monday. Meanwhile they could holler for *habeas corpus* all they wanted.

A loud knock on the door aroused Bill Haywood at 11:30 P.M. Saturday in his Denver rooming house. "I want to see you, Bill," called a deputy sheriff. "I want you to come with me."

At the local jail he found Moyer and Pettibone already in custody. A few hours standing around, then they were taken in the early dawn to the Denver depot. A special train was waiting, steam up. They were hauled aboard, followed by a swarm of Idaho deputies, Pinkertons and minor officials.

The train shot off into the early morning, blinds drawn. There were no stops till they crossed the state line, then only brief pauses for coal and water at small mountain crossroads. Early Monday morning they pulled into Boise and were taken by carriage to the penitentiary. As they reached the gray stone walls, Haywood glanced ruefully at the sign over the gate: "Admittance Twenty-five Cents."

High-handed, but it would be unfair to label the arrest merely a sample of "Idaho justice." Behind it lay deep feelings not confined to any one state—not directed at any one union. It was the lingering belief, shared all over the country, that somehow unions were wrong.

To many people they seemed to deny the very premise of America: that there was no working class, that anyone could reach the top. For more than a century men had struggled to build the country, cheered on by this hope. To join a union—the acknowledged defender of a working class—meant giving up on this best dream of all.

So men clung to it, long after new factors—mechanization, immigration, great business consolidations—suggested that it no longer held true. Unionism, they still said, was defeatism. President Eliot of Harvard called the strikebreaker the true American hero. Woodrow Wilson of Princeton declared, "I am a fierce partisan of the Open Shop and of everything that makes for individual liberty."

The nation's courts felt the same way. When Congress tried to stop the railroads from forcing their workers to sign a "yellow dog contract"—that is, an agreement not to join a union—the Supreme Court threw the law out. The reason: it interfered with "the right of a person to sell his labor upon such terms as he deems proper." When some Danbury hatters struck in 1903, urging a boycott on their company's products, the court declared that the union was, of all things, violating the Sherman Antitrust Act. When workers at the Buck Stove & Range Company went on strike, the court barred the A.F. of L. from putting the firm on its "unfair list." Federation president Sam Gompers did it anyhow and was held in contempt of court. In sentencing him to a year in jail, the judge called Gompers "a leader of the rabble who would unlaw the land, bring hideous pestilence and . . . subordinate the law to anarchy and riot."

Yet Gompers was the most conservative of union men. A dynamic, bullet-headed little Jewish immigrant, he had organized the country's skilled workers into the American Federation of Labor in 1886. Realizing from the start that the big problem was to make unions "respectable," he welded his group to the capitalistic system. He divorced it completely from politics. He stood for "pure and simple" unionism— pure of radical ideas, simple because he preached nothing more complicated than better pay, hours, and working conditions. If his carefully coached, skilled craftsmen were "rabble" spreading "hideous pestilence," then where did the millions of unskilled industrial workers stand?

The answer was—nowhere. Even Gompers wasn't interested in them, trusting vaguely that if the skilled workers got ahead, the unskilled would follow along. But it didn't work out that way, for other more powerful forces were pushing them back. The constant flow of new machinery weakened their bargaining position. A flood of immigrants —eighteen million between 1880 and 1910—further swelled their ranks. Absentee ownership in the new giant corporations made it ever more difficult to deal with the boss. As the rest of the country surged forward, the vast army of the unskilled straggled painfully behind.

Startling disparities arose. One Massachusetts mill, worth some $24 million, handed out $45 million in profits over a ten-year period. Yet it paid its lumpers 14 cents an hour . . . its 1,200 unskilled millhands $7.70 for a 55-hour week.

Just to stay alive meant endless, weary hours of toil. Many Pittsburgh steelworkers sweated through a 12-hour day, 7 days a week. New England textile workers labored 60 hours a week . . . railroad men 70 hours . . . New York bakers 84 to 100 hours.

And when they were finished, what did they have? In 1905, the Census Bureau estimated that the average American worker earned $523.12 a year. Yet all the sociologists agreed that a family needed $800 a year for a decent standard of living. In desperation, some men began flirting with the idea of tearing the whole system apart.

None were more bitter than the leaders of the Western Federation of Miners. In 1897 they pulled out of the A.F. of L., fed up with Gompers' policy of nuzzling with the capitalists. In 1903 they declared for Socialism, and tough, growling Bill Haywood didn't hesitate to say where he stood—for violence and direct action. The miners tried plenty of both in Cripple Creek that year, when they struck for the eight-hour day promised under the Colorado Constitution. But the Mine Owners Association fought back with troops and Pinkertons. In the end the strike was beaten, the Federation crushed, and some 238 union men run out of the state.

The leaders now knew that little could be accomplished alone. They would have to join others who felt the same way. The chance seemed to come in 1905, when they were invited to help launch a broader organization that would include all industrial workers.

It was an oddly assorted group who convened in Chicago that June 27—Eugene V. Debs, leader of the Socialist party . . . quaint little

Mother Jones, who had given most of her seventy-five years to the Eastern coal miners . . . black-bearded Father Thomas Haggerty, the radical ex-priest . . . nearly 200 others whose only bond in common was a hatred of the system. Haywood—holding the chair by virtue of his 28,000 miners—brought the meeting to order, whacking a rough board on the speaker's table. He obviously meant business—and so did the new union they set up. The preamble left no doubt: "The working class and the employing class have nothing in common."

They called it the Industrial Workers of the World, and it was against everything the American Federation of Labor stood for. Instead of catering to skilled workers, the I.W.W. appealed to the unskilled, the loggers, the miners, the boomers, the restless migratory men of the West. And instead of welding itself to the established order, it repudiated capitalism completely:

> We hate their rotten system more than any mortals do.
> Our aim is not to patch it but to build it all anew.
> And what we'll have for government when we're finally through
> Is One Big Industrial Union!

Guilty or not, this was the hymn of Haywood, Moyer, and Pettibone. And the courts knew how to handle the men who sang it. The three union leaders quickly discovered this when they arrived in Boise and demanded their release, charging illegal arrest. It did no good to go to court in Idaho, because the arrests were made in Colorado. But they couldn't go to court in Colorado, because they were now in Idaho. And when the case finally reached the U.S. Supreme Court, it ruled that the arrest might be illegal, but once in Idaho the men could be tried anyhow. The court wouldn't ask how they got there.

None of this was a surprise to the big, shambling man who turned up from Chicago to help defend them. Clarence Darrow had spent much of his forty-nine years fighting uphill battles on the labor front. He had fought for the union men convicted of the Haymarket bombing . . . he had defended Debs for violating the court injunction in the Pullman strike . . . he had represented the anthracite coal strikers in 1902.

By now he was considered the country's leading labor attorney—more than that, a brilliant trial lawyer. He had a way with juries, even though his technique ran against almost all the accepted rules. Other lawyers went in for purple prose and pear-shaped tones; Darrow's drawl was smooth as syrup. Others dressed in flaming elegance; Darrow's spotted vest and tie almost boasted sloppiness. The others brushed their hair; Darrow's thin gray shock fell casually over his forehead.

These little traits—many of them carefully cultivated—led some people to call him just an actor. Actually, he had one of the shrewdest legal minds in the business—good enough to have once excelled as corporation counsel for the Chicago & Northwestern Railway. He was eloquent, indeed, but it was his attention to detail—his complete mastery of all the evidence in a case—that made him so good.

On reaching Boise, Darrow quickly saw the key to the case against Haywood, Moyer, and Pettibone. It had to be backed up by someone besides Orchard. For he was an accomplice, and under the law no man could be convicted on the uncorroborated testimony of an accomplice. The state knew this too and had wangled a confession from a miner named Steve Adams, implicated by Orchard in some of his other crimes. Adams hadn't been in on the Steunenberg murder, but he said he knew about it and he backed up a good part of Orchard's story.

Clarence Darrow immediately set about getting Adams to repudiate his confession—that would leave Orchard without support. He couldn't get to see Adams himself (the miner was a "guest" in the Boise jail), but he managed to contact him through his uncle James Lillard, an Oregon rancher. Lillard reported that Adams had confessed only to save his skin and would gladly repudiate his statement if assured a decent defense. Darrow was happy to oblige.

By midsummer the state suspected what was up and frantically tried to hold Adams in line. McParland delivered one of his fatherly lectures; Adams cried, said the old man was his "best friend," but refused to talk any further. Later McParland wooed him with pipe and tobacco—that had worked before. More tears, but no change of heart.

Philosophically, the great detective wrote off the $3.65 invested in the pipe.

Truth was, McParland had met his master in the gentle art of persuasion. Once Clarence Darrow managed to reach his client—indirectly at first, later in person—Adams was lost to the prosecution. On September 12 he publicly announced his confession was false.

The state immediately arrested Adams for the murder of an obscure claim jumper named Fred Tyler, one of the crimes he had admitted. If convicted, perhaps he would change his mind about repudiating his confession. Men had been known to do such things with the noose hanging over their heads.

But he wasn't convicted. Darrow didn't get him off, but he got a hung jury—almost as good. There would be no retrial for months; meanwhile the state no longer had a club to hold over Adams' head. He stuck to his guns—there was no truth to his confession.

By now it was early 1907. First the battle over illegal arrest, then the Adams case had eaten up a whole year. There could be no more delay, or the public might believe the defense claim—that the prosecution was merely stalling while it searched for better evidence. This was perfectly true, but secretly Darrow too was pleased about the delay. It gave him time to build his own case. Even more important, it gave him the chance to do what he did best—dramatize the clash . . . strip it of criminal trappings . . . clothe it with dignity and meaning . . . turn it from a simple murder case to a Cause, affecting the rights of all men everywhere.

"It is not for him, a humble almost unknown workman," he told the Adams jury, "that all the machinery of the state has been set in motion. It is because back of all this, and beyond and over it all, there is a great issue of which this is but the beginning . . . a great fight, a fight between capital and labor, of which this is but a manifestation up here in the woods and the hills."

That was the aura he gave it, and as he spoke, workers all over the country began to listen. Where men weren't sensitive or deep enough to grasp the meaning of Darrow's beautiful words, Big Bill Haywood —a born pamphleteer—put the message in meatier terms. "ARISE YE

SLAVES!" ran the poster he composed in jail, "THEIR ONLY CRIME IS LOYALTY TO THE WORKING CLASS!" Underneath was a picture of "The Kidnapers' Train," carting the three union leaders, all heavily handcuffed, off to their doom in Idaho.

The effect of all this was electric. Haywood, Moyer, and Pettibone suddenly symbolized the injustice and frustration other men had felt for years. Emotions, no less real for lying dormant, all at once exploded. Unknown, unsung workers everywhere responded to the call for funds. A Massachusetts brewers' local raised $7.25 . . . the Greenwood miners of British Columbia sent $1,000 . . . Bill Eddy, a lonely boomer on a Western Pacific construction job near Chilcott, California, mailed in 25 cents.

Their letters showed how they felt. Mostly their protest was intensely, pathetically personal: "There are three of us, all poor men, and we just want to help a little by sending a dollar apiece." Or, "May our brothers be freed and restored to their family circle." But occasionally someone bitterly scrawled, "Three cheers for the Revolution!"

The whole nation was soon aware. Ads urged, "Union Men—smoke the Moyer Cigar!" Maxim Gorki, visiting New York, sent the prisoners a wire of encouragement, saw it boomerang when it focused attention on his common-law wife living with him in the hotel. The press clucked its disapproval and Gorki had to leave. If there was anyone who hadn't yet taken sides, President Roosevelt fixed that. He released a letter lumping Haywood, Moyer, Debs, and E. H. Harriman all together as "undesirable citizens." This made everybody mad.

Excitement mounted when fierce, dramatic Bill Haywood was named the first to be tried, and the date was set for May 9. Parades wound through the nation's streets in a final, bitter show of protest. Small towns, huge cities—the scene was repeated everywhere. In Rochester, New York, marchers packed the Cook Opera House, where they raised $744, after subtracting $1.50 for a drummer and another $1.50 for his drum. In Boston, some fifty thousand tramped behind the biggest band ever seen in Massachusetts. It was an impressive sight—fifteen thousand teamsters . . . Sunday-school children marching fifty abreast . . . women holding out blankets to receive the nickels and pennies that showered down from the tenements along the line of march.

San Francisco police broke up a rally there, but usually there was little commotion. Thousands of onlookers quietly lined the curbs, amazed to find their fellow citizens harboring such resentment. They were astonished by the red banners and streamers that bloomed among the marchers. They were awed and frightened by the bands that played the "Marseillaise."

For that was always the tune. In this confident era when political and social patterns seemed so firmly set, men had to go back more than a hundred years to find the music that could express their anger. But they got across the point. Watching the New York parade sweep up Lexington Avenue on a warm May evening, the Reverend Henry Brann was shocked. "Are we going to substitute a foreign hymn identified with bloodshed, strife and carnage for our own national anthem?" he asked his congregation next morning. "This is precisely what that horde did last night. One band played 'My Old Kentucky Home,' and I heard another play 'Hail Columbia,' but the 'Marseillaise' was dinned and dinned upon us everywhere."

It had been a hymn of revolution, and indeed there was now a whisper of revolt in the air. Eugene V. Debs egged it on with his most violent manifesto: "Arise ye slaves!" he began as usual, but the rest was more alarming. If the mine leaders were convicted, he threatened to lead an army of workers to Idaho to rescue them from the noose.

And even the most moderate press accepted their execution as a foregone conclusion. The *Outlook* brushed aside the possibility of acquittal in spelling out the issue for its readers: "Shall death on the gallows end the career of the leaders of the worst criminal conspiracy that can be conceived, or shall the lives of innocent men be sacrificed in the furtherance of a counter-conspiracy?"

In sharp contrast to the rest of the country, the scene of the trial was curiously calm. Boise never looked greener than it did this spring. The lazy river, the shady streets, the comfortable porches lent a tranquil touch scarcely in keeping with the momentous event about to take place. It was hard to believe that the old brick courthouse, standing in the square among the dandelions, was to be a testing ground for the system that governed the nation.

It took the visitors to break the spell. They were pouring in now—lawyers . . . correspondents from fifty-four papers . . . magazine writers . . . reformers . . . a "people's jury" sent by the Socialists, presumably to render separate judgment.

The prosecution staff swarmed over the Idan-ha Hotel, which soon matched Versailles as a center of gossip and intrigue. The regular county attorney had long since been brushed aside in favor of James H. Hawley, who was named special prosecutor for the state. Hawley was a pioneer of the old breed. His fiery oratory, huge bulk, and walrus mustache had dominated many a Western courtroom. But even Hawley was eclipsed by his brilliant young associate, William E. Borah. Here was a man whose lionlike features had suggested an elder statesman even at the age of twenty-one, whose rich voice commanded instant respect. He had just been elected to the U. S. Senate—this trial would cap a splendid career at the Idaho bar.

But there was much to be done first. Steve Adams' repudiation had weakened the state's case. Now Orchard's confession must be corroborated bit by bit from dozens of sources. Detectives roamed everywhere—trailing new witnesses, checking new evidence, watching other detectives who were in turn watching them.

A more select group, under James McParland's personal supervision, took on the assignment of penetrating the defense. They did a good job too. Not just screening wastebaskets and steaming open letters—Darrow expected that—but actually joining the defense staff. "Operator 28" regularly sat in on the most secret strategy sessions, faithfully reporting the results to the prosecution. To this day, the identity of "Operator 28" remains unknown, but there's no doubt about his reports.

It was just as well the defense never knew. They had worries enough already. Orchard's confession had never been released, so endless hours were spent trying to fathom the state's case. Other hours were devoted to squabbling. Chief defense counsel was Edmond Richardson, long the miners' attorney; Darrow on the other hand was more celebrated. Each had his own idea on how to present the case.

Only Haywood seemed perfectly relaxed. After years of rough-and-tumble fighting, he suddenly discovered blissful tranquillity in jail. He browsed through *Sentimental Journey;* he caught up on Voltaire; he planted a garden and trained nasturtiums. In what was for him an incredible display of Victorian sentiment, he even collected rose petals, made a little cushion and sent it to his wife. For the first and only time in his life, Haywood was utterly at peace with the world—this could go on forever.

It all came to an end at 10:00 A.M. on the morning of May 9, when Judge Fremont Wood took his seat in court and asked in his clear, firm voice: "Are you ready, gentlemen, to proceed to trial?"

"We are," replied Hawley and Richardson, and the trial of William D. Haywood for the murder of ex-Governor Frank R. Steunenberg formally began.

Haywood, of course, sat at his lawyers' table. Directly behind him was his invalid wife in a wheel chair. Completing the family scene—for Darrow wouldn't miss a chance like this—were his little daughters Vernie and Henrietta.

But what good would it do if the trial were fixed? And that was already the firm belief of the left-wing press. "The pins have all been set for conviction," cried *Appeal to Reason,* a violently radical journal published in Kansas. "The fair trial assurance may satisfy children and idiots, but the facts all combine to give it the lie." Why, Governor Gooding had even picked his own judge—everyone knew Fremont Wood could be had.

Perhaps it was this contempt for the judge that led Darrow to add Wood's long-time law partner, Edgar Wilson, to the defense staff. Certainly there seems no other reason than the hope of influencing the judge, for Wilson had never done any criminal work and took almost no part in the drama to come. In any event, Darrow couldn't have made a worse mistake. Wood was, as the leftists knew, a very conservative man; now he was highly insulted as well. The trial proceeded with the judge able—but barely able—to conceal his anger.

Now for the job of choosing the jury—a slow process since

practically everyone in the county had already made up his mind about
the case. When some of the talesmen admitted they might have difficulty believing Orchard, the state invited the press to meet him and
see how completely he had reformed. The interview went off beautifully—the correspondents reported Orchard a changed man; anyone
could safely believe him.

One by one the jurors took their places—old Sam Russell, a sixty-
five-year-old G.A.R. veteran whose flowing beard gave him the look
of a Biblical patriarch . . . wiry Finley McBean, a blue-eyed Scot who
farmed ten acres just outside town . . . tall, rangy Daniel Clark, the
only one of the group under fifty. When the last man entered the
box on June 4, it was a jury composed almost entirely of small ranchers
and farmers.

Most had also been good friends of Steunenberg. James Robertson,
the seventy-two-year-old Scotch blacksmith, had even boarded the Governor at his home for two years. "We loved him as one of us," he
sternly told Clarence Darrow during examination.

"Twelve dupes," cried the loggers' paper *National Rip-Saw*. And
that was about the mildest comment from the left. "PACKED JURY AND
BRIBERY," screamed the *Appeal to Reason*. The article went on to describe how, "according to a Boise man," the prosecution was offering
each juror $5,000 to convict.

The preliminaries over, the state lost no time getting down to business. Harry Orchard took the stand on June 6 and spent two days
describing his work as trigger man for the miners' federation. Dressed
in a gray tweed suit, speaking quietly and without emotion, he seemed
more inscrutable than ever. The whole courtroom played the game of
trying to figure him out. Hugh O'Neil of the Denver *Post* detected
"fathomless, fearless wide-set eyes, believing in the Everlasting God."
Bill Haywood, his face muscles tense with hatred, noticed only that
those "fathomless eyes" always avoided his own.

Now for the cross-examination. As chief defense counsel Edmond
Richardson advanced to tackle the witness, hope ran high among Hay-
wood's supporters. Richardson was a savage, slashing trial lawyer.
Many thought his brand of hell-and-brimstone oratory would go over

better with this Western jury than Darrow's Chicago sophistication.

But the result was a complete disaster for the defense. The more Richardson sneered and snarled, the calmer and more convincing Orchard grew. He stuck to his story perfectly. He handled every barb with devastating courtesy—once when Richardson caustically asked if he had been coached as usual by McParland that morning, Orchard said no, politely explaining that the detective had a bad cold. In the end, he was even helpfully correcting Richardson on errors in the trial transcript.

The rest of the state's case against Haywood was not quite so successful. It was mainly an attempt to corroborate Orchard's story, and somehow everything fell just a little bit short. There was a letter from Haywood to Mrs. Orchard clearly showing that the men knew each other—but the union boss admitted that already. There was the wire Orchard said Pettibone sent him the day of the Steunenberg murder —but it was unsigned. There was evidence that Orchard did indeed blow up the Independence depot—but it also came out that the mine owners had a cute trick of wrecking their own property to create anti-union feeling. And there were plenty of witnesses who supported his story of bombing Fred Bradley in San Francisco—but Bradley himself, oddly enough, felt it might have been a gas leak.

When the state finished its presentation on June 21, the defense made what it considered a clever move. Nudged by Clarence Darrow, Edgar Wilson arose for the only time in the trial and asked his long-time law partner to direct a verdict of not guilty. Certainly there was little corroborating evidence, and Judge Wood later admitted that he might well have granted the motion—if it had come from anybody else but Edgar Wilson. But this was too much. The utter transparency of it— the contempt for his integrity—the way it would always look if he complied. Coldly he announced that the trial would go on.

"Capitalism deals with judges as it does with Pinkertons," sighed the *Appeal to Reason*.

On June 24 Darrow opened for the defense. Normally he would have gripped the attention of everyone in court. But not that day. Instead, all eyes were on the radiantly lovely girl in the tan linen suit, sitting in the front row of spectators. Ethel Barrymore had come to town for a one-night stand in her great hit *Captain Jinks of the Horse Marines* and was taking in the trial that afternoon.

Sitting between Mrs. Borah and another distinguished visitor, Gifford Pinchot, she carefully studied Harry Orchard ("a little like Mr. Hobbs in *Little Lord Fauntleroy*") and Clarence Darrow ("he had all the props"). But most of all, she was taken with the jury—"the most wonderful-looking men I've ever seen . . . the bluest eyes, used to looking at great distances."

Miss Barrymore's appearance was one of several interludes that relieved the strain of the courtroom sessions. On another hot June night the road company of Oscar Wilde's *Salomé* performed at the Columbia Theater. The *Evening Capital News* assured its readers that "the objectionable features of the play have been eliminated."

Then there were more informal evenings. This was the era when people made their own entertainment, and even the visitors were expected to contribute. Clarence Darrow, who enjoyed a far more cordial welcome than later stories indicated, gave a lecture on Walt Whitman. Pinchot was roped into speaking before the Commercial Club on "Our Forest Reserves."

But the biggest break, of course, was the Fourth of July. The trial and everything else in Boise stopped for a rousing, walloping celebration. The reformers and detectives and big-city newsmen gaped in wonder—they had forgotten, or never knew, what the "Glorious Fourth" meant to a small American town.

The festivities were in full swing by the night of the third. Crowds surged down Main Street, beating time to the Columbia Military Band, cheering the awesome fire-swallowing act of Professor Fra Diavolo. At 9:45 the Fire Department galloped out on an exhibition run, clearing the way with Roman candles as it swept down the street.

Next morning the traditional pie-eating contest . . . the fat man's race . . . "A Greased Pig Race; prize: the pig." Then the parade, with every store in town contributing a float . . . the ball game at Riverside Park . . . the Mammoth Pyrotechnical Display in the evening. And all of it repeated on Friday the fifth.

With the holiday over, the trial dragged on through the weary dog days of July. To Darrow, nothing seemed to go right. When he tried to show that Orchard had his own motive for killing Steunenberg—that the Governor's crackdown in 1899 had cost him a share in the fabulous Hercules mine—the state proved that Orchard had sold out a whole year earlier. When he showed that Orchard had taken money from the mine owners' detectives, the state proved that this was before he ever met Haywood.

As always happens when things go wrong, serious dissension broke out in the defense "family." Haywood no longer spoke to Moyer. Darrow took an intense dislike to Haywood—the man might be innocent in this case, but he certainly was all for blowing up things. Richardson and Darrow also drifted further apart; the old Denver labor lawyer seemed an impossible ham. Only Pettibone remained blissfully content. "Cheer up, Clarence," he admonished Darrow one day. "Don't you know we are the ones they are going to hang?"

To many, it looked more and more that way. Noting that both the jury and the state administration were Republican, the *Miners Magazine* observed, "It requires no extraordinary amount of mental activity to arrive at a conclusion as to how it became possible for eight Republicans to find seats in the jury box. The political ring of Idaho has based its political future on the results of this trial." As usual, the *Appeal to Reason* went even further: "The men on the jury have already made up their minds, and they have decided to win the approbation of Gooding and his gang of timber thieves by handing to the 'Colorado anarchist' a sample of Idaho justice."

Darrow's analysis of the jury was somewhat more searching. In fact, he studied them all the time. He thought old Sam Russell had a "kindly face"—yet these G.A.R. men were always conservative. He saw tears fill O. V. Sebern's eyes when the miners' sufferings were described—yet on another jury Sebern had once voted to hang a man. He thought Finley McBean was impressed by his arguments—yet it was hard to tell about these expressionless Scotchmen.

All of Darrow's hunches, all of his theories about these men, went into his closing argument for the defense. He began on the morning of July 24, pacing up and down before the jury box as he talked. His left hand was thrust into the pocket of his crumpled gray coat, his right pounded the air to emphasize his points. The loose wisp of gray hair never looked more unruly.

The courtroom was packed, and a large overflow spilled into the yard outside. There they sat on the grass, or in the trees, listening carefully to the man from Chicago. It was stifling hot, and they could hear him quite clearly through the big open windows.

First came a call for fair play. Darrow said he realized Steunenberg was the jury's friend, had even boarded at the home of one of them—he shot a quick look at Sam Russell. Then a shrewd reminder of how much prosecutor Hawley's efforts had already cost the taxpayers —this time a glance at McBean, the canny Scot.

Now they were in the mood, and it was time for the meat of his argument: there was nothing to the state's case but Harry Orchard. "Perjured monster" . . . "miserable wretch" . . . "brute" . . . "liar" . . . "unspeakable scoundrel"—Darrow never lacked words to describe him. "If you men can kill my client on his testimony, then, peace be with you."

Could such a man suddenly get religion? Could he—as the state contended—have really seen the light and now be telling all to cleanse his soul? "I might have a little more confidence in this if he had not confessed to the Pinkertons before confessing to the Saviour."

Then as proof that the conversion was a sham—that there still wasn't an ounce of decency in Orchard—Darrow struck a note that was so novel, so unexpected, yet so convincingly simple that the whole courtroom leaned forward in hushed attention. He pointed out that all through the ages even the worst criminals had gone to their deaths protecting their name—the only thing they had left. But Orchard had gladly said who he really was—Albert Horseley of Ontario. He had long ago deserted his family—no one back home knew he was a famous criminal—why bring such shame upon them now? Not because it was necessary to his confession; just because it would help sell his story to *McClure's,* just because the "miserable, contemptible Pinkerton detective" thought it might sound better in court. "Gentlemen, am

I wrong? Is there any sane man who can ever think of Harry Orchard except in loathing and disgust?"

Next day Darrow was still going strong, by this time on the subject of Haywood. Again and again he pointed out that it was not this one man who was on trial but the whole Western Federation of Miners. The rights of all labor were at stake. But even if Haywood were hung, the battle would go on: "There are others and these others will come to take his place; they will come to carry the banner when he can hold it up no more."

He had talked for nearly eleven hours. Now he soared to his climax, off on one of those eloquent flights that electrified his listeners . . . that made them forget they were there to decide whether one man killed another . . . that made them feel they had a thrilling opportunity to serve the cause of freedom:

The eyes of the world are upon you—upon you twelve men of Idaho tonight. If you should decree Bill Haywood's death, in the railroad offices of our great cities men will applaud your names. If you decree his death, amongst the spiders of Wall Street will go up paeans of praise for these twelve good men and true. In every bank in the world, where men hate Haywood because he fights for the poor and against that accursed system upon which the favored live and grow rich and fat—from all those you will receive blessings and unstinted praise.

But if your verdict should be "Not Guilty" in this case, there are still those who will reverently bow their heads and thank these twelve men for the life and reputation you have saved. Out on our broad prairies where men toil with their hands, out on the wide ocean where men are tossed and buffeted on the waves, through our mills and factories, and down deep under the earth, thousands of men, and of women and children will kneel tonight and ask their God to guide your hearts—these men and women and these little children, the poor, the weak, and the suffering of the world, are stretching out their helpless hands to this jury in mute appeal for Bill Haywood's life.

Borah's turn came in the evening. Again the place was packed, but the Senator—who also knew a little about courtroom dramatics—managed to get Steunenberg's widow in a seat near the jury. Calmly, dispassionately he went to work stripping the emotional frills from the case: "We are not here to fight organized labor. This is simply a trial for murder. Frank Steunenberg has been murdered and we want to know."

He then reviewed Orchard's trail of crime, showing that he must have had help from somewhere. But where? The evidence supplied the answer. Orchard's base for all his missions was Denver—home of the miners' federation. Letters, money orders and telegrams linked him to the federation leaders. Wherever he went he found a friendly reception at local federation headquarters. He had no victims but federation enemies; no possible motive but federation orders; no income but federation funds. It was all a conspiracy—it had to be—there was no other explanation. And that being so, it must be stamped out. "I only want what you want—the gate which leads to our homes—the yard gate whose inward swing tells of the returning husband and father shielded and guarded by the courage and manhood of Idaho juries."

"Terrific, crushing, destroying" enthused the *New York Times*. And indeed it was a masterly job of marshaling the evidence. When, at one point in Borah's speech, Haywood's mother fainted, J. R. Kennedy of the Associated Press sternly declared, "This woman fainted because Mr. Borah's argument convinced her of her son's guilt."

The harangues, the speeches, the fireworks were over. Nothing remained but Judge Wood's instructions to the jury. He addressed them slowly and quietly on Saturday morning, July 27. The jurors must remember, he said firmly, that the defendant was considered innocent unless proved guilty beyond a reasonable doubt. And the testimony of an accomplice was often questionable, since he might be merely seeking to save himself. Even if the jury believed Orchard, the judge stressed, they must not convict unless his testimony was corroborated by other independent evidence. And that evidence had to link Haywood to the Steunenberg murder itself, not just anything else that may have happened in Idaho or Colorado. He finished at 10:59 A.M. . . . the jury filed out . . . and the waiting began.

Time passed slowly that July afternoon. In the courtroom, Judge Wood sat almost alone, staring moodily at the empty seats. Outside, little knots of people stood in the yard, peering up at the jury room windows, but not a clue drifted down through the hot still air. Under a tree in the yard Haywood rested with his family on the grass—it looked like a picnic—until his mother again fainted, and this time was taken to the hospital. At 3:30 a note came down from the jury room . . . the crowd stirred excitedly to its feet . . . but it was only a request for cushions.

Night fell, and still no word. Gradually the crowd drifted home. Even the lawyers retired—Richardson said he was satisfied that he had done his best and he might as well go to bed. But Darrow could not sleep. All night long he paced the streets, wondering and worrying. From time to time he slipped over to the courthouse yard and gazed up at the brightly-lit jury room windows. Then off again into the dark. Once, at 2:00 A.M., he picked up a disquieting rumor from the few night-hawks that lingered around. The jury, they said, stood ten to two for conviction.

Well, it figured. The Boise papers were all confident of a guilty verdict, and the visiting correspondents seemed to think so too. As for the labor press, it was wild with frustration. The *Appeal to Reason* felt that the instructions to the jury were outrageously weighted in favor of the prosecution: "With the autocratic power assumed by the capitalistic judiciary, Judge Wood assumed the function that belongs to the twelve men in the jury." Not that it made much difference, for the jurors were hopelessly "bamboozled." The case was bound to be lost, but someday there would be an hour of reckoning before "The Real Jury—the American People." Eugene V. Debs muttered about a general strike all over the United States, to begin when Haywood was convicted.

It was 7:05 the following morning when the break came. Weary, snow-bearded Bailiff Maginty, dozing against the locked door of the jury room, was startled into action by a loud knock from inside. The jurors were ready.

Judge Wood arrived in twenty minutes . . . then Darrow . . . then most of the other lawyers. Haywood entered at 7:45 and slumped carelessly in his seat, his right elbow hung over the high back of his chair. It looked like a supreme effort at studied indifference.

At 8:00 the tired, haggard jurors filed in. As soon as they were settled, Judge Wood cleared his throat: "Gentlemen of the jury, have you agreed upon a verdict?"

"We have," responded foreman Gess, and he handed over a long white envelope. Fremont Wood tore it open, and the room fell so silent that the tick of the wall clock seemed like a sledge. Then, looking up in amazement, the judge exclaimed: "Why, there's nothing in here!"

As the spectators gasped, juror Russell called over to Gess, "There's the right envelope still in your coat pocket." The flustered foreman fished it out, Judge Wood gave a quick glance and handed the paper to clerk Peterson to read: "We the jury find the defendant, William D. Haywood, not guilty."

Haywood leaped up, utter disbelief written over his face. For a second he stood alone, hat in hand, not knowing what to do. Next instant his lawyers were all over him, shouting, laughing, pounding him on the back. Richardson turned to address the jury, thought better of it, and hugged Haywood instead. Darrow broke away and sat down dissolved in tears.

Off to one side, the prosecution staff sat shocked and silent. Borah was spared the nightmare—he hadn't reached court yet—but the rest looked stricken. Finally, Hawley slipped out to Judge Wood's chambers. There he had to break the news to Governor Gooding, who was expecting something entirely different.

Gooding was no more surprised than anyone else. As the "extras" appeared on the streets of Boise, people could hardly believe their eyes. Although it was Sunday, crowds packed Main Street, excitedly asking each other how on earth it could have happened. It was the same throughout the country. "Not anticipated, not at all," gulped the *Independent*. "Orchard was unquestionably the tool of other men, and it is these men who most deserve to die."

The jurors were closely questioned. Could there have been any tampering? Not at all. It turned out, in fact, that eight of the jurors had been for acquittal from the start. And the pre-dawn hours had largely been spent trying to win over Sam Gilman, the last holdout. Surprisingly, most of the jury felt that Haywood was guilty; but they must obey the law, and the law said there had to be proof "beyond a reasonable doubt"—something just not there. They also were inclined to believe Orchard, but again, they must follow the law, and the law said his testimony had to be corroborated—and it simply wasn't.

It turned out that Judge Wood too had believed Harry Orchard: "No man living could conceive the stories of crime told by him and maintain himself under the merciless fire of cross-examination, unless he was speaking truthfully." But this was his personal opinion, and it had no place in his instructions to the jury. Nor did his personal bitterness about the way the defense used Edgar Wilson. Wood was a judge—his sacred trust was to administer the law—and the law was very clear about corroboration.

This stand of an honest jury and a conscientious judge was lost on many people. The New York *Sun* warned: "The momentous consequences we have cause to fear, when a case apparently so strong ends in a way to please the enemies of a system of government whose chief function it is to throw safeguards around the life of the citizen."

In London, where the trial caused great excitement, the press could only see the storm of passion that surrounded the case. The *Daily News* felt that the whole trial "has illustrated the insecurity of authority in America." The *Star* simply concluded, "The country cannot digest itself."

American Socialists regarded the acquittal as a big step toward the Promised Land. When a huge crowd welcomed Haywood back to Denver, the *Miners Magazine* happily announced: "The ovation that was tendered to William D. Haywood last Sunday night must have made him feel that there is a fraternity among the laboring people that will one day crystallize into a strength that will sweep the present murderous system from the face of the earth and usher in a civilization where the brotherhood of man shall be a reality and not a mere and miserable delusion."

This turned out to be a total miscalculation. Actually, the verdict took the wind out of the radicals' sails, restoring a wavering faith in capitalism. For months the left-wing press had driven home the point that Haywood couldn't get a fair trial under the capitalist system of government—and now he was acquitted. "It is made known by this great trial," declared the Springfield *Republican,* "that the courts of this country are still open to do justice to the working man as to all others."

So the law of the land was the same for everyone. And the law alone was enough to win justice. There were still many thousands who believed in a basic conflict, but surely even the most left-wing political groups included men who now believed that basic change could be won within the law.

Millions more—the vast majority of the labor movement—actually veered to the right. The I.W.W. lost its magic. For the next twenty-five years, the course would be set by Gompers and his "pure and simple unionism."

Meanwhile the capitalists had some problems of their own.

1907

Panic

"If there ever was a general in charge of any fight for any people that did more intelligent, courageous work than Mr. Morgan did then, I do not know of it in history."

—FINANCIER GEORGE W. PERKINS

Even Big Bill Haywood never spoke more vigorously about the denizens of Wall Street than Theodore Roosevelt. In 1906, for instance, he bitterly complained to William Howard Taft about "the dull, purblind folly of the very rich men."

And as business slumped in 1907—the first bad year in a long while—Roosevelt stepped up his attacks. The responsibility, he wrote on March 28, lay "upon the railway and corporation people—that is, the manipulators of railroad and other corporation stocks—who have been guilty of such scandalous irregularities during the last few years." In another barrage the following month, he pointed out that these financiers had "no moral scruple of any kind whatsoever."

The decline continued through the summer, and in August the President added a darker thought: "It may well be that the determination of the government to punish certain malefactors of great wealth has been responsible for something of the troubles, at least to the extent of having caused these men to bring about as much financial stress as they can in order to discredit the policy of the government."

The "malefactors of great wealth" had a different view of the subject. "I would hate to tell you," remarked E. H. Harriman as Union Pacific skidded twenty-five points in one day, "where I think you ought to go for an explanation of all this." Others were less cryptic. The Augusta *Chronicle* bitterly called the President, "our chief panic-maker."

Actually, neither Wall Street nor the President was very much to blame. The money shortage behind most of the trouble stemmed from deeper causes: the costly Russian-Japanese war . . . the job of rebuilding San Francisco . . . several big railroad expansion programs . . . a late crop season tying up the farmers' cash. All these forces, and more, were operating at the same time to drain the world's supply of capital.

The result was inevitable. Stocks fell because no one had the money to buy them. Building plans were postponed because no one had the money for construction. Bonds went begging because no one had the money to lend—when the Union Pacific tried to float a $75 million bond issue in September, there were takers for only the first $4 million. In short, there just wasn't enough money to run the economy.

It was unfortunately a problem which Roosevelt was poorly equipped to meet. No one was more socially or politically conscious, but economics left him cold. "I am not an expert in financial affairs," he confessed; and he might have added they bored him. He paid lip service to the need for a more elastic currency, but that was about all. His last message to Congress had suggested giving national banks the power to issue notes in a crisis, which would later be taxed out of existence. It was a vague scheme at best, and certainly he never pushed it. Now, on October 1—with the financial outlook darker than ever—he romped off to hunt bears in Louisiana.

That same day another train rolled southward with an almost equally distinguished passenger. J. Pierpont Morgan was on his way to the triennial Episcopal Convention in Richmond. With him went his usual guests—two private carloads of bishops.

When Theodore Roosevelt once spoke disparagingly of "Pierpont Morgan and so many of his kind," he couldn't have used more inept phraseology. There were absolutely no others like Morgan—anywhere. The great financier was over seventy now, semi-retired, but still a man of thundering authority. One look at his blazing eyes and fierce red nose left no doubt about that. He moved in a world apart—proudly, regally alone.

Yet there was always the touch of small boy in him too, and perhaps that was why he enjoyed these church conventions so much. They gave him the chance for an outing, to get in a world where—for a little while at least—he could be an equal instead of a symbol of overwhelming but lonely power.

This trip had started pretty much like all the others. As always, Louis Sherry himself came along to look after every need. And as always, a house had been rented for the Morgan party. This had been a little difficult, for Richmond really had nothing on the Morgan scale, but in the end the problem was solved. They took the old Rutherford place on Grace Street, and to make it more palatable for a three-week stay, Morgan had the stairs recarpeted and an extra bathroom installed.

The sessions proved pleasantly uneventful, and for a while Morgan enjoyed himself immensely. He argued ecclesiastical questions . . . played dominoes in the evening . . . and lounged on the Rutherford porch, contentedly puffing his long cigars. Only occasionally would he turn and glower at the people who flocked by for a glimpse of him.

Then around the middle of October, Morgan began to receive a flood of telegrams from New York. At first he only glanced at them, but gradually he grew morose and silent. When a wire came during dinner, he would read it and stare straight ahead for minutes at a time. Usually the room fell uncomfortably silent, and once a well-meaning prelate ventured to inquire: "Mr. Morgan, you seem to have bad news?" The old banker merely shot his devastating glare at the man, and as Bishop William Lawrence later recalled, "No question of that sort was asked again."

The news was indeed bad. On October 16 two of Wall Street's most reckless operators, the dashing F. Augustus Heinze and stocky little Charles W. Morse, had tried to corner United Copper. They missed, and as the stock tumbled, Heinze's Mercantile National Bank sent a frantic call to the Clearing House for cash.

The whole Street was jarred, for the incident focused attention on the irresponsible way Heinze and Morse were using the banks they controlled. These, in fact, were no longer banks but mere reservoirs of money, to be tapped for any plunge that suited the two men's fancy. For even greater freedom, they had centered much of their influence around trust companies, which enjoyed more leeway under the law. An ordinary bank, for instance, had to keep a 25 per cent cash reserve, but a trust company could slide by with 2 per cent or 3 per cent. Nor were there any curbs on how the depositors' money might be used. It could produce fantastic profits—like the time Morse captured all the ice business in New York. Or it could go down the drain—like this futile attempt to corner United Copper.

None of this was lost on the more astute depositors. By Wednesday afternoon, October 16, they were quietly getting their money out of the Heinze-Morse banks. The Mercantile National's call to the Clearing House was the tip-off. Clearly, its cash had been used up in the copper fiasco—no telling how far the trouble might spread.

October 17 saw the financial storm blow harder. Heinze's brokerage firm went under; then at noon Heinze himself resigned as president of the Mercantile National. This turned out to be the price exacted by the Clearing House Committee for any help in the crisis. These conservative bankers had never liked Heinze (nor the competition he gave them), and this was the perfect opportunity to polish him off. Nor were they through. Next day they made the Mercantile National's whole board of directors resign, and on Saturday the 19th they forced Morse out of all his banks as well. Chairman Nash of the Clearing House Committee cryptically observed that changes in several other banks "might be of distinct benefit," and all over town people began wondering what really went on behind those marble façades.

All these events, of course, were reported in the stream of wires that flowed south to Richmond. And it was on this same Saturday that Pierpont Morgan could stand the mess no longer. That morning he told Bishop Lawrence he was taking the noon train back to New York. The bishop persuaded him to wait until evening—it was the last day of the convention anyhow—but there could be no more delay than that: "They are in trouble in New York; they do not know what to do, and I don't know what to do, but I am going back."

As the train rolled northward, Morgan was again in a wonderful mood. He was above all a man of decisive action, and every click of the wheels must have soothed him, telling him that something was being done . . . that he was no longer just there on the sidelines. The departure had pleased him too. He had a passion for order—for having things done just right—and Louis Sherry never managed better. With practically no warning, the versatile caterer had the cars coupled up, the galley stocked with Richmond's best, and the excited bishops all packed and bundled aboard. That kind of well-oiled efficiency always left the old man mellow and relaxed.

He was still aglow the following morning. As the train crept through the yards toward the Hoboken ferry, Morgan invited several of the churchmen to his car for coffee. They found him sitting at the table, holding a tumbler upside down in each hand, happily chanting a tune that defied recognition.

Reaching Manhattan, he politely put them all into cabs. As he waved them off, someone asked if he would be at St. George's services later in the morning. "Perhaps so," he replied, but church was the last thing on Pierpont Morgan's mind that Sunday. He rushed across town to his new marble library on East Thirty-sixth Street. He charged up the steps, through the Florentine bronze portals, and burst into the silk-lined West Room. The partners and friends already on hand surged forward to greet him. The commander had returned, and the troops couldn't have been more relieved.

One by one they told him the story . . . showed him the balance sheets . . . briefed him on the latest developments. It was clear that Morgan & Company was perfectly safe—unless everything went. But that was just the danger. Panic was in the air. The week's events had shaken the public completely. As banker after banker quit under fire, lines began forming at any institution that was mentioned in the papers. And even the safest banks couldn't stand the drain if everyone wanted his money at once.

Lunchtime came, and the others drifted off. Soon Morgan was completely alone in the big room, thoughtfully puffing his cigar as usual.

It was an odd setting to ponder a financial crisis—the red silk walls . . . the huge marble fireplace . . . the lovely kneeling angels on the mantel. Yet somehow it suited Morgan perfectly, even at a time like this. He was so majestic he seemed born to study balance sheets under a carved ceiling from Cardinal Gigli's palace in Lucca.

At the moment, however, he wasn't studying balance sheets at all— he was playing solitaire. As soon as the last visitor left, his valet brought in his favorite card table and the little silver box with the two packs inside. Now Morgan sat by the fire, laying the jack on the queen, the ten on the jack . . . puzzling what to do. It was an odd sort of therapy; his son-in-law Herbert Satterlee felt it reflected perfectly his love of order. In any case, it was no recreation. For his hardest thinking on his biggest problems, Morgan almost invariably turned to solitaire.

By mid-afternoon the cards had disappeared, the table was gone, and the bankers were back. No longer just his friends and partners, but all the major figures of the financial world. By instinct—there were no agreements or resolutions—they automatically turned to Morgan for leadership. In a way, he had always been their leader, although in ordinary times men like James Stillman and George Baker were too proud to admit it. But these weren't ordinary times, and there was no point in fooling themselves. They respected each other's ability, but Morgan was the only one they all looked up to. He was no angel— and they knew it. He took his profit along the way—and they expected it. But he was a giant among them—his bank, his record, his manner, his eyes all added up to immense strength; and that was what they needed now.

It was midnight by the time the last visitor left the library. All through the evening Morgan had listened, rarely saying anything but occasionally jotting down a figure or two. Now the talking was over, and he was expected to do something. Wearily he trudged across the lawn to the Satterlee house next door, where he was staying until his own could be opened. It had been a hard day for a man over seventy— fifteen hours of conferences after an all-night train trip. Even so, he didn't go to bed right away. Those eyes still flickered with fire as he picked up a deck of cards for one final game of solitaire.

At breakfast next morning—Monday, October 21—he outlined his
first step to George W. Perkins, the nimble Morgan partner who usually
served as his chief lieutenant. They must recruit the best young banking minds in the city, put them to work examining everybody's books.
Only then would it be clear who really needed help and how much.

Would the big financial houses go along with this plan? Would they
turn over their most secret records to these men? It never occurred to
Morgan that they might not. Of course they would; he was telling them
to—and he was right.

But rumor moved even faster than Morgan's flying squads. Late that
morning, word spread that the great Knickerbocker Trust Company
was in trouble. At first glance it seemed incredible: the Knickerbocker
had 18,000 depositors, $67 million in deposits, a magnificent new palace
on Fifth Avenue just across from the Waldorf. Yet President Charles
Barney was indeed a close crony of the discredited Charles Morse—
who knew how he had been spending the bank's money? When Barney
admitted that he had made heavy advances to Morse's ice company—
that he was involved in other Morse speculations—the damage was
done.

It did no good for Barney to resign. Or to point out that the bank's
assets were sound, even if there wasn't much cash on hand. That afternoon the National Bank of Commerce announced it would no longer
clear checks for the Knickerbocker. When asked why, a spokesman
ominously declared that the action spoke for itself. The remark was
hardly calculated to reassure the Knickerbocker's depositors. Long lines
began forming at the withdrawal windows.

Around dinnertime the directors made a final bid for help at the
Morgan library. The old man was personally against aiding the bank.
There had been no time to inspect its books and he wouldn't go on
guesswork. He only knew that Barney had been close to Morse and the
Bank of Commerce thought there was no hope. But it was just possible
that the Knickerbocker might be healthier than he suspected. He advised the directors to hold a meeting, examine the day's figures, and
decide whether they could possibly carry on. But with these rumors
flying, there was no time to lose; they must be decisive, they must meet
right away.

They chose—of all places—Sherry's Restaurant. At 9:00 that night the Knickerbocker directors crowded into an upstairs private dining room and began dissecting the affairs of their bank. Downstairs there were the usual fashionable dinners, the usual laughter and conversation. The Sherry regulars practically lived on gossip, and it was inevitable that word should drift down of the interesting meeting upstairs. The idle and the curious—and more than a few Knickerbocker depositors—excused themselves and slipped up to see what was going on. No one had bothered to close the door, and now little groups clustered about the entrance, wide-eyed at this public airing of the Knickerbocker's $67 million problem.

Soon the onlookers could restrain themselves no longer. They flowed into the room . . . stood on chairs to get a better view . . . shouted advice at the harried directors. The session became a grotesque "town meeting," broken only by the departure of occasional spectators who hurried off to spread the news or lay plans for saving their own money.

George Perkins, sitting in for Morgan, left in disgust at 11:00. He brought back to the library a harrowing picture of the meeting. Morgan, with his love of order, must have been appalled. In any event, he decided that the Knickerbocker was gone . . . that it should get no aid from him. In reaching his decision, he grimly ignored one consideration which might have weighed heavily with others: an important Knickerbocker stockholder, and a man bound to lose if it failed, was Pierpont Morgan himself.

The meeting at Sherry's finally broke up at 1:30 A.M., with the directors loudly boasting of the Knickerbocker's $8 million reserve. Certainly the bank would open as usual—there was plenty of money. But the assurances had a hollow sound that came through all too clearly in the morning *Tribune*. Even less inspiring was ex-President Barney's farewell statement to the press: "These are perilous times, and perhaps someone else can fill the position better." But the most discouraging item of all concerned Luther Mott, the state's new Superintendent of Banks. He had come down from Albany, taken one look at the Knickerbocker, and quit his job.

Reports from other cities were equally disconcerting for anyone with money in a bank. Frightened by the news from New York, there were runs in Providence, Pittsburgh, Butte, Montana. Stocks were shaky everywhere, and Westinghouse seemed in serious trouble.

Down in Louisiana, Theodore Roosevelt emerged from the cane-brake, happily oblivious of the erupting chaos. His views on other matters, however, were dutifully reported. Possum? "Absolutely the best dish we had, excepting bear liver!"

There was just about time this Tuesday morning, October 22, for a Knickerbocker customer to digest these stories, have breakfast, and be at the main uptown branch in time for its opening. Perhaps that was why so many depositors turned up together shortly after 9:00 A.M. At that, there were others before them—the Sherry diners, the inevitable "insiders," the messengers from various banks holding Knickerbocker checks. Whoever they were—whenever they got there—they had but one thought in mind. They surged into the great marble hall and headed straight for the paying teller windows.

The line grew much faster than it could be paid off, and it soon spilled through the bronze doors into the street. A steady stream of motorcars, taxis, and carriages rolled up, discharging innumerable veiled ladies and derbied gentlemen who quickly took their places in the ranks. There was never a more stylish-looking bank run, but then this was Fifth Avenue. A big crowd watched from the sidewalk, and others gazed down from the windows of the nearby Waldorf. It reminded at least one observer of an opera opening.

It was bad advertising, to say the least, and inside the Knickerbocker Vice President Joseph Brown desperately applied his theories on mob psychology. He added extra tellers—but the line still grew. He stacked bundles of banknotes for all to see—but nobody left. He pulled the line off the street to make the event a little less public—but this was the strategy of an ostrich. The whole city knew.

By 11:30 the place was jammed. The line curled round and round the great hall, twisted about the handsome green columns, finally tapered off at a glass-topped table in the center of the bank. Here the latecomers slumped in discouragement, pushing onto the floor the neat little piles of deposit slips. It didn't matter—no one had any use for these slips today.

All the formalities of banking evaporated. The crowd surged into the executive offices. They swarmed over the thick green carpet of the vice presidents' room. They lounged in the deep leather chairs normally reserved for visiting financiers. The usual buffers of office boys and secretaries completely disappeared. The harried vice presidents stood back to the wall, fencing off the excited men and women who clamored for their money.

Around noon Vice President Brown squeezed his way to the center of the room, mounted a chair and read the State Banking Department's opinion that everything was all right. There was a smattering of applause . . . cries of "Good for the Knickerbocker!" . . . and in the ladies' department handkerchiefs fluttered in appreciation. But nobody left the line.

At 12:30 Mr. Brown again mounted his chair with an entirely different announcement: "There will be no more payments today."

So this was it. The ladies put away their handkerchiefs and cried, "Shame, shame!" A few hisses, boos, and catcalls pierced the air. But now that it had happened, the crowd was remarkably well behaved. The hard fact—that the Knickerbocker had really failed—seemed easier to take than the hours of uncertainty that had gone before. Besides, the fashionable—even when broke—had a way of carrying things off. As the crowd slowly melted away, one lady announced with charming feminine logic that since she had no money, she might as well go shopping.

The end wasn't as decorous at the Knickerbocker's uptown Harlem branch. The butchers, the small shopkeepers, the Italian immigrant women refused to believe that they couldn't have their money. Police reserves were called out. A sweating bank official begged everyone to be patient. He shouted that Morgan's "influence" was behind the Knickerbocker, that it would all come out right in the end. Nearby a ferret-like man glided about, offering to buy anyone's deposits at eighty cents on the dollar.

With the Knickerbocker gone, the post-mortems began. Some blamed Barney's slow-yielding investments . . . others the slender reserves . . . others the trust companies' reluctance to band together in emergencies

("Reluctant is no name for it," acidly remarked the unfortunate bank's unfortunate new president, Foster Higgins). But the Knickerbocker's fourth vice president William Turnbull knew the blame lay elsewhere. The disaster was entirely due to "the destruction of the credit system of this country by one man."

"Do you mean President Roosevelt?" a reporter gingerly asked.

"You know perfectly well whom I mean!" exploded Turnbull.

The "one man" was now working his way back to Washington, praising Confederate heroes at every stop along the way. Never had a Republican President received such ovations in the South, and Roosevelt was having a glorious time. It wasn't until Nashville that he even took note of the financial crisis. Then he dusted off a favorite metaphor: "All I did was turn on the light; I am responsible for that but not for what the light showed." Clearly, it was just another example of the evil wrought by "Pierpont Morgan and so many of his kind."

That night, writing his son Ted, Roosevelt was back on the bear hunt: "I shot it in the most approved hunter's style. . . ."

One Washington official who had the panic very much on his mind was Secretary of the Treasury George B. Cortelyou. His quiet diligence had carried him far since the days when he was McKinley's personal secretary. Still, he too knew little about finance, and as the walls came tumbling down, his first thought was to get to New York and offer his services to someone who understood. He let Pierpont Morgan know he was taking the four o'clock train.

While waiting for Cortelyou, Morgan continued organizing his rescue operation. The statistics gathered by his bright young men would show how much was needed to shore up the weaker banks; now to collect the money. One after another he called in the city's leading bankers; one after another they gave him their books, let him fix the share each must contribute to the general fund.

Next to enlist the government. Cortelyou checked into the Hotel Manhattan about 9:00 P.M., and Morgan went right over with Baker, Stillman, Perkins, a few selected others. Closeted in the Secretary's room, he explained what had been done, what was still needed. Cortelyou had already deposited $6 million of Treasury funds in the city's national banks . . . more was available . . . all was at Morgan's disposal. When the old banker left the hotel at 1:00 Wednesday morning, he virtually had the keys to the Treasury in his pocket.

It probably never occurred to Morgan that this was unusual. He took authority for granted. Besides, tonight he was in no mood for reflection—he was fighting a wretched cold. The hours, the strain of the past few days had finally caught up with him. Nevertheless, back at the library he struggled through another long conference. Then at 3:00 A.M., he dragged himself to bed without even his final game of solitaire.

At the Manhattan, Perkins was left to deal with the press. He bubbled with hope and confidence. He offered a brief statement which, he felt, was bound to reassure everyone. The "sore point," he explained brightly, was now the Trust Company of America—but there was no need to worry. It would certainly get cash "pending an investigation." And there was every reason to believe it would be cared for "in any eventuality."

The depositors took one look at their morning paper and bolted for the Trust Company offices. Perkins might have felt his statement was helpful, but to thousands of jittery people it only focused attention on one more bank in trouble.

By 9:00 A.M. Wednesday, October 23, they were storming the firm's main branch on Wall Street. The big men of the financial district crowded their windows to watch. They knew all about bank panics— maybe had started a few—but until now they had never seen one. It proved quite a shock. One executive impulsively rushed out and gave his office chair to an elderly lady waiting in line. An empty gesture, perhaps, but somehow symbolic. The thought was dawning that all this involved more than securities and pieces of paper—these were people.

Meanwhile Oakleigh Thorne, the Trust Company's stylish president, was frantic. True, he had lent money to the Knickerbocker's Charles Barney. And maybe he was a little friendly with the Heinze crowd. But the bank was safe. His investments were sound . . . his reserves totaled $11 million . . . yesterday's withdrawals were modest . . . he certainly hadn't asked for help. But how could you reason with this mob that surged against the doors? When a young man appeared who actually wanted to make a deposit, the crowd yelled, "Let him in—let him in! There'll be that much more for us to take out!"

A different kind of crisis beset the Satterlee house uptown. No one could wake Pierpont Morgan up. He seemed in a daze—a stupor—racked with fever and his cold. Satterlee worked over him, finally got his eyes open, asked him a few simple questions. His voice came in a whisper; he was dreadfully sick. Desperate calls for Dr. Markoe . . . then sprays, syrups, gargles. Slowly, painfully the old man dragged himself to his feet, managed to dress and stumble down to breakfast.

A few cups of coffee and he began perking up. By 10:00 he was downtown, glaring at the crowds across the street storming the Trust Company of America. In his office he found Harriman, Thomas Fortune Ryan, other leading financiers already waiting. Then George Baker arrived and, best of all, James Stillman with a $10 million pledge from the Rockefellers. Thoroughly scared, they all came to Morgan that day.

Oakleigh Thorne appeared shortly after 11:00 A.M. . . . he simply had to have help. This was his only hope, although he darkly suspected that Perkins' "sore point" statement had been a Morgan plot to put him out of business. He learned with relief that this was not the case.

Morgan seemed even hopeful. He explained that he had called a meeting of the trust company presidents; he would urge them to raise a fund to help Thorne through. Meanwhile he told his investigating team to hurry its examination of the beleaguered firm's books.

The trust company presidents poured into his office at 12:30—a dozen pale and thoroughly frightened men. Morgan quickly discovered that there was no hope at all of getting them to organize. They didn't even know each other.

If the Trust Company of America was to be helped, he would have to do it himself. But was this the place to draw the line? If he moved too soon and poured millions into a bank that couldn't be saved, he would just be throwing good money after bad. On the other hand, if he acted too late, people would be needlessly hurt. He refused to act on sentiment or guesswork; he'd wait for his investigators to report.

These specialists—young Benjamin Strong and Willard King—had been working on the Trust Company's books since 4:00 A.M. They still hadn't finished, but time was running out. The mob was growing . . . the company's funds were melting fast . . . Thorne was on the phone begging Morgan to hurry—his reserves were now down to $1,500,000.

Morgan quickly ordered Strong and King to come back with whatever information they had. King was sent to soothe the trust company presidents; Strong was brought to an inner office, where he found Morgan, Stillman, and Baker grimly awaiting him. It was now 1:00 P.M. and Thorne phoned again to say his reserves were down to $1,200,000.

"Is the Trust Company solvent?" Morgan asked right away. Strong hesitated—his opinion depended on the value of some securities he knew little about. He asked Baker's and Stillman's opinion, and the three huddled over the question for interminable minutes. Morgan remained silent, puffing his cigar while the clock ticked away. It was almost 1:30 when Thorne called again to say he now had only $800,000.

The decision had to be made, and Strong faced up to it. Yes, he slowly declared, he thought the bank was solvent. Morgan barely knew Strong, but he was Baker's man and that was good enough. So the old banker now asked the question on which his whole strategy depended: "In your opinion, do you think it would be safe for us to see them through?"

There was no more hesitation. Strong quickly answered, "In my best opinion, yes."

"This, then," boomed Morgan, "is the place to stop this trouble."

He flashed word to Thorne to send over his best collateral—cash was on the way. Baker and Stillman rushed back to their banks to collect the money. Messengers soon were racing to the besieged Trust Company with satchels of gold and greenbacks. They fought their way through a cheering, handclapping crowd to the pay tellers. And they were none too soon—when the first installment arrived at 2:15 the bank was down to its last $180,000.

The lines were drawn now, and Morgan swept into action on every front. He stormed at the trust company presidents . . . drove them at last to form an association. He pounced on the bears, swore that if they tried to break prices and throw the market into a panic, he would crush them. He looked at the frightened men who were hoarding their money: "You ought to be ashamed of yourself to be anywhere near your legal reserves! What is your reserve for at a time like this except to use?"

That evening after dinner he lectured the newly-organized trust company heads: this was *their* panic, he had saved them today, they had to take over from here. And their course was clear. He was arranging for Cortelyou to deposit $10 million in the national banks, which could in turn be borrowed and used to support the Trust Company of America. That ought to see Thorne through, and he planned to sit here until they agreed to do it.

The presidents haggled and argued—they might need that $10 million to save themselves. The hours dragged by and the air grew heavy with smoke. Morgan was tired, dead tired . . . his cold was worse . . . his eyes so watery he could hardly see. As the talk droned on, his head sank on his chest and the famous cigar for once went out. But he stayed, and even asleep he loomed over everyone in the room—an awesome reminder that they had to act. They finally raised $8.25 million, but that was all. Morgan blinked, shook off his sleep, announced that he, Baker and Stillman would put up the rest. Then back to the library for a final game of solitaire to wind up this awful day.

In Washington Theodore Roosevelt happily greeted the press on his return from the South: "I have had a delightful time; I am extremely gratified that I got a bear."

Thursday, October 24, was a day that showed how a panic could spread. The mob outside the closed Knickerbocker branch in Harlem overflowed in front of the nearby Dollar Savings Bank, triggering a run on that. A newspaper picture of this new run carried the caption "a Harlem savings bank." This was immediately misread as "The Harlem Savings Bank," triggering a run on that. These two new runs started others, and before the day ended, three more Harlem banks went under.

Psychology also started a new run in Manhattan. The Lincoln Bank & Trust Company, organized by proprietor George C. Boldt of the Waldorf-Astoria, had won a great following among the fast, slick set who patronized the Waldorf bar. Quite an asset while things were going well, but now these men were utterly discredited. Their soiled reputation quickly spread to their bank, and the Lincoln's depositors— once so satisfied with its daring policies—rushed to get their money.

Meanwhile the run on the Trust Company of America continued, and the Knickerbocker's depositors had humiliation piled on insolvency. As they stood outside the closed doors of the Fifth Avenue branch, a sightseeing bus passed by and the barker cried, "On your left you see a run on a bank. The people in line are men and women who have lost all their savings."

Fear was everywhere, when Morgan set sail that morning to renew the battle. He and Satterlee rode downtown to Wall Street in the Union Club brougham, and as they rolled south on Broadway, police and cabbies shouted encouragement. Now they were nearing Trinity Church and dozens of excited people ran behind and alongside the carriage urging it on. Turning into Wall Street, they found a big crowd already gathering outside the Morgan offices. Seeing the carriage, the people yelled and cheered this latter-day knight riding to the rescue.

As Morgan climbed out, the crowd fell silent, then let out another whoop as he disappeared inside the bank. Throughout the whole demonstration he stared straight ahead—never paid the slightest attention—but Satterlee, who knew him well, felt that he was immensely pleased.

Just as well, for grim news awaited him. Now the stock market was collapsing. In the scramble for cash, people were unloading their holdings and prices were tumbling. And there was no call money to finance transactions. Dozens of brokers, unable to borrow on any terms, were heading for bankruptcy. President R. H. Thomas of the Exchange rushed across the street calling: "Mr. Morgan, we will have to close!"

The old banker was thunderstruck. That would destroy any confidence left . . . undo everything he had done so far. But Thomas wailed that there was no other course. It was now 1:30 and the time for settling accounts was 2:20. How could money be raised in the meantime?

Morgan simply told him to go back and announce that help was on the way; then he summoned all the Street's bank presidents to his office immediately. He explained the emergency, pointed out that it was now two o'clock, and said he had to have $25 million in fifteen minutes. It seemed an impossible challenge, but driven by the sheer force of Morgan's personality they more than matched the need—they produced $27 million in five minutes.

"MORGAN & COMPANY SAVE MARKET" ran the *Evening Post*'s headline that afternoon, and indeed it was true. When word was flashed that the money was available, a wild shout of relief swept the floor. The scramble was so violent that broker Amory Hodges lost his coat and vest. But there was enough for everyone and the call rate fell from 100 per cent to 10 per cent. The market closed at 3:00 P.M. as usual, and when the bell sounded a great yell went up that could be heard clear across the street. Asking what the noise was all about, Pierpont Morgan learned that the cheers were for him.

That night in the library he faced a new crisis. The jittery city was no longer using its banks at all. Every safe deposit box in town had been rented and virtually no deposits were being made. This meant that there was almost no currency left for normal commercial life. Something had to be done.

While the leading bank presidents huddled in the East Room trying to devise a solution, Morgan sat alone in the West Room playing solitaire. Back and forth between the two rooms shuttled a fascinating figure—Miss Belle da Costa Greene, Morgan's devoted librarian. Ordinarily she kept track of his collections—often entrusted with decisions involving thousands of dollars. Tonight, she served as messenger. From time to time she ushered some banker into the West Room with a new proposal for solving the currency shortage. Invariably Morgan would say, "No, that won't work."

Finally Miss Greene could contain herself no longer: "Why don't you tell them what to do, Mr. Morgan?"

"I don't know what to do myself," he replied, "but sometime someone will come in with a plan that I know *will* work, and then I will tell them what to do."

Which is exactly what happened. Eventually it was suggested that the Clearing House issue script as a sort of emergency currency. Morgan was unenthusiastic, but at least it would "work." He nodded his approval, and the bankers poured out of the Library at 1:00 A.M.—happy schoolboys dismissed by the teacher.

Friday, October 25. Again the stock market almost ran out of money. Again Morgan summoned the city's leading bankers, this time to a meeting at the Clearing House. He laid it on the line—$15 million needed immediately. But for the moment even his magic was wearing thin—the bankers weren't able to raise more than $13 million. He rushed it over anyhow, hoping for the best, and with the luck that sometimes follows the bold, it proved just enough.

Striding back to his office—completely absorbed in his plans and thoughts—he cut an unforgettable figure. Satterlee, tagging along, later recalled it vividly:

With his coat unbuttoned and flying open, a piece of white paper clutched tightly in his right hand, he walked fast down Nassau Street. His flat-topped black derby hat was set firmly down on his head. Between his teeth he held a paper cigar holder in which was one of his long cigars, half smoked. His eyes were fixed straight ahead. He swung his arms as he walked and took no notice of anyone. He did not seem to see the throngs in the street, so intent was his mind on the thing that he was doing. Everyone knew him, and people made way for him, except some who were equally intent on their own affairs; and these he brushed aside. The thing that made his progress different from that of all the other people on the street was that he did not dodge, or walk in and out, or halt or slacken his pace. He simply barged along, as if he had been the only man going down the Nassau Street hill past the Subtreasury. He was the embodiment of power and purpose.

In Washington, President Roosevelt was fully aware now, but he never felt more helpless. This Friday he sent Cortelyou a letter designed to "restore confidence." But it was his only idea, and his covering note showed how remote he felt. He let Cortelyou decide what to do with his letter: "You can judge better than any of us here."

The letter itself was a far cry from the old days. There were no blasts this time at "malefactors of great wealth"; only warm congratulations for "those conservative and substantial businessmen who in this crisis have acted with such wisdom and public spirit."

But the "conservative and substantial businessmen" had almost run out of ideas. They had pumped millions into the banking system—and it scarcely made a dent. They had rushed to the rescue of the trust companies—and the lines were as long as ever. They had twice saved the Stock Exchange—and clearly didn't have the cash for a third try. Only Morgan still sounded defiant; the others turned to faith healing.

Over the weekend one group of financiers called on the press and begged the editors to be more encouraging. Others visited the clergy and requested a few kind words from the pulpit on Sunday. "I have confidence in the banks," complied Archbishop Farley.

It did little good. Monday, October 28, saw the line still riveted to the Trust Company of America. Depositor Burnett Milburn—a $500 check pinned to his coat—had the honor of being first. He had spent the whole weekend in the vestibule wrapped in a red-and-black blanket. Now some seventy others stretched behind him, stamping and blowing on their fingers in the cold, wet dawn.

The bank opened as usual at 10:00, but no line ever moved more slowly. The Trust Company officials had abandoned any hope of building confidence through fast service. Now the idea was to conserve cash by paying out as slowly as possible. They tried everything—closed most of the teller windows, made endless verifications, paid off in the smallest gold coins. The tellers became especially adept at stacking the coins . . . spilling the pile . . . then doing it all over again.

All the time a stream of Morgan messengers dashed in from his offices at 23 Wall Street, bringing new cash reserves. Others headed uptown, where the same scenes were repeated at the Lincoln Trust Company. Here, in fact, it was worse, for George Boldt, the innkeeper turned banker, now had a thorough case of cold feet. It required a volcanic display of Morgan wrath even to keep his doors open.

On top of all this came a new crisis. Mayor McClellan of New York raced to the library at 4:00 P.M. to announce that the city was about to go broke. He needed $30 million immediately to pay off some short-term bonds. Morgan thought about it overnight, called the city officials to the West Room the following afternoon. As they sat nervously around his desk, he scratched out in longhand an agreement to furnish the $30 million at 6 per cent interest. At the time no one knew where the money would come from—and it never would materialize, unless conditions improved—but Morgan never doubted this for an instant. All that was needed was the strength and will power to ride out the gale.

But the storm was far from over—in fact, it was roaring to a climax. Toward the middle of the week the brokerage house of Moore & Schley suddenly faced bankruptcy. This firm had financed the group controlling the Tennessee Coal & Iron Company. These financiers had put up TC & I stock as collateral, and Moore & Schley had in turn used the stock as collateral for its own loans. Now these loans were due and Moore & Schley had no money. Worse, the TC & I collateral turned out to have no market. Selling it off would not only ruin Moore & Schley—it would wreck the banks and houses that held the stock as collateral . . . it would jolt the whole stock market, probably starting another crash. In these dark, fear-clad days there seemed no end to the dreadful possibilities.

On Saturday, November 2, Lewis Cass Ledyard, a shrewd lawyer acting for Mr. Schley, visited the Morgan Library with an interesting proposition. Why not have U.S. Steel take over Tennessee Coal & Iron? Moore & Schley could then substitute Steel securities for the TC & I stock as collateral on their loans. This would help everybody: Moore & Schley would be saved . . . the banks would get decent collateral . . . the market would be bolstered. And, he added mildly, U.S. Steel would gain a new and valuable property.

Morgan saw it all at once. Apart from his enormous interest in U.S. Steel, the many facets of a deal like this always appealed to him. He would carry it even further—he saw the opportunity for one of those sweeping master strokes he loved so well. By now it was clear that the two main trouble spots were the stock market and the trust companies. Both, he decided, should be tackled together. He would advance the $25 million needed to purchase TC & I and support the market, while the sounder trust companies raised another $25 million to save their wilting brethren. The combined outlay of $50 million should be enough to break the back of the panic for good.

First to make sure he could carry out his part of the plan. Morgan had put together U.S. Steel, but still he felt he ought to consult its officers. Saturday afternoon he called the steel company's finance committee to the library. To his astonishment, Judge Elbert Gary and Henry C. Frick, two key members of the group, didn't like the deal. Morgan didn't expect them to grasp the over-all picture, but he did think they would see the great advantages to U.S. Steel—fabulous coal and ore deposits that could be picked up at a bargain. They remained leery, and the best Morgan could do was to call another meeting the following day. Meanwhile, he went to work pulling together facts and figures that might make a better impression.

Sunday afternoon, November 3, the committee returned to the library. The breathing spell had not been wasted—Morgan produced the sort of facts that were bound to impress any good steel man—the TC & I property had perhaps 500 million tons of iron ore, more than a billion tons of coal. Its Birmingham plant could produce pig iron at $9 a ton—$2 less than its competitors. In the end Frick and Gary gave in. Perhaps they were convinced; perhaps just overwhelmed. The old man had a way of doing that.

There was one last hitch. How would the government take all this? Roosevelt's trust-busting campaign was in full swing—Judge Landis had just fined Standard Oil an astronomical $29 million. Washington must not be allowed to think that U.S. Steel was merely gobbling up another company. Roosevelt's blessing was essential.

At 10:00 P.M. Judge Gary was on the phone with presidential secretary William Loeb. Could he and Frick have an appointment first thing next morning? Gary didn't explain why, but they desperately needed Roosevelt's approval by the time the market opened at 10:00

A.M. Otherwise, Moore & Schley might collapse—and the market crash —before help could come.

Loeb made the appointment and word was flashed to the Pennsylvania Railroad to get an engine ready. Gary and Frick reached the station at midnight, and minutes later a one-car special train—that inevitable prop in every turn-of-the-century drama—hurtled off into the dark. The signal lights flashed green . . . the way was clear . . . at least as far as the White House door.

Back in the library, Morgan turned his attention to the trust company side of the problem. Now the job was to persuade the various presidents to take on their share of the rescue work . . . specifically, to put up the $25 million needed to bolster the Lincoln and the Trust Company of America. It would not be easy. These men had seen too many multi-million-dollar funds vanish in the last few days. Still, the old man was determined. He assembled some 125 bankers in the building— everyone who could possibly help—and to make sure they didn't squirm out of their responsibility, he took the most literal precaution imaginable. He locked the library door and put the key in his pocket.

In the lofty East Room were the Clearing House bankers, who were needed to help wind up the TC & I deal. In the West Room nervously sat the trust company presidents. Morgan himself retired to Miss Greene's cubbyhole, in the rear of the marble hall between the two main rooms. From time to time he summoned some trembling financier to this inner sanctum, while the others would watch—half envious, half glad it wasn't themselves.

Among those who waited in the West Room was young Ben Strong. He had gone without sleep for two days, completing a fresh examination of the Trust Company of America books. Now he could hardly hold his head up. As he sat there nodding, James Stillman eased down on the sofa beside him. Normally Stillman was perhaps the coldest fish on Wall Street, but the pressure had finally gotten him too. Not knowing they were all locked in together, he smiled at the exhausted Strong and suggested he get some sleep: "The country isn't going to smash just because you've gone home to bed."

In Miss Greene's room Morgan alternately cajoled and rumbled at the trust company men. Why couldn't they see that he had already done his part and they just had to do theirs? Especially since they faced no real danger. What if the management of the two trust companies was terrible? Ed King of Union Trust was taking over, and you couldn't want a safer man than that. What if the public didn't think the firms were solvent? Ben Strong had spent two days going over their books, and he said they were all right, and he ought to know. Looking up sharply, Morgan called for somebody to get Strong.

Once again the young banker stood in the glare of those fierce, blazing eyes. Deftly, he outlined the situation—the Trust Company of America was certainly solvent, and the Lincoln was perfectly salvageable, although it might end up about a million dollars in the hole if every depositor demanded his money. Strong had said his piece, and Morgan quickly nodded him out.

The hours dragged on. At 2:00 A.M. the Trust Company of America directors, who had been in separate session at the Waldorf, came over and joined the rest. At 3:00 A.M. Strong, feeling that he had done all he could, decided to go home. It was then that he discovered that the door was locked.

On the street outside, a little knot of newsmen whiled away the cold November night. Everyone who entered the library—and the few who emerged on authorized missions—were closely questioned, but reporters have rarely had a more frustrating assignment. When George Baker was momentarily cornered, he assured them that the meeting had nothing to do with the trust company situation—"it was simply a conference of bankers on private matters, which would not be of interest to the public."

Now it was 4:30 A.M. Miss Greene's door opened and Morgan himself came out. He headed straight for the West Room, where the trust company presidents still babbled in hopeless indecision. He had talked to them individually; now he put it to them all. Again he emphasized that he was getting up at least $25 million to save Moore & Schley and support the stock market; they simply had to match it with the $25 million needed for the trust companies. He pointed to a subscription form, and he walked over to Ed King, leader of the trust company committee. Morgan's voice this time had none of its famous thunder. Instead, it had a curious warmth that was typical when he talked to children but rarely evident in his business transactions. "There's the place, King," he coaxed, "and here's the pen."

Of course, King signed. They always did in the end. And one after another the rest of the bankers fell in line. It was just a little after 5:00 A.M. when Morgan finally had the doors unlocked and sent everyone home. Waving them off into the cold gray morning, he called cheerfully to Lewis Cass Ledyard, "You look tired. Go home and get a good night's rest—but be back here at nine o'clock sharp."

He himself retired to the Satterlees' for a few hours' sleep. At 8:30 he was up again for breakfast. Then he sat around waiting fretfully for first word of the President's reaction to the Tennessee Coal & Iron deal.

In Washington, Frick and Gary were equally impatient. By 9:00 they were at the White House, begging to see Roosevelt right away. Loeb briefly objected; the President couldn't possibly see them till 10:00. But they persisted, and Roosevelt finally appeared. Quickly they outlined their story: a certain business concern "of real importance" was about to fail; it could be saved only if U.S. Steel bought the firm's heavy holdings in Tennessee Coal & Iron. It was not a good buy, they declared, but the purchase would be "an important factor in preventing a break that might be ruinous," and they were willing to take the step as their contribution to business recovery. They pointed out that the purchase wouldn't raise U.S. Steel's share of production above 60 per cent. How, they asked, did the President feel about it?

This, of course, was a rather carefully edited version of the situation. Frick and Gary did not mention that the firm in danger was a brokerage house—knowing Roosevelt, that would have been fatal. Nor did they even hint that its senior partner was a brother-in-law of George Baker, who almost certainly qualified as one of the President's "malefactors of great wealth." And naturally, they said nothing about the enormous potential value of TC & I to U.S. Steel. Still, in fairness to both men, they personally hadn't wanted to make the purchase, and their description at least reflected some of their own misgivings.

Even so, Roosevelt felt on the spot. Since Attorney General Bonaparte was out of town, he called in Root (that old corporation hand) to get his view of the matter. The steel men told their story again, but Root had little to offer. Inevitably this sort of decision had to be made by the President himself.

And time was running out. If approved, Judge Gary pointed out, word had to reach New York before the market opened at ten. Otherwise the firm—it was never named—might go under before help could come. Around 9:50 Roosevelt made up his mind. His language, normally so emphatic, suggests the pressure he was under: "I do not believe that anyone could justly criticize me for saying that I would not feel like objecting to the purchase under the circumstances."

Hardly a strong endorsement, but good enough. With less than ten minutes to go, Gary dashed to the phone . . . got Perkins, who was already waiting on the other end of the line. No time for details or explanations; the judge simply gave the prearranged signal that conveyed the Presidential blessing: "All is well."

And all was well. Perkins efficiently leaked the good news and the market opened strong. Moore & Schley was saved; its creditors relaxed. Tuesday was a holiday—Election Day—and that helped too, for it gave the exhausted bankers a chance to catch up on their sleep and their perspective. Wednesday brought more glad tidings—the Cunarder *Lusitania* was on the way with $10 million in gold specie. At a time when London was still the financial capital of the world, this support from the Bank of England did wonders for morale. The lines outside the Trust Company of America and the Lincoln Trust miraculously melted away; in an incredibly short time the panic was a memory.

How could it fade so quickly? There was no careful recovery program; in fact, it was almost all improvised. But that in itself was partly the answer—the Morgan instinct for the right step at the right moment. It was as he had told Miss Greene: he didn't know what to do himself, but he would know when someone came up with the right idea. And that was just what happened. When Ledyard suggested the TC & I deal, Morgan saw the solution and acted.

Later men would speak harshly of his motives. And Morgan's decisions did indeed reflect self-interest—he wasn't made any other way —but that didn't lessen his contribution in stopping the panic. At the height of the crisis he filled a gap that neither the President nor anyone else could fill.

This was all very clear at the time—when memories were fresh and before men could indulge in the luxury of leisurely sniping. A relieved and rescued nation was only too glad to give the old man credit. "Morgan clears up the whole trust situation," ran the headlines. "He was the leading spirit," acknowledged Secretary Cortelyou. And proud, stolid George Baker was happy to call Morgan "the General" and himself "a mere lieutenant." Even Roosevelt quieted down for a while, and a few weeks after the crisis invited Morgan to a small dinner at the White House.

But for Morgan, probably the finest tribute came from none of these great men. It turned up instead from a most unexpected source. At the time of the meetings in the library, Satterlee mused rather snobbishly that none of the magnates present could appreciate the beauty and taste of their surroundings. This, however, was not so. For on New Year's Day, 1908, Morgan received a small, exquisitely bound volume of Shelley's *Prometheus Unbound*. It was from banker Edward W. Sheldon, one of the 125 locked up that famous night. On the flyleaf were the words that must have pleased Morgan the most: "It was a memorable fact for us all that in those dark autumn days, our financial Prometheus was also unbound and ready to use his titanic power unceasingly and so wisely for the country's good."

Faith restored, the New Year looked bright for everyone. "Sunshine movements" and "Prosperity Leagues" blossomed once more throughout the land. Nickelodeons winked on every side street, and in a burst of enthusiasm the press referred to them as "the university of the poor." On Broadway at somewhat higher prices, a tingling new show was presented to the public—the first Ziegfeld *Follies*.

It was a cheerful season in the White House too. Christmas-time was always a big production for Theodore Roosevelt. Best of all, he had turned from economics to something he really enjoyed—sending the fleet around the world!

1908=1909

The Great White Fleet

"Always ready at the drop of a hat, for either a fight or a frolic."
—REAR ADMIRAL ROBLEY D. EVANS

Traditionally the United States fleet had always been concentrated in the Atlantic, the only conceivable setting for a sea fight. But in the summer of 1907, in a characteristically dramatic gesture, Theodore Roosevelt ordered it to prepare for a cruise to the Pacific Coast. His motives were varied—he wanted to impress the Japanese, who seemed to be feeling their oats; he hoped to give the fleet some practice; he wished to dramatize the Navy and get the money he needed to keep it up-to-date.

There had, of course, been the usual objections. Some feared "waving the fleet in Japan's face." Others worried about the tricky current in the Straits of Magellan, for the Panama Canal was still unfinished. Others shuddered at "denuding" the Atlantic defenses. Senator Hale of the Naval Appropriations Committee even threatened to refuse any funds for the trip. Very well, replied the President, he had enough to send the fleet out—let Congress get it back.

It wasn't as easy to dispose of the Japanese menace. It was all very well to impress Tokyo, people said, but maybe this was going too far. Why, even now Admiral Togo's torpedo boats might be lurking somewhere along the route. The European press was practically licking its chops. "This American fleet," declared the London *Daily News,* "would crumple up and disappear before the forces of the nation which hitherto has never thought it necessary to declare war before commencing hostilities."

The French also predicted a quick Japanese victory. The Paris paper *La Libre Parole* contributed perhaps the most ingenious analysis: "Is the fleet being watched by the Japanese from some dangerous ambush? Will Admiral Evans, when he arrives in April or May, find the Japanese already occupying Hawaii or the Philippines? Edward VII, Japan's ally, could possibly answer these questions. Wilhelm II, who we believe is united by secret treaty with Washington, may have a fine opportunity to try his new fleet."

While in no sense an ally, the Kaiser was indeed trying to be helpful. He offered an endless supply of court gossip, faithfully forwarded by U.S. Ambassador Charlemagne Tower, surely the world's most gullible envoy. The November crop of Berlin rumors had Japan planning to seize the Panama Canal, presumably while the fleet was rounding the Horn.

There were similar stories at home—all ignored by Roosevelt as preparations went ahead for the cruise. In the end only one precaution was taken, but that was shattering to the fleet's more urbane officers. The superbly efficient Japanese wardroom stewards were left behind.

Any lingering doubts vanished as the day of departure drew near. Excitement swept the base at Hampton Roads, where the fleet had assembled. Liberty parties roamed the streets, singing the songs that showed how they felt. The tune was borrowed from "The Kid That Built the Pyramids," but the words were strictly their own:

> Old Japan can lick our Navy,
> She can? Yes? Like Hell she can!

In the stodgier dining room of the Chamberlin Hotel at Old Point Comfort, the officers danced the new one-step. The prettiest debutantes of New York and Washington were down to see them off, and surely it was worth the effort. Who knew when they would see again these dashing figures with their epaulets and jangling swords?

December 16, 1907, dawned warm and partly cloudy. Snatches of boom of dynamite, the harsh scraping of trunks dragged along the winter sunshine danced off the white hulls; gusts of wind whipped at the bright pennants that flew from every mast. At 9:45 A.M. the anchors clanked up, and in single file the fleet slowly moved down the harbor. Passing close to shore, the bands saluted the cheering crowds with "The Girl I Left Behind Me." On the bridge of the flagship *Connecticut* Rear Admiral Robley D. Evans—"Fighting Bob" to his fourteen thousand men—froze to attention as he led his ships by the Presidential yacht *Mayflower,* anchored near the mouth of the harbor. Alone on the yacht's bridge stood a solitary figure, resplendent in top hat, frock coat and striped trousers. Theodore Roosevelt proudly watched his fleet steam to sea.

The long line turned south and grew smaller. The white hulls, the buff funnels and masts slipped over the horizon, and soon only a trace of smoke remained. Then this too was gone.

But not the pride that surged through the families along the shore, the sports in naphtha launches, in fact the whole nation. These sixteen splendid battleships were more than the country's first line of defense—they were its new symbol of greatness. Together they cost a breathtaking $100 million (the next generation would pay $250 million for one carrier), but this mighty armada would never be used for crass self-interest. It was a shining sword to uphold "honor" and "righteousness," and for most Americans the cruise had an almost knightly quality. "The departure of that fleet was momentous," declared the Reverend Robert MacArthur of New York's Calvary Baptist Church. "It drove me to prayer. I could see in it America's assertion of her right to control the Pacific in the interest of civilization and humanity."

With such a lofty mission, it was rather a blow to find that Trinidad, the first stop, couldn't have been less interested. Warships were nothing new to these tight-knit British colonials, and besides, it was Christmas race week. Local society was completely engrossed in imitating the traditions of Epsom and Derby; it had no time for American visitors. For a while the lonely bluejackets hovered on the fringe of the promenaders at the Queen's Park Hotel, then gave up and went back to the fleet. Perhaps it was better that way, for their

Christmas turned out to be a charming family affair—rowboats of sailors drifting among ships banked with palm leaves, serenading each other with guitars and mandolins.

Their friendly enthusiasm was shared by all of Latin America. The sophisticated British colonials might not care, but certainly everyone else did. Country after country begged Washington for a visit from the fleet. Apparently no one was suspicious of "battleship diplomacy" —there was only the fear of being left out. From Chile, Minister Hicks wrote Secretary Root a personal plea that the fleet revamp its schedule to include Valparaiso—"the Chileans would consider it a great feather in their cap." When Minister Fox failed to get even one ship to stop by Ecuador, the local government lodged a formal protest. Most insulted of all was Buenos Aires. The whole fleet was going to Rio de Janeiro, but not even the accompanying torpedo boats planned to visit Argentina. Their itinerary was quickly rearranged, but the Argentines remained sulky . . . certainly Brazil seemed to be getting all the excitement.

The point was strikingly emphasized by the crash of glass in a Rio waterfront saloon on the evening of January 13—the bluejackets' first night of liberty. Two Brazilian longshoremen had been arguing. One hurled a bottle at the other . . . missed . . . and in the classic tradition of every good barroom brawl, hit an innocent bystander. In this case the bystander happened to be a sailor from the *Louisiana*.

The sailor's buddies rallied around, the longshoremen called for reinforcements, and by 8:30 bricks and stones were flying. Nobody remembered very clearly what happened after that, although both sides retained a vivid picture of a big marine from the *Vermont* swinging a chair over his head, threatening to kill anyone who came near him. The Shore Patrol finally got everybody back to the ships, all liberty was canceled, and the usual inquiry launched. Master-at-Arms R. A. Hunter of the *Louisiana* loyally testified that in his unbiased opinion "the civilians seemed to be the aggressors."

The Brazilian officials generously agreed and invited twice as big a liberty party the following day. From here on, all was sweetness and light. In their enthusiasm parties of American sailors even joined local political parades, carrying banners, shouting slogans they didn't remotely understand. The Brazilians were enchanted. President Penna toasted the "glorious American Navy," and his foreign minister loudly proclaimed that these "Northern friends" were "the pride of the Continent."

One person not completely happy was "Fighting Bob" Evans himself. He had been confined to his cabin almost from the start, and even the glowing tributes of the fleet's correspondents couldn't conceal the unglamorous nature of his ailment—the gout. Moreover, he was secretly bitter that he was still a rear admiral. Surely, he felt, anyone in charge of so important an expedition should have three stars. And it seemed like rubbing it in when the Italian cruiser *Puglia* breezed into port one day and gave him a vice admiral's salute.

On top of all this, Rio's chief of police suddenly announced that he had foiled an "anarchist" plot to blow up the fleet. Washington frantically cabled for details, and Evans dragged himself out of bed. There was a day of scurrying about, chasing down "suspects"; then, the plot simply evaporated and the celebration went on.

More rumors of trouble when the fleet weighed anchor January 21 and continued south toward the Straits of Magellan. That afternoon the U.S. naval attaché in Berlin cabled Washington that he heard the fleet had been attacked. He would appreciate, he added laconically, "official confirmation or denial." A few days later the Kaiser came up with another of his chilling reports—ten thousand Japanese were planted in Mexico about to attack the United States. They were cleverly disguised, but his agents had detected them by the brass buttons they forgot to take off their coats.

About the same time Dr. Nevy Churchman, a Portland dentist, wrote the Secretary of the Navy, describing a subtler form of peril facing the fleet. The doctor warned that "off-color prostitute women" might easily slip into the engine rooms and mix giant powder in the coal.

None of these evils came to pass, and as the fleet steamed through the balmy South Atlantic, the only incident was another unfortunate salute to "Fighting Bob" Evans. On January 27 four Argentine cruisers appeared, and as they passed the flagship *Connecticut,* they banged out seventeen guns—an honor normally reserved for a full admiral. Once again Evans was reminded that his long-coveted promotion hadn't come through.

It was February 1 when the ships finally reached Punta Arenas and the Straits of Magellan. They had been making only ten knots, but even so, the *Maine*—a phenomenal coal eater—almost ran out of fuel. It was with a long sigh of relief that Admiral Evans sighted the faithful British colliers patiently waiting at anchor.

Now discussion raged over the coming passage through the narrow part of the straits. The Japanese menace, of course, cropped up again— the *New York Times* reported a Tokyo "observer" recently seen in Punta Arenas. But the straits themselves posed the real problem. Dotted with names like Delusion Bay, Desolation Island, Point Famine and Dislocation Point, they seemed to offer every hazard known to navigation. There were stories of whirlpools that could twist a ship completely around . . . of wild winds called "Williwaws" that could hurl a vessel onto the rocks. The French Admiral Gervais warned of "perplexing currents." The *Western Morning News* of Plymouth, England, pictured the scattered ships ramming each other. The Sacramento *Union* conjured the worst nightmare of all—shipwreck and cannibalism: "We don't want any of our jackies eaten by the terrible Tierra del Fuegans."

Needless to say, nobody dined on the bluejackets. Chile thoughtfully dispatched the cruiser *Chacabuco* to guide the fleet through, and she skillfully led it by Cape Forward, through the S-curve of Crooked Reach and out into the Pacific.

Heading north, there was soon another scare. It seemed the Japanese steamer *Kasato Maru* was acting "suspiciously" off the Chilean coast. She too was safely passed, and the squadron continued on, firing a barrage of salutes off Valparaiso harbor. It was quite a gesture, for U.S.-Chilean relations had been somewhat stormy over the past thirty years. "But," enthused the New York *Sun*, reflecting the country's mood perfectly, "what is the use of being a big nation if you can't be big-hearted with it and show that you don't hold resentments?"

The fleet reached Callao, Peru, on February 20, setting off a wild celebration that lasted nine days. All business was suspended. George Washington's birthday was proclaimed a national holiday. The Peruvian composer César Penizo whipped up a two-step called "The White Squadron," and a small tug churned around the ships in the harbor, its crew mysteriously adept in Cornell football cheers.

Once again both hosts and visitors plunged into the barrel of superlatives. Rear Admiral Thomas, pinch-hitting for the gout-ridden Evans, declared that the visit had established "a tradition of friendship to be handed down not only to our children but to our children's children." For its part, Lima's leading paper *El Diario* was happy to concede where supremacy lay. It greeted the fleet "with the sympathy and respectful admiration which the example of the great and lofty North American virtues awaken in our mind."

From Peru the fleet pushed on north to Magdalena Bay and a month of target practice. There were rumors that $300,000 worth of shells would be fired, and that seemed a dreadful waste of the taxpayers' money.

All of this was forgotten on March 13. That day the country was electrified by the announcement that the fleet would return by way of Suez. Roosevelt, of course, had planned it all along, but this was the country's first inkling that the ships would go completely around the world. The nation swelled with pride—and a lot more speculation as to what the Japanese might do.

Tokyo's reaction came almost at once: a cordial invitation to the fleet to visit Japan. Washington accepted with thanks—and went into a dither of secret indecision. Could the overture be just a diabolical plot to lure the squadron into a trap?

Even Roosevelt was worried now. He had planned this cruise partly as a lesson to the Japanese—he had shrugged off the endless alarms that filled the early stages—but now this unexpected Japanese invitation almost threw him. Early in April he wrote Rear Admiral Charles Sperry, who was slated to replace the sick and bitter Evans. The President pointed out the delicacy of relations with Japan and wondered whether some group of "fanatics" could successfully attack the fleet.

In any event, he questioned whether the men should be given any shore leave.

Sperry's reply was wisdom itself. He was sure that Tokyo's invitation was sincere, and "in regard to any fanatical attack upon the vessels, we shall take every possible precaution and the Japanese government will doubtless guard the fleet by means of a very quiet but very effective patrol of picket boats as was done in Rio."

As for limiting the men's liberty, Sperry had no fears on that score: "Our men are intelligent, good-humored, actively interested in seeing the world and without a trace of any feeling stirred up by newspaper discussions." Reassured, the President decided the visit should come off as scheduled and the men should get "a moderate quantity of leave."

A far more imminent peril awaited the fleet along the coast of California. A half-dozen chambers of commerce were jockeying for position in an all-out drive to capture the ships for the greater glory of their communities.

Ulysses S. Grant, Jr., fired the first shot for San Diego. While the squadron was still pounding targets in Magdalena Bay, he wrote Theodore Roosevelt, urging that the fleet abandon its plan of anchoring off Coronado. Instead it should come right into San Diego, to show how deep the harbor was. The President—always a good politician—sounded out the Navy Department. Regretfully, he learned that the gesture might permanently mire the ships in California mud. San Diego would just have to get along with the honor of being the first U.S. port of call.

The loudest whistle in town gave sixteen blasts as the first plumes of smoke appeared on the horizon April 14. Thousands of San Diegans flocked to the waterfront to greet the nation's heroes. As the anchors rattled down off the Hotel del Coronado, small boats swarmed around each of the shining vessels. A fruit committee flooded the sailors with free lemonade; a flower committee pelted them with blossoms "worthy of California."

"Flower battle duty" the Navy Department sourly called such welcomes, and one old sundowner estimated that they robbed the fleet of most of the sharpness developed during the cruise. Perhaps so, for the men were swamped with hospitality as each new city tried to outdo the last. At Los Angeles, for instance, the entertainment included a balloon ascension, prize fights with Jeffries refereeing, and for the more discriminating, a fencing match between Professor Victor de Lambertini and the equally skillful Professor Harry Uytennhover. Then the whole affair was capped by a giant Spanish barbecue, from which the men could barely waddle back to their ships.

As the fleet moved up the coast the rivalries grew more intense. The Humboldt Chamber of Commerce wired Washington a desperate plea —the county had only thirty-five thousand people, but that was why they needed a visit so badly; the publicity value would be immeasurable. Santa Cruz felt more sure of itself. When it was reported that only half the ships planned to stop there, the city fathers wrote Admiral Thomas, temporarily in charge, threatening to call off the whole reception if the entire fleet didn't come. The Navy quickly surrendered, and from then on Santa Cruz turned its attention to crowding Monterey out of any share in the glory.

It was a brisk, glorious day when the sixteen battleships finally steamed through the Golden Gate and anchored off San Francisco. The hills were jammed with people—sixty special trains brought thousands into the city—and the celebration was the wildest yet. Old-timers still insist that the forty-eight-hour ball at the Fairmont Hotel was the best party they ever attended.

The welcome was especially taxing, since nearly everything had to be done twice. Mayor Schmitz—having enjoyed his hour of glory during the earthquake—had returned to his corrupt ways, and now a group of reformers were trying to clean up the city. Each faction offered a welcome, and the Navy didn't want to offend either. First came a $20-a-plate dinner given by the "bad millionaires," who included the shady traction men and a number of indicted politicos. The "good millionaires" clucked their disapproval at such extravagance and gave a $10-a-plate dinner shortly afterward. Whatever their differences, both groups were practical enough to use the same table decorations.

More than one chamber of commerce remained unappeased when,

on July 7, the Great White Fleet began its odyssey across the Pacific. For others the departure meant more than lost business. "For God's sake and the sake of our helpless people," wrote Kane E. Marvin of Kalispell, Montana, to the Secretary of War, "do not allow our fleet to go to China or Japan. If they *do* go there, they are lost, and we also. . . . You may want to know how I know all this . . . I am a seer and the great privilege has been given me to be the means of helping to save our nation. Now don't say he's a crank, but be up and doing."

But the die was cast . . . there would be no turning back. July 16— they arrived at Honolulu, where a group of the younger officers picnicked by a charming bay in the midst of cane and palms; it was called Pearl Harbor. August 9—they reached Auckland, New Zealand. Here, as a special treat, Admiral Sperry and his staff were conducted to a Maori village for a tribal ceremony. It was just what might have been imagined—painted warriors, native dancers, pounding tom-toms. As Sperry turned to leave, however, an incident occurred showing that the personality of Theodore Roosevelt may have penetrated even to this backwater of civilization. A painted tribesman suddenly bounded forward flashing his teeth and shouting, "Bully!"

On to Sydney, August 20, and the greatest welcome yet. Some 250,000 people stayed up all night to greet the fleet at dawn. After eight days of non-stop celebration a sailor was found fast asleep on a Sydney park bench. Above his head was a boldly lettered sign that summarized the story of Sydney's welcome:

> YES, I AM DELIGHTED WITH THE AUSTRALIAN PEOPLE.
> YES, I THINK YOUR PARK IS THE FINEST IN THE
> WORLD. I AM VERY TIRED AND WOULD LIKE TO GO
> TO SLEEP.

Melbourne's welcome was almost a duplicate. A single statistic drove home its irresistible quality: when the fleet finally left, a total of 221 men failed to turn up in time to sail.

More coaling . . . a brief stop at the Philippines . . . and the squadron at last turned toward Japan. As the ships approached Yokohama, even

Admiral Sperry—once so confident in his assurances to Roosevelt—began to feel some qualms. No incident must be allowed to start any trouble. For liberty, the admiral designated "only first-class men whose records show no evidence of previous indulgence in intoxicating liquor." As for the big reception scheduled in honor of the crews: "The men will be made to understand that this, though an entertainment, is a matter of military duty." But even after all precautions had been taken, there remained the haunting question: How did this unpredictable nation really regard the American visit?

"Fleet Banzai Number!" proclaimed the Yokohama *Boyaki Shimpo* on October 17, and the fact the paper appeared a day too soon only emphasized Japan's eagerness. On October 18, the actual day of arrival, the *Bakan Mainichi Shimbun* went all out. Numerous ads saluted the ships and Dr. T. Ikada announced he was ready to solve the fleet's dental problems. The editor, unable to offer such a tangible gesture, made words do almost as well: "Despite the loneliness of the autumn days, a brilliant sight catches our eyes. It is the glorious fleet approaching our waters, with the Stars and Stripes flying at their mastheads. On this propitious day it behooves us to welcome them with overflowing joy. . . ."

Overflowing joy indeed. The admirals were put up at the Emperor's Palace, the captains in suites at Tokyo's Imperial Hotel. The temperate seamen selected for liberty were greeted by ten thousand Japanese schoolchildren, carefully tutored to sing "Hail, Columbia" in English. Junior officers got railroad passes; the men (with fine distinction of rank) free trolley rides. Admiral Togo gave a garden party, Premier Katsura a formal ball, and fifty thousand citizens of Tokyo saluted the fleet with a mammoth torchlight parade that ended in a near riot of ecstasy.

Only Admiral Sperry himself suffered a moment of peril, and that really couldn't be helped. It happened on the last night of the fleet's visit, when he was guest of honor at a champagne party on the Japanese battleship *Nikasa*. A group of Imperial cadets suddenly picked him up and hurled him into the air three times, happily shouting "Banzai!" A great tribute, carefully explained his hosts, as the admiral came down the last time, a gasping tangle of sash and ribbons.

But it remained for an American enlisted man to make the greatest contribution to international relations. In Tokyo on the night of October 22, a flimsy arch honoring the fleet caught fire. A large crowd watched impassively as the flames crackled upward toward a Japanese flag flying from the top. Suddenly out of the dark raced three American sailors and a marine. Climbing up the blazing pile the marine managed to save the flag. The crowd instantly caught the symbolic overtone and went mad with enthusiasm. They hoisted the marine on their shoulders and paraded him about, delirious with joy. When the ships set sail two days later, there was not a Japanese who didn't agree with the *Bakan Mainichi Shimbun*'s appraisal: it was in truth a "glorious fleet."

Everything afterward was easy—even the banquet of sharks' fins at Amoy—although there was admittedly an embarrassing moment when the Chinese government realized that only half the ships were visiting its shores. Peking was touchy about such things, but the government saved face by telling the public that the rest of the fleet had been lost in a typhoon.

The squadron slowly moved on across the Indian Ocean to Ceylon, where it was swamped with complimentary tea from Sir Thomas Lipton. Then up through Suez and into the Mediterranean. Another round of calls . . . an errand of mercy at earthquake-torn Messina . . . and a final stop at Gibraltar. It was February 9, 1909, when the sixteen battleships—a little grimy but still bravely white—hoisted anchor for the last time and headed into the Atlantic, their bands playing "Home, Sweet Home."

February 22, and it seemed as if all America had crowded into Newport News. All America, that is, except "Fighting Bob" Evans, who coldly sent his regrets. He was on a lecture tour and just couldn't interrupt it. That missing star still rankled.

Launches, skiffs, rowboats, anything that would float bobbed in the harbor that raw gray morning. The *Mayflower* was there, of course, with the President impatiently scanning the sea. At 10:20 the first faint smudges appeared in the mist . . . 10:45, the ships were passing the capes . . . 10:58, the *Connecticut* reached signaling distance. A thundering crash, and the entire fleet began a twenty-one-gun salute to its proud Commander in Chief.

The ships were close to shore now, just as when they steamed out a year and sixty-eight days ago. But the music was no longer "The Girl I Left Behind Me." This time the air bounced with the lively beat of "Strike Up the Band" . . . then a pause . . . then the slow, heartfelt strains of "There's No Place like Home."

And at first glance home did seem very much the same as always. "School Days" still tinkled on every Pianola—certainly America hadn't lost its sentimental streak. The Merry Widow hat still graced countless fair heads—women's tastes were as ludicrous as ever. Prohibition was still spreading—clearly the country retained its abiding faith in simple moral panaceas. In a well-meant burst of paternalism, Henry Clay Frick even ordered his steelworkers to stop drinking, whether on or off duty. The national obsession with morality popped up in other areas too—a wide reaction against horseracing and, in New York City, the Sullivan law forbidding women to smoke in public.

But the law against women smoking was more than evidence of the same old moral streak. It was also evidence of deep, underlying change —one of a number taking place while the men were away. For this law was a futile attempt to halt a quickening of pace, a bursting of bonds that had been gathering momentum during the year. It was all very well to keep Woman on a pedestal in the nineteenth-century tradition, but this was the twentieth century, and she wouldn't stay put. There was this trend to smoking, and more—the new sheath dress, daring dances called the Bunny Hug, the Grizzly Bear, the Turkey Trot.

As the tempo grew faster, the world grew smaller—and this was another change going on while the fleet was away. In 1908 Wilbur Wright broke all records by flying 75 miles in 113 minutes, and everyone now knew that the airplane would revolutionize travel. Visionaries even began talking of night flying as a distinct possibility. "At night," prophesied aviation writer W. B. Kaempffert, "a trailing line will be cast overboard, fitted with some electrical indicator, which will ring a bell if some object should be struck, to warn the pilot that he is flying too low."

At sea, the Great White Fleet itself experimented with a device which could also prove a miraculous bridge between peoples—the radio telephone. The New York *Sun* reported, "There was a division of opinion among the officers as to the real value of the invention." Concerning that other electrical marvel, the wireless, there was no longer any doubt. When the White Star liner *Republic* was rammed and sunk just a month before the fleet returned, nearly all aboard were saved because her Marconi operator, Jack Binns, flashed a timely call for assistance.

The automobile too was helping draw the world closer together. On February 12, 1908, six cars started off on, of all things, a race from New York to Paris. Originally it had been hoped to go by way of Alaska, over the Bering Sea on icecakes, and then on across Siberia. This ambitious scheme was later modified, and the cars crossed the Pacific by steamer. Perhaps it was just as well, for it took two weeks to get to Chicago.

Still it was quite a race, and the whole nation glowed with pride when the American Thomas Flyer lunged ahead of its German, Italian, and French rivals. It seemed a particularly fine achievement, since the Thomas was widely advertised as "an ordinary stock car," while the others obviously had special equipment. The French De Dion, for instance, carried a sail and a Norwegian explorer to help negotiate the snowbound Rockies.

Despite such competition, the Thomas steadily increased its lead. There were no roads (not to mention road maps) west of Laramie, but driver George Schuster wangled a good set of Union Pacific charts and was even allowed to use the railroad's tunnel at Aspen. Unfortunately the Thomas did so much damage to the tracks that the U.P. threw it off the right-of-way and wouldn't let the other cars have the same edge. There were cries of protest but not too loud—nearly all the contestants had something to explain. The German Proust, for instance, arrived in Seattle by rail and was penalized seven days for such questionable tactics. Less justifiably, the Thomas crew was awarded a twenty-two-day bonus for making a reconnaissance of Alaska by steamer.

Once in Siberia the race dwindled to a duel between the Thomas and the Proust. One of the Frenchmen who had withdrawn caused some mischief by trying to corner all the gasoline in Vladivostok, but chivalry reasserted itself twenty miles from the city, when the Thomas pulled the Proust from a mudhole. Lieutenant Koeppen, the very correct Prussian officer in charge of the German car, was fully up to the occasion. He produced a bottle of champagne and the two teams toasted each other.

On they sputtered, sometimes bouncing along the ties of the Trans-Siberian Railroad, sometimes pulled through bogs by singing Cossacks, always facing new and unusual hazards. George Schuster still shudders at the swarms of gnats and the problem of making repairs while swathed in yards of mosquito netting. But his persistence won out; the Thomas was declared the winner when it finally reached Paris on July 30. True, the Proust got there first, but not after counting the various bonuses and penalties. Besides, the spirit of *revanche* was growing and what Frenchman was willing to hail a German car?

At the inevitable reception on Sagamore Hill, Theodore Roosevelt proudly congratulated the Thomas crew for "putting America to the front in automobile manufacturing." But a far more significant development in this direction was taking place quietly, with no fanfare at all. In 1908 the young automobile builder Henry Ford decided that it was time for a cheap car and produced the first Model T. Until then, the automobile industry had never really found itself; in this same year, for instance, the Cadillac dealer in Berthoud, Colorado, was a thirteen-year-old boy. But from the Model T on, it was clear that the automobile would be not a novelty, not a rich man's plaything, but an integral part of the American scene, promising a fuller life for everybody.

This fuller life, extending the pleasures of the few to the many, was another change that gathered momentum while the fleet was away. Until recently, for instance, sports had been enjoyed mainly by the rich. Suddenly they were becoming part of the American scene. When

Fred Merkle failed to touch second in the Giant-Cub game that cost New York the 1908 pennant, more than baseball fans were aroused. The whole country discussed Merkle's "bonehead" play; everyone argued whether Chicago's Johnny Evers had really used the same baseball when he stepped on second to force Merkle out. The World Series gate at one game that year was only six thousand; it was never anything like that again. By 1910 (the next five-game series) attendance was double 1908 figures, and the pattern for the future was set.

Of course, the excitement stirred by Merkle's blunder didn't cause the change, but it was certainly symptomatic. It showed that the general public was eagerly moving into an area that had previously been monopolized by the rich. Big stadiums began blossoming over the land . . . poor boys started taking up tennis . . . the seeds were planted for the age of Red Grange, Babe Ruth, and Bill Tilden.

It was somehow fitting that the same autumn which saw signs of this new era should also see an emphatic punctuation mark placed on the old. On October 28, 1908, Mrs. William Waldorf Astor—*the* Mrs. Astor—quietly passed away in her Fifth Avenue mansion. For fifty years she had been the acknowledged queen of Society, and although a trio of duchesses now fought to take her place, nobody really could. With the queen gone, the social pinnacle would never again be quite so alluring—or quite so difficult to reach.

But the biggest change of all was the passing of another figure, far more important than Mrs. Astor. Theodore Roosevelt was leaving the White House. Seeing his familiar figure bounding about the *Mayflower*—just as on the day the fleet left—it was hard for the men on the ships to believe. Yet it was so. In another two weeks he would be out—his place taken by the ample figure of William Howard Taft. It was a change not only the fleet but the whole country found difficult to grasp.

For Roosevelt himself, it was especially difficult. He had flatly declined a third term . . . handed the torch to Taft . . . said he didn't plan to be "officious or a busybody"—yet he just couldn't bow out. All during the 1908 campaign he sent his hand-picked candidate a steady stream of advice and comment: "Stay in hotels" . . . "Stop citing court decisions" . . . "Say nothing, not one sentence, that can be misconstrued" . . . "Let the audience see you smile *always*."

And as the campaign drew toward its climax, a special caution: "The folly of mankind is difficult to fathom; it would seem incredible that any one would care one way or the other about your playing golf, but I have received literally hundreds of letters from the west protesting about it. . . ." The problem was serious enough to send editor Mark Sullivan as a special emissary with an additional message: "I myself play tennis, but that game is a little more familiar; besides, you never saw a photograph of me playing tennis. I'm careful about that; photographs on horseback, yes; tennis, no. And golf is fatal."

None of it did much good. Taft couldn't have been more colorless. He ultimately won, but by only half the GOP margin in 1904. At that, he ran ahead of his ticket—partly because the Democrats were so uninspired (they again came up with William Jennings Bryan), but mostly because Roosevelt injected so much of his own fire into the campaign.

Certainly no one was better qualified to explain how to be memorable. Roosevelt put his special stamp on everything he touched. Other men urged enforcement of the Sherman Act, but "trust busting" made the battle glamorous and exciting. Others preached equal rights for management and labor, but "the Square Deal" had a ring to it that made the goal worth fighting for.

It was the same in foreign affairs. Other Presidents had strong policies, but not his spark and zest. Surely no one else could have matched his unique brand of indignation when Colombia refused to cede the Canal Zone ("We may have to give a lesson to those jack rabbits"). Or the picturesque flow of epithets he continually hurled at His Excellency President Cipriano Castro of Venezuela ("unspeakably villainous little monkey").

Many of these explosions Roosevelt brought on himself. In 1904 he extended the Monroe Doctrine to cover Latin American countries that misbehaved toward European powers. Since we wouldn't let others intervene, we'd have to keep order ourselves ("It will show these Dagos that they will have to behave decently"). The net effect kept the President constantly embroiled in the Caribbean, but it's difficult to sympathize—he exhibited too much obvious relish for the assignment ("Some time soon I shall have to spank some little international brigand").

Most of these remarks were uttered more or less in private, but his gusto was a trademark he couldn't hide. In fact, it infected everyone else down the line. When the Moroccan bandit Raisuli kidnaped an American ex-patriot Ion Perdicaris in 1904, the normally suave John Hay demanded "Perdicaris alive or Raisuli dead!"—a remark so Rooseveltian that Hay never got credit for it. Again, when some Santo Domingo insurgents threatened a town with important American interests during the 1905 intervention, the local U.S. Navy commander quickly called both sides together. He told them he would not allow any firing in the streets, but would set aside a field where they could fight it out . . . the winners to get the town. The arrangement worked perfectly and delighted the White House.

Nor was the Roosevelt touch limited to relations with banana republics. He used his "Big Stick" with equal fervor in dealing with major powers. When the Kaiser blockaded Venezuela in 1902 to collect a few overdue debts, Roosevelt hauled in the German ambassador, told him that Berlin must arbitrate immediately or face Dewey's battleships. "You gave that Dutchman something to think about," remarked the awed presidential secretary William Loeb. And perhaps he was right, for Germany agreed at once to go to the conference table.

Again, when England stoutly defended Canada's claims in the Alaskan boundary dispute that same year, Roosevelt dashed to the fray with buoyant abandon. He ordered troop reinforcements to southern Alaska, later appointed three heavily biased representatives to the board of "impartial jurists of repute" who would decide the case. When the United States won, few noticed that this was due to the integrity of Lord Altmore, Britain's Chief Justice, whose vote swung the decision. To most people, "Teddy" had simply done it again.

But above all—and entirely apart from the conduct of his office—Roosevelt put an inimitable stamp on the country's daily life. He seemed to get into everything. In a typical two-week period, he helped a schoolmarm win a job teaching in the Philippines ("her father was a splendid soldier") . . . he met with the coaches of Yale, Harvard and Princeton to reform football . . . he broke up a bankers' meeting on hearing that one of the financiers had eight children ("Hurrah for the Olivers!") . . . he toured New Orleans . . . he starred in a shipwreck. When a freighter rammed the lighthouse tender *Magnolia,* which was bringing him back north, Roosevelt rushed to the bridge in white pajamas, took over from the startled captain, and "saved" the vessel.

In the midst of all this, he somehow found time for another piece of extracurricular work always close to his heart. He initiated Robert Bacon, his Assistant Secretary of State, into the "Tennis Cabinet." This was done by taking Bacon on one of the famous presidential point-to-point walks. When they came to the Georgetown Canal, Roosevelt offered to let Bacon cross by a bridge further down. "Not by a darn sight!" cried the new recruit. "Bully!" shouted the President, plunging in. A few seconds later they emerged on the opposite bank, Bacon's patent leather shoes and dark serge suit dripping. French Ambassador Jules Jusserand, once faced with the same challenge, handled it differently. Before swimming across, he carefully removed all his clothes except his gloves. "I might," he explained, "meet some ladies."

The "strenuous life" the President called this sort of pastime, and he automatically bestowed its virtues on the causes he favored—these were "vigorous" . . . "robust" . . . "virile." By the same token, the policies and people he opposed were usually "soft" and "unmanly." Anti-imperialists were "physically timid" . . . the editors of a critical newspaper "had led lives of bodily ease and avoidance of bodily risk" . . . the advocates of arbitration (when American interests were involved) were "usually men of soft life."

Such emphatic views led to endless scrapes and tangles—some ridiculous, all a sheer delight to the press and public. In 1908 while the fleet was away, perhaps the liveliest scuffle was with the venerable Charles Eliot, President of Harvard. Two undergraduate crewmen had been suspended for minor infractions of university rules. Roosevelt vigorously protested, partly because he thought the punishment too severe but also because he wanted to see the crew win ("like most sane and healthy Harvard graduates"). Eliot replied with a stuffy telegram about the need for "a sense of honor." These were fighting words, and the President thundered back. He buttonholed any Harvard man within reach, took informal polls of his friends, decided Eliot's act was "unjust, unwise, improper and harmful." The country watched with glee as the university president and its most distinguished alumnus hammered away at each other. Then as always, the squabble simply evaporated as some new adventure with the "Tennis Cabinet" took its place.

And now he was going. "Ha! Ha!" Roosevelt wrote Taft. "*You* are making up your Cabinet. *I* in a lighthearted way have spent the morning testing the rifles for my African trip."

"Health to the lions," Pierpont Morgan was supposed to have rumbled. But most people went along with John L. Sullivan, who dropped by and handed the President a gold-mounted rabbit's foot.

The greatest tribute, however, came at the very end. On the morning of March 4, 1909—Inauguration Day—brittle old Henry Adams emerged from his home on Lafayette Square in Washington. A wet, sticky snow was falling, and down the avenue the bands were already playing. Slowly he trudged across the street and entered the White House. Seven years had passed since Adams' first visit, when he had such misgivings about young men in high office. Now he hardly knew what to say. Sentiment never came easily to him; affection, as Owen Wister noted, dwelt "deep inside him, hard to reach." Finally he blurted the six simple words so many people felt: "I shall miss you very much."

The White House would never be quite the same, nor in a very real sense would the fleet Roosevelt so proudly sent around the world ("the most important service that I rendered to peace"). For along with the fun, the music, and the bunting, there had been some serious thinking—pointing to the need for changes. A lot were technical: recommendations for cage masts, improved conning towers, armor for the wireless shacks, new speaking tube arrangements, better protection for the telescopes. But one change at least had symbolic as well as practical significance. The day the fleet returned, orders were issued to take these pretty white ships with their gay gilt bowsprits—so in keeping with the country's own bright spirit—and paint them a dull, stern, businesslike gray.

1909

The Dash to the Pole

"This work is the finish, the cap and climax of nearly four hundred years of effort, loss of life, and expenditure of fortunes by the civilized nations of the world, and it has been accomplished in a way that is thoroughly American. I am content."

—ROBERT E. PEARY

As the Great White Fleet left San Francisco on July 7, 1908, another auspicious departure was taking place across the continent, on the sheltered waters of Long Island Sound. But the lone vessel preparing to leave Oyster Bay was a far cry from the glittering battleships that headed into the Pacific. She was squat and stubby; her black hull relieved only by a narrow white stripe. Toward her stern rose an awkward smokestack, and the sails that adorned her three masts suggested some lack of confidence in the engine below.

Along her cluttered decks wandered a distinguished visitor. Theodore Roosevelt, now in his last summer as President, happily inspected the crew, the boilers, the supplies, and especially a pack of yapping dogs. Beside him walked a tall, bristling man in a crumpled linen suit and floppy straw hat. Eventually it was time to say good-by, and the man's words were a curious mixture of stiltedness and deep feeling: "Mr. President, I shall put into this effort everything there is in me—physical, mental, and moral."

"I believe in you, Peary," Roosevelt called as he went over the rail, "and I believe in your success, if it is within the possibility of man."

The President had reason to be enthusiastic. Commander Robert E. Peary was off on the sort of adventure Roosevelt loved—an expedition to discover the North Pole. And he was bringing to the project a quality the President also loved—fierce, matchless determination. Twenty-two years had passed since Peary, then a young naval engineer surveying Greenland, first dreamed of reaching the Pole. In seven arctic journeys, he had inched closer and closer—always learning but always falling short. Now at fifty-two, he was setting out for one more try—the very embodiment of what Roosevelt meant when he lectured countless schoolboys to "hit the line hard!"

But except for this all-consuming drive, the two men had little in common. Peary would never have qualified for membership in that most amiable fraternity, the President's "Tennis Cabinet." He was aloof and preoccupied—had always been, even in his college days at Bowdoin. He had an unpleasantly vain streak too; on his early expeditions he affected a bamboo baton with a silk guidon and embroidered star. Above all, he was painfully, disagreeably uncompromising. There was the time, for instance, when he felt the Norwegian explorer Otto Sverdrup was encroaching on his projects. The two parties met in the frozen wilderness west of the Kane Basin, and although they were the only human beings within hundreds of miles, Peary refused to join Sverdrup in a cup of coffee. It was a slight the Norwegian was not likely to forget.

As sometimes happens, however, Peary's stiff, unbending manner cloaked a strain of gentleness that continually emerged in moments of trial and danger. Then, no sacrifice was too great to help a colleague. Once, during his 1892 survey of Greenland, Peary and the expedition doctor—an amiable Brooklynite named Frederick A. Cook—were caught in a blizzard on the open ice. As Cook began to freeze, Peary dug a hole in the snow, put the doctor in it, and covered the makeshift shelter with his own trousers. Then, to give still more protection, Peary curled himself around the windward side of the hole until Cook revived.

Also buried deep within him ran a strong romantic streak. It had always been there. When he was seventeen, he penned a rapturous description of a sunrise in his diary. As a Bowdoin undergraduate, he wrote poetry full of medieval knights with "plumèd heads" and "lances couchant." Later there were occasional valentines flowing with grace and sensitivity. Now this same romantic streak drew him inexorably toward the Pole. It was "the goal of the world's desire" . . . "the last of the great adventure stories" . . . "the one dream of my life."

Other men also longed to stand on top of the world, but they were merely dreamers. Peary was different because he had the drive and experience to make the dream come true. It was this rare combination of qualities that made people believe in him . . . that led millionaires to form the Peary Arctic Club . . . that kept the money coming year after year, in spite of heartbreaking defeat.

But faith has its limits. After the failure of the 1906 expedition even Peary's greatest admirers began to lose heart. His ship the *Roosevelt* had returned badly battered; it needed an expensive overhaul. Then a set of new boilers failed to arrive on time, forcing him to postpone his plans for 1907. On top of everything came the death of Morris K. Jessup, head of the Peary Arctic Club, who was to pay for the boilers and much, much more. Another important source of funds—Peary's book about the 1906 try—proved a disappointment. It appeared that the public only wanted to read about successful explorers.

Preoccupied with these disasters, Peary paid little attention to another sailing for arctic waters that summer of 1907. His old colleague Dr. Cook headed north with a millionaire sponsor named John R. Bradley, ostensibly on a hunting trip. Even after Bradley returned and announced that Cook was really going for the Pole, Peary took only scornful note. The doctor had no ship, little equipment and less organization.

So Peary worked on through the winter—begging, scraping, scrapping for his own expedition. As always, his persistence finally won out. Mr. Jessup's widow came through with a generous check; others, captivated by the sheer doggedness of the man, sent more. Peary was never good at public relations, but in the long run that mystical zeal was perhaps more important. By the spring of 1908 the *Roosevelt* was again ready, and the commander turned to recruiting his team.

"If you are still interested in arctic exploration," ran the telegram to Donald B. MacMillan, a young prep school master at Worcester Academy, "come to see me at once, Grand Union Hotel, New York City." Peary had known about MacMillan for years, and he was just the type needed—the deserving son of a ship captain lost at sea, a star athlete at Peary's own alma mater Bowdoin. His character and physical ability were all known qualities.

It was the same with the other men already lined up. Captain Bob Bartlett had taken the *Roosevelt* up and back in 1906. He was only thirty-three but of old Newfoundland stock—the arctic practically ran in his blood. Ross Marvin, Peary's secretary, had also been with him last time. He was a brilliant young Cornell engineer who excelled at the meteorological calculations that always seemed to bore the commander. Dr. J. W. Goodsell was new, but he had the kind of Anglo-Saxon pioneer background Peary liked, and he specialized in microscopy, which should be useful in medical research.

Matthew Henson, Peary's Negro servant, was another natural. He had been along on all but one of the commander's polar trips. By now he boasted qualifications far beyond those of an ordinary valet. He was, for instance, an expert sledge maker and a superb dog driver. Henson was also what was known at the time as a "nice colored man." His views on integration were built around the theory that in every great achievement the white man always had a Negro servant. As for looking after Peary: "With the instinct of my race I recognized in him the qualities that made me willing to engage in his services."

There was nothing logical, however, about Peary's selection of the sixth and last man for his team. Twenty-two-year-old George Borup was chosen purely on whim. Borup—one year out of college—combined all the good and none of the bad qualities of an era when undergraduates were glad to "die for dear old Rutgers," although in his case it happened to be Yale. He was appropriately strong and true, but he had a puppylike cheerfulness not always found in the Eastern college man of the period. After graduation he tried his hand at working for the Pennsylvania Railroad, but the routine was intolerable. With his love of sports and the outdoors, he began haunting Peary to go along on the trip. For a while it was an imaginative but futile campaign, including one wire which ran, "Have just shot a hole-in-one—now will you take me?"

A more effective lobbyist was his father, Colonel Henry D. Borup, a ramrod-straight West Pointer, who had his heart set on helping his son. The colonel spent long painful hours in Peary's hotel room, stiffly pleading the boy's case. His awkward but intense sincerity impressed the commander and finally an interview was arranged.

Late that spring young Borup appeared at the Grand Union Hotel, uncomfortably neat in a new gray suit. But nothing could hide his boyish charm and the outcome was inevitable. The expedition was already full . . . Borup had no experience whatsoever . . . he contributed nothing but desire—so Peary told him to pack his things and come along.

The team was complete now, and once again Bob Bartlett felt "the suspense and eagerness that go before the departure of an Arctic expedition." It was a feeling shared by the whole country. People were entranced by polar exploration—the way they would feel about transatlantic flights in the twenties or space travel a generation later. It was the big news story of the period and rightly so—the only part of the world not yet conquered by man . . . a target for national rivalries . . . a dangerous game played by princes, scientists, and unemployed warriors.

As sailing day approached, an excited nation showered Peary with helpful suggestions. Inventors came up with flying machines, icemobiles and mysterious cannon guaranteed to lob the commander direct to the target. Another correspondent urged him to set up a soup kitchen at his base and pump hot consommé to the party struggling toward the Pole. Peary was especially amused by one man who had the absurd idea of going to the Pole by submarine.

Actually, no one was ever in less need of advice. Peary knew exactly what he wanted to do. Through years of experience he had perfected a plan that was original, imaginative, and immensely practical. First, he would drive his ship as close to the Pole as possible—not just to the Kane Basin as others did, but through the ice to Point Sheridan, some 350 miles farther north. Next, he would copy the Eskimos—use their food, clothes, dogs, sledges, methods, and help. After all, they lived in the arctic and ought to know best—a simple idea that never occurred to any other explorer. Finally, he would use a carefully organized system of pioneering and supporting teams that would put him within 150 miles of the goal with practically no effort on his part. With any luck at all, he should then be able to make it to the Pole and back.

"I'll see you up there," called a water-front drunk as the *Roosevelt* backed away from her pier on the afternoon of July 6. It was the hottest day of the year, but the blazing sun didn't wilt the enthusiasm that swept the harbor. Crowds cheered along the East River shore . . . every whistle seemed tied down . . . the presidential yacht *Mayflower* banged away with its signal gun. As the ship passed the city jail on Blackwells Island, even the prisoners swarmed to their windows and waved.

The *Roosevelt* now headed for Oyster Bay, where Peary and his wife dined at Sagamore Hill the following day. Then came the President's inspection of the vessel named in his honor . . . the official farewell . . . the sighs of relief, as the ship's company realized that the formalities were over and they could get down to business.

A brief stop at New Bedford for whaleboats . . . another at Eagle Island for a spare rudder . . . then on to Sydney, Nova Scotia, the traditional jumping-off place for every arctic expedition. It was July 17 when the *Roosevelt,* loaded with last-minute supplies, finally headed out. Close astern followed a small tug, chartered to take off the Peary family, Colonel Borup, and a few other friends. As the tug eased alongside, Colonel Borup sat with George on the quarterdeck, stiff as ever but betraying his feelings by holding his son's hand in his own.

The last partings over, the *Roosevelt* turned north and pushed on to Labrador. At Cape St. Charles she took on seventeen thousand pounds of whale meat for the Eskimo dogs, and at Hawke Harbour farther up the coast, she joined the steamer *Erik,* chartered by the Peary Arctic Club as an extra supply ship. The *Erik* was loaded with coal—and twenty-five more tons of whale meat. She also carried three paying passengers—the young New Haven millionaire Harry Whitney and his friends Walter Larned and George Norton. They had nothing to do with the expedition; they simply craved excitement and a little big-game hunting. Peary had worries enough without becoming a cruise director, yet they were willing to pay $1,500 apiece and he needed every cent he could get. At the moment, as they sat among the rotting whale blubber, they must have wondered whether the cruise was worth the price.

As the two reeking ships lay at anchor together, a dainty white vessel steamed unexpectedly into the harbor. This was the Harkness yacht *Wakiva*, proudly flying the New York Yacht Club pennant. She was far from home, but with polar exploration all the rage it had become fashionable for millionaires to cruise the northern waters. True, they never saw the real arctic—or even a polar bear—but there were occasional icebergs, the barren coast, the screaming gulls, the mysterious long twilights of the midnight sun. Certainly enough to regale the crowd at Sherry's the following winter.

But no one had bargained for this. These two black, foul-smelling ships were impossible. Yet it was too late to turn back without causing offense—after all, Peary was a very distinguished man. So Mr. Harkness and his guests, including several ladies in fluffy white dresses, steeled themselves for a courtesy call. The men on the *Roosevelt* did their best to rise to the occasion. From the rail to Peary's cabin, they laid a plank across the mass of jellylike blubber. The ladies paled but made it, and no one in either group ever mentioned the incredible stench. It was perhaps an all-time high in observing social proprieties.

On to Turnavak still farther up the coast, where Captain Bob's father ran a trading station. (Sometimes it seemed as if the Bartletts ran everything in Labrador.) After picking up fifty pairs of sealskin boots, the *Roosevelt* finally headed for Greenland.

A grinding crash shook George Borup the first afternoon out. He dashed from the little cabin he shared with MacMillan, half expecting to find the *Roosevelt* aground. To his delight the ship was merely pushing aside her first ice. "She bucked that piece good and hard and went through for a touchdown," he later noted, dipping into his endless supply of sports analogies.

On August 1, the *Roosevelt* edged through the ice into Cape York Bay. As she crept toward the shore, Bartlett sounded the whistle, and from the hills a dozen tiny figures came running down to the beach, piled into kayaks and paddled out to greet the ship. For the Smith Sound Eskimos, this was the great day—"Pearyaksoah" had returned.

For eighteen years Peary had worked among this gentle tribe that roamed the coast from here to Etah, a tiny settlement two hundred miles farther north. He nursed them, fed them, gave them guns, knives, and lamps. In return, they clothed him, hunted for him, provided his dogs, handled his sledges, and were willing to follow him literally to the end of the earth. As Peary himself put it, up to Cape York his success depended on the things civilization supplied; north of the cape, it hinged on the skill and help of these charming, childlike people.

Peary knew them all—who were the good sledge drivers . . . who owned the best dogs . . . who had the temperament for the long, dangerous trip across the sea ice. Now he set about recruiting the ones he wanted. And it was easy to persuade them to come. They were only too anxious to get the hardware that waited at the end of the rainbow. They had no homes to leave behind—they were nomads. There was no question of abandoning wives and children—Peary needed the women to sew.

So the *Roosevelt* and the *Erik* steamed slowly north, dipping in and out of ice-packed coves, picking up Eskimos and dogs. One of the first to come aboard was Seegloo, the old campaigner who stuck by Peary all through the awful days of 1906. Now he was willing to try again, and for two rifles he threw in his fine pack of dogs. Farther up the coast they picked up Kudlooktoo, the only Eskimo who had ever bothered to learn English . . . then "Harrigan," who understood no English but had mastered perfectly the song he was named after.

At North Star Bay they found sturdy young Ooqueah, the only Eskimo who came along for as complicated a motive as love. Ooqueah was wooing the tribal patriarch's daughter, but the old man considered the boy too poor. A year with Peary would fix that. The knives and

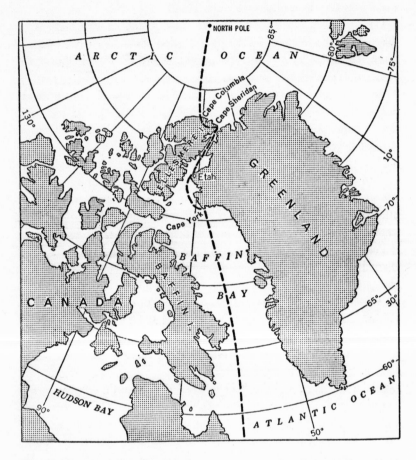

Peary's Route to the Pole: The Commander steamed north to Cape York, where the first Eskimos were recruited . . . then to Etah, where supplies were shifted . . . then to Cape Sheridan, where the Roosevelt *was based. The polar party next sledged ninety miles west to Cape Columbia, the final jumping-off point. From here Peary crossed 413 miles of shifting sea ice to the Pole itself.*

guns and whaleboat promised anyone who reached the Pole would make him the richest man for miles around.

During this brief stay in North Star Bay, Peary made an interesting discovery. In a native tent he found an ordinary American trunk, marked simply "F. A. Cook, Brooklyn, New York." The doctor, the Eskimos vaguely explained, had passed through the previous year.

Well, no time to wonder about that. There was too much to do before winter set in. Hunting fresh meat, for instance, to see them through the long arctic night. When they spotted a herd of walrus on August 5, Borup and MacMillan took off in a whaleboat. They managed to bag several in a wild, confused chase, with the Eskimos screaming encouragement and Borup firing his pistol with happy abandon. ("Our magazines were as empty as a Princeton man's pocketbook after the Yale football game.")

The *Roosevelt* reached Etah on August 7, and the *Erik* joined her on the eleventh. The next week the two little ships lay side by side, while the *Roosevelt* got ready for the final push north. This was the last chance to take stock—the northernmost settlement in the world. At that, there were only a few Eskimo families here, but the harbor was perfect—an ink-blue fjord cut deep into rugged hills that were splashed with orange lichen. Strangely beautiful surroundings for the dirty work at hand. The *Roosevelt's* men sweated through the twenty-four-hour daylight . . . cleaning the furnaces, restowing cargo, shifting fifty tons of whale meat from the *Erik,* plus some three hundred tons of coal.

Another fifty tons of coal were cached on the shore. This extra supply would be a godsend on the trip back. To guard it Peary detached Bo'sun John Murphy and cabin boy Billy Pritchard. Seeing them set up camp was too much for sportsman Harry Whitney. He was due to return on the *Erik,* but he dearly wanted polar bears and musk oxen for his collection of stuffed heads. This might be his only chance to get them. He begged Peary to let him stay too, and the commander agreed. The other two tourists, Norton and Larned, had roughed it enough; they were only too glad to go back.

Another return passenger appeared most unexpectedly. Just before the ships parted at Etah, an American dory appeared from the north with a ragged, frantic figure at the oars. This turned out to be Rudolph Francke, Dr. Cook's only white companion the previous winter. Cook had left him in charge of some supplies at Anoratok several miles up the coast, but it had been a dreadful year for Francke. Hating walrus meat, he tried living off canned goods; now he was half starved and racked with scurvy. He begged Peary to let him go back on the *Erik*.

The commander lectured the wretched man on duty—the obligation to carry out an assignment. But Francke had a letter from Cook releasing him, and it seems clear that Peary's reluctance really stemmed from his resentment of the doctor's expedition. In any case, Peary finally relented and let Francke on the ship. Then—with his knack for poor public relations—he billed Cook's benefactor, John R. Bradley, $100 for passage home.

There were no more complications, and at 4:45 P.M. on August 18, the *Roosevelt* continued north in a driving sleet storm. Ahead lay the treacherous, ice-jammed currents of Kane Basin, Kennedy and Robeson channels. Only four other ships had ever made it through here, and the *Roosevelt* herself was almost crushed in 1906. Yet if she could fight her way to Cape Sheridan, the prize would be well worth the risk. She would then be at the edge of the Arctic Ocean . . . less than five hundred miles from Peary's dream, the Pole itself.

The scene on the *Roosevelt* belied her peril. She looked like a slovenly excursion boat. Her deck seethed with laughing, yelling Eskimos—forty-nine altogether. The waist of the ship was a bedlam of dogs—246 in a furious free-for-all. The quarterdeck reeked worse than ever with seventy tons of whale meat and the blubber of fifty very dead walruses. That evening Bob Bartlett had peaches for dessert; he ate them all right, but the smell was so awful he couldn't even taste the flavor.

Soon the ice was too thick to dodge. Smashing and grinding her way ahead, the *Roosevelt* now plowed right into the floes. Sometimes she couldn't get by at all and had to try again. Then she would back up and plunge forward once more, bucking and battering the ice until at last she was through. From a barrel rigged high on the mainmast,

Bob Bartlett searched for open water or some weak point in the barrier. He called orders to his helmsman through a big megaphone, but often he simply implored the ship: "Rip 'em, Teddy! Bite 'em in two. That's fine, my beauty. Now—again!"

August 29, they couldn't move at all . . . a nerve-racking day completely hemmed in by the ice. But it was Robert E. Peary, Jr.'s fifth birthday, and no emergency was allowed to interfere with that. Summoning to his cabin Henson and Steward Charles Percy—the little boy's two best friends—Peary broke open a bottle of champagne.

When they were still frozen fast on the 31st, MacMillan could stand it no longer. Bursting with animal energy, he took off for the shore and raced aimlessly over the hills and rocks. He had no hat, no coat, no protection at all, and since it was 17° below, he inevitably came down with a high fever the following day. Peary could have lectured him, but with the gentleness he always mustered when his men were really down, he said nothing. Instead, every evening he sat at the Pianola and pumped out MacMillan's favorite song, "The Wedding of the Winds."

Finally they began moving again, and on September 5 Borup opened the cabin door and yelled, "We're there, Mac!" MacMillan was still too weak to care where, but the silent engines and the noise of unloading told him anyhow. The *Roosevelt* had made it; they were at Cape Sheridan.

The ship had done all it could do—no base could be farther north. The rest of the way they must go by sledge, more than four hundred miles over the polar sea ice. But they couldn't possibly start this year—it would soon be too dark to travel. Their first chance would come at the end of next February, when it grew light again. Then they must get there and back before the April thaw broke up the ice that formed their highway to the Pole. Meanwhile, they had to wait out the long winter night.

Occasionally they played, even though the temperature now hovered between 20° and 50° below. They dressed ship on little Marie Peary's birthday and celebrated with polar bear steak and frosted cake. On December 22—the shortest day of the year—Peary staged such a dramatic ceremony that one Eskimo ran south to meet the returning sun. MacMillan, ever the physical director, held a track meet on Christmas, and Borup—perhaps dreaming of those bright college weekends—organized some Eskimo girls into a Floradora sextet. Quiet, conscientious Ross Marvin tutored Henson in mathematics, and Bob Bartlett—who had an appreciation of the niceties of life that could only come from years in the wilderness—amiably lectured the group on their table manners.

But usually they were hard at work. At one time arctic explorers did nothing during the long winter night. It was a dreary period of depressed spirits, frustrating idleness. Peary changed all that. He made the dark months a time of constant, absorbing activity. When the moon was out, parties were off hunting, or taking tidal observations, or shifting supplies ninety miles west to Cape Columbia, the jump-off point for the Pole. When there was no moon, they had plenty to do around the ship—making sledges, sorting provisions, humoring the Eskimo women who sewed their furs. And for the new men, there were always the long, fascinating hours of training—learning how to build an igloo . . . drive a dog team . . . cook their food . . . wear their clothes . . . manage the Eskimos. So many details—boots were drier with a little grass inside . . . an igloo stayed warmer if the sleeping platform was high . . . good elbow motion was the secret to snapping a dog whip.

Peary was busiest of all, constantly studying new ways to save weight and time. He taught the men to use their *kooletahs* instead of sleeping bags . . . saving sixteen pounds on every sledge. He invented an alcohol stove that boiled water in only nine minutes—that would save over an hour a day in making tea. He made the Eskimo sledge more maneuverable by lengthening it to twelve feet and rounding off the ends—that should save time too . . . maybe the difference between victory and defeat.

By late February, everything needed had been moved to Cape Columbia. The polar party—Peary, his six assistants and seventeen Eskimos—huddled in a bleak community of igloos bravely christened Crane City. The supplies were stacked in neat piles, the nineteen sledges in good repair. Many of the dogs had died during the winter, but 133 were in excellent shape—easily enough for the trip.

As the day approached, George Borup sensed the exhilaration men have always felt on the brink of a great adventure. To cap it off, one morning he saw the ruddy glow of the returning sun. He reacted the only way he knew—he gave "the long Yale cheer with three 'suns' at the end."

February 27, the day before starting out, they loaded the sledges. Again, Peary proved a master of detail. Each sledge was arranged with meticulous care—500 pounds of "dog" pemmican in red tins on the bottom . . . then 50 pounds of "man" pemmican in blue tins . . . then cans of milk, tea, and alcohol . . . then rifle, snowshoes, boots, tools, all covered by a small fur rug. It added up to a compact 650-pound load, without an inch of wasted space. Even so, Dr. Goodsell managed to find a chink in his load where he quietly slipped a small leatherbound set of Shakespeare.

That last night they all gathered in Peary's igloo. The time was past for technical advice; this was a moment for words from the heart. Peary was never much at oratory (on the lecture circuit he depended largely on his dogs), but this was the most important thing in his life—his last shot at the Pole—and he became touchingly eloquent. He said he had always believed in action—not hot air. He told them the next weeks would be "undiluted hell"—but other brave men had come through worse. He played on their emotions like a skillful coach, reminding Borup of "the way a football team gathers round its leader just before trotting out on the field for a big game."

Late that evening Marvin, MacMillan, and Borup slipped into Bartlett's igloo for a smaller, more intimate session. Over the months these four men had become utterly devoted to each other, and this last night called for something special. Bartlett, who had a self-educated man's wistful respect for formal education, hesitantly suggested that the others sing their college songs. When this was done, they all joined hands, and each man led his own college cheer. The lump in Bartlett's throat was heavy as he listened and tried to follow—"I could make as much noise, but somehow it wasn't organized when it came out of my throat."

Then they quietly pledged themselves to give their all for Peary, and shaking hands, they joined in one last song. Through the igloo doorway and out across the bitter arctic night drifted the words they sang with such feeling:

> *Amici usque ad aras*
> Deep graven on each heart,
> Shall be found unwavering true
> When we from life depart.

"Forward! March!" Peary's crisp command seemed almost too dramatic, as Bob Bartlett started out next morning. The plan was for the captain to lead the way. He would pioneer the trail . . . hack a path through the tumbling, jagged offshore ice, camping about ten miles out. The others would start later—first Borup, then everyone else the following morning. The main party would trace Bartlett's course and use his igloos at night. Meanwhile the captain would be trail-blazing the next day's march. He would keep ahead of them until he wore out; then his place would be taken by somebody else.

"Forward! March!" Again the order came, as George Borup started off two hours later. His party included four sledges with three Eskimo drivers and himself. They were to stick with Bartlett for three days, then stockpile their supplies and return to Cape Columbia for more. A lot of responsibility for a novice, but Borup wasn't in the least concerned. As he cheerfully told the commander, this was his sister's birthday, and she had always been his lucky mascot.

"Forward! March!" The familiar words rang out a third time at 6:30 the following morning, March 1. Slowly the fourteen sledges of the main party formed in single file and set out over Bartlett's trail. The weather had been fine, but now a biting wind howled in from the east. "The perversity of hard luck," thought Peary; "A good omen," philosophized Henson, who recalled that all the commander's great marches had begun under stormy skies.

Peary, Henson, and their specially selected Eskimos brought up the rear of this slow-moving caravan. Ahead were units led by Marvin,

MacMillan, and Goodsell. Together with Borup and later Bartlett, they were the "supporting parties." Each had the job of keeping Peary's unit fed for five days . . . then back to Cape Columbia, ultimately leaving the commander to carry on alone. But by that time he should be within 150 miles of the Pole, in excellent physical shape, and with a well-marked route back.

As they headed out across the ice, they had easy going at first, for they were still on the glacial fringe that bordered the coast. But once on the polar sea it was a different story. No matter how cold the weather—no matter how frozen the water—the wind and tides were always at work. They slammed floes together, piling up huge pressure ridges . . . or pulled them apart, forming the deadly lanes of water that arctic men call "leads."

Panting and sweating even in the bitter cold, the main party wrestled their sledges over this jumble of ice. It took constant attention to keep the traces straight, the dogs in check, the sledges upright. A moment's lapse, and some frozen spur would catch the runners and dump the whole load . . . or perhaps even worse.

Two of the Eskimos smashed their sledges almost at once and trudged back to Cape Columbia for spares. Peary was furious. Taking aside Kudlooktoo, one of the culprits, he chewed him out unmercifully. When it was a matter of interfering with "my life's dream," the commander was no longer the Great White Father, generously dispensing hardware to the natives. He was a hard, harsh master, capable of brutal words and decisions. The tirade over, Kudlooktoo continued on back, sullen and abashed.

On March 2 they met their first lead, a black ribbon of water that cut squarely across the trail. MacMillan, using the delay to take a sounding, suddenly tripped and fell in. Marvin yanked him out, but there he stood—a sopping bundle of fur at 40° below. He raced back to camp, to find Peary already waiting with a dry change of clothes. When it came to helping the men who backed him up, there was nothing the commander wouldn't do. Yanking off the ice-coated boots, he warmed MacMillan's freezing feet against his own bare chest.

Next day the lead closed and they were on their way again. But

March 4 brought more trouble. The temperature suddenly shot up—it stood at a sultry 9° below—and leads were forming on all sides. Soon the men reached a harrowing stretch of water—so broad they called it the Big Lead. Here they found Bartlett, already held up for twenty-four hours. There was nothing to do but wait together, hoping the lead would close.

Day after day they waited—Peary pacing up and down the ice . . . Dr. Goodsell reading his leatherbound Shakespeare . . . Henson studying the Bible . . . MacMillan, still the physical director, trying to divert the men with a track meet. But the Eskimos grew more and more restless. Every time they looked at this forbidding barrier, they realized they were now far out at sea. In the constantly shifting movement of the polar ice, leads might open up anywhere, any time—even right under them—pitching them into the freezing water.

Some of the Eskimos began to grumble, arguing that the whole expedition ought to retreat. On March 7 Peary had enough. He sent Panikpah and Pooadloonah, the two loudest troublemakers, back to the *Roosevelt* in disgrace. With them went a note, ordering the crew to put them and their families off the ship. Stiff punishment, for it meant expelling them three hundred miles from home without food or equipment. But Peary was adamant—nothing must threaten this final try for the great prize.

March 11, and at last the Big Lead closed enough for the party to cross. But at this point a new problem arose. Borup had missed them on his way back to the cape for his second load; Marvin had been sent after him with instructions; now a week had passed and neither man had reappeared.

Should they wait any longer? If they did, they would have all the more trouble reaching the Pole—the ice was already starting to melt. But if they didn't, everyone might freeze to death. Borup was bringing the fuel they needed to make hot tea—considered a "must" to survive in the arctic. For Peary, the decision was easy. "I don't know how long a man can work and live at 50° and 60° below without a hot drink," he told MacMillan. "We may find out."

The crisis never arose, for they were finally overtaken by Borup and

242

Marvin on March 14. The two men had also been held up by leads, and it took some magnificent marching to catch up with the main party. Happy, boyish George Borup was overjoyed. Clapping Marvin on the back, he paid the quiet engineering professor the best compliment he knew: "Cornell always was strong on cross-country!"

One by one the "supporting parties" began to go back. March 14—Dr. Goodsell, who was really too heavy for sledge work anyhow. March 15—MacMillan, after one more sentimental rendition of *"Amici usque"* in Bartlett's igloo. March 20—Borup, delighted to have carried the Yale colors farther north than they had ever flown before. March 26—Marvin, with Peary calling after him, "Be careful of the leads, my boy." Bartlett's last words to Marvin were more aphoristic: "I'll see you again in one of three places—Heaven, Hell, or the *Roosevelt*." He never dreamed that it wouldn't be the *Roosevelt*.

Now only Bartlett and Henson were left. On they plodded with the captain usually pioneering. In this desolate waste the eye played crazy tricks—an empty pemmican can lying in the snow might look as big as a house. And always there was the biting, stinging wind. So cold, the men's beards froze stiff. So cold, the bottle of brandy that Peary kept "warm" against his chest was frozen solid.

April 1, and it was Bartlett's turn to go back. For a while the captain wistfully hoped he might go all the way. Certainly Peary was fond of him, but what chance did sentiment have when Henson was the better dog driver? As the commander explained, "It's all in the game and you've been at it long enough to know how hard a game it is."

Bartlett knew, but still it was difficult. He started out slowly, unconsciously hanging back in case some new summons might come from the north.

But Peary was no longer even thinking of him. All his attention was turned toward the Pole, now only 133 miles away. To make it, he had Henson, the four most eager Eskimos, forty dogs, five sledges, enough food for fifty days. Best of all, he was fresh. The "supporting parties" had done their work well—taking all the strain, catapulting him within easy reach of his goal.

Pulling his belt in another notch, Peary began his final dash on

April 2. For the first time he was in the lead. Striking out under the pale, cold sun, he felt a strange exhilaration. Suddenly he was young again; his mind drifted back to the early days in Greenland—"perhaps a man always thinks of the beginning of his work when he feels it is nearing the end." He tramped on, in a world of his own. Occasionally, they stopped to rest, but Henson doubted if Peary ever slept an hour.

For once the arctic seemed on his side. The wind died down; the ice turned smooth. The sledges fairly streaked over the flat surface. April 3, twenty miles . . . April 4, twenty-five miles . . . April 5, again twenty-five miles . . . April 6, over thirty miles. Now even the Eskimos grew excited. Occasionally they scrambled to the top of some pressure ridge and searched the northern horizon, hoping for a glimpse of the Pole.

At ten o'clock on the morning of April 6, Peary ordered the party to halt and make camp. As they unloaded the sledges, he carefully pulled a small package from under his *kooletah*. Lovingly, he unfolded the old silk American flag he carried on every expedition. Mrs. Peary had given it to him fifteen years before, and he had left a piece of it at each of his "farthest norths." Now the flag was patched and discolored, but it still snapped in the breeze as he proudly planted it on his igloo.

"This, my boy," he told Henson, "is to be Camp Morris K. Jessup, the last and most northerly camp on earth." A fitting honor for Peary's greatest benefactor, yet not quite at the Pole. When he took his noon observations, Peary discovered he was at 89°57′—still three miles to go.

Most of the next thirty hours he marched and countermarched over a ten-mile area. Twice he started out walking north, then without changing direction ended up walking south. He took four different sets of observations—thirteen single altitudes of the sun—all putting him at or near the Pole. Overdoing it, perhaps, but he wanted no arguments back home. No one must question his victory.

"We will plant the Stars and Stripes—*at the North Pole*," Peary announced when finally satisfied on the morning of April 7. Then, he led Henson and the four Eskimos to a hummock not far from camp. It wasn't exactly the Pole, but for photographic purposes it would do. He raised Mrs. Peary's flag, and others too: the Navy League, the Red Cross, the D.A.R. peace emblem, the colors of the D.K.E. fraternity— his old house at Bowdoin.

Next he had Henson lead "three rousing cheers." The Eskimos were delighted to oblige. They were a little bewildered—this wasn't quite the way they imagined "The Big Nail"—but they vaguely realized they were at the top of the world. More important, they knew that Peary had achieved his goal. Ootah, Egingwah, and Seegloo had all been with him before; Ooqueah was new but no less ardent—his reward should easily win the girl he courted at Cape York.

Now for the marker traditionally planted at the scene of every discovery. Peary used a glass bottle, cramming into it a diagonal strip of his flag and two separate statements, written just after his arrival the previous day. The first listed the members of the party (carefully noting, "Matthew Henson, colored"). The second formally took possession of the North Pole "for and in the name of the President of the United States of America." A little high-handed, since in effect he was claiming a part of the ocean.

Peary also wrote another message, but this was more personal and kept with his other belongings. It was, of all things, a post card to his wife. Nothing remarkable; just the kind of card any lonely husband might send after a successful business trip: "I have won out at last. Have been here a day. I start for home and you in an hour...."

It was a vastly different Peary who got under way at four o'clock that afternoon. Now that he had won "this splendid jewel," an overwhelming reaction set in. To Henson, he seemed in a daze; after the first two southbound marches he became practically a dead weight, usually riding on top of a sledge.

But it didn't matter. Bartlett had done a superb job of knitting the trail. The igloos built on the way up served perfectly on the way down. The weather behaved—no dangerous leads to block them. And best of all, they were going home.

They made spectacular time: occasionally 40 miles a march. On April 23 they were back at Cape Columbia—413 miles in just sixteen days. Here they slept the sleep of winners, and Peary quickly recovered his energy. On April 25, he led them on the final lap: two more long marches to Cape Sheridan and the *Roosevelt*.

The smell of hot coffee and good tobacco drifted to meet them, even as they sighted the ship. On board, the Eskimos—always the first to see anything—began shouting and pointing. Bartlett—usually the first to act—vaulted the rail and raced out on the ice. Extending his hand, he spoke with the breathless formality men sometimes use to hide their excitement: "I congratulate you, sir, on the discovery of the Pole!"

"How did you guess it?" Peary asked.

But Bartlett changed the subject to the awful news that had haunted him for days: "Have you heard about poor Marvin?"

Of course Peary hadn't, and the story came out swiftly. Marvin had died, returning over the polar ice. No one knew exactly how it happened—only the story told by his shaken Eskimos, Kudlooktoo and "Harrigan." They reported that Marvin, traveling ahead of them both, had crashed through the thin ice of the Big Lead. When they reached the spot, it was already too late to save him.

Peary was stunned. He admired Marvin greatly, and in addition this shook his professional pride. He considered himself the safest of arctic explorers; until now he had lost only one man in eighteen years. It would have been small consolation had he known the story that came out later. When Kudlooktoo was baptized in 1926, he confessed that Marvin had not drowned—he was shot. The Eskimo said he murdered the professor at the climax of a bitter dispute between Marvin and "Harrigan."

Whatever happened, everyone else was safe on the ship except Mac-Millan and Borup. They were on the Greenland coast laying down emergency supplies in case the polar party returned that way. Peary sent them word to switch to tidal observations—a change the happy-go-lucky Borup found immensely tedious. At one point in the record book they were keeping for the Coast and Geodetic Survey, he noted, "I do not know whether this Goddamn tide is going up or down."

Peary would have sympathized. He too was bored by the scientific side of these expeditions. It was just something that had to be done. The Pole was the real challenge, and that had been won. At the first chance he reassembled everyone on the *Roosevelt,* and on July 18 the ship started back on the long trip south.

August 8, they reached Nerke on the Greenland coast. Here they found three Eskimo families who gave them some interesting news.

It seemed that Dr. Cook, who had disappeared so mysteriously over a year ago, was safely back with his two native companions. According to the Eskimos, Cook said he had been "a long way out on the sea ice . . . far north."

They learned much more when they met sportsman Harry Whitney at Etah on August 17. He had enjoyed his year in the wilderness, but the conversation quickly switched from his toll of musk oxen (many) and polar bears (none) to the return of Dr. Cook. Whitney reported that the doctor and his two Eskimo boys stumbled in from Ellesmere Land the previous April. Before heading on south to catch a whaling ship to Denmark, he told Whitney a momentous secret—he had reached the North Pole on April 21, 1908.

If true, this was a whole year before Peary—a sickening blow for the man who had just achieved "the thing which it was intended from the beginning that I should do." The commander quickly launched a little detective work. Henson and MacMillan questioned Cook's Eskimos—they laughed and said they were never far north, or even out sight of land. Borup examined Cook's sledge—it was hardly scratched, certainly not battered the way a sledge should be after a thousand miles across the polar ice.

Peary relaxed. Still, he was bitter at the very thought of this man trying to rob him of the great prize. When Harry Whitney asked permission to carry back some of Cook's things on the *Roosevelt,* Peary coldly refused.

They pushed on south, unexpectedly meeting the schooner *Jeannie* with mail and supplies on August 23. In the excitement of this first contact with the outside world, Cook for the moment was forgotten. MacMillan read with interest that Taft was President . . . that a frightful earthquake had ravaged Messina. For Borup there was news of a far worse disaster. Harvard had beaten Yale in football ("It took me so by surprise I couldn't get used to it").

More mail was waiting at Cape York on the 25th. Rummaging through the pile, Peary handed one of the letters to MacMillan. It was from Captain Adams of the whaler *Morning* and described meeting Dr. Cook in South Greenland. The captain reported that Cook was definitely claiming the Pole. "Do you think," MacMillan asked, "he will carry that story home?"

"Absolutely," was Peary's answer.

"Reached the North Pole," Cook cabled the Brussels Observatory on September 1 from the little port of Lerwick in the Shetland Islands. He was now en route to Copenhagen on the blubber ship *Hans Egede,* and this was his first chance to claim success.

He also cabled a summary of his triumph to the New York *Herald,* which turned out to have exclusive serial rights. It was an amazing story: He and his two Eskimos left Anoratok in February, 1908 . . . sledged west to the tip of Axel Heiberg Island . . . crossed the sea ice to the Pole . . . lost their way on the return trip and ended up in Jones Sound, far to the south. Here they wintered and eventually beat their way back across Ellesmere Land to Etah.

An epic story, well worth the *Herald*'s $20,000 investment, although Cook's description of the Pole itself was surprisingly drab: "What a cheerless spot to have aroused the ambition of man for so many ages. An endless field of purple snow. No life. No land. No spot to relieve the monotony of the frost. We were the only pulsating creatures in a dead world of ice."

Later he improved on this considerably: "We all were lifted to the paradise of winners . . . the ice under us seemed almost sacred. . . . At last we step over colored fields of sparkle, climbing walls of purple and gold—finally under skies of crystal blue, with flaming clouds of glory, we touch the mark!"

Whatever it looked like, the world was electrified. Long before the *Hans Egede* reached Copenhagen, congratulations poured in from everywhere. The English-speaking press was especially gratified. "It is good to think that the Anglo-Saxon race has always been a pioneer in Arctic discovery," gloated the London *Chronicle.* The paper added that although America had finally won the race to the Pole, "We may be glad the victor is at least of our blood."

Governor Claude Swanson of Virginia went further: Cook showed "the dash and daring only found in the soul of an American." Scholars and scientists were less chauvinistic, but equally satisfied. "YALE PROFES-

SORS EXPRESS DELIGHT," proclaimed the *Herald* on September 2, and the only dissenting note appeared in the next column: "NEWS RECEIVED IN DOUBT AT HARVARD."

Cook had an answer for these Cambridge kill-joys. When he reached Copenhagen September 4, he declared: "Let skeptics who disbelieve my story go to the North Pole. There they will find a small brass tube which I have buried under the flag."

A more convincing rebuttal lay in the almost universal acclaim Cook received at Copenhagen. After all, these Scandinavians had the arctic in their blood, and they ought to know. The Crown Prince met the doctor's ship. The King received him at a state dinner. The explorer Knud Rasmussen endorsed him completely. Otto Sverdrup backed him to the hilt—and no one recalled that the great Norwegian was still smarting from that time in the Kane Basin when Peary wouldn't have coffee with him.

In the general rejoicing, hardly anyone (except some London papers) commented on Cook's failure to produce his records. After all, there was plenty of time. Yet it did pose a question. As explorer Evelyn Briggs Baldwin put it, "It is perfectly easy for a man to go to a certain point and then to say that he has reached the Pole. How is he going to prove it? Is not Peary likely to return soon and say that he, too, discovered it?"

"I have the Pole, April six," Peary radioed the *New York Times* on September 6, as soon as the *Roosevelt* touched Indian Harbor. This was the first wireless station on the way back, and the commander lost no time spreading the glad tidings. To the Associated Press: "Stars and Stripes nailed to the Pole" . . . to the New York Yacht Club: "Steam yacht *Roosevelt,* flying club burgee, has enabled me to add North Pole to club's other trophies" . . . and of course to the patient, long-suffering Mrs. Peary: "Have made good at last. I have the old Pole."

The news reached Copenhagen that evening during a formal dinner to Dr. Cook at the Tivoli Casino. As the doctor—submerged in a garland of pink roses—modestly blushed at the toasts and compliments, whispers suddenly flew through the room that Peary was back . . . also claiming the Pole. Cook heard but made no comment in his carefully-prepared address. He simply said he owed everything to his friends Sverdrup, Bradley, and the Eskimos.

Afterward there was a rush for the dais, and the doctor smilingly faced the correspondents. What did he think of the news? "I am proud that a fellow American has reached the Pole. There is glory enough for us all." Did he really believe Peary got there? "If Mr. Peary says he has reached the Pole, I'm sure he has." Later the doctor sent a gracious cable to the *New York Times*: "Glad Peary did it. Two records are better than one."

He neatly side-stepped every attempt to stir up a controversy: "I am not a doubting Thomas . . . three cheers for him and the Stars and Stripes." The New York *Herald* nodded approvingly and added, perhaps with crossed fingers: "It is a foregone conclusion that Commander Peary will hail Dr. Cook's achievement in the same ungrudging spirit."

"Cook's story should not be taken too seriously," Peary wirelessed the Associated Press on September 7, answering an urgent request for his views. Another message to Mrs. Peary was stronger: "Don't let Cook's story worry you. Have him nailed."

As the *Roosevelt* headed on south, the commander's indignation grew. Cook's story was so preposterous—how could anyone believe him? Yet here was this pile of inquiries, all of them asking for comment. Borup was calling Cook's claim a "gold brick"—perhaps that was the phrase to use. Yet it did seem a little undignified. Peary asked Mac-Millan for a better word, but the schoolteacher had no suggestions. Anyhow, it was the truth, and hadn't he always faced facts? When the ship reached Battle Harbour on the 8th, he grimly fired his next barrage. It was to the *New York Times;* they had the serial rights to his own story and might need a little encouragement: "Do not trouble about Cook's story or attempt to explain away discrepancies in his installments. The affair will settle itself. He has not been to the Pole on April 21st, 1908 or at any other time. He has simply handed the public a gold brick."

In Copenhagen Dr. Cook watched the fireworks with an air of injured bewilderment. Summoning the press on the 8th—the day Peary's charges appeared—he said how sorry he was. As for himself, he tried to be more open-minded. For instance, he never complained about the commander seizing his supplies at Anoratok. If the press happened to mention this, he hastily added, "Please don't say anything disagreeable about Peary."

When the doctor reached New York on September 21, a thousand fans steamed out to greet him on the excursion boat *Grand Republic*. She was chartered by the Arctic Club, a sort of Cook claque, but there was nothing staged about the 100,000 cheering people who lined the water front. They were there to pay homage to this modest man who, in the *Herald*'s words, "stood for American pluck and endurance and for manly dignity."

There were those, unfortunately, who demanded something more tangible—like polar observations. All scientific evidence of Cook's discovery remained exasperatingly elusive. At first he said he left his notes with Harry Whitney. Even before the young sportsman denied this, others asked how anybody could leave behind such valuable data. This led to a new stand—the notes didn't matter anyhow; he had copies of everything. When would they be available? Well, his notes must first be submitted to the University of Copenhagen. How long would that take? At least a month.

Meanwhile he picked up some excellent backing. America's two most venerable arctic explorers, General Adolphus W. Greely and Admiral W. S. Schley, were loud in their praise. It was perhaps a coincidence that both had been grievously offended by Peary. The commander was openly scornful of Greely's work and had Schley's name erased from the maps. (True, Peary proved "Schleyland" was nonexistent, but he might have done it a little more tactfully.) In any case, both of these distinguished warriors now wrote off Peary and jumped enthusiastically on the Cook bandwagon.

That was good enough for most people. Dr. Oscar Treder, rector of St. Luke's at East Hampton, Long Island, ceremoniously placed Cook's account in the cornerstone of his new church. When the Toledo *Blade* polled its readers on who discovered the Pole, the vote came out Cook 550, Peary 10. A similar poll in Pittsburgh gave Dr. Cook a 10 to 1 margin. Crowds stormed the St. Louis Coliseum and the Cleveland convention hall to hear the doctor, who lost no time reaping a harvest on the lecture circuit.

And he put on a magnificent show. By now his description of the final dash was better than ever ("the young Eskimos, chanting songs of love, came with easy step"), and of course, he was always so nice about Peary. "Dr. Cook," declared the Buffalo *Commercial,* "is behaving like a man; Peary like a very naughty or ill-bred child."

Amiable jeers and catcalls greeted the returning *Roosevelt* when she steamed up New York harbor on October 1, buried deep in a naval parade honoring the Hudson-Fulton Exposition. As the indignant crew turned to shout back, Peary sternly called a halt: "It does them more harm than it does us."

Brave words. Actually, no one could have been hurt more than Peary by the taunts, and certainly none could have been more surprised. He was so sure he had stopped all this nonsense by his barrage of wires from Labrador. Yet every passing excursion steamer seemed full of Cook supporters, loud and insulting as ever. Then to cap the commander's humiliation, the *Roosevelt*—having weathered every arctic peril—broke down in the middle of the Hudson and had to leave her place in line.

Even worse was to follow. Until now, the doctor's friends merely argued that Peary reached the Pole a poor second; soon they began hinting that he never got there at all. They pointed out that the only inspection of his instruments took place in the unscientific confines of a railroad baggage room . . . that he was sometimes fuzzy on his dates . . . above all, that he claimed to have sledged incredible distances. For Peary to have returned 133 miles on his first three marches from the Pole, he must have averaged 44 miles a day—yet even the great Fridtjof Nansen said his best record was only 25 miles. It did no good for Peary to point out that he had revolutionized the whole technique of sledging . . . that under his system even inexperienced "tenderfeet" like Borup and MacMillan averaged 34 miles. The public knew only that competent authorities were dubious—the pros and cons were all too technical.

But there was nothing technical about the other charges raised against Peary. Everybody understood these—that he was a poor sport . . . that he wouldn't bring back Cook's belongings (not even his American flag!) . . . that he charged $100 to rescue the doctor's scurvy-ridden assistant Rudolph Francke. And people lapped up stories that he was a tyrant to the Eskimos—a martinet who exploited them ruthlessly at the cost of a few pans and knives. "His deportment has all the conqueror's traits of character," declared the Danish explorer Dr. P. H. P. Steensby. "This year will bring to the Eskimos the great satisfaction that they have seen for the last time Peary."

Only his own men (the stories ran) had been treated worse. The New York Herald—perhaps protecting its investment in Cook's serial—claimed that Perry didn't pay his men, that he delayed writing Ross Marvin's mother, that he shamefully mistreated the loyal Bob Bartlett in not taking him to the Pole. The hostile press shed many tears over Bartlett, and it did no good for the captain to deny that his feelings were hurt. Hounding Peary, the great English journalist W. T. Stead thundered, "He is a bounder. When the story of how he had treated Bartlett was published, there was only one sentiment throughout the civilized world—and that was one of regret that such a man had ever come back to live among men."

Worst of all, the press pointed out, Peary had taken a colored man to the Pole. This was regarded as a selfish device to capture all the glory for himself, for it was generally acknowledged that Negroes didn't count. Even Peary seemed to agree. When asked why he didn't have along a "white witness," he was quoted as saying, "Because after a lifetime of effort I dearly wanted the honor for myself." Lost in the shuffle were the very valid points that Henson was the most skillful sledge driver and easily the best at handling Eskimos.

The country had yet to feel any pangs about racial intolerance, and even Peary's friends found Henson a bit embarrassing. As for the commander's enemies, they happily sharpened their knives. When Henson reported that Cook's native boys told him they never went near the Pole, the Herald printed a cartoon showing a hulking Negro threatening two little Eskimos with a razor.

Peary met these attacks with scornful silence—he refused to publish anything until the National Geographic Society judged his claim—but his supporters struck back with a vengeance. The New York Times raked over Cook's questionable expedition up Mount McKinley . . . later uncovered two mathematicians who said they worked out the doctor's polar observations in New York. The pro-Cook *Independent* counterattacked, claiming that the manufactured data was a Peary trap. No one was neutral—all the great guns of journalism were now lined up, hurling broadsides at each other. Watching the uproar from the quiet sidelines of Newfoundland, Bob Bartlett's mother could only write her son, "I am beginning to think that somebody ought to be spanked. Send me a letter and let me know whether it's you or not."

Events gradually supplied the answer. As early as October, arctic expert George Kennan published two devastating articles attacking Cook's sledge loads, times, and distances as completely impossible. Then Admiral Chester offered figures showing that, to work out certain of his claimed observations, the doctor must have made the sun stand still for twelve days. Later someone noticed that Cook's "North Pole" picture showed the Eskimos wearing musk-oxen trousers, although the doctor himself said they killed none of these animals until the following winter at Jones Sound.

By October 17 Cook decided to cancel his lecture tour and concentrate on preparing his case for the University of Copenhagen. The time could not have been very well spent, for after receiving the data in late December, the university took only two days to conclude that his observations proved nothing. The official report was coldly tactful, the committee members far less so. Chairman Strömgren called the case "shameless," and Cook's old friend Rasmussen did a complete somersault, terming the presentation "most impudent."

The discredited doctor dropped from sight. The papers which praised him so loudly no longer mentioned him at all. The honorable and distinguished societies expelled him. When he turned up again a year later, he was no longer the calm, collected man who played it so cool. Now he bitterly lashed at Peary, but no one was interested; *Hampton Magazine*'s offer for his story fell from $100,000 to $4,000. Even then it caused only a mild ripple, although mislabeled his "confession." To all intents and purposes, the field was left to Peary.

But it was a hollow victory for the commander. True, the National

Geographic Society completely accepted his claims . . . scientific bodies hailed him all over the world . . . and Teddy Roosevelt sent a cable from Nairobi. But this wasn't the way this stern, remote, but impeccably honest man had pictured it. He felt none of that first splash of golden glory his romantic mind envisioned for so long. And the sordid squabble, the suspicious press, the insults and mudslinging simply appalled him. As the *Nation* summed it up, "the joy of the acclaim that should have greeted him at the triumphant close of his twenty-three year quest can never be his."

Yet the goal was won, and to the country that was what counted. Best of all, it was done by Americans. As Peary pointed out, the *Roosevelt,* the supplies, in fact everything on her was American . . . except her crew. But this was all right, he hastily added, for they were Newfoundlanders—"essentially our first cousins."

With the flag flying safely over the Pole, there seemed nothing left to discover. The South Pole, of course, was still there, but it somehow never had the mystery or appeal of the arctic. Even Roald Amundsen, its ultimate discoverer, conceded that. When he reached there two years later, he regarded it as strictly a consolation prize—at best a publicity stunt to win him support for another try at the arctic. It took tragedy to give the South Pole any glamour—the glorious failure of Britain's Captain Robert F. Scott, who died showing "that Englishmen can endure hardships, help one another, and meet death with as great a fortitude as ever in the past."

But it was the North Pole that stood as the symbol of conquest, and with the battle now won, the country settled back for a quiet spring —*The Chocolate Soldier* . . . "Down by the Old Mill Stream" . . . the latest mystery by that promising new writer Mary Roberts Rinehart. A quiet spring indeed, broken only by that startling phenomenon Halley's Comet. When its tail brushed the earth on May 18, fortune-tellers predicted the end of the world, Kansas farmers retired to their cyclone cellars, and Broadwayites flocked to the Astor Roof. The more sophisticated smiled tolerantly, and no one—not even the wisest— thought that this visitor from outer space could possibly be the herald of a whole new world yet to conquer.

1910=1912

The Cosmopolites

"I am interested to see how extensive American influence is, and in how many directions it is felt. Among the novels I see in the houses, no English ones are more common than for instance, David Harum, or Winston Churchill's—I mean, of course, our Winston Churchill, Winston Churchill the gentleman."

—THEODORE ROOSEVELT

"The only thing wanting to make the gathering complete in all respects was the presence of King Edward," declared the *New York Times,* describing Commander Peary's triumphant reception at London's Albert Hall on May 4, 1910. The paper went on to explain that His Majesty had planned to attend, "but at the last minute he found himself utterly unable to do so."

The *Times* gave no reason, but the truth was written in the worried faces, the soft footsteps, the hushed voices at Buckingham Palace. Edward VII was desperately sick. His old trouble, bronchitis, the doctors said, but this time he couldn't shake it off. Years of rich food, hard work, and play were at last taking their toll.

Still, he tried to carry on. This Wednesday he couldn't make the Peary reception, but he somehow got through his daily audiences— hoarse and wheezing, his great bulk heaving with labored breath. Thursday, he could barely speak, and that afternoon the royal family began to gather. Then, at 7:30 P.M. came the first medical bulletin: a simple announcement that the King's condition "causes some anxiety."

Laconic, but London instinctively understood. And in the mysterious way that such news travels, word spread instantly all over the capital. Crowds began converging on the palace, and once again the world witnessed the sight of Englishmen drawn physically—almost by magnet—to the royal family in time of stress.

Friday, May 6, found thousands waiting in the bright morning sun—first the costers, clerks and chars on their way to work . . . then a sea of women . . . finally the polished carriages and motorcars of the fashionable. By noon traffic was hopelessly snarled, but everyone was very, very patient . . . hardly even a sound, except the hum that rose whenever some high official whisked through the gilt-tipped gates.

Inside the palace, the King struggled grimly, pathetically to get through another day. He insisted on keeping an appointment with Sir Ernest Cassel, but confessed he was "miserably ill." He fainted twice that afternoon but revived long enough to smile when his horse Witch of the Air won at Kempton Park. Toward evening he lapsed into a coma, murmuring softly, "I shall go on."

It was raining now. In the square the crowd huddled under umbrellas and newspapers. Many were in evening clothes, dressed for the theatre or the Savoy or Romano's. But they no longer felt like going, and stood quietly with the rest . . . waiting, watching, wondering. At 7:45 the Archbishop of Canterbury left "greatly affected" . . . 7:55, the Duchess of Albany emerged in tears . . . 8:00, the Home Secretary hurried in, pale and serious. No one saw another visitor who slipped in a little later—the King's great and good friend Mrs. Alice Keppel, summoned by that most understanding of women, Queen Alexandra herself.

In the palace courtyard the *Daily Chronicle*'s brilliant young reporter Philip Gibbs paced up and down. His orders were to stay put—no matter what—but so far there was nothing new. Only the shadowy visitors who rushed in and out . . . the crowds beyond the dripping fence . . . the glare of headlights on the wet pavement.

Now it was 11:45, and as Gibbs restlessly smoked a last cigarette, a royal carriage suddenly appeared from the gloom of an inner court. It rolled silently by, and in the pale light of a lamppost he caught a fleeting glimpse of the Prince of Wales and Princess Mary—their faces streaked with tears. With the instinct of a good journalist, Gibbs quickly slipped into the palace and asked for any late news. "Sir," replied an equerry with broken voice, "King Edward died two minutes ago."

America was almost as shaken as Britain herself. When the news reached New York that evening, most Broadway theatres played "God Save the King." Next day many business operations were suspended—not just the New York Stock Exchange where British influence was strong, but the Philadelphia, New Orleans, Chicago, and Baltimore exchanges too. Wall Street itself was plunged in gloom; flags flew at half mast, and the J. P. Morgan offices were draped in black.

It was more than a matter of sentiment. These were the days when few kings were figureheads, and Edward was a powerful man indeed. In his short nine-year reign people came to regard him as far more than a magnificent clotheshorse and connoisseur of pretty women; his warmth and tact made him a force for stability throughout the world.

No one knew how George V would do. Business spokesmen like Judge Gary and Isaac Seligman assured the country that there would be no panic, but financial circles still worried. It was said that the new King was "unfriendly," that he was "undependable," that Queen Mary was cold and remote. Wall Street discussed the implications in the most specific terms—the danger to the boom in rubber and oil . . . to Kuhn, Loeb's new issue of B & O bonds. "It is recognized as a possibility," warned the business-minded New York *Tribune,* "that the accession of a new King, of whose personality and whose attitude toward other powers little is publicly known, may prove an obstruction to the negotiations pending for the placing of various issues of American railway bonds abroad."

The man in the street ignored such subtleties. Far more wisely, he assumed business would go along pretty much as always. As for the change in kings, he cared only that a great and colorful personality was gone. In this last era when the poor gained pleasure from simply watching the rich, he knew only that a giant had passed from the scene. Now he was mainly interested in the appointment of the U. S. representative to the funeral.

The choice was obvious. More than a year had passed since Theodore Roosevelt left office, but he remained easily the best-known American in the world. In Africa, no lion had "done its duty"; on the contrary, seventeen fell before the Roosevelt onslaught . . . with every victim faithfully reported by the press. When the *Herald* hopefully predicted that the Cook-Peary controversy would end these "African stories," the prophecy proved quite wrong. Within a week the Colonel was back in the headlines, riding a locomotive cow-catcher to Nairobi.

Now he was touring Europe, irrepressible as ever. In Rome he quarreled with the Pope ("a worthy, narrowly limited parish priest"); in Paris he lectured at the Sorbonne; in Copenhagen he lost his evening clothes. When Edward died, he was in Oslo staying with Haakon VII. The King proved a splendid but mildly baffled host. "Colonel Roosevelt," he once asked, searching for some way to please his guest, "wouldn't you like a cup of tea?"

"By George, Your Majesty, the very thing I should like!" cried the Colonel, but he soon began romping with seven-year-old Crown Prince Olaf.

All this was interrupted by Edward's funeral on May 20—but not before Roosevelt fitted in one last military review with the German Kaiser. Then he turned to the solemn occasion at hand.

"What will Theodore Roosevelt wear?" the *New York Times* asked, and the whole country wondered. It was generally assumed that the Colonel had his khaki Rough Rider uniform with him—but he certainly couldn't wear that. Yet the alternative was to put on civilian evening dress and not ride horseback at all—equally unthinkable. The nation was wrong on both counts. The Colonel did not have his Rough Rider suit along (Mrs. Roosevelt had vetoed the idea); moreover, he was perfectly willing to wear the prescribed evening dress and sit in a carriage. On state occasions, Theodore Roosevelt liked to be scrupulously correct.

And there never was more of a state occasion. Over twenty-eight thousand red-coated troops—arms reversed, colors dipped—stood at attention along the route from Westminster Abbey to Paddington

Station, where the cortege would continue by train to Windsor Castle. Thousands of Londoners jammed the streets . . . filled the temporary stands . . . packed the roofs and windows that dripped with crepe. They pushed and strained and shoved—but rarely said a word. Long after all else was forgotten, people recalled the quiet of this solemn day.

At 9:30 A.M. the silence was broken by the dull boom of minute guns . . . the tolling of bells . . . the majestic strains of Chopin's "Funeral March." The procession began to move and the crowd shoved all the harder as the honor guards filed slowly by: Territorials . . . Indian Gurkhas . . . Royal Hussars . . . two coldly correct German naval captains . . . the magnificently uniformed Inspector of Cavalry of the Imperial Bulgarian Army. Next, the highest-ranking British officers— with Lord Kitchener more bristling than ever—and then the royal household itself: the gentlemen-at-arms, the Lord Chamberlain, the captains of the Yeomen of the Guard.

Now at last came the khaki-colored gun carriage, drawn by black horses instead of the usual creams. Atop the casket lay the crown and the insignia of the Garter. Just behind walked a riderless horse—Edward's favorite charger. But what tore every heart was the small white terrier that trotted mournfully in the rear. On his collar was the simple inscription: "My name is Caesar. I belong to the King."

The tears were soon forgotten in the stunning sight that came next— the mounted guard of kings and princes who had come to pay their last respects.

They were all there—George V, looking strangely small . . . the moth-eaten King of Greece . . . the dazzling Kaiser . . . the willowy young King of Portugal with his sad, weak face . . . nine kings and forty-four royal princes altogether. There were familiar monarchs like Alfonso XIII of Spain—and strange new figures like the stiff, reserved Archduke Franz Ferdinand of Austria. With curious perspicacity, the New York *Tribune* identified him as "destined to make history in southeastern Europe."

Behind this splendid assemblage rolled a dozen carriages—heavy with gilt and mourners. Queen Alexandra rode in the first, bowing and smiling from force of habit. Next, six more coachloads of royalty, including a Chinese prince or two. Then, far in the rear, an eighth carriage with three oddly contrasting figures. In the jump seat sat Prince Sanad Khan Montas es Sultaneh of Persia, looking withdrawn and frightened. Opposite him was French Foreign Minister Pichon, looking very animated. And alongside him sat the third figure, betraying no emotion whatsoever. The only man who wasn't gorgeously arrayed—just a civilian wearing evening clothes in the middle of the day—he seemed at first glance to be in the wrong procession. But those flashing teeth and glasses explained everything. Even in a closed carriage at the end of the line, no one could miss Theodore Roosevelt.

This time there were no vigorous gestures. He seemed stern, serious, perhaps bowed with grief. The New York *Tribune* felt he was "deeply interested." The *Times* found him "somber" . . . his face "very grave." But it took Conan Doyle, writing for the London *Daily Mail*, to do full justice to the Colonel's stoical bearing. Doyle carefully noted "the strong profile of the great American set like granite, as he leans back in his carriage."

"I laughed until I almost cried," Roosevelt later confided to President Taft, describing his experiences riding with Pichon and the Persian prince. In fact, the Colonel enjoyed the whole funeral immensely, and it was all he could to keep his solemn appearance. Not that he was callous; it was just that the occasion had long since lost its meaning as a funeral and was now a mammoth pageant. Kings and princes forgot their grief and jockeyed endlessly for position, prerogatives and political advantage. With no stake himself, Roosevelt sat back and enjoyed the show.

He had an especially good time at King George's reception the previous evening. The royal guests happily fawned on the famous American, asking his opinion on their various problems. Roosevelt was delighted to oblige. To one: "Oh, I would never have taken that step at all, if I had been in your place, Your Majesty!" To another: "That is just what I would have done; quite right!"

As they swarmed around, the Kaiser appointed himself Roosevelt's protector and did his best to ward off royal riffraff. When Czar Ferdinand I of Bulgaria sought a few words, Wilhelm blocked him off com-

THE GOOD YEARS

pletely: "That man is entirely unworthy of your acquaintance. I should not spend any time talking to him. He is a poor creature."

Through it all Monsieur Pichon kept sidling up, complaining about affronts to French national honor. As the only other representative from a republic, Pichon assumed that Roosevelt was a natural ally and desperately tried to win his support. The Colonel couldn't have cared less. Finally, when Pichon pointed out that their coachmen wore black instead of the usual red, Roosevelt said he was perfectly willing to have his man wear green with yellow spots. He paid a price for his levity: Pichon thought that Roosevelt not only agreed but was demanding green and yellow livery for himself.

Next morning Pichon was still complaining. He protested that their carriage was inferior . . . that the Chinese were placed ahead of them . . . that, even worse, the Persian prince ("ce Perse") was going with them. He then scrambled into the carriage to keep "ce Perse" from taking the seat of honor; and it was at this point that Roosevelt confessed he almost exploded with laughter.

Somehow he kept his dignity intact, leaving Doyle to create his flattering impression. Nothing else was as difficult—even the private audience with Queen Alexandra, when she persisted in describing how "wonderfully preserved" the royal undertaker had left Edward. It was difficult, though, and as the audience neared its conclusion Roosevelt found himself easily distracted by a series of squeals outside the chamber door. Emerging, he discovered his small friend Crown Prince Olaf of Norway.

Another romp was inevitable. Roosevelt tossed him in the air, rolled him on the floor, while the little boy shouted with delight. In the midst of the rumpus they glanced up to find the Empress Dowager of Russia standing in a doorway, staring at them. The Colonel guiltily stopped in his tracks, but Olaf wasn't in the least nonplused: "You aren't going to stop playing just for her, are you?"

Olaf, of course, was right. It really didn't matter. From the royal family down, everyone was delighted with the buoyant visitor. The English loved it when he teased the Cambridge undergraduates. They were delighted when he singled out the song of the blackbird while walking with Sir Edward Grey. They were astonished but secretly pleased when he offered some free advice on British policy in Egypt. "Roosevelt has turned us all upside down," wrote Cecil Spring Rice that June. "He has enjoyed himself hugely, and I must say by the side of our statesmen, he looks a little bit taller, bigger and stronger."

It was in fact part of a general awakening in England, a growing awareness of America. Until now the British had tended to be a little superior . . . to regard Americans as frontiersmen . . . or worse, as bores. The two countries might be of the same blood—and certainly should stand together on world issues—but generally speaking, "the States" had little to offer. Suddenly all this was changing.

Edward VII, of course, had helped with his penchant for Americans . . . especially pretty heiresses. So had old Pierpont Morgan—his Princes Gate establishment was anything but that of a frontiersman, or even a parvenu. Whatever the reasons, the evidence of this new interest was everywhere. Peary won acclaim for his polar triumph far beyond anything he enjoyed at home. The Wrights were lionized for their aerial feats. The Broadway hit *The Pink Lady* played to packed houses in the West End. American sportsmen were appearing on fields hitherto sacred to Englishmen; in 1909 the U.S. polo team defeated Britain for the first time in history.

Of course, not everything that came from America was welcome. When "Alexander's Ragtime Band" reached London in 1911, it launched a new kind of dancing that shocked Mayfair. The situation was not helped by the subsequent arrival of the Bunny Hug. The *New York Times* Society correspondent flashed back a stern warning: "There is a growing feeling of resentment among hostesses at the extraordinary dancing which is now obtaining among quite young people. The introduction of various coon dances is not approved of, and this is not to be wondered at."

Such warnings were important. For there was an awakening in America too. More and more people liked the British and wanted the British to like them. Old suspicions were dying, the old feeling of inferiority vanishing. It was no longer a crime "to act like an Englishman." In fact, the growing leisure class turned to Britain for its model. Giant new liners made it easy to see things first-hand, and the new

British outlook insured a friendly reception. Fashionable Americans came to feel as much at home on Park Lane as on Fifth Avenue or Bailey's Beach.

Edward's death strikingly illustrated how far this process had gone. "Blow to Social Season," ran a *New York Times* headline, declaring that the event was bound to change American plans. The *Tribune* went into greater detail, explaining that it was especially unfortunate because "The London season gave promise of proving more American than ever. King Edward's demise changes all this, and the season is virtually dead. The result will cause Americans to cancel their projects for spending the next few months in the British metropolis and recuperating afterward at Marienbad."

In England there were those who understood all too well. "London Fears American Exodus," ran the headlines, and it was little consolation to have Manager Kroell of the Ritz point out that things could be worse. "People must eat," he declared hopefully, "and those who don't have town houses simply must eat at hotels."

American Society suffered a further blow when King George indicated that the coronation would be held in October instead of the following spring. "This change," the *Tribune* declared, "bids fair to affect the plans of New York society almost as seriously as the death of Edward VII, for it will have the result of taking to London in the fall a number of well-known persons from here who are accustomed to spend the autumn at their country seats on Long Island, Westchester, and on the other side of the Hudson."

But everything turned out all right in the end. In a few days the coronation was again scheduled for June, 1911, as originally planned. Society sank back in relief, happy to settle for the novelty of an all-American summer.

As America and Britain drew closer, the evidence spread far beyond the Society columns. London's Berkeley Hotel took full-page space in the New York dailies. Bond Street clothing, leather, lace, and silver shops also advertised regularly. The steamship lines were represented as always, but there was no Madison Avenue message about "Half the fun is getting there." The day Edward died (and too late to take out) the Cunard Line ran a large advertisement in the New York *Post* boldly headed, "The London Season." It listed various coming events, carefully assuring the readers that the Royal Academy exhibit "may be termed a society function."

But the most spectacular feature of this Anglo-American entente was the marital spree it produced. Theodore Roosevelt might rant against it, but the flood of international marriages increased. By 1903 *McCall's* could list fifty-seven such matches. Now the flow was faster than ever—with a new and perhaps refreshing frankness in arranging the details.

"I have so far interested myself in the young people's affairs as to cable my representatives in London for information regarding the standing of the Collins family," millionaire John H. Parks told the New York *World*, as the city buzzed with rumors concerning his lovely stepdaughter Clara and the dashing Captain Charles Glen Collins, formerly of the Cameron Highlanders. Mr. Parks added that he had already met the captain's sister, "and there can be no possible doubt as to her high breeding."

In this case it wasn't necessary to prove the other essential ingredient—the bride's wealth. It was well known that Mr. Parks was rich. He had been in on some of "Bet-You-a-Million" Gates' best coups. And in the intricate labyrinth of business combinations, Parks was understood to be the key man in the "tack trust" and more recently, in the "wrapping paper trust."

The Parks-Collins affair was soon forgotten in the excitement surrounding the most brilliant of all these Anglo-American unions. On February 6, 1911, Vivien Gould, granddaughter of fabulous Jay Gould himself, married John Graham Hope Horsley-Beresford, D.S.O., fifth Lord Decies and Major of His Majesty's Seventh Hussars.

This one was really breathtaking. It was said that 225 seamstresses worked on the bride's trousseau. The cake alone cost $1,000, with its electric lights and tiny bisque cupids bearing the Decies' coat-of-arms. The presents were equally spectacular—Mrs. Stuyvesant Fish's gold toilet set for motoring . . . the Duke of Connaught's solid gold inkstand . . . the diamond coronet that George Gould gave his daughter for the coming coronation. As they pored over the details, most New Yorkers wallowed in sentimentality.

Most, but not all. "Cad that you are," an anonymous dissenter wrote the groom, "you are here to marry an American girl for a fortune that was made in America—that you may return to your native lair and there spend your days and this American girl's fortune. Well, let this convey to your mind the positive assurance that you are not going to marry Miss Gould (and get away with it). Not if well devised plans and positive determination may count—regardless of the cost."

On top of this came a challenge to a duel from one John Madison Thomas, who identified himself as "the scion of an ancient Virginia house." He explained that the step was inevitable "in view of your attention to the youthful and obviously unsophisticated daughter of an American house." When no ducal reply was forthcoming, the Virginia "scion" mailed carbons of his challenge to the press. The reporters got busy but could find no trace of him in the Social Register, or even the phone book.

Lord Decies took the threats lightly. He was inclined to think that the weapon for the duel should be chocolate éclairs. His corps of English ushers were less amused. "I wonder that the authorities in America allow these cranks," said Captain Edward Lamb of the Royal Life Guards. "They don't bother us much in England, because the bobbies take care of them good and well."

New York's finest did the next best thing. On the afternoon of the wedding they kept the uninvited a block from Saint Bartholomew's. Thousands pressed against the barriers, watched from rooftops, even climbed chimneys and lampposts with spyglasses, but only one group managed to break the blockade. Just before the ceremony, a flying squad of fifteen women dashed through the lines, raced into the church and began frantically plucking the Easter lilies from the nave. At this point, the Goulds fell back on their own resources. Dozens of private detectives—immaculately clad in cutaways and gloves—charged the invaders and wrestled them out of the building.

Less could be done about the guests themselves. As the bride came down the aisle, Society forgot its manners completely. Matrons and men-about-town jumped on the pews, clawed one another for a better view of the famous fifteen-foot train. In the melee one lady put her Parisian heel clear through an unidentified gentleman's topper.

After a three-month honeymoon, the newlyweds moved into the Decies ancestral home, where Vivien did her best to live like a titled English lady. To redo the place properly, she spent hours studying the paneling at the Victoria and Albert Museum, then hired only the best contractors. The $25,000 overcharge was perhaps inevitable, but English justice prevailed. "There are certainly real grounds for complaint," declared the judge. "When I sat in the drawing room I could hear a plug being pulled in a bathroom."

The coronation of George V was a far happier experience for Lady Decies. On June 22, 1912, she joined the other American peeresses in Westminster Abbey, where they made a sparkling addition to the pageantry of crowning a new king. "The Duchess of Roxburgh (nee May Goelet) and the Countess of Granard (nee Beatrice Mills)," gushed the New York *Tribune,* "supported America's reputation for perfection of costume and jewels."

Their fathers had seen to that, but most of the group gave themselves away by an awkward habit of clutching and straightening their coronets. Only the lovely Lady Ashburton seemed completely at home, and she was no heiress but Florence Belmont of the original Floradora sextet.

Still, it was a proud day for them all. Americans might be "everywhere," but few others made the Abbey. The unofficial guests were limited to two or three perennials like Pierpont Morgan, who arrived in full court dress—black velvet knee breeches, silver buttons and a sword.

"Mr. Morgan," whispered an English acquaintance, "what would people say if they saw you like this on Broadway?"

The old banker gave no answer but did manage a smile, perhaps at the thought he might ever be seen on Broadway at all. Then he slipped into his seat, which was farther back than last time—a sure sign that the old regime was over.

Morgan saw to it that he had no back seat at the procession that followed. He rented two floors of Gloucester House for $5,000—about equal to four months' rent. Alfred G. Vanderbilt paid another huge sum for the top floor of the same building, and jealous Londoners enjoyed the rumor that he was too high to see anything. Other fashionable Americans simply took hotel suites, stayed with their English in-laws, or attached themselves to the diplomatic colony. In an unguarded moment Mrs. John Hays Hammond, wife of the Special American Ambassador, generously announced, "I want all my American friends about"—dozens took her at her word.

As they watched the glittering troops, cheered the gilded coach, sighed over the Prince of Wales, these Americans felt they were more than mere visitors. That tingle didn't come from watching someone else's parade—in a very real sense, it was their coronation too. "Hands across the sea," enthused the New York *World,* "seldom have met so closely and warmly. Society is thrilled at the consciousness that it has helped make history."

Nor was this mood surprising. In the past ten years a large set of fashionable people had developed a pattern of life that went far beyond the boundaries of any one nation. Americans, British, and a sprinkling of Continentals, they lived an international life of their own . . . restlessly migrating from country to country, from season to season. They were extravagant, frivolous, often foolish, but they were perhaps the most truly cosmopolitan group the world has ever seen.

The coronation was a natural rallying point, but this set needed no special event to get together. Even when nothing was happening, they made their rounds; and even when they didn't do anything, they still were news. "Mrs. Stuyvesant Fish has made no plans to spend the summer in Europe," the New York Times breathlessly announced as the 1911 season approached.

Most of the group ran more true to form, and once the coronation was over resumed their regular orbit. In June it might be Newport, but more likely it was Paris, for it was already time for the racing at Longchamps.

In August, it was Cowes for the Regatta. Or perhaps Aix-les-Bains, or Lucerne, or the French channel resorts. In 1911 Dinard was especially popular, and here too the American influence was strong. Everyone danced the "Triple Boston," and all efforts failed to start something else . . . although not entirely due to the new step's beat. "An attempt was made this week to introduce the latest dance, The Tango," reported the *New York Times*; "after a few experiments, however, it was discarded, as the majority of dancers found it a little risque. . . ."

September found everyone "taking the cure" at Marienbad, Carlsbad, Homburg, and the other German baths. This was perhaps the most essential part of the whole routine, for at these resorts Society was literally flushed out and prepared for another year of Seasons. The "cure" could apparently do anything. According to an ad in the *Tribune,* Marienbad (Edward's favorite resort) was good for "Corpulence, gout, anemia, chronic appendicitis, constipation, arteriosclerosis, women's diseases, heart diseases, kidney trouble, nerves, etc."

Autumn was a time for Americans to return home. They entertained on weekends . . . served enormous breakfasts . . . played the new auction bridge . . . and when in town, caught up on the theatre. It was a miserable season on Broadway this fall, but those who suffered through *The Hen Pecks* at least discovered a thrilling new dancer named Vernon Castle.

New Year's, 1912, found the group on the go again. The restless Wideners and a few others gingerly nibbled at Palm Beach, but most fashionable Americans headed straight for the Riviera—Cannes, Nice, Menton, and above all, Monte Carlo. There they rejoined their English and Continental cohorts, who arrived on trains so luxurious that the passengers dressed for the dining car.

April, and the sun again touched Paris. One by one the great houses opened, and the usual round of salons and soirées began. The hotels were rapidly filling too, crowded with people returning from the south—Lord and Lady Decies at the Meurice . . . the John Jacob Astors at the Ritz. The Astors, however, would not stay long. One glance at the bride—or the proud, beaming colonel—quickly told why. "They will return to America," the *Times* coyly announced, "where an interesting event is likely to occur shortly."

Mrs. Charlotte Drake Martinez Cardeza was another fashionable

American heading back this April. In her case there was no impending "event," but she had been abroad ten months, and even the most inveterate members of the coterie liked to check home once in a while.

For Mrs. Cardeza this was no simple matter. Like the rest of the international set, she traveled with a fantastic amount of baggage. Every time she moved, fourteen trunks, four suitcases, three crates, and a medicine chest went along. Now it was time again. Once more her long-suffering maid packed the wardrobe that so accurately etched the world she knew—the latest creations from Worth . . . the blue satin tea gown from Ungar of Vienna . . . the white China silk waist from Carlsbad . . . the parasol from Lucerne . . . the ermine muff from Dresden . . . the baby lamb coat from St. Petersburg. It all added up to seventy dresses, ten fur coats, thirty-eight large feather pieces, twenty-two hat pins to keep them in place, ninety-one pairs of gloves, and innumerable trifles to amuse her, like the little Swiss music box in the shape of a bird.

Somehow it all was packed and loaded aboard the tender that bobbed out from Cherbourg in the early April twilight. Now as they chugged through the harbor, Mrs. Cardeza—like the Astors and everyone else there—must have felt the thrill that always comes with the start of an Atlantic voyage. No matter how often they did it—no matter how blasé they were about this endless round of Seasons—the ocean trip always seemed new and exciting. They felt it as they looked up from the tender at the forest of masts and funnels . . . the hundreds of portholes twinkling in the dusk . . . the bright ribbon of light that marked the promenade deck, lined with friends already on board.

And tonight there were many familiar faces in the crowd—people who had started earlier from Southampton. The George Wideners were there—they had gone to London for a suitable trousseau for their daughter Eleanor. So was Clarence Moore of Washington, who had been buying up English foxhounds for the Loudoun hunt . . . and Archie Butt, President Taft's stylish military aide.

The trip couldn't help but be fun, and all the more if you were young and attractive like Gretchen Longley of Hudson, New York, a pretty American student in Paris. In her little cabin she excitedly tore open a final bon voyage letter. It came from a friend left behind, who sent her a separate good wish for each day of the voyage:

Good weather
Refreshments (chocolate cakes)
Every desire
Tommies to burn
Chocolate ice-cream
Heavenly evenings
Entire meals
No regrets.

There was no chance to get farther than "chocolate ice cream," for this was the *Titanic,* and on the fifth night out the great new "unsinkable" liner had a rendezvous with ice in the black, lonely waters of the North Atlantic. Two hours later—while her band played pleasant music on the sloping deck—she slipped beneath the sea. In this most unbelievable of disasters, over fifteen hundred people were lost—including the cream of a confident, complacent Society that never felt completely sure of anything again.

1912

Women Triumphant

"Sensible and responsible women do not want to vote. The relative positions to be assumed by man and woman in the working out of our civilization were assigned long ago by a higher intelligence than ours."
—GROVER CLEVELAND

Lida Stokes Adams, a prominent advocate of woman's suffrage, took a dim view of the chivalry displayed on the sinking *Titanic*. "I think," she declared, "the women should have insisted that the boats be filled with an equal number of men."

For embattled feminists like Miss Adams, the disaster came at the worst possible time. They were planning a "mammoth" suffrage parade up New York's Fifth Avenue, to be held Saturday, May 4, 1912. Now—with the great day less than three weeks off—the *Titanic* raised all sorts of problems. The entire country was carried away by the gallantry of men who died that women might live. At such a time, how did it look to raise the cry of equal rights?

Some leaders like Lida Adams merely regretted that the woman passengers had failed to demand an equal chance to drown. But others felt that there was something ungrateful—almost blasphemous—about parading at this particular moment. Annie Nathan Meyer, founder of Barnard College, indignantly returned her pledge card, noting, "After the superb unselfishness and heroism of the men on the *Titanic,* your march is untimely and pathetically unwise."

It was decided to carry on, but now other fears arose. It was said that Tammany Hall, always against suffrage, planned to station rowdies along the line of march. It was rumored that the Socialist working girls hoped to make some political hay—wear red sashes and sing the "Marseillaise." And when Theodore Roosevelt declined "with thanks" an invitation to join the men's brigade, it seemed another ill omen. After all, the colonel had a reputation for sensing which way the wind blew.

And in fact, many people did have strong ideas on the subject. At the turn of the century, the American woman of the upper brackets lived (or was meant to live) a curious cocoonlike existence, lovingly preserved by the men in her life. "It is exceedingly bad manners," explained Edward Bok's *Ladies' Home Journal,* a leading proponent of shelter, "for a girl to slap a man on the back, or lay a hand upon him in any way, or for him to touch her except for a friendly handshake."

"Ladies" were guarded by maids, chaperones, or older gentlemen ever ready to "offer their services." The middle-class housewife was less elaborately convoyed, but she was also far less exposed. She was mostly relegated to a service function—basically dreary, even though one of her "services" was to provide, as always, the feminine love and support without which heroes fail. The working-class woman was nowhere at all . . . she was almost literally a slave whose reward if any was to be found in heaven.

Some, of course, had to work. But far better if they didn't. "Men," observed Henry Finck in the April, 1901, *Independent,* "want a girl who has not rubbed off the peach blossom of innocence by exposure to a rough world."

An emphatic answer came the following August when Anna Edna Taylor, a 160-pound Texas schoolmarm, shot Niagara Falls in a barrel. An unimportant achievement by an unknown woman, but a good opening gun for the revolution that was starting. The ladies just wouldn't stay put any longer. All kinds were bursting to the forefront—Carry Nation smashing saloons . . . Ida Tarbell dissecting business . . . Mrs. Thomas Hitchcock riding cross-saddle . . . Emma Goldman preaching anarchy . . . Jane Addams plunging into settlement work . . . and everybody's idol, the demure Gibson Girl, taking up golf and tennis.

Bewildered males found a dozen reasons for the eruption. The bicycle craze encouraged simpler clothes. New appliances gave housewives more leisure. Immigration brought in women who didn't know better. New office machinery meant that even a girl could be a secretary. Probably all played a part, but whatever the explanation, the march was on ... although frequently interrupted by cries of astonishment, indignation and sometimes the law.

"You can't do that on Fifth Avenue!" thundered one of New York's first mounted policemen at a lady cowering in the rear of an automobile, trying to sneak a cigarette. And he was right—she was promptly arrested. This was September 27, 1904; and four years later the police were still at it, when the city passed the Sullivan Ordinance forbidding women to smoke in public. But the ladies fought on, and by 1910 had invaded the White House itself. At an official dinner that January, Baroness Rosen, wife of the Russian ambassador, asked President Taft for a cigarette. As everyone watched, the President smilingly surrendered and sent his aide Archie Butt to borrow one somewhere. Thanks to the orchestra leader, Butt was successful and excitedly wrote the news that night to his sister-in-law Clara. "I am glad to say," he primly added, "that the American women did not indulge."

Clothes provided another lively battlefield. Bit by bit the women chipped away at the old restraints—the rainy day skirt in 1902, the hobble skirt in 1909. Yet there was always stubborn opposition. Dr. Edward Bruce of the New York Board of Education was particularly shocked by the trend to bloomers. Perhaps permissible in the privacy of a gym, but on a public playground they were certainly "giving the children a false notion."

On the beach, it was more than a controversy over costume. The question was the propriety of swimming itself. Traditionally a lady might dip and wade, but not much more. Now women were also demanding the freedom of the seas. In 1904 the magazine *Outing* capitulated, deciding that if they had to swim they should at least know how. "The beginner should first enter the water gradually," the editor advised, "wade out to her knees, to her waist, and finally to her neck. Then, stooping until she is entirely submerged, she should remain so for a second. For the first time or two it is permissible to close the nose with thumb and finger before sinking."

Automobiling was an even more exciting way to enjoy emancipation. The Gibson Girl soon appeared behind the wheel, crumpling the fender of a Richard Harding Davis–like male—whose only reaction was blind, instant love. It pointed up a theory which gained prompt and lasting acceptance: Women just weren't good drivers. On March 9, 1908, Mayor Markbreit of Cincinnati declared flatly: "No woman is physically fit to run an auto."

Markbreit was a politician, so it was perhaps no coincidence that woman's hardest battle was on the political front. Ever since the Civil War a small ardent band of suffragists led by pioneers like Susan B. Anthony and Elizabeth Cady Stanton had been fighting an uphill battle for the vote. After 480 campaigns they still could boast only four victories—Wyoming, Colorado, Utah, and Idaho. Now these old leaders were dying—Mrs. Stanton in 1902, Miss Anthony in 1906—and the opposition remained as implacable as ever.

To a certain extent the foe was organized, well-heeled, and a little sinister. The early suffragists were great reformers, and from this the more powerful lobbies drew the flattering deduction that all women voters would want reform. The timber, beef, and especially liquor lobbies fought hard against suffrage. But opposition also came from the most respectable quarters.

Bishop John H. Vincent, founder of the Chautauqua movement, thought that woman suffrage would deprive man of his most exalted role: "It is his glory to represent her. To rob him of this right is to weaken both." James M. Buckley, brilliant editor of the *Christian Advocate,* was a little less gallant: He felt that you couldn't tell one woman from another, and multiple voting would result.

"Jackasses," snorted Father Vaughan, a Boston priest, offering his opinion of women as voters. Others were more tactful, but there was no doubt how they felt. "We all know how much further women go than men in their social rivalries and jealousies," Grover Cleveland gently explained in the October, 1905, issue of the *Ladies' Home*

Journal. The ex-President went on to stress, "Sensible and responsible women do not want to vote. The relative positions to be assumed by man and woman in the working out of our civilization were assigned long ago by a higher intelligence than ours."

The place "assigned" to woman was, of course, The Home. To leave the home and enter the voting booth couldn't help but be disruptive. Some declared that women would lose their femininity. Humor magazines like *Life* depicted legions of tough battle-axes bullying meek little men; and in 1906 an unknown wit defined a suffragette as "one who has ceased to be a lady and not yet become a gentleman."

The suffragists' bitterest blow was that so many women were unsympathetic. Mrs. Charles B. Gulick of the Massachusetts Public Interest League asked, "Why add a perfectly useless body of voters?" Ida Tarbell (of all people) declared that it was simply unfair to ask women to do men's work. Mrs. Clarence H. Wildes distributed pictures showing a Denver lady accepting a box of chocolates in payment for her vote. Vassar girls paraded about the campus carrying mops, banging pans, singing "Home, Sweet Home." One of them also brandished a sign bearing the dark warning: "Remember that suffrage means office holding."

This, of course, referred to the worst fate of all. Women would not only stray from the home, but fall into the filth of political life. It made some ladies indignant just to think about it. As Gail Hamilton wrote, "Women have a right to claim exemption from political duty and responsibility; and men have no right to lay the burden upon them."

The "burden" of the ballot was a familiar American theme, but Englishmen were less protective. Watching the same struggle unfold in Britain, Sir Almroth Wright was anything but solicitous. The trouble was, he declared, women no longer knew their place. Too few learned about "the defects and limitations of the feminine mind." Too many suffered from "the failure to recognize that man is the master."

But the British women didn't seem to understand. "I shall spit at you!" screamed twenty-six-year-old Christabel Pankhurst at the perspiring constable trying to get her out of a 1905 political meeting in Manchester. Miss Pankhurst was being expelled for asking about votes for women, and her assault on the bobby was part of a careful plan. Her mother, Mrs. Emmeline Pankhurst, was a dedicated suffragist who had given up trying to win the ballot by sweet reason. Her group, the Women's Social and Political Union, would dramatize the cause by violence.

The idea caught fire immediately. Women flocked to Mrs. Pankhurst's green, white, and purple banner. Militancy spread—to use Lloyd George's rueful simile—"like hoof-and-mouth disease." The Suffragettes (as the *Daily Mail* christened them) stormed Parliament, heckled candidates, broke up political meetings everywhere. It did no good to try and keep them out—they hid under platforms, popped out of organ lofts, slipped in as messenger boys. And it was useless to arrest them. They seemed to thrive on night sticks, arm twisting, rabbit punches, and jail.

More was to follow. When Minister Haldane spoke at Liverpool's Sun Hall in 1909, the dashing Mary Leigh mounted the next-door roof with a hatchet, chopped up the slates, and hurled them down on the auditorium skylight. At the Lord Mayor of London's dinner that November, two Suffragettes got in disguised as charwomen, smashed a banquet hall window, and raised their howl of defiance. A little later Emily Davison started burning mailboxes, and at Great Western Station young Theresa Garnett whipped Winston Churchill with a riding crop.

The news spread across the Atlantic—an electric jolt to the drooping American movement. These Englishwomen were no burly Amazons or dowdy teachers: Mrs. Pankhurst was deftly graceful . . . Christabel had a radiant sprightliness . . . Lady Constance Lytton was as patrician as they came. They set American imaginations spinning.

The dedicated Harriot Stanton Blatch soon revamped her moribund group along English lines. Spirited young women like Alice Paul, a battling Quaker from Pennsylvania, quickly joined the fight. Mrs. O. H. P. Belmont—at loose ends since the death of her husband—rushed to London, picked up some pointers from the Pankhursts, returned to form her own Political Equality Association. Mrs. Clarence Mackay was not far behind. She, of course, couldn't be under Mrs. Belmont, so she set up the Equal Franchise Society. As the two squared off, old-line suffragists enjoyed a rare treat—all the money and ingenuity that once went into social rivalry were now poured into "the cause" instead.

Suffrage became fashionable. Attractive Society girls like Inez Milholland and Portia Willis entered the fold, adding a glamorous touch that was badly needed. And if there was still any doubt that the movement was feminine as well as feminist, it vanished the day Lillian Russell joined up.

An ever-growing army of young Progressives were also intrigued. They discovered that suffrage wasn't a mere political artifact left over from Abolitionist days. As practiced by the English, it was something new . . . part of that brighter world ahead—like initiative, referendum, recall, and direct primaries. Dreary clerics like the Reverend Buckley might still hang back, but the brilliant young Rabbi Stephen S. Wise saw it clearly. So did the engaging Foster Peabody and dozens of other enthusiastic reformers.

By 1910 Mrs. Blatch decided it was time for the Americans to try some dramatics of their own. She announced that her Women's Political Union would lead a parade down New York's Fifth Avenue. Not quite like smashing up Parliament, but still it was a start.

The other leaders were shocked. Militancy, it turned out, was inspiring—three thousand miles away. To walk down the middle of the street themselves was a different matter. The distinguished pioneer Dr. Anna Howard Shaw feared "so radical a demonstration." Mrs. Mackay pounded the table in helpless rage. Mrs. Belmont retired to Long Island, coldly announcing that "ill health" prevented her from attending.

Only a few hundred ladies were in line when America's first suffrage parade got under way on the afternoon of May 21. A cold, penetrating drizzle drenched the gowns of the college women, left the bunting wilted and soggy. A few younger girls like Portia Willis felt the exaltation of early Christians, but dozens deserted the ranks or took to limousines. Some of the scanty crowd clapped, more jeered, but for the most part, the women suffered the cruelest blow of all—they were ignored.

In 1911 Mrs. Blatch grimly announced they would try again. Once more Mrs. Belmont and Mrs. Mackay begged off. Once more the city looked the other way; Mayor Gaynor, invited to review the parade, refused to have anything to do with it.

Yet there were grounds for hope. During the past year Washington had gone for suffrage—the first state since 1896—and this time the weather was mild and sunny. On Saturday, May 6, about three thousand women were ready at the appointed time, awaiting only the signal to march.

"Young man," exploded seventy-year-old Emma Butterworth Danforth several hours later, "if you say anything to make this parade look ridiculous, I'll never forgive you." The *Tribune* reporter was only too happy to surrender: "Her warning was unneeded. One cannot ridicule one's grandmother."

But it was all too clear that the parade had again been less than successful. Although the crowds were certainly bigger, the jeering was far worse. "The barber shop wit was out in force," the New York *Tribune* observed, "and the brass foundry humorist manned every street corner, bellowing his ancient and bewhiskered jests at the loudest of his raucous voice."

The ninety-four members of the Men's League for Woman Suffrage, who bravely marched as a unit, suffered especially. "Lizzie!" was the mildest thing they heard, and as they passed the Waldorf, a wet Turkish towel came hurtling down from above. Nor did it help when Oswald Garrison Villard was assigned to carry a banner that read, "Men have the vote—why not we?"

Most galling of all, the parade didn't start on time. Scheduled to begin at 3:30, it didn't get under way until 4:10. True, there was a good excuse—the weary tail-enders of a marathon race still monopolized the avenue—but few people swallowed that. Everyone knew that women were never on time; that was one more reason why they shouldn't vote.

Yet the movement would not die. Sometimes a brave try can achieve more than a gaudy triumph, and even the opposition *New York Times* conceded that the women "did not lose but gained respect." That November they won California, and as 1912 dawned new campaigns were launched in six Western states. Across the ocean their English allies also stepped up the attack. On March 1 the Suffragettes smashed shop windows all over London's West End; a few days later Nurse Pitfield introduced a new note by trying to set fire to the General Post Office. Lecturing in Michigan, Sylvia Pankhurst noted that the new British outbreaks stirred tremendous excitement . . . but serious misgivings too.

Suffrage was in fact at the crossroads. California had been won—but by the narrowest of margins. If the outlook was bright in Oregon, it was all too dark in Wisconsin. Militancy clearly surpassed the old debating society approach, yet pushed too far it might be disastrous.

No wonder the leaders were on edge as the day of the 1912 parade drew near. No wonder they worried about the *Titanic,* Socialist demonstrations, and Colonel Roosevelt's absence. And as if all that wasn't enough, a host of little things went wrong. The Finnish delegation, subjects of the Czar, refused to appear under the Russian flag. Mrs. Clarence Mackay again said she wouldn't march. The lovely Inez Milholland—suffrage's answer to the Amazon charge—came down with a bad cold and was ordered to bed by her doctor. All the women were up in arms against the official 37-cent hat, lovingly if impractically concocted to give the parade some semblance of uniformity.

"Uniformity of dress was the dream of artists for us," Mrs. Blatch conceded in her final orders the night before the parade. Then she added a bright thought: "Distaste for conforming may be but the promise of independence in a future voter."

Mrs. Blatch had come a long way as a diplomat. Daughter of the sainted Elizabeth Cady Stanton, normally she was fiercely inflexible in the old feminist tradition. She had fought this fight on every front— even battling the English school system for giving the girls easier arithmetic than the boys. She was not known for her open mind, but this time was different. It was so important to co-operate that she buried her instincts, working smoothly and tactfully with a dozen willful groups. She was even willing to compromise with Mrs. Jean Penfield, whose Woman's Suffrage Party wanted a torchlight parade so badly. Mrs. Blatch stuck them at the end of the line, where they could march in the dark to their hearts' content.

On only one point was she absolutely adamant. The parade must start on time—"at five o'clock and not one minute later." There must be no repetition of last year's tardiness—the howls of male derision still rankled. "Remember," she beseeched in her final instructions, "the public will judge, quite illogically of course, but no less strictly, your qualification as a voter by your promptness."

At exactly 4:57 P.M. on the sunny afternoon of May 4 two long bugle blasts sounded above the bedlam that swirled around New York's Washington Square. "They're coming! They're coming!" cried the crowd that lined Fifth Avenue. And sure enough, at 5:00 on the dot, a cavalry detachment clattered past Washington Arch (known by the zealots as "Martha Washington Arch") and swung up the Avenue.

Fifty women made up this mounted vanguard. A year ago none had been willing to ride; now they wore three-cornered hats at a cocky angle and some even sat astride their horses. Proudly leading the troop was Mrs. Charles E. Knoblauch, whose husband had appropriately been a Rough Rider. But most eyes were focused on the girl just behind her. There, miraculously risen from her sickbed, was the radiant Inez Milholland.

Years afterward it would be difficult to decide just how beautiful Miss Milholland really was. According to legend, she inspired at least one novel and her glance could reduce the toughest legislator to a blushing schoolboy. On the other hand, a contemporary recalls, "She was stylish and attractive but not that remarkable." It is a matter of record, however, that in 1910 Miss Milholland's mere appearance was enough to break up a Republican rally.

On this lovely May afternoon she was at her best. A photographer dashed up for a picture and by the time she could break away the cavalry was two blocks ahead. Galloping to catch up, she got a big hand from the crowd. A small incident perhaps, but it showed an important change that was taking place. This year instead of the usual good-natured hoots, the people were cheering.

"Everybody's Doing It" the Old Guard Band played, marching just behind the cavalry; and as the cheering spread, it finally seemed that the song might be right. Just after the band came Grand Marshal

Josephine Beiderhase of the Women's Political Union ... then Eleanor Brannan, carrying the WPU banner of green, white, and purple. Traditionally the suffrage color was yellow, but Mrs. Blatch had scornfully tossed it aside. She felt that everything about the old movement was insipid, and for her organization she adopted the colors of Britain's militant Suffragettes.

Indomitable as ever, Mrs. Blatch herself marched just behind the flag with her executive committee. Having urged everyone to wear white, she turned up in her black Vassar cap and gown. The inconsistency went unnoticed; for they were pouring by now—political workers from Albany ... the group from Finland (having finally found a Finnish flag) ... two hundred trained nurses in their starched uniforms ... Mrs. Otis Skinner and the actresses ... teachers ... the Washington Irving High School students in their middy blouses ... Ida Freese and her tearoom girls ... band after band thumping out "What Am I Going to Do to Make You Love Me?"

"Boilermakers!" roared a dissident at the corner of Thirtieth Street.

"Frankfurter makers!" added a companion.

"I'd like to bite their ears off!" shouted still another in the group.

Three detectives rushed over and arrested them for disorderly conduct. This too was something new. In the past, the women were fair game for taunts and insults—the cruder the better. Now the crowd cheered as the hecklers were hauled off to the stationhouse.

The parade rolled on—typists ... chocolate dippers ... tired factory girls from the East Side sweatshops ... then an open carriage covered with lilacs and dogwood blossoms. Half buried in the flowers sat a wrinkled old lady waving a white shawl. It was the Reverend Antoinette Brown Blackwell, eighty-seven years old and the last of the 1848 suffrage pioneers. Originally, it was planned to have twenty maidens draw the carriage, but Mrs. Blackwell was shocked. "Let women be beasts of burden?" she cried. "Why, I wouldn't even let a man do a thing like that."

Representatives from the six suffrage states followed, drawing almost as much attention. The crowd pushed and shoved, trying to get a better look at a real live woman voter.

Next came a chipper little figure walking alone in cap and gown. It was Anna Howard Shaw leading her National Woman Suffrage Association. These were the people Mrs. Blatch called soft—but there was nothing weak about them today. They wore their yellow daisies and jonquils and buttercups with martial pride. They even kept step. Dr. Shaw herself was waving and smiling at everyone. High above her head she held a small sign. Referring to Peking's current experiment with universal suffrage, the message said simply, "Catching up with China."

This breezy slogan clearly followed Mrs. Blatch's shrewd advice: "As this is an advertising age, leaders of any movement do well to study somewhat the methods of the press agent." Most of the banners, however, showed the need for further study: "By Keeping Women out of Politics, the Soul of Our Country Is Diminished by One-Half" ... "A Democracy That Recognizes Man Only Is a Dangerous Error" ... "To Create Sex Antagonism Is an Unwise Precedent."

It was twilight now, but still the women flowed past—the non-suffrage states, including a group unaccountably from the Argentine Republic ... Miss Annie Peck, the noted mountain climber ... Mrs. Marie Stewart, portraying that original Suffragette, Joan of Arc. As Mrs. Mackay's Equal Franchise Society marched by, everyone noticed that its fashionable leader had again remained aloof. But this year she at least chose her marshal well. Miss Elizabeth Burchenal of the Public School Athletic League was a master at precision drilling; her charges put on a great show.

"Where are your trousers?" cried a caustic Englishman who had somehow turned up in the crowd near St. Patrick's Cathedral. The writer Inez Haynes Gilmore darted from the ranks, grabbed him by the shoulder, gave him a piece of her mind. The crowd laughed its approval, once again showing its change of heart. The march continued, the bands played on—"Oh, You Beautiful Doll" ... "Some of These Days You're Gonna Miss Me, Honey" ... "What's the Matter with Father?"

The music was lost in the uproar that greeted the next contingent. To an ever-swelling tumult of cheers, catcalls, and yells of pure excitement, the Men's League for Woman Suffrage came swinging into view. Led by the Parkville Fife & Bugle Corps, they marched with heads erect, eyes front—just as Mrs. Blatch had ordered. No longer a beleaguered handful, this year 619 men proudly flaunted the daisies that symbolized their cause.

Nor were they just the innocent crackpots described by anti-suffragists. Leaders in every conceivable field turned up. Hardened politicians like W. C. Amos, head of the 19th District Republican Club, marched with the poet Richard Le Gallienne. Montague Glass, author of the trivial *Potash and Perlmutter,* strode beside economist Henry Rogers Seager. And still they came—philosopher John Dewey ... Rabbi Wise ... two troops of Boy Scouts ... Robert Bruere, expert in that interesting new field, industrial relations . . . nine Harvard undergraduates ... editor Max Eastman ... T. E. Mahan, the admiral's son . . . an unidentified grandfather carrying a baby.

"That's what the rest of us will be doing soon!" shouted a heckler, and whatever the rules on insulting women, it was clear the men were still a valid target:

"Who got the breakfast this morning?"

"Don't forget to do the dishes tonight!"

"Oh, you daisies!"

But rising above the taunts was the strange new sound of cheering. The men had never heard it before, and it was not a bad sensation. More pleasant surprises lay ahead. As they passed the Waldorf, instead of last year's wet towel they were greeted with applause. As they marched by the Union League Club, some of the old gentlemen in the windows even waved. And when they reached Delmonico's, they got the biggest jolt of all. The popular humorist Gelett Burgess, famous for his attacks on the cause, was leaning out the window, tirelessly waving a large yellow suffrage banner.

It was dusk by the time the Woman's Suffrage Party came tramping by. They had wanted a torchlight parade and now they got it. Grand Marshal Augusta Hughston waved an electric torch, and instantly the long line blazed with flares and Japanese lanterns. In the flickering glare, the women swept on—Mrs. George Arliss with the 15th Assembly

District brigade . . . a big yellow auto scattering leaflets . . . shirtwaist workers from the Woman's Trade Union League. In the fading light it was difficult to see the banners carried by the factory girls, and perhaps—for the sake of harmony—it was just as well. One of them ignored suffrage entirely, simply depicted a poor woman crushed by a capitalist pig tagged "Exploitation." But at least the union didn't carry out its threat to turn the affair into a Socialist rally. The band that played the "Marseillaise" the loudest belonged to Mrs. Mackay.

In the gathering darkness no policeman recognized the dumpy little lady who slipped through the barrier at Forty-first Street, as the Political Equality Association came marching by. Her white silk suit was three years old; her huge white hat was no more outrageous than any of the others; she seemed just another late recruit. But the women knew, and as she took her place in line, a great shout went up. Mrs. O. H. P. Belmont—that devastating autocrat who despised the mere idea of marching in public—had joined the parade.

She walked alone, at the head of the brigade. She seemed cool, poised, completely unperturbed. It was only years later that she confessed to her daughter Consuelo, "To a woman brought up as I was, it was a terrible ordeal."

Certainly no one knew it that night. When Mrs. Belmont did something, it was done with all the boundless energy and tactical skill she possessed. It was that way when she took on Mrs. Astor and successfully stormed Society. It was that way when she married off Consuelo to the Duke of Marlborough. It was the same in this parade. She deftly bolstered her unit by stealing a whole brigade of Swedes from Mrs. Blatch. She angrily turned on a tired patrolman, who wasn't giving her girls enough marching room: "The police protection is most inadequate!"

But for once, someone was up to her. "Never mind, lady," the officer replied. "Next year you'll all be policemen."

It certainly looked that way. The women stormed Carnegie Hall, where the march ended, and speaker after speaker promised the birth of a new era. When Mrs. Blatch was interrupted by a Tammany heckler (the only one who dared appear), the audience howled, "Eat him alive!"

—and seemed to mean it. Other lady orators mounted soap boxes on almost every Broadway corner and harangued fascinated crowds far into the night.

"Woman suffrage marched yesterday in the most significant demonstration ever attempted by it in this country," the *World* declared next morning. "The greatest demonstration of women in all American history," proclaimed the *Tribune*. And all the papers noted the immense change in the crowd's mood from a year ago. "The march stirred the minds of the beholders as no other pageant seen in the city streets had done," the *Press* observed; "Manhattan was brought for the first time to a realization of the strength of the suffrage movement, its universality, and its grip on the minds of its adherents."

Typical was the reaction of Inspector McCluskey, in charge of the police detail. The inspector was a seasoned veteran . . . he had seen lots of parades . . . he wasn't moved easily. But now, surveying the yellow streamers, the confetti, the litter left in the wake of the march, he could only say, "It's about time to give them the vote. I wish to God they would. I'd be with them."

The opposition *New York Times* understood all too well. "The situation is dangerous," the editor warned. "We often hear the remark nowadays that women will get the vote if they try hard enough and persistently; and it is true that they will get it, and play havoc with it for themselves and society, if the men are not firm and wise enough and—it may as well be said—masculine enough to prevent them."

It was a voice from the grave. The day had passed for putting the issue in terms of masculinity. If the parade accomplished nothing else, it convinced people that the suffragists weren't merely a band of hulking females trying to wear the pants in the family. The long ranks of shop girls, factory workers, nurses, clerks, artists, housewives—to say nothing of Inez Milholland—were proof enough of that.

This great mixture was important. For the affair also offered dramatic proof that suffrage wasn't merely Society's latest toy. "All classes of women were in that parade," the *Tribune* pointed out. "This is the significant thing for politicians and 'antis' to stop and think about —that all classes are united in this fight for a principle."

"The solidarity of womanhood," Mrs. Blatch called it, and to the suffragists the thought carried far beyond the fight to get the vote. After that was won, the women would continue working together for a better, finer, more beautiful world. It never occurred to them that they might be absorbed into the Democratic and Republican parties. On the contrary, they would vote as a bloc. There would be Democrats, Republicans—and Women. In this alignment the women would hold the balance, always throwing their weight on the side of truth and light. United this way, there was no limit to the good they could do.

As a starter, they would end crooked politics. They were sure they could do it, although they admitted it would be a hard fight. "The lowest grade of politician," explained Mrs. Laidlaw of the Suffrage Party, "the one who is on the side of graft and corruption, which he knows will end when the women vote, he'll get into his war clothes and fight us harder than ever." But the battle would continue until finally, as the writer Belle Squire put it, "the boss shall be no more."

The knell would also sound for prostitution. "That is one question the women could settle if they had votes!" cried the Reverend Anna Garlin Spencer at the Carnegie Hall rally. Dr. Shaw had an even better idea: "If you want the 'white slave' traffic stopped in New York, give us a woman Police Commissioner."

And all this was only the beginning. The women would close the saloons. They would stop government waste. They would introduce a new note of economy. (After all, the argument ran, government is just another form of housekeeping.) Best of all, they would end war —what woman would vote to send her son off to be shot?

And now it was all within their grasp. The parade left no doubt. Over 15,000 marchers, against a mere 3,000 last year; 500,000 cheering spectators, against an indifferent handful in 1911. Yes, that glorious afternoon made it clear that the battle would be won. Perhaps not this year . . . maybe not next . . . but it was coming, it was coming.

No wonder Mrs. Edith Seldon Rogers of the WPU felt so exalted: "Never was the outlook brighter for the welfare of humanity." No wonder the women of Pittsburg, Kansas, chose such a special way to celebrate their victory the following November. When word spread that Kansas had definitely gone for suffrage, the ladies gathered around a great community bonfire. Then, at a given signal, they threw their old bonnets into the blaze. As the flames rolled skyward, all of them could plainly see the passing of the old and the coming of a golden new day.

1912

Big Man off Campus

"We are witnessing a renaissance of public spirit, a reawakening of sober public opinion, a revival of the power of the people, the beginning of an age of thoughtful reconstruction that makes our thoughts hark back to the age in which democracy was set up in America."
—WOODROW WILSON

"I'm a Bryan man," chirped the dedicated suffragist Mrs. Mary Arkwright Hutton of Spokane, Washington. Mrs. Hutton was more than that; she was one of only two woman delegates at the 1912 Democratic Convention in Baltimore. As such, she attracted even more attention than her scarlet suit and awesome straw hat would naturally warrant. Everywhere she went, reporters crowded around, plying her with questions. Since Bryan said he wasn't running, how did she feel about Woodrow Wilson, Governor of New Jersey, former president of Princeton, and the cherished hope of reformers, Texans, and all true sons of Old Nassau?

"No man," Mrs. Hutton declared, "who has been a schoolmaster all his life is quite big enough to be President of the United States."

A lot of people felt the same way. After all, until he was elected Governor in 1910, what had Wilson done? Erudite son of a Southern clergyman, he had indeed spent most of his life in the cloistered halls of Johns Hopkins, Bryn Mawr, Wesleyan, and his own alma mater

Princeton. True, he proved a dazzling college president, but did even that prepare a man for the White House? Wilson himself dryly observed that college politics were the best preparation of all, but many remained unconvinced.

Others had different complaints. Dean Andrew F. West, who had defeated Wilson's own plan for the Princeton Graduate School, felt he was dictatorial and deceitful. Old Tigers, who saw their eating clubs threatened by Wilson's drive for college "quadrangles," were sure he was a dangerous radical. Editor George Harvey of *Harper's Weekly,* who was bumped off the original Wilson-for-President bandwagon, thought he was ungrateful. New Jersey boss Big Jim Smith, who put Wilson over as governor, sadly discovered he wouldn't play ball. And William Allen White had a Kansan's suspicion of anyone with a handshake "like a ten-cent pickled mackerel in brown paper."

Yet the Wilson movement rolled on, for he also had qualities that thousands of Americans found irresistibly appealing. If he was aloof, he could certainly unbend—take that cakewalk he danced with Senator Frelinghuysen. If he looked professorial, he was also the man who once coached the Wesleyan football team. And though his words were often lofty, he remained a master at rough-and-tumble campaign speaking. Who could forget the night in Jersey City when he derided the state bosses as "warts on the body politic"?

Above all there was that magic touch with people . . . that art of making them want to join him—work with him—in bringing about a better day. He had a curiously convincing way of linking everything he believed with human progress, and he could make any goal seem so exciting—so easy to reach—that men could hardly wait to follow him, wherever he might lead.

It had always been that way. As Princeton's president, he electrified the men he wanted for his faculty. "Had Woodrow Wilson asked me to go with him while he inaugurated a new university in Kamchatka or Senegambia," declared the young English preceptor Robert K. Root, "I'd have said yes without further question."

And there was that night in Trenton in 1910 when Big Jim Smith put him over as Democratic candidate for Governor. Smith thought

Wilson would be an easily-handled puppet, but the candidate accepted the nomination with a ringing declaration of independence. Reformers who had bitterly fought him an hour before listened in astonishment. Joe Tumulty cried to Dan Fellows Platt, "Dan, this is one of the happiest days of my life!" Judge Crandall, another liberal who had fought Wilson's nomination, waved his cane with joy: "I am sixty-five years old and still a damned fool!" All over the Taylor Opera House men wept and shouted, "Thank God, at last a leader has come!" Long after Wilson had finished his speech, they stood on their seats and in the aisles crying, "Go on, go on!"

It was the same in 1911, as he toured the country expressing his ideas, seeking the support that would make him President. The message was simple enough—the cure for the evils of democracy was more democracy; not controls, but greater freedom. Yet it was not the doctrine but the way he said it that stirred men's souls. He spoke in Denver the night the first long-distance line was hooked up with the East. Marking the occasion, a reporter phoned from New York and asked perfunctorily, "What is the news in Denver?" Back over the wire came the faint, static-filled answer: "The town is wild over Woodrow Wilson!"

It was this way everywhere—immense crowds and enthusiasm—and perhaps that was just the trouble. The party's conservative block had never taken to Woodrow Wilson's lofty talk; these huge ovations made them worry more than ever. The big city machines took one look and knew they could never control the man—it would be New Jersey all over again. Still other leaders—slighted by the tactless Governor somewhere along the way—watched the ovations with growing jealousy. It was all very well for the New York *World* to say that ingratitude was a cardinal virtue in a politician, but "Marse Henry" Watterson of the Louisville *Courier-Journal,* who had felt Wilson's cold shoulder, didn't think so at all.

By March, 1912, new candidates were blooming like the spring blossoms. There was Ohio's Governor Judson Harmon, choice of most staunch conservatives. There was Indiana's bland, amiable Governor Thomas R. Marshall. There was the South's favorite son, Oscar W.

Underwood, Congressman from Alabama and the only man who, if locked in a closet, could still come up with a perfect tariff schedule.

And most important of all, there was Missouri's Champ Clark—Speaker of the House . . . old-time liberal . . . party wheelhorse . . . choice of William Randolph Hearst . . . ringing orator whose slightly dog-eared lecture "Signs of the Times" had echoed through a hundred county fairs.

Clark had come from nowhere this spring, easily overtaking Wilson's early lead. The Governor had popular appeal, all right, but it couldn't beat organization. Clark lieutenants knew every district leader from Bangor to San Diego. Even his black slouch hat and his long, old-fashioned coat seemed to spell party regularity. In four momentous weeks he swept eleven primaries, picked up 324 delegates.

Now, as the delegates began coming to Baltimore the week before the convention opened, Clark men swarmed all over town. An advance headquarters blossomed at the Emerson Hotel on June 20. The Speaker's good friend William Randolph Hearst moved into an adjoining suite. Supporters from Clark's home state Missouri poured from a stream of special trains, scarcely noticing the Democratic emblem of two thousand flowers that the B & O groundkeeper had lovingly planted on the slopes of Mount Royal station. Up and down Charles Street they marched, singing and shouting the song that had become their man's trademark:

I don't care if he is a houn',
You gotta quit kickin' my dawg aroun'.

Wilson fortunately didn't have to hear it. He had gone to the Governor's summer cottage at Sea Girt, New Jersey, to sit out the convention. Here he was exasperating his family and staff with an attitude of exaggerated indifference. But his worried supporters in Baltimore grew frantic as the Clark boom continued to build up steam. One frustrated Wilson delegate seriously considered getting a hound dog and kicking him around Bolton Street just to see what would happen. The Clark men were wild enough, he was warned; don't stir them up any more.

Outyelled, but possessing certain advantages of his own, Tammany Boss Charles F. Murphy rolled into town on the evening of June 21. With him on his special train came New York's ninety delegates—a group of cheerful men who amiably discussed their preferences. Most were for Harmon, but they freely admitted they would do whatever the Big Chief ordered. On the way down they were summoned from time to time to his drawing room. When they emerged, they always seemed quieter than before.

Perhaps this was natural. Charlie Murphy was the most reticent of men. Not at all the traditional brassy type of boss, he was polite and silent. His political demise had been predicted for years, but he always grew stronger. Now he had moved from saloonkeeper to water-front man to country gentleman. The new role went well with his courtesy, his pleasant smile, his nice gray eyes. There was absolutely nothing sinister about him. He was just awfully quiet.

Sitting in the drawing room, he politely parried a reporter's questions. Who would get New York's ninety votes? "I really don't know." Could he give any hint? "Any good man . . ."

Later he briefly dropped his guard. When Mrs. Borden Harriman cornered him in the Emerson and asked why he wasn't for Wilson, Murphy answered softly, "The boys don't want him."

The delegates were pouring in now—loud Westerners in their soft felt hats . . . Princeton students yelling for Wilson . . . Cap Mitchell, who walked the whole way from Oklahoma with a Clark houn' dawg. The Cook County Democratic Club of Chicago arrived behind a fifty-piece band, defying the heat with toppers, Prince Alberts and white four-in-hands. New York delegate August Belmont quietly holed up in the Belvedere Hotel. His Wall Street friend, Thomas Fortune Ryan, mysteriously turned up in the Virginia delegation—the state convention thought it had elected his son. Mississippi's colorful Senator-elect James K. Vardaman swaggered about in a cream-colored flannel suit, roaring the virtues of Oscar Underwood.

And people listened, for these days the South was riding high. It had at last recovered from the Civil War; it had not yet run into the problems that undermined its political power a generation later. At the moment, Georgia had more delegates than California; Kentucky more than Connecticut and Oregon combined. No one ever said, "You can't elect a Southerner."

Vardaman himself mirrored this Southern resurgence. His flowing locks and even more flowing speech carried over the old days; his cocky manner reflected the new. He was a bundle of contradictions, drawing a fascinated audience wherever he appeared. What sort of campaign lay ahead? "Progressive, of course!" How about the colored vote? "Why, sir, every patriotic white man knows that God never intended a Negro to take part in the government of this or any other country."

A very different type of Southerner was William Gibbs McAdoo, who arrived on June 22. McAdoo grew up in Georgia, moved to New York, built the Hudson Tubes, and earned a reputation as a progressive by his startling slogan, "The public be pleased." He was one of the first on the Wilson bandwagon, and during the past year had grown closer and closer to the Governor.

Checking into campaign headquarters at the Emerson, McAdoo was appalled at what he found. There just didn't seem to be anyone in charge. Wilson's manager, William McCombs—always jealous and high-strung—was now a nervous wreck. He had so little to offer bosses like Taggart of Indiana and Sullivan of Illinois, and they always wanted so much. Good steady Joe Tumulty, who might have been a help, was holding Wilson's hand at the Governor's cottage in Sea Girt. The only real professional, the mysterious Texan Colonel Edward M. House, was in mid-Atlantic on the Cunarder *Laconia*. The frail colonel felt he had done all he could and was now bound for a vacation in Europe. He left behind instructions for such details as "flying squadrons" on the convention floor, but what good did they do at this point? Wilson had less than a third of the delegates . . . not even enough to exercise a veto.

And yet there was hope. There had to be, with that vast groundswell of support throughout the country. The voters wanted him—everyone knew that. But the barriers of pledged delegates had to be broken. The time-honored mechanics of the convention had to be thrown aside. The

torrent of popular support had to be let loose by something—or someone.

On the afternoon of June 23 a balding, pasty-faced man in a
crumpled alpaca coat stepped off the train at Baltimore's Union Station
and blinked at the crowd rushing toward him. William Jennings
Bryan—three times Democratic candidate, three times disastrous loser
—was meant to be all through . . . a thoroughly shopworn standard-
bearer. Woodrow Wilson privately called him "The Great Inevitable."
Yet to the thousands who now swarmed around him, he clearly remained "The Great Commoner" . . . "The Peerless Leader."

They swept him along the platform, up the stairs, out into the street
where a touring car was waiting. He sat in back, smiling and waving
as the crowd lining Charles Street passed the word along: "Here he
comes! Here comes the Leader!" It was twilight by the time the procession reached the Belvedere, but for William Jennings Bryan the sun
was far from setting.

In the lobby ardent party leaders climbed on chairs, the cigar counter
—even the office safe—carried away by excitement. On the ninth floor
bellboys and chambermaids joined the horde of well-wishers who
cheered him to his suite. Inside it was a madhouse. Wherever he
stayed, Bryan's rooms were always as public as a railroad station—the
door open, strangers milling in and out—this time was no exception.
In one corner Mrs. Bryan desperately fended off reporters: "You can
look at me if you want, but I won't answer any questions." In the
center, Bryan himself embraced the blind Senator Gore of Oklahoma.
Outside, a grizzled sentry in blue flannel shirt vainly tried to keep
some sort of order. But the uproar continued, and above the general
din came the distinct cry, "Bryan, our next President!"

This was the last thing he wanted, he insisted. As he told his wife,
"The other boys have been making their plans; I would not step in
now." He was just here as a delegate from Nebraska . . . just here to
help choose a truly progressive candidate . . . just here to make sure
there was no repetition of the Republican Convention in Chicago.
There, as a special correspondent, Bryan saw the Old Guard steam-
roller Taft through . . . then watched the Roosevelt progressives stalk

out to form a new party. This must not happen to the Democrats. If they were to win, Bryan felt they had to be united behind the type of liberal he thought the country wanted.

Yet there were already signs of trouble. While Bryan was still in Chicago word came that the Democratic National Committee planned to install Judge Alton B. Parker as temporary chairman of the convention. A small matter to most men—the job was honorary and only lasted a day—but not to Bryan. Parker was New York's choice; he stood for Augie Belmont, Thomas Fortune Ryan, Tammany, all those conservative Easterners who led the party to ruin in 1904. Convinced they were trying to seize control again, Bryan wired the leading progressive candidates to help him block the move.

A hot potato for them all. If they joined him, they risked any hope of getting those ninety New York delegates; if they refused, they risked the wrath of the Peerless Leader. Marshall preferred a shot at the ninety delegates and came out firmly for Parker: "I do not see how his selection will result in a reactionary platform in 1912." Clark tried to play it safe—a vague appeal to avoid controversy "in the interest of harmony." At Sea Girt Wilson hesitated for hours. Tumulty begged him to back up Bryan; McCombs urged him to dodge the whole mess. Finally he turned to his family. It was his wife Ellen who broke the ice: "There must be no hedging."

Sitting on the edge of his bed, the Governor then took a pencil and began scribbling his answer to Bryan: "You are quite right. . . ."

At Wilson headquarters on the tenth floor of the Emerson, McCombs was appalled when he read the reply. He always felt that the Governor's only chance lay in winning over the big party bosses. Now it would be harder than ever. He threw himself on a bed and lay there sobbing.

McAdoo stood uneasily by, fumbling for something to say—he never knew what to do with weeping men. Besides, he felt that Wilson had done the right thing. McCombs looked up and blurted brokenly "All my work has gone for nothing."

He slowly rose and moved to the window. Down below the Clark legions were marching—neat ranks of political club members, proudly swinging their canes. They were the men that Wilson needed, the powerful men so hard to catch. "The Governor," sighed McCombs, "can't afford to have a row."

"The Governor," answered McAdoo, "can't afford to have anything but a row." By now he was convinced that Wilson's chance lay not in winning the machines but beating them. "The bigger the row the better for us."

At exactly 12:16 P.M. on Tuesday, June 25, Democratic National Chairman Norman E. Mack called the convention to order in Baltimore's Fifth Regiment Armory. Over fifteen thousand delegates and spectators were packed in the hall, but it's safe to say that not one of them heard him. That electronic miracle, the public address system, had yet to be invented; anyone who wanted attention depended on megaphones, lungs of leather, and endless patience.

At 12:20 Mack was still pounding his gavel. Completely oblivious of the hammering, Delegate Platt of New Jersey stood directly below, tossing bananas to the crowd. The fruit made a pungent contribution to the already stifling atmosphere, for air-conditioning was something else that hadn't been invented.

At 12:25 Mack's weary arm still pounded in vain. On the floor Master-at-Arms Martin now took over. He used the tactics of a lion tamer, prodding and bullying his charges into their seats. Miraculously he began getting results, and by 12:30 the convention was as orderly as it ever would be—a restless sea of sweating people. Despite the heat, the women wore heavy dresses, the men stiff collars and black winter suits. Seersucker was still another marvel yet to come.

Cardinal James Gibbons now came forward, a colorful splash of scarlet against this dark background. A respectful hush fell over the armory, as he prayed for wisdom, guidance, and calm deliberation.

Assistant Secretary Smith followed with a list of officials. "Temporary Chairman," he began, "the Honorable Judge Alton B. Parker of New York." The band instantly burst into "Oh, You Beautiful Doll." Tucked away deep in the New York delegation, Judge Parker blushed happily. Boss Charlie Murphy smiled, and the cardinal seemed pleased with this early sample of calm deliberation.

But as Smith finished, a familiar figure in an alpaca coat suddenly appeared in the middle of the stage. He seemed to come from nowhere (actually, he had very carefully picked a hidden side entrance), and perhaps this touch of magic gave his arrival extra impact. Not that he needed it—William Jennings Bryan always had the knack of setting a crowd off.

Instantly thousands of people were on their feet, cheering, booing, stamping, whistling. These were the days when a man was willing to sacrifice his hat to a cause, and dozens of skimmers sailed off into the armory haze. The New York delegation roared with rage; his old friends from Texas yelped with joy. The Peerless Leader benignly surveyed the scene, head erect and one foot forward like a statue from Ancient Rome. His right hand toyed with a palm-leaf fan, which he occasionally raised in mild protest. This only made the crowd shout louder.

When he finally began to speak fifteen minutes later, his rich ringing voice needed none of the yellow and white bunting spread over the ceiling for better acoustics. It was the most famous voice in the land. It carried to the farthest corner of the building. It quivered with indignation as he explained why he, "a mere delegate from one of the smaller states," demanded that the reactionary Judge Parker be rejected, that Senator John Kern be named temporary chairman instead.

" 'He never sold the truth to save the hour'—that is the language of the hero of Monticello," thundered the Commoner, pointing to the inscription above a large portrait at the end of the hall. Actually it was a quote from Tennyson and the picture was of Andrew Jackson, but nobody cared. The Texans yelped louder than ever; the New Yorkers gave exaggerated groans of boredom. On the platform one cynic dryly remarked to his neighbor, "I told them that he would use that quotation if they put it up there."

"The Democratic party is true to the people," Bryan roared on, "you cannot frighten it with your Ryans nor buy it with your Belmonts." Again, the hall was swept with cheers and groans, and the place seemed a madhouse by the time Bryan finished. Senator Kern came forward, failed to get Parker to join him on a compromise candidate, then dramatically announced that the Commoner himself should be the temporary chairman: "There is only one man fit to lead the interests of progress. That man has been at the forefront for sixteen years—William Jennings Bryan!"

The Tammany men cursed and howled. At last it was out—Bryan wanted the job for himself. "All I know," answered Cone Johnson, the human foghorn from Texas, "is that the fight is on; Bryan is on one side and Wall Street the other." As the uproar spread, the peace-loving Cardinal Gibbons gathered his robes and fled in dismay.

When they finally voted, Parker beat Bryan 579 to 508. So the New York crowd won—but it was close. And very revealing. The Wilson delegates stuck by Bryan to a man. Most of the Clark voters went over to Parker. Ever since the Speaker's cautious wire to Bryan, there had been rumors of a Clark-Murphy deal. Was this it? Was Old Champ selling out to Tammany in return for New York's ninety votes?

Certainly the answer wasn't written in the blank face of the pinkish old gentleman who ambled to the stage as temporary chairman. Judge Parker was perhaps the least memorable of all presidential candidates, and he never seemed more forgettable than now. He began his keynote speech at 3:40 P.M. and within seconds the crowd was yawning. If anyone was satisfied, it must have been Bryan, who had feared a ringing declaration of conservatism. All that came, however, was a fast, low, unintelligible monotone that quickly emptied the building.

At 4:17 Congressman Fitzgerald of New York decided that the travesty had gone far enough. He moved for adjournment, suggesting that the judge try again after supper. With a yell of relief the delegates poured out, leaving Parker alone on the stand gazing at the empty seats.

Buoyed by the "William Tell Overture," Parker began again that evening. This time he finished, although he still had his troubles. Once when a photographer set off some flash powder too close to the speakers' stand, the judge disappeared completely in a cloud of smoke. When he was visible (and audible), he stuck to an innocuous plea for harmony. "We had our little differences here this afternoon," he said lightly.

It wasn't that easy. Bryan was now thoroughly aroused. He had tried to keep clear of the Clark-Wilson fight. He felt they were both liberals, and if anything, he leaned toward Clark. As a Nebraska delegate he was pledged to Clark and certainly no one had a better party record. Wilson, on the other hand, was new, unpredictable, and just a little bit aloof in an Eastern sort of way. But this afternoon was an eye-opener: 228 Clark men went over to the enemy. In a burst of bitterness that night Bryan told a Wilson supporter, "I know what has happened; I am with you."

Actually he hadn't gone that far. But he was impressed. And even more impressed after calling Sea Girt for Wilson's views on the permanent chairman—a job that really counted. The Governor smoothly suggested Bryan's great friend, Congressman Ollie James of Kentucky.

"But, Governor Wilson, Mr. James is in the convention as a Clark man."

"It does not matter, he is our kind of fellow. . . ."

Bryan had never known a politician quite like that. Maybe this was the genuine liberal the people wanted. And they certainly seemed to want one, judging by the wires coming in. Messages from farmers, millhands, clerks, ordinary citizens everywhere. All over the country they were down at the local telegraph office, checking the latest convention bulletins. Then, whenever they didn't like something, they chipped in together and fired off a wire to their delegate. A new practice, but in keeping with the new spirit that a man could and should help shape his own destiny. As these telegrams poured into Baltimore, they all seemed to say one thing: Give the nation a progressive candidate running on a progressive platform.

The delegates could almost feel the note of exasperation that ran through the wires. The liberal tide was never stronger, yet events of the past four years convinced many people that shadowy forces were at work, deliberately subverting the reforms. The country wanted a lower tariff—but it got the Payne-Aldrich travesty, actually increasing most rates. It wanted conservation—but it saw the dismissal of Garfield, Pinchot, and other officials seeking an effective program. It wanted social welfare—but just this past year the courts threw out New York's new minimum wage law. It wanted a tough antitrust policy—but the latest Supreme Court decision said trusts were only bad if "unreasonable." To many that seemed like opening the gates.

Searching for an explanation, most eyes focused on Wall Street. Here were the men who controlled commerce and industry. And the 1907 panic showed that they also controlled the nation's money and credit. Many authorities felt that this "credit monopoly" was the most important of all. If these men had all the money, why wouldn't they spend it to get the business and political climate they wanted? Oversimplified perhaps, but an easy idea to grasp, and the wires that poured into Baltimore dripped with hatred of Wall Street.

Spurred by this bombardment, on Wednesday, June 26, the progressives won their first major victory. A wild battle developed over the convention's seventy-six-year-old "unit rule." Under this system a state cast all its votes the way the majority of its delegates wanted. This meant that Ohio had to give Governor Harmon all forty-eight of its ballots, even though the state primaries had instructed nineteen delegates to vote for Wilson. Led by Cleveland's young Mayor Newton D. Baker, the Wilson men revolted and took the fight to the convention floor. In the vote that followed, nearly all the old-line party men went for unit rule. But dozens of independents—impressed by the wires pouring in from home—joined the Wilson and Bryan forces supporting the rebels. In the end unit rule was beaten, 565½ to 492⅓—the first clear-cut progressive victory.

But the biggest event of the day was not the unit rule fight; it was the interruption that came in the middle of it. Ohio's John W. Peck was speaking—a long, dull argument in favor of the rule. By now it was evening, and the galleries seemed bored and listless. Peck's voice droned on above the hum of conversation, the scraping chairs, the occasional coughing. Driving home one of his innumerable points, he casually observed, "This is the position taken by the distinguished Governor of New Jersey—"

"Wilson!" roared a man in the gallery, and suddenly—incredibly— the whole armory went wild. It was the first time the Governor's name had been mentioned, and the crowd made the most of it. Senator John

Sharp Williams of Mississippi raced to the stage and led cheers with his big planter's hat. In the balcony the Princeton men yelled their locomotives. The band burst into "Maryland, My Maryland," and the Baltimoreans went crazy. From somewhere above, a blizzard of Wilson pictures floated down. A lady grabbed one and climbed on a chair. Two men lifted her up and began parading her around. Delegates poured into the aisles trying to follow. Wilson opponents tried to sabotage the demonstration by getting the band to play the "Star-Spangled Banner," but it took more than the anthem to stop this.

Five . . . ten . . . fifteen minutes went by, and still the crowd pushed and shoved. "Good old Texas—40 votes for Wilson" . . . "Give us Wilson and we'll give you Pennsylvania"—dozens of banners surged back and forth in a sea of yelling people. No organized march ever got started simply because there was no organization. This was spontaneity in its purest form.

Twenty minutes passed, and the demonstration at last began to lose steam. But at that moment a great orange and black banner appeared in the west gallery: "Staunton, Virginia—Woodrow Wilson's birthplace." The band crashed into "Dixie" and the crowd was off again.

A flying wedge brought the Staunton banner down to the main floor, and the more dedicated tried to plant it on the press stand. Even the pro-Wilson newsmen took a dim view of this—that is, all except L. T. Russell, owner of the Elizabeth, New Jersey, *Daily Times*. He was for the Governor beyond all else, and threw himself into the fray. Rushing up and down on top of the tables, he trampled typewriters, telegraph keys, and reams of copy.

The reporters cursed and shouted, but nobody did anything until Russell had the audacity to step on even Arthur Brisbane's copy. The great Hearst editor jumped up, tackled Russell and brought him crashing down on the Alabama delegation.

"Rush up twenty-five men from every police station," Floor Marshal Farnan frantically called headquarters in downtown Baltimore. But long before Lieutenant Scott's men arrived, the crisis had passed. Brisbane return to his place and calmly resumed writing as though nothing had happened. Russell was taken in tow by Nellie Bly, invariably identified as "the newspaperwoman."

The whole demonstration lasted thirty-three minutes, the statisticians said, and the exhausted crowd was ready to believe it. Only the Tammany and Clark delegates seemed fresh. Through it all they sat passively by, watching the show with great indifference.

Bryan now suspected more strongly than ever that a Clark-Tammany deal was brewing. And when he returned to the Belvedere at 3:00 A.M. his brother Charles confirmed his fears. Charles had heard that Murphy would throw New York's ninety votes to Clark at some early stage, putting the Speaker under obligation to Wall Street. To smoke out the conspirators, Charles had a bright idea: Why not offer a resolution to expel Belmont and Ryan from the convention? If the Clark men voted against the resolution, it would mean that the Speaker had indeed sold out.

Bryan went along with the idea and next morning, the 28th, drafted his resolution. It put the party on record against any candidate "who is the representative of or under obligation to J. Pierpont Morgan, Thomas Fortune Ryan, August Belmont, or any other member of the privilege-hunting and favor-seeking class." Getting down to specifics, it demanded the withdrawal of any delegate "constituting or representing the above-mentioned interests"—in other words, Ryan and Belmont.

Those who had a chance to see the draft were shocked. States' rights were still sacred to every good Democrat, and that, of course, included the right of a state to choose its own delegates. The resolution seemed an outrageous interference. But Bryan no longer cared. When he entered the hall for the evening session, his big jaw was clamped tight, his lips pressed in that hard, thin line that always formed when he was angry. No doubt about it, he was going to introduce his resolution.

The New York delegation was in caucus in an anteroom when the session opened. There were procedural matters to discuss, and everyone knew nothing important ever happened the first few minutes. They were still at it when a white-faced man burst into the room, shouting that Bryan had just introduced a resolution that was an insult to all

New York. Murphy's men tumbled back into the hall and found the place in wild tumult.

"You have heard of bedlam," McAdoo later recalled, describing the scene. To Josephus Daniels it was like Dante's *Inferno*. Hundreds of cursing delegates surged about the floor. One man stood on a chair, shouting that he would give $25,000 to anyone who killed Bryan. Another scrambled onto the stage and stood swearing at the Commoner until he literally frothed at the mouth and was led away by his friends. Hal Flood of Virginia was up there too, dramatically refusing an offered handshake. Down on the floor one man was dashing wildly about shouting, "Lynch him!"

Others seemed to have the same idea. Sometimes Bryan completely disappeared in the midst of the fist-shaking men who milled around him. Big Cone Johnson of the foghorn voice and some of the Commoner's more rawboned friends rushed forward to protect him. Police and marshals dashed about the floor. The bewildered Ollie James kept pounding his gavel. Slowly the crowd retreated and order was restored.

Bryan finally withdrew the second part of his resolution—he no longer demanded that any delegate get out. This left only the first part, putting the party on record against any candidate under obligation to Morgan, Ryan, Belmont, "or any other member of the privilege-hunting and favor-seeking class." Few could argue with that, and the emasculated resolution passed easily 883 to 201½. Even Tammany went along; as Boss Murphy cast his ninety votes he caught Belmont's eye and smiled, "Now, Augie, listen to yourself vote yourself out of the convention."

So Bryan had to back down—or did he? McAdoo for one, was sure that he never expected Belmont and Ryan to be expelled. All he really wanted was to alert the country that a conspiracy was afoot. Certainly the resolution did that. More than ever, people saw the issue as Wall Street against Freedom; more than ever they looked to Bryan and Wilson to protect them from the rascals. The flood of wires increased; the crowds at the telegraph tickers watched their delegates even more carefully.

"The old lion at his best," mused Woodrow Wilson at Sea Girt.

304

It was hard to believe that these words came from the man who once hoped that the Commoner would be "knocked into a cocked hat." Or who less than a year ago compared Bryan's cluttered home to his state of mind. With so much at stake, it was easy to discover new virtues and forget old flaws in such a valuable ally.

In Baltimore the convention moved on to the business of nominating the candidates. It was nearly 11:00 P.M., but no one thought of adjourning or even saving any breath. Young William B. Bankhead took over thirty minutes to portray the virtues of Oscar W. Underwood, then the crowd cheered for another half hour. At that, the demonstration seemed a little genteel—the high point came when a lady set loose a flock of white doves.

There was nothing genteel about what happened next. At 11:55 P.M. Arkansas yielded to Missouri, and Senator James A. Reed launched a thundering speech for Champ Clark. "Give me no political dilettante," he sneered, and the Speaker's delegates yelled in agreement. They were at fever pitch when he finished at 12:25. Into the aisles they poured braying the "Houn' Dawg Song." They seemed to keep marching forever—12:40 . . . 1:00 . . . 1:25.

At Sea Girt Joe Tumulty leaned over the special ticker, keeping track of every minute. Pocket watch in hand, he was a picture of dejected agony. Wilson himself seemed hardly to notice. He always had the knack of looking especially calm when others were most excited. Hearing that young Genevieve Clark was riding around the hall wrapped in an American flag, the Governor merely said to his own daughters, "Now you will understand why I wouldn't allow any of you to go to the convention."

The demonstration finally ended at 1:30 A.M.—after lasting an hour and five minutes—and the delegates slowly got back to business. Connecticut put up her favorite son, Governor Baldwin . . . the roll of states continued . . . Delaware yielded to New Jersey . . . and at 2:08 A.M. Judge John W. Wescott took the stand to nominate Wilson.

He never even got started. Wilson banners rolled down from the gallery rail . . . a fifteen-foot portrait of the Governor appeared at the west end . . . hundreds of shouting delegates poured into the aisles.

Texas led the way . . . then Pennsylvania . . . then no one could keep track any longer. A half-dozen different parades were under way. Around and around they marched amid an endless uproar of horns, whistles, rattles and Princeton locomotives.

Anything to keep going longer than the Clark men. Some genius set a live rooster loose in the crowd. The band contributed a musical answer to the houn' dawg—it steadily pumped out "School Days." From the stand Chairman Ollie James watched benignly. He was a Clark man, but he made no attempt to stop the show. He understood these games . . . probably enjoyed them more than the issues. And above all, he wanted to be fair. As Wilson told Bryan, "He's our kind of fellow."

At Sea Girt Tumulty excitedly studied his watch. At 3:13 A.M. he let out a yelp of joy. The demonstration had beaten Clark's record. He rushed upstairs but was unable to break the good news. The Governor had gone to sleep.

It was 3:20 before Judge Wescott was able to start speaking . . . 4:00 when he finished. It was a deeply moving if somewhat flowery effort, but largely wasted on the crowd. The long, hot night had taken its toll. The sweating delegates slumped wearily in their seats. It was so muggy that the steam from their wringing clothes rose in a cloud toward the grimy canopy.

The hours wore on—hours of interminable eloquence. In the humid galleries, mothers fanned the children who slept in their laps. Fathers foraged for cold water or sarsaparilla. On the stage, prominent women who had "kalsomined" their faces against the heat, sat like powdered mummies . . . afraid to move lest they spoil what they felt was a dainty appearance. Their unappreciative escorts lay sleeping on side benches —so many battlefield casualties. After every oratorical outburst the dozing reporters roused themselves long enough to flash "release speech," then sagged back at their tables. Even the policemen were stretched out on chairs, their pistols under their heads.

Yet hardly anyone left. They didn't dare to go. There had already been too many unexpected explosions, too many rumors of sinister plots. When big Ollie James persistently refused to adjourn, the story spread that another trick was afoot: a vote would be called unexpectedly and the nomination quickly rammed through. Nobody wanted to be caught that way; so, tired as they were, the crowd hung on.

Dawn was breaking when Senator Shively nominated Indiana's Governor Marshall at 5:00 A.M. A band appeared in an ill-starred attempt to stir some enthusiasm, but all it got was shouts for quiet. Through it all, only one man never seemed to tire. Tammany's Charlie Murphy sat bolt upright the whole night long . . . his quick gray eyes darting here and there, his bright mind obviously spinning with plans everyone longed to know.

At 7:00 the last speech was over, and James called for the first ballot. Magically, the hall snapped back to life—voices babbling everywhere . . . delegates rushing to their seats . . . messengers running up and down the aisles on tantalizing errands. The roll call began; Wilson and Clark instantly took the lead; the others lagged far behind. From time to time there were cheers at some unexpected vote . . . then a great hush as New York's turn came. In a loud, calm voice Charlie Murphy called, "Ninety votes for—Judson Harmon."

So Murphy wasn't trying a stampede after all. There would be nothing decisive this time. The crowd relaxed, hardly listening to the rest of the ballot, which ended up Clark 440½, Wilson 324, Harmon 148, Underwood 117½, Marshall 31.

Out into the sun they poured, finally released by Ollie James at 7:20 A.M. They had been at it all night, but as they gulped in the cold, clean air of the morning, they were no longer in the mood for sleep. They could only wonder what Murphy was up to. Was there nothing to those rumors of a Clark-Tammany deal? Was the Big Chief really for Harmon after all? Was he playing for a deadlock, giving him a chance to put his man over? Certainly Harmon was Augie Belmont's choice, and that was where the money lay. To say nothing of Thomas Fortune Ryan, who sank $77,000 into Harmon's campaign (while hedging his bet with another $35,000 on Underwood). Or was there indeed a deal with Clark? Was Murphy just biding his time? Waiting for the right moment to shift his ninety votes and start a Clark landslide?

At Sea Girt, Wilson took no apparent interest in any of these intriguing questions. He had just discovered a new way to tease Joe Tumulty. This was to hum the "Houn' Dawg Song" whenever his harassed secretary entered the room.

Friday afternoon the convention reconvened, with the delegates tensely expecting some break. But the fifth ballot still found Clark and Wilson about the same, still found Murphy monotonously calling, "New York casts ninety votes for Harmon."

Nor did the supper recess make any difference. The sixth, seventh, eighth, ninth ballots all told the same story—minor changes here and there, never anything important. Whenever New York's turn came, the armory fell quiet, but as always, Murphy merely called, "New York casts ninety votes for Harmon."

It was 1:00 A.M. by the time the tenth ballot began. Again the states rolled by, again the usual adjustments—Marshall took seven from Underwood in Connecticut . . . Wilson lost two in Michigan. Now it was New York's turn, and once more the hall grew quiet to hear the dry, flat voice of Charlie Murphy: "New York casts eighty-one votes for Champ Clark—"

The shift really meant all ninety votes for Clark, since New York still preferred the unit rule, but this was a minor detail—Murphy had made his move. Old Champ had New York. With an ear-splitting yell, the Clark men surged into the aisles.

Missouri's standard bobbed into the lead. Then Arkansas, Iowa, Kansas, Kentucky; the parade was on. The band blasted away with "Tammany" in tribute to Murphy's statesmanship. Genevieve Clark reappeared with her American flag. The New York standard-bearer scaled the stage, and other states swarmed up too, swamping the party dignitaries. In the most literal sense, Clark was taking over the convention.

The band swung into the "Houn' Dawg Song," and the marchers were wilder than ever. At 1:30 A.M. some New Yorker tried to tear up a Wilson banner hanging near the Nebraska delegation. Someone rushed over and knocked the man down. Revealingly, the Wilson supporter turned out to be William Jennings Bryan, Jr.

The Governor's men desperately battled back all over the hall. One group fought to hold the Massachusetts standard in place. "Alfalfa Bill" Murray stopped a break by Oklahoma: "We won't put our stamp of approval on Wall Street!" A friendly policeman hurled the Rhode Island standard-bearer down from the stage. William McAdoo made the shrewdest move of all. He rushed to the press stand, confidentially announcing that New York's ninety votes would be transferred to Underwood on the next ballot.

At the height of the uproar, Bryan raced into the hall. He had been at a committee meeting, caught completely off guard. Now he was trying to make up for lost time, bellowing against any candidate "besmirched" by New York's vote. As he watched the excitement swirl around him, he remembered a lesson he once taught others: how easy it was to stampede a convention with some dramatic, unexpected move.

Then and there Bryan vowed this wouldn't happen here if he could help it. He decided never again to leave the floor during a session. From this moment on, he remained rooted in the Nebraska delegation —a bottle of lukewarm water under his seat, sandwich crumbs liberally sprinkled over his famous alpaca coat.

Gradually the hall quieted down, and Ollie James resumed calling the roll. It was North Carolina's turn next, and the crowd listened tense with excitement. Until now she had given seventeen of her votes to Wilson, but Murphy's shift was designed to trigger a general rush to Clark. Here was the test. "North Carolina," announced a calm, cool voice, "casts eighteen votes for Wilson. . . ."

North Dakota stood firm too, and the pair of votes lost in volatile Ohio seemed like getting off easily. Then came Oklahoma, another big Wilson state. A Clark member, trying to blast loose some votes, demanded that the delegation be polled. "Alfalfa Bill" Murray leaped to his feet, shouting, "We do not intend to be dragged into Tammany Hall!" This set off a fifty-five-minute Wilson demonstration, giving the Governor's men valuable time to bolster their position.

So the lines held; there was no stampede. But the tenth ballot showed Clark 556, Wilson 350½, everyone else left in the dust. The Speaker now had a majority of the 1,088 delegates. True, the rules said he needed two-thirds—or 726—to be nominated, but for the past sixty-eight years any candidate with a majority had gone on to win. In fact, it had become the accepted thing, and all good progressives said that was the way it ought to be. Now the Clark men clamored for the Governor's surrender. The Wilson leaders scoffed at the idea, but they squirmed a little too—as recently as March 11, Woodrow Wilson said a majority was the fair way to decide the nomination.

Thanks to newly discovered virtues in the two-thirds rule, the Governor was still hanging on when the convention adjourned at 4:03 A.M. after the twelfth ballot. The delegates poured out into the pre-dawn darkness and scattered to the traditional "smoke-filled rooms." Munching Georgia watermelon in the Belvedere, William McCombs put on a brave front, but his heart must have been heavy.

He was on the phone to Sea Girt by breakfast time that morning, Saturday the 29th. As Wilson listened calmly in the little phone booth under the stairs, McCombs explained that the case was hopeless, that the Governor had better release his delegates. Possibly he might like to ask them to vote for Underwood on the long shot that a complete outsider could still beat Clark. No, answered Wilson, that wouldn't be fair. "Please say to them how greatly I appreciate their generous support and that they are now free to support any candidate they choose."

Overhearing the Governor from the next room, great tears welled in the eyes of Ellen Wilson.

Breakfast began, heavy with gloom. Mrs. Wilson, daughters Margaret, Jessie, and Eleanor, glumly toyed with their food. After asking Tumulty to draft his congratulations to Clark, Wilson joined them and immediately plunged into the job of cheering them up. Finding a coffin advertisement in the morning mail, he laughed with delight, "This company is certainly prompt in its service."

The joke didn't go over very well, but the Governor wasn't about to give up. Taking a new and softer tack, he reminded Ellen of the beautiful summers they had spent in the English Lake Country. "Do you realize," he said gently, "that now we can see our beloved Rydal again?"

There was no one to cheer up McCombs in Baltimore. When McAdoo dropped by headquarters about 10:00 A.M., he found the manager in a state of collapse: "The jig's up; Clark will be nominated. All my work has been for nothing."

McAdoo was amazed; he himself felt rather optimistic after four hours' sleep. But McCombs went on to explain that even Wilson had given up. He described his phone call to Sea Girt and told how the Governor agreed to release his delegates.

McAdoo exploded. He accused McCombs of "betraying" Wilson, of "selling him out." Unfair charges, and McCombs flared back. But there was no time to stand there arguing. Word of the release might get out any minute. McAdoo raced to the phone and got Sea Girt. In another minute he had Wilson on the line. "I'm dumbfounded," he told the Governor and begged him to ignore McCombs' advice, to cancel the authority releasing his delegates. "You're gaining all the time. Clark can never get two-thirds. . . ."

It was all too much for Wilson. He countermanded the release, but turned to his family in a daze. He told them it was high time for a vacation . . . urged them to take up something healthy. He himself wandered off for a round of golf.

In Baltimore, the crowd packed the armory for the thirteenth ballot on Saturday afternoon. The Clark men were confident—in Washington the Speaker was already writing his telegram of acceptance.

At 1:06 P.M. Ollie James began his roll call. Again the crowd hung on every state's answer, but the result was an anticlimax. Clark picked up only seven more votes.

Fourteenth ballot. Again James started down his list, again nothing sensational. Wilson gained a vote in Connecticut; Clark took one from the Governor in Michigan. Now it was Nebraska's turn. Senator Hitchcock interrupted the call, asking that the delegation be polled.

Instantly Bryan was standing on his chair, waving his palm leaf fan, demanding the right to explain his vote. He was hopelessly out of order, and Congressman Sulzer (spelling Ollie James for a moment) refused to recognize him. It didn't make the slightest difference. Ignoring the chair, the Commoner began, "As long as—"

His voice was drowned in a torrent of jeers and catcalls. Finally

Senator Stone of Missouri interceded, suggesting that since this was a democratic meeting, Bryan be allowed to proceed. Another roar of dissent, which Sulzer met with majestic disdain: "The chair hears no objection."

From the platform, Bryan now began again: "As long as Mr. Ryan's agent—as long as New York's ninety votes are recorded for Mr. Clark, I withold my vote from him and cast it—"

Once more his words were lost in the howls that swept the hall. Now Bryan pulled a prepared statement from his pocket—enough of a switch to quiet the crowd and give him a chance to go on. When instructed to vote for Clark, he shouted, he gladly supported the Speaker as a progressive. But Murphy's shift changed everything: "I shall withhold my vote from Mr. Clark as long as New York's vote is recorded for him." The same, he added, went for any other candidate under obligation to the Tammany-Wall Street combination. "Having explained my position, I now announce my vote for—"

For the third time his voice disappeared in a storm of angry protest. Only his chief target Charlie Murphy seemed completely unperturbed. Through it all, he presided over a quiet huddle with his chief lieutenants. Finally the hall calmed down again, and this time Bryan got it out: "I cast my vote for Nebraska's second choice Governor Wilson."

The Wilson supporters exploded with joy . . . poured into the aisles, dancing and hugging each other. In their excitement, they failed to notice that Bryan hadn't endorsed the Governor at all. His switch was clearly labeled a vote against Tammany and Wall Street—not a vote for Wilson. Was he really biding his time for a moment when he could step in and walk off with the nomination himself?

Whatever his motives, the effect was spectacular. Once again the wires began pouring in, backing his stand, demanding that the delegates cleanse themselves of Wall Street. Slowly Clark's vote began falling. Sixteenth ballot 551 . . . Seventeenth 545 . . . Eighteenth 535—now for the first time since Murphy's shift, the Speaker no longer had a majority.

At first Clark's losses were not Wilson's gains. Many of the deserters were just conservatives looking for someone Bryan wasn't mad at. For several ballots the Wilson total hovered around 360. Then the chanting galleries, the wires from home began to have their effect. Nineteenth ballot: Clark 532, Wilson 358. Twenty-first ballot Clark 508, Wilson 395½. On the twenty-fourth, the Governor passed 400 for the first time, and the galleries went wild. In Sea Girt, Wilson dryly told his family, "I've been figuring it out. At this rate, I'll be nominated in 175 more ballots."

Watching the ticker in Washington, Champ Clark was desperate. Suddenly the thought occurred: a dramatic appearance at the armory might turn the tide. Normally, candidates didn't plead their own cause, but it was easy to feel that this time was different. He raced to the station, jumped aboard the first train out. Thirty-nine minutes later, Clark leaped to the platform in Baltimore—only to discover that the convention had just adjourned for the weekend.

Sunday, June 30, proved no day of rest; there never was a Sabbath more shattered by deals, plots, bargains, and intrigue. Clark's able lieutenant "Gum-Shoe Bill" Stone worked on the Harmon and Marshall die-hards. Thomas Fortune Ryan did his best to corral the Underwood men—after all he had given them that $35,000. Charlie Murphy played a subtler game—he engineered a meeting with Mitchell Palmer, suggesting that if he deserted Wilson, he could have the nomination himself. Palmer indignantly declined.

Meanwhile the Wilson forces were far from idle. Senator Saulsbury of Delaware worked on the border states most of the morning. McCombs polished up a promising deal with Tom Taggart of Indiana: if the Hoosier boss would deliver his thirty delegates, Governor Marshall could have second place on the ticket.

McCombs also dickered with Murphy, ignoring the fact that if the Tammany leader did come over, Bryan and his followers would pull out. Small loss, felt Wilson's manager; he far preferred the scores of disciplined votes that could be instantly produced by a strong political boss. And when these leaders began putting on the pressure—saying they would never fall in line until Bryan was shelved—McCombs quickly called Sea Girt. He explained that he could get those badly-needed Eastern votes only if Wilson promised *not* to name Bryan Secretary of State.

Wilson was shocked. The whole idea violently clashed with that inflexible Calvinist streak that ran so deeply in him—sometimes his greatest strength, sometimes a heartbreaking weakness. He had showed it as Governor when he risked political suicide by vetoing an unfair grade-crossing bill. He showed it as president of Princeton when he fought his losing battle against Dean West's separate graduate school. Once over a game of billiards, a faculty friend tried a gentle word of advice: "There are two sides to every question." Wilson gave him an icy glance: "Yes—the right and the wrong."

It was the same now. Rejecting McCombs' suggestion, he turned to Tumulty and sternly declared, "I will not bargain for this office." It was ironical, of course, that unknown to Wilson, his friends were bargaining all over Baltimore. But in the last analysis, their combined manipulations produced nothing compared to the votes he won as the uncompromising champion of political cleanliness.

The blizzard of telegrams increased—110,000 that week, 1,182 for Bryan alone—most of them clamoring louder than ever for Wilson. And if there was any delegate who failed to grasp the meaning, the press was happy to let him know. Charles H. Grasty's Baltimore *Sun*, the paper read by every delegate, slanted its columns heavily for the Governor. (Old *Sun* men still enjoy the hatchet job they did on Thomas Fortune Ryan.) The New York *World* now called Wilson's nomination "a matter of Democratic life and death."

Monday, July 1. The weary delegates, the wilted spectators trudged back to the armory for another day of balloting. The band was gone—no more money to pay it—and many of the camp followers were going home too. But if the carnival touch was missing, the battle itself was tenser than ever. Twenty-seventh ballot: no major change. Twenty-eighth: Indiana suddenly bolted for Wilson. Tom Taggart, it seemed, was a man of his word.

Now it was the thirtieth ballot. Suddenly most of Iowa switched from Clark to Wilson . . . then Vermont, Wyoming, Michigan in quick succession. The armory was in an uproar as the Governor forged into the lead 460-455.

"You've passed him! You've passed him!" yelled the reporters at Sea Girt. They crowded around Wilson, begging for a statement. "You might say," he suggested, "that Governor Wilson received the news that Champ Clark had dropped to second place in a riot of silence."

Oddly enough, the Wilson lead was deceptive. He had gone about as far as he could without a major shift somewhere. But Murphy was out of the question, and the Underwood men still banked on a deadlock. The only hope was Illinois's crafty old boss Roger Sullivan. His fifty-eight delegates were in the Clark column, but he had occasionally flirted with Wilson's managers.

Monday night they tried every conceivable pressure. Mrs. Sullivan and his son Boetius—both avidly for the Governor—added their weight. A caucus showed the delegates too wanted Wilson. Finally, Sullivan said he would shift in the morning, but he didn't seem particularly enthusiastic.

McCombs worried the night away, and by Tuesday morning, July 2, he was near hysterics. "Roger," he cried, "we've got to have Illinois, or I'll withdraw!"

"Sit steady, boy," was all the old man had to say. But true to his word, Illinois came over on the forty-third ballot . . . making the count Wilson 602, Clark 329.

Even now, it wasn't all over. First, the Underwood crowd had to be won, and never were men more stubborn. They still clung to the hope of deadlock and compromise. All during the forty-fifth ballot Mc-Combs, Palmer, the other Wilson managers feverishly worked on the Alabama delegation. And as the delay grew longer, the wildest rumors spread: Sullivan would shift his vote to Underwood next ballot . . . no, he would switch them back to Clark . . . the Speaker was in an anteroom about to make his long-advertised dramatic appearance.

At 2:45 P.M. Ollie James stood by, ready to take the roll for the forty-sixth time. But before he could start, old Senator Bankhead of Alabama got permission to say a few words. Underwood, he declared, wanted an end to sectional prejudice far more than the nomination . . . Under-

wood would gladly forgo the honor if the country was united . . .
Underwood never entered the race to defeat any man. . . .

No doubt about it—he was withdrawing. Murphy darted down the
aisle to pay his last respects to the Missouri boys—he was abandoning
ship. The Clark forces began cursing and heckling. The Wilson rooters
rocked the hall with their cheers.

The landslide began. Trying on his new loyalty, Murphy's lieutenant
John Fitzgerald suggested that Wilson be nominated by acclamation.
But the Missouri delegates refused—they wanted to cast "one last vote
for Old Champ Clark." Few others were as sentimental. State after
state fell in line, including New York.

The forty-sixth ballot ended Wilson 890, Clark 84. Her honor intact,
it was Missouri that now suggested the nomination be made unani-
mous. The delegates roared their approval, and at exactly 3:30 P.M., a
hoarse, weary Ollie James shouted above the din, "I declare Woodrow
Wilson the nominee of this convention!"

At Sea Girt Joe Tumulty was waiting. At his frantic signal, a band
stepped out from behind a clump of bushes blaring "Hail, the Conquer-
ing Hero Comes." Wilson merely asked what the band would have
done if he had lost.

Instantly the broad lawn seemed to fill with people. Reporters and
friends crowded around. A passing Pennsylvania Railroad train came
to a stop, the engineer and fireman abandoned the locomotive and
rushed across the field to congratulate the Governor. Wilson mechanically greeted them all. He seemed in a daze, repeating over and over,
"Well, well, is it really true?"

But he wasn't so stunned that he failed to recall that gloomy breakfast just three days ago. Turning to his wife Ellen, he smiled and said,
"Well, I guess we won't go to Rydal after all."

"The most remarkable demonstration of the people's influence upon
a national council of a national party in the history of the republic,"
proclaimed the Baltimore *Sun* the day after Wilson's nomination. The
whole country seemed to agree. Everyone gloried in the thought of
amateurs beating professionals . . . of the man in the street routing the
interests . . . of David thrashing Goliath.

The stand against Murphy was compared to Thermopylae (but with a happy ending) . . . to Garibaldi's liberation of Italy. Joe Tumulty went even further—he thought it was like the Crusades.

The Crusades, in fact, were always a favorite progressive image. There was something more exhilarating than mere reform in this battle for social justice. It was a Mission, a Holy War. The theme ran through the whole Wilson campaign, and it positively saturated the new Progressive party launched by Theodore Roosevelt.

Roosevelt's Progressives gathered in Chicago on August 5, and from the start it was less a convention than a religious revival. "We stand at Armageddon and we battle for the Lord," the Colonel had cried, and his followers took the cue. The band blared "Onward Christian Soldiers." The crowds sang "The Battle Hymn of the Republic." Senator Beveridge's keynote speech sounded the call—"we battle for the actual rights of man." Roosevelt himself delivered a "Confession of Faith." Wallowing in evangelism, the Progressives nominated the Colonel, and for the first time in years a third-party candidate posed a serious challenge.

Poor Taft was crushed. It inwardly killed him to hear those slashing attacks from his old friend Roosevelt. He hated running for office anyhow. Everything he did seemed to go wrong. Even when he sat in the baseball bleachers—presumably a safe course for any politician— he was criticized for wasting his time at ball games. Sadly he wrote to Helen Taft, "I think I might as well give up so far as being a politician is concerned; there are so many people who don't like me."

Wilson and Roosevelt soon forget about him, traveled all over the country happily battering each other. For some observers it was difficult to understand how two progressives could so violently disagree, yet each represented an entirely different branch of the movement. Roosevelt and his New Nationalism stood for government as a positive force, looking after the people's needs through social welfare laws. Wilson and his New Freedom saw the government more as a referee, hired to keep the game clean. The Governor argued that if Washington wiped out special privilege, free men could look after themselves.

Roosevelt derided Wilson's theory as "rural Toryism"—an effort to

turn back the clock. By now the Colonel took monopolies for granted—
the solution was to make them behave. Wilson rejected this flatly—the
solution was to abolish them: "If America is not to have free enterprise, then she can have freedom of no sort whatever."

The people listened—intrigued as ever by this eloquent man who
spoke so glowingly of freedom. And they enjoyed more and more the
way he slugged it out with the rambunctious Colonel. The schoolmaster turned out to be an incredibly good campaigner. "Ladies and
gentlemen in the boxes," he saluted the agile souls perched on boxcars,
when his campaign special stopped at Willimantic, Connecticut. And
when a would-be assassin wounded Roosevelt in Milwaukee, Wilson
reaped enormous dividends by a dramatic display of sportsmanship. He
announced he would simply mark time until the Colonel was back in
action—"my thought is constantly of that gallant gentleman lying in
the hospital. . . ."

Fighting this sort of campaign—and with the Republicans hopelessly
split—Wilson won easily. Even the surprisingly large Socialist vote—
showing that at least some people were still dissatisfied with the system
—didn't dampen the enthusiasm of this first Democratic victory in
twenty years.

That November 5 was a glorious election night at Wilson's home
in Princeton—the students cheering outside . . . the college band playing . . . the old bell tolling on Nassau Hall. Swept up in the thrill of
the victory, next morning's New York *World* saw no limit to the
possibilities ahead: "a new era . . . a new vindication of republican in-
stitutions . . . a new birth of freedom."

"New" was the keynote. And not merely in politics, where this new
administration heralded its New Freedom. In every field the country
was bursting with fresh, exciting ideas. New theatre—J. M. Synge's
outspoken *Playboy of the Western World*. New music—Irving Berlin
changed America's whole taste in popular tunes with "Alexander's
Ragtime Band." New art—in February, 1913, New York's Armory
Show introduced the nation to a revolution in painting. When the
show went on the road, 400,000 people in Chicago alone flocked to see
pictures by men with unfamiliar names like Matisse and Cézanne.

Everyone talked about "Nude Descending a Staircase" and tried to find either the nude or the staircase. (The public was much more shocked by a recently-discovered picture that anyone could understand—"September Morn.")

The same month as the Armory Show, the country faced still another innovation—a new kind of levy called the "income tax." When Delaware gave its approval on February 3, 1913, the Sixteenth Amendment went into effect, and Washington turned its thoughts to the provocative concept of taxing people according to their ability to pay. Conservatives howled with dismay when it was reported that the rate would run as high as 2 per cent on incomes from $20,000 to $50,000.

But the liberals were in the saddle now, and they brushed aside complaints. There was a better world ahead, and they could hardly wait to get going. Swarming down Pennsylvania Avenue on Inauguration Day, March 4, they crowded behind the barriers on the east side of the Capitol.

Shortly after 1:10 P.M., Woodrow Wilson took his place on the temporary stand. Chief Justice White administered the oath; the crowd cheered, then fell silent to hear the Inaugural Address. But Wilson's first words were no speech at all. Noticing the huge throng behind the distant barrier—and supremely mindful of all he stood for—he turned to the guards and calmly ordered, "Let the people come forward!"

1913

Children at Work

"The golf links lie so near the mill
That almost every day
The laboring children can look out
And see the men at play."

—SARAH N. CLEGHORN

Woodrow Wilson stood for freedom; so it was not surprising early in 1913 when a group of social workers asked him to help free the children from the nation's factories. The new President politely declined. No one was more idealistic, but an important part of his idealism was a deep, almost sacred belief in states' rights. "It is plain," he told the reformers, "that you would have to go much further than most interpretations of the Constitution would allow, if you were to give the government general control over child labor throughout the country."

So the children worked on, unhampered by federal interference. Twelve-year-old Owen Jones tore and bruised his hands in the breakers of a West Virginia coal mine. Tiny Anetta Fachini twisted the stems for artificial flowers under the lonely lamp bulb of a New York tenement sweatshop. Eleven-year-old Sam Bowles did his best in the weaving room of Georgia's White City Manufacturing Company—for forty cents a day.

At an Atlanta cotton mill one nimble-fingered boy stretched three thousand flour bags a shift; but he had plenty of practice, for he worked a sixty-hour week. In Pittsburgh an unknown little girl rolled one thousand stogies a day—which meant, looking at it another way, that one thousand times a day she had to bite off the end of a cigar.

Somehow in these years of thrilling reform, there were still areas of extreme poverty. Worst of all, children were lost in the shuffle. Perhaps the economists were bored—it was so much more stimulating to rewrite the tariff or draw up the Federal Reserve. Perhaps labor was to blame; Samuel Gompers was a rugged individualist who had little use for social welfare laws. Perhaps the children were too quiet.

In any case, by 1913 some 20 per cent of all the children in America were earning their own living. And the number was growing all the time. In 1900 the Census listed 1,750,178 "gainfully occupied children aged ten to fifteen"; in 1910 the figure jumped to 1,990,225. To many this was sad but inevitable. The average family needed $800 a year to get along, yet most unskilled jobs paid less than $500 a year. Unless general wage levels went up, the children had to fill in the gap. As the Clarke County Mississippi *Tribune* realistically asked, "What are the children going to do to keep from starving and going naked?"

A small band of dedicated people refused to go along with all this. They felt that child labor was one reason why wages were so low; get the children out of the factories and the general level would rise. These reformers had set up the National Child Labor Committee in 1904, and in the years since then had waged a tireless crusade. They roamed through the factories. They talked to the children. They heard out the foremen. They prepared model bills. They badgered state legislatures. And occasionally they even pushed through a law.

But so many of the "victories" were hollow. Massachusetts had only eighteen inspectors for fifty-six thousand plants. The New York law against tenement work listed some ninety exceptions. In Alabama a twelve-year-old girl might still put in a sixty-hour week.

The cotton mills posed the biggest problem. Hot competition and little call for skill—the perfect climate for cheap child labor. And the children came: five thousand little girls between ten and twelve worked at the spindles in Southern plants. In the North, nearly seventeen thousand mill hands were under sixteen.

More meaningful, perhaps, were the figures on injuries. One Southern surgeon estimated that he had amputated the fingers of more than one hundred children. "We don't have many accidents," a mill foreman countered, "once in a while a finger is mashed or a foot, but it does not amount to anything."

No wonder the reform groups were elated in 1913 when two leading cotton textile states—Massachusetts and Georgia—began to consider stronger child labor curbs. Best of all, public interest was growing, and this time it looked as if something might really be done.

The Massachusetts bill came up first. It restricted street trades, raised school requirements, and most important of all, set an eight-hour day for anyone under sixteen—the highest standard yet reached by a cotton mill state. As expected, the law passed in June, and the New England conscience basked in a glow of self-congratulation.

All eyes now turned to Georgia. The bill here was not quite as strong—it gradually raised the working age to fourteen—but it was a big step forward and its prospects were bright. Early in August the Atlanta *Journal* predicted that the measure would definitely pass, and child labor groups everywhere prepared to celebrate the biggest victory yet. Then, on the afternoon of August 5, word was flashed that the Georgia State Senate had unexpectedly killed the bill.

What had happened? Many Southerners were sure that the Senate had discovered in the nick of time that child labor reform was really sponsored by hypocritical Yankees, hoping to increase Southern labor costs and cut the South's competitive advantage. Northerners were equally convinced that Georgia's failure to act was one more example of Southern backwardness.

Actually, both theories were wrong. No Northern mill ever gave a dollar to the National Child Labor Committee. And some of the most active reformers—not only in the South but throughout the nation—were dedicated Southerners . . . men like Senator Hoke Smith of Georgia, Dr. A. J. McKelway from Atlanta, and Dr. Edgar Gardner Murphy, the Alabama clergyman who organized the whole movement.

Moreover, the men who led the fight against reform in Georgia were not necessarily "backward" Southerners by any means. Often they were upstanding New Englanders who pointed with pride to "enlightened Massachusetts" . . . but applied different standards to the mills they ran down South.

There was, perhaps, no nicer man in Columbus, Georgia, than Frederick B. Gordon, a transplanted Bostonian who ran the Columbus Manufacturing Company's cotton mill. Active in civic affairs, Mr. Gordon helped found the Primary Industrial School. His big new plant, a local historian proudly recorded, "responds liberally to all civic calls—even some that do not directly benefit its own business." And it prospered mightily . . . quickly repaying its Northern investors dollar for dollar, plus a 100 per cent stock dividend. Relaxing in his colonnaded mansion appropriately called "Gordonido," Mr. Gordon undoubtedly fitted the description supplied by his authorized biographer: "He possesses a genial, sympathetic nature and has found life well worth living, making the most of it every day."

Down at the factory, life was a little different. "I have never seen so many children in any one mill as there were here," wrote the Reverend Harvey P. Vaughn, a gentle Tennessee minister, after a visit in April, 1913. The children worked, it turned out, a twelve-hour day—from 5:30 A.M. to 5:30 P.M. There was no time off even for lunch; if anything went wrong while they were snatching a bite, they had to stop eating to fix it.

When Dr. Vaughn indelicately asked how many of the mill hands were under fourteen, Mr. Gordon politely declined to answer. As he once explained, "The millowners do not feel that there is any reason for spasms on the part of the paid agitators, the newspaper preachers, or our gentle and zealous friends, the clubwomen."

Mr. Gordon had always felt that way. It was 1902 when he first tried to set the record straight. Writing to the magazine *Social Service,* he denied that the children were exploited. On the contrary, they were often hired "purely as a matter of charity" and they were much better off in the mill than running loose, "learning the first lessons of a vagrant's life."

As for the people stirring up all this trouble, Mr. Gordon felt that at best they were "a noble and disinterested class made up of the clergy and the clubwomen, with whom it is quite a drawing room fad." At worst, they were "paid and prejudiced agitators." And with perhaps a slight bow toward the Confederate flag, he added that these agitators were "backed to some extent by New England competitors of Southern mill interests." This was always a good argument in Georgia, and Mr. Gordon wisely did not add that he was a Northerner backed by Northern capital.

As for any abuses, he pointed out that the millowners had a "gentleman's agreement" that was far more effective than any law. It limited the employment of ten-year-olds to sixty-six hours a week . . . and the owners could be trusted to observe it. "Legislation based on over-sentimentality and disregard of actual conditions," Mr. Gordon concluded sternly, "would prove a severe menace to Southern industrial progress."

Feeling as he did, Frederick Gordon was naturally on hand when the state legislature began considering child labor curbs in 1905. Introduced by young Representative Madison Bell, the bill set the age limit at twelve, except sometimes ten would do. It didn't seem particularly harsh, but Mr. Gordon eloquently marshaled all his arguments against the measure.

Nor was he alone. Also testifying against the bill was Mr. Austin of the Whittier Mill, who declared, "I know the mill laws of Massachusetts, and there is no doubt that those mills up there want to get the Southern mills put on the same footing with themselves, so as to embarrass us in competing with them." A little misleading, for at this very moment Mr. Austin was representing not Southern but Northern interests. The Whittier Mill's largest stockholder happened to be Paul Butler, son of the South's anathema General Ben Butler of Massachusetts.

Another spokesman against the child labor bill was kindly Harry Meikleham, agent of the Lindale Mills. Earlier he had signed an open letter to the people of Georgia, blaming the agitation on "the energy of our competitors in the North and East." Again, a little misleading.

Mr. Meikleham's Lindale plant was entirely owned by the great Massachusetts Mills of Lowell.

As the time for voting neared, a Mr. J. J. Spalding checked into Atlanta's Kimball Hotel and added his own special talents to the assault on the bill. Jack Spalding was reputed to be the most effective lobbyist in the state, and at the moment was serving as chairman of the Legislative Committee of the Georgia Industrial Association. This group, which bitterly opposed the bill, happened to be quietly but strongly influenced by Northern-owned mills.

This combination of forces proved too much for the more inexperienced Georgia progressives supporting the measure. It was beaten in the State Senate 23-17. Rehashing the defeat, Dr. McKelway tried to be understanding, but he couldn't help thinking, "It does rather rile a Southern man to have a Massachusetts Corporation with good laws in its home state, come to Georgia, employ children at tender ages and at long hours, such as would not be permitted in Massachusetts, and then resist the effort of the Georgia Legislature to pass an effective child labor law."

It also "riled" a spirited Boston lady named Mrs. Glendower Evans, who had great pride in Massachusetts and a conscience to go with it. For years Mrs. Evans had assumed, like many other Bostonians, that the fight against child labor reform in Georgia was led by purely Southern interests. And like many other Bostonians, she also assumed that New England mill men were far more idealistic on this matter. "Massachusetts has led the way in this country in restricting the age and hours during which children may do factory work. . . . This is a record in which Massachusetts glories."

The eye-opener came on a trip down South in 1903. Mrs. Evans was surprised to discover that Northern mills, with good standards in Massachusetts, were taking a leading part in the fight against child labor reform in Georgia. And she was positively appalled to learn that one of these factories—the Massachusetts Mills of Lindale, Georgia—was a company in which, through family inheritance, she was a stockholder.

Returning to Boston, Mrs. Evans took new interest in developments in Georgia. She was dismayed by the Lindale Mills' role in defeating the 1905 bill. Nor was she mollified when Manager Meikleham supported a mild bill that passed in 1906. It still let ten-year-olds work, and Mr. Meikleham undermined any good effects by commenting that the whole law was "worthless."

With mounting indignation, even shame, Mrs. Evans began writing letters to the directors of her Massachusetts companies. She begged them to abandon their double standards . . . to apply Massachusetts age limits in their Southern mills . . . above all, to fight for, rather than against, child labor reform in Georgia. "It would be a new and higher achievement if Massachusetts capital were to carry the Massachusetts conscience with it wherever it may be invested, and make its influence count in favor of humane conditions such as already exist in so high a degree for the working people of this state."

Her pleas had little effect. Visiting the Lindale Mills a few years later, investigator Lewis W. Hine saw "youngsters by the dozen, tiny little chaps, sweeping, doffing, spinning—there were twenty-five of them that I judged to be under twelve in the three spinning rooms alone, and I found some more in the weave rooms, helping."

At that, the Lindale management was more advanced than some, for at least it allowed Hine to poke around. Other mills didn't let outsiders in, and since they usually owned not only the factories but the houses, stores and streets as well, their orders were final. When the Reverend Alfred E. Seddon visited the Porterdale Mills in 1908, he was refused a room at the local hotel and advised to take the next train out of town.

Whole communities seemed mesmerized. In Winona, Mississippi (not Georgia, but typical), a local doctor declared that the longer children were in a factory, the healthier they grew. "Why, one bright little girl told me she gained ten pounds in four months after going to work in the mill."

In 1911 Georgia again considered the child labor question, and the reform groups again found themselves up against ingenious opposition. This time petitions poured in to the legislature ostensibly from mill workers all over the state. They begged the lawmakers not to shorten hours, not to stop night work, not to set any age limitations. Some were all signed by the same hand, but others seemed genuine— painfully scrawled signatures by the few who could write, rows of X's for the many who couldn't.

Somewhere along the line the owners also picked up a poet laureate. He was Thomas Dawley, who specialized in obtaining rapturous testimonials from enthusiastic child workers. One little victim of reform in Tennessee was quoted as pleading, "Oh, kind sir, can't you do something to have the law changed so that I can go back to the cotton mill?"

Against this sort of talent not much could be done. By the end of the 1911 session the reform elements did manage to win a sixty-hour work week. But the eleven-hour day remained, and it was still legal for a ten-year-old child to work in a Georgia cotton mill.

But the reform groups kept chipping away, and in 1912 it seemed as if something might be done. The progressive movement was at flood tide and, best of all, the millowners appeared to see the light. Not just liberal manufacturers like Harry L. Williams of Swift Company—he had always understood—but even Frederick B. Gordon, the transplanted Bostonian. As president of the Georgia Cotton Manufacturers Association, Mr. Gordon indicated that his organization would not oppose a reasonable bill.

Just to make sure, the reformers met with the association's officials and went over the provisions together. When the manufacturers objected to parts of the proposed bill, a compromise was worked out. In its final form the measure gradually raised the age limit to fourteen. Everybody seemed agreeable.

The bill sailed through the House with one minor amendment— store help was exempted to allow for delivery boys, bootblacks, stock clerks, and the like. Although disappointed, the progressives felt half a loaf was better than none and let the change stand.

But not Frederick B. Gordon. He vigorously complained that the bill was no longer in its original shape. Then he appeared at the Senate hearings on behalf of the children who worked in the stores, as the reform leaders watched in wide-eyed amazement. They soon learned what was up. Since these lads in the stores weren't covered, Mr. Gordon felt reluctantly compelled to withdraw his support. The Cotton Manufacturers Association fell in line and the bill was defeated. Once again Georgia had no effective child labor law.

When the Reverend Harvey Vaughn resumed his tireless investigations of mill conditions the following April, Mr. Gordon cheerfully described his role in beating the 1912 bill. But he announced that he was now definitely going to work for a law. Hence the reformers' optimism when the new bill came up in August, 1913—and their surprise when it lost like so many of the others. They might have known better, for certainly the pattern was familiar: Again a compromise approved by everybody . . . again a minor amendment . . . again defeat.

Senator Spinks, one of the measure's opponents, tried to placate the progressives. He said that the bill was "beautiful in theory but it would not stand the test." And he added that Georgia was not ready.

Maybe not, but almost. Each successive defeat had awakened more interest, and now public support was strong. Georgia labor leaders and newspapers threw their weight behind the battling clergymen and progressive politicians.

By December sentiment was hot enough for an interesting meeting to take place at the National Child Labor Committee headquarters. Mr. Edward Lovering of the Massachusetts Mills of Lowell and Harry Meikleham of the firm's Lindale Mills (he who had earlier warned so darkly of Northern mills) together called on the committee leaders and strongly complained about the drive. They especially resented any comparison of the company's Massachusetts and Georgia mills. They couldn't see why the same age limits should apply to both. The committee couldn't see why not.

The movement continued to build up steam, and in the summer of 1914 the Atlanta *Georgian* went all-out in support of reform. All through July the paper ran immensely effective articles, editorials, and cartoons. By August the battle was won. A new bill was proposed and this time passed by the Legislature. There were loopholes—and the educational requirement was a little weak—but at least children under fourteen (with a few exceptions) were kept out of the mills and factories. Georgia at last had its law.

A great day, but poor children were still a long way from rich children. The upper-class child was, in fact, as sheltered as the working child was exposed. Parents were rarely seen—except at appointed hours—and often life was spent in the hands of English nannies, German governesses, and French maids.

Everyone seemed to conspire to preserve this cotton-padded world, so removed from reality. *The American Boys' Handy Book* devoted a chapter to putting on "Puss 'n' Boots." *Saint Nicholas Magazine* overflowed with gentle yarns—like Richard Harding Davis' story of the little invalid befriended by the wealthy Princeton football captain. And, as Eleanor Roosevelt recalled in her own recollections of childhood, "babies dropped from heaven or were brought in the doctor's satchel."

It's not surprising that the neat school compositions of wealthy children (even when written early in their teens) were so often devoted to brownies, little creatures of the forest, and fairy princes. "Where, oh where, do the fairies meet . . ." began a thirteen-year-old's poem in 1905.

But if America was still a land of extremes, there was at least a great moral awakening. Ordinary people in every walk of life felt a growing sense of social responsibility. It was not so much a political movement as a purely humanitarian revolt against poverty . . . a warmhearted crusade for a finer, cleaner life.

Child labor reform was only one sign. Another was the spate of laws governing factory safety, minimum hours for women, and workmen's compensation. Sometimes it took a vivid tragedy like New York's Triangle Waist Company fire to get action. In this holocaust 146 workers—mostly young girls—died because of overcrowding, cluttered rubbish, lack of exits, miserable working conditions. But usually no dramatic event was needed. Some civic league simply prepared the groundwork; the people's conscience did the rest.

This moralistic revival extended far beyond labor problems. It popped up in every phase of daily life. The New Orleans city fathers banned "September Morn"; the Bishop of Nashville forbade the tango. And Secretary of State Bryan dismayed the diplomatic set by serving only grape juice. But apart from his personal conviction, Bryan knew the public mood; he realized that prohibition was now sweeping the land. Reviewing the fervid feeling of the times, the January 24, 1914, issue of *Collier's* proudly declared, "Fifty years from now the future historian will say that the ten years ending about January 1, 1914, was the period of the greatest ethical advance made by this nation in any decade."

But all too soon no one even noticed. For in the hot, languid summer of 1914—in fact on the very day the Georgia Senate Committee finally approved the child labor bill—Germany unexpectedly invaded Belgium, and within a few brief years the tramp of marching feet stamped out such pleasant thoughts.

1914

The Last Summer

*"Let us wear on our sleeves the crepe of mourning for a civilization
that had the promise of joy."*

—HAROLD BEGBIE

Child labor, reform, causes—they all seemed far away in Atlanta
on the morning of Sunday, June 28, 1914. It was a lazy summer day
and hard to get worked up over anything more serious than last week's
arrest of Harris G. White, the prominent real-estate man, for wearing
a sleeveless bathing suit in Piedmont Lake.

The massive Sunday paper was by now an American institution,
and Atlantans waded through feature stories like "The History of
the Elberta Peach" or read how Jack Johnson, the Negro heavyweight
champion, easily outpointed Frank Moran in Paris, France. Clearly,
boxing fans would have to wait a little longer for the already long-
awaited "White Hope."

The fight was the big sports story for most of the country, but in
Baltimore local baseball fans happily read that their new rookie, young
Babe Ruth, had just pitched the minor league Orioles to a 10-5 victory
over Buffalo.

By eleven o'clock it was time for church, and all over the nation
people answered the tolling bells. In Muskogee, Oklahoma, the Rev-

erend James K. Thompson delivered what was surely neither the first nor the last sermon ever to be called "Whither Are We Drifting?"

Forty-eight hundred miles away, it was also a hot, lazy Sunday in Sarajevo, capital of the Austro-Hungarian province of Bosnia. Here too the day had dawned bright and sunny. Here too the people had flocked to their churches. But not everybody, for the morning offered an interesting counter-attraction. The Archduke Franz Ferdinand and his wife, the Duchess of Hohenberg, had arrived from Vienna—hoping to cement the ties that bound Slavic Bosnia to the Empire . . . trying to curb the growing sentiment for a union with Serbia.

And the people's mood seemed all too clear. Driving to a morning reception at the City Hall, Franz Ferdinand barely escaped an attempt to blow up his car. "Herr Burgermeister," he greeted the unfortunate mayor, "we have come here to pay you a visit and bombs have been thrown at us. This is altogether an amazing indignity!"

Undeterred, the mayor gamely stuck to the script of his prepared address: "All the citizens of the capital city of Sarajevo find that their souls are filled with happiness, and they most enthusiastically greet Your Highnesses' most illustrious visit with the most cordial of welcomes. . . ."

Amenities over, Franz Ferdinand decided to visit an aide wounded by the misdirected bomb. Once again he climbed into the back of his big gray touring car, and with the Duchess sitting beside him, the official party set off down Appel Quay.

Then a wrong turn, and the car stopped to back. As it did, it drew opposite a young man named Gavrilo Princip. He was one of seven pan-Slav nationalists on hand that day for the express purpose of killing the Archduke. He just happened to be standing where the car stopped, but given the chance, he knew exactly how to use it. He stepped out from the curb, drew a Belgian pistol, and fired two quick shots at point-blank range.

Shouts, pounding feet, slashing sabers. Princip disappeared under an avalanche of surging, shoving, fist-swinging guards. The Archduke's car roared into reverse, spun around, and raced across the Lateiner Bridge toward the Governor's Palace. In the back seat, the Duchess of Hohenberg's head slumped between her husband's knees. Blood spurting from his own throat, Franz Ferdinand gasped, "Sophie dear! Sophie dear! Don't die! Stay alive for our children!"

Around eleven o'clock they were both carried into the palace, to die a few minutes later. Outside, the only signs of the hatred that seared central Europe were a few green feathers from the Imperial helmet, scattered on the floor of the empty touring car.

Next day, the news caused a brief flurry in the American press. The more romantic editors recalled Mayerling and dwelt on "the curse of the Hapsburgs." Other papers speculated about the political effect. Although cold and aloof, Franz Ferdinand had seemed the only man firm enough to hold the crumbling Austro-Hungarian Empire together. The New York *Sun,* however, felt that the removal of such a strong personality would in the end make for greater peace in Europe.

But it all seemed so far away. Even on the evening of the 29th, the Atlanta *Journal* didn't consider the assassination front-page news. And next morning Atlantans were far more interested in the park board's denunciation of Judge Nash Broyles for condoning Mr. White's sleeveless bathing suit. By July 1, the nation's press had all but forgotten Franz Ferdinand. As the Grand Forks, North Dakota, *Herald* put it: "To the world, or to a nation, an archduke more or less makes little difference."

Behind the heavy paneled doors of Vienna's ornate Foreign Ministry, men had other ideas. It was now definitely known that the assassination had been engineered in Serbia—the work of Slavic conspirators seeking to wrest Bosnia from the empire. The lights burned late, as Austria's statesmen began planning appropriate counter-measures.

America moved into a sleepy, typically hot July. Little to worry about beyond the next predicament of Miss Pearl White in *The Perils of Pauline,* the exciting new movie serial that was sweeping the country. "Pauline flees to the shore," ran the producer's blurb for the ninth episode, "persuades a hydroplane pilot to take her to safety. As they soar aloft, he lights a cigarette, flicks away the match, which lights on one of the wings, and in a few minutes the machine is in flames. Coward that he is, he grabs the only parachute and leaves Pauline to her fate . . ."

All this for only five cents, but then so many prices seemed reasonable. In Washington, D.C., eggs were 21 cents a dozen, a shoulder of lamb 16 cents a pound. In Houston, Texas, the Yale Painless Dentists offered gold fillings for 75 cents. Atlanta barbers gave haircuts for 15 cents, a Denver store advertised, "Ladies' house dresses 98¢."

Perhaps it was just as well, for a want ad in the Washington *Post* sought an industrious girl to cook and do housework—for $10 a month.

It was clearly big money, then, when the nation's top automobile drivers raced for $25,000 at Sioux City, Iowa, on the Fourth of July. The country briefly awoke from its torpor—it always did on the Fourth—and watched with interest as Eddie Rickenbacker drove his big Dusenberg Special to victory. He averaged seventy-eight miles an hour over the three hundred-mile course—quite a feat, even though Barney Oldfield, the greatest legend of them all, was forced out by engine trouble early in the race.

Back to the hammock, and hours equally tranquil whether a man was humble or high-placed. Writing from his post in Germany on July 7, Ambassador Gerard told Colonel House how a pleasant sail with the Kaiser was interrupted by Sarajevo . . . how tennis was responsible for his wretched handwriting . . . how everybody had left town: "Berlin is as quiet as a grave."

Ambassador Gerard hadn't noticed anything unusual, but the day before he scribbled his letter, the Kaiser and Chancellor Bethmann-Hollweg held an important meeting with Austrian representatives at Potsdam. Mighty Germany was Vienna's only real ally, and it meant a great deal when the Kaiser gave Austria *carte blanche* to punish Serbia any way she liked for Franz Ferdinand's murder.

"RABASA HOPES FOR PEACE" ran the headline in the New York *Post* a few days later, but the story had nothing to do with Austro-Serbian relations. It was about the Mexican Revolution, which gave the July dog days a little seasoning this summer. The revolution had raged for over a year . . . Wilson had occupied Vera Cruz . . . and now the

Mexican dictator Huerta seemed near defeat, with an end to the bloodshed in sight.

The globe was full of such irritating trouble spots this summer—any of them good for a short front-page item from time to time. There was the Ulster crisis, with civil war threatening in Ireland. There was great disorder in Haiti and Santo Domingo, with Washington preparing once again to land the Marines. And, of course, there was Eastern Europe. "Is Another Balkan War Near?" ran the title of an item in the July *Review of Reviews*. The article, however, said nothing about Bosnia; it referred to wrangling over Albania and the perennial threat of Greco-Turkish hostilities.

All this seemed far away too, and America continued its placid summer. In Grand Forks, North Dakota, the Sells-Floto Circus arrived on July 11, with Buffalo Bill himself leading the traditional parade. But the great frontiersman looked a little old now, and some found more excitement trooping behind the Giant Serenadum, a magnificent calliope that shot out jets of steam with every piercing note.

This same week in Cheyenne, Wyoming, another tent went up, but for a different kind of show. The Chautauqua was in town, presenting its incredible mixture of education, entertainment, and sawdust. The season ticketholder faced a succession of Hawaiian minstrels, minor government officials, acrobats, stumping ministers, and (this week, anyhow) Kiyo Sue Inui, vaguely identified as "the Japanese Orator."

Carried away by the galaxy, the local *State-Leader* crowed, "Some have wondered how Cheyenne was able to secure as good talent as this." Nevertheless, tickets moved slowly, perhaps because they were advertised the same day as an accessory every woman simply had to have—the $4.00 Tango and slit skirt mesh bag, "very nobby and all the rage."

The ad was right. This was indeed the summer of the tango. At first a fad of the fashionable, the new dance spread like a prairie fire. Gone were the days when the Bishop of Nashville could banish it with a wave of his hand. Now it was everywhere. At Coney Island, couples tangoed up and down the stairs of the Castle Summer House. In Denver, thousands tangoed in the streets on the final night of the Elks' jamboree. At Brighton Beach, couples tangoed in the sand. In

Little Rock the press worried about the "tango face." And in Muskogee, Oklahoma, this problem was explained a little more clearly by the *Daily Phoenix:* "The effort of trying to look proper while dancing the tango must be very trying to the facial muscles of the up-to-date woman."

Not that morals had collapsed. The tango was simply taking its place in the procession of great American fads. Otherwise the country remained eminently proper. West Virginia joined the growing list of dry states. Lillian Russell wrote a syndicated article called "Drink and Be Ugly." Chicago prohibited men and women from bathing together on municipal beaches. And in St. Paul, Minnesota, a convention of educators condemned (of all things) foundation grants as "menacing academic freedom."

Part and parcel of the penchant for purity was a new vogue for classical dancing. In Newport, Society girls temporarily abandoned the social whirl and pranced barefoot about the lawns, smothered in togas and laurel wreaths.

But Newport was still Newport, and interest soon returned to parties, Bailey's Beach, and above all, Sir Thomas Lipton's coming assault on the America's Cup. On July 18 word came that the new challenger *Shamrock IV* had started from Portsmouth on its trip across the Atlantic.

That same day in St. Petersburg, the Czar's Foreign Minister Sergei Sezinov delivered a stern warning to the Austrian Ambassador. The Russian government had heard rumors that Vienna planned strong measures against Serbia. The ambassador must be reminded that Russia, the protector of the Slavs, "would not be indifferent to any attempt to humiliate Serbia. Russia could not permit Austria to use menacing language or military measures against Serbia."

America dozed on. The West moved into one of its patented heat waves, and most people found it too hot even to read the papers. Nothing in them anyhow. That is, unless one read the financial pages very, very carefully. Here, there were odd, cryptic little items, buried deep in dispatches from abroad. On July 18 Serbian bonds dropped from 78½ to 76½. On July 20, the New York *Post's* financial correspondent in London spoke vaguely of "heavy Vienna selling due to the Austria-Serbian situation"—no further explanation. Foreign dispatches to the Chicago *Tribune* described the Paris, Berlin, and Vienna markets as "demoralized"—again, no further explanation. Heavy shipments of gold began moving out of New York for European destinations . . . no one tried to explain this either.

Even if anybody had been interested, it would have been hard to get at the facts. There was no tighter fraternity in the world than the small group that bound together European politics and finance. In every nation, the great figures who set the political course also determined financial policies—and in many cases had vast fortunes of their own at stake too. What they learned they kept to themselves and quietly took whatever steps seemed necessary.

July 23. Houston's Montrose Embroidery Club met as usual. In Philadelphia, Chief Bender pitched the A's to a 9-2 win over Cleveland. "Little Mary Pickford" thrilled her fans in Washington, Denver, probably fifty other cities. In Little Rock the latest bargain was the "Castle Walk Shoe"—another tribute to Vernon and Irene Castle's influence in dancing. But as a reminder that at least some old ideas still prevailed, the San Francisco *Chronicle* headed a feature story, "Disadvantage of Being a Lady—When Hungry: If rich relatives won't keep you and you're asked to go to work."

At Lake Forest, Illinois, tennis enthusiasts watched Australia's awesome Davis Cup team trounce Canada in the first challenge round. The Chicago *Tribune* assured its readers that the event attracted "practically all Society folk still in town."

That evening Vienna finally showed its hand. At 6:00 P.M. the Austrian ambassador in Belgrade handed the Serbian government a document that astounded anyone accustomed to the usual niceties of diplomatic language. In the harshest terms, it blamed Serbia's "culpable tolerance" for harboring the movement that led to Franz Ferdinand's assassination. It called on Belgrade to repudiate all anti-Austrian activity and to punish the guilty parties. It insisted that Serbia accept Austrian police help in doing this. And it demanded compliance by 6:00, July 25—just forty-eight hours off.

This was more than an ultimatum. The humiliating language was obviously designed to be unacceptable . . . thus giving Austria a long-awaited pretext to march in and crush the pan-Slav movement herself. A mammoth storm was clearly blowing up.

"ALL CHIEFS FAVOR PEACE," the New York *Post* proclaimed the following day. But again, the paper was referring not to Europe but to Mexico. Austria's ultimatum drew little attention anywhere. The Muskogee, Oklahoma, *Daily Phoenix* gave it ten lines on page six. And lest it seem unfair to take such a small paper, the mighty Chicago *Tribune* didn't mention it at all.

So America continued to drift—another untroubled day of Eskimo Pies . . . droning electric fans . . . open-air trolley rides . . . winding up the Victrola to hear "Sylvia" just once more. The big event of the day—and front-page news nearly everywhere—was Mrs. O. H. P. Belmont's fabulous Chinese Ball at Newport. Once more the country interrupted its simple pleasures to enjoy the spectacle of Society at play.

No one was disappointed. Mrs. Belmont converted Marble House into a reasonable replica of the Imperial Palace at Peking (actually, not very difficult to do) and added pelicans for extra authenticity. Mrs. Stuyvesant Fish came in robes that once belonged to a daughter of the Empress Keen-Lung. Smiling pleasantly—as though nothing were going on behind the scenes—Baron Kurt von Lersner of the German Embassy (in blue silk mandarin coat) chatted amiably with Joseph Loris-Melikoff of the Russian Embassy (in robes of purple and gold).

The following morning, July 25, the country suddenly woke up. Long before Vienna's ultimatum technically expired, word came that Serbia, though conciliatory, couldn't yield all the way . . . that she was backed by Russia and France . . . that Austria wouldn't give an inch . . . that she was backed by Germany.

"ALL EUROPE ON VERGE OF WAR," ran the shocked headline in Denver's *Rocky Mountain News,* and the words were repeated with little change all over the nation. People were stunned by the lack of warning—it was like a train plunging suddenly into a tunnel—but there was no doubt it was so. The headlines grew blacker with every edition. Foreign news bureaus, asleep for weeks, suddenly gushed out a torrent of late flashes, inside stories, background data, and interviews with that inevitable "authoritative spokesman who must at present remain unidentified." Dazed and overwhelmed, the American people picked up the threads as best they could.

And it wasn't easy, for events were now racing with lightning speed. On July 28 the *New York Times* optimistically declared, "A general European war is unthinkable . . . Europe can't afford such a war, and the world can't afford it, and happily the conviction is growing that such an appalling conflict is altogether beyond the realm of possibility."

But that very day Austria declared war on Serbia, and one by one the major European powers—chained together by interlocking alliances —tumbled into the fight. August 1, Germany against Russia . . . August 3, Germany against France. Britain tried to stay clear, but it was hopeless—she was bound to protect Belgium against German invasion, and was tied to France by interests as strong as any formal alliance. At eleven o'clock on the evening of August 4, London declared war on Germany; and the great general conflict that seemed so impossible had at last begun.

"It is almost inconceivable," declared the Houston *Post*. "This incredible European catastrophe," Woodrow Wilson wrote his friend Mary Hulbert. "Unthinkable, if it did not happen before our very eyes," sighed the Arkansas *Gazette*. "The war of nations has discovered the poverty of the language. Words are insufficient for the job," philosophized the Chicago *Tribune*. Maybe, but the Cedar Rapids, Iowa, *Gazette* made a brave try: "Blood-mad monarchs prepare dread sacrifice. Fifteen millions facing death. Royalty forces wreck and ruin on fated lands. Stubborn rulers play subjects as pawns."

A little lurid, perhaps, but a favorite theme. America was fascinated, if appalled, by the spectacle of these closely related kings and princes leading their subjects to war. Why, the Kaiser and the Czar even called each other "Willy" and "Nicky." It all seemed so outdated, so archaic, so hideously medieval to a country fairly bursting with progress.

Of all these royal figures, the Kaiser seemed the most preposterous.

He was so completely the antithesis of everything the new America stood for—those ridiculous uniforms, the spiked helmet, the constant flow of personal messages to God. Wilhelm tried hard to win American sentiment, but he never had a chance. Long before the "rape of Belgium," few could swallow this bombastic man who was not only an Emperor but twice a grand duke, eighteen times an ordinary duke, ten times a count, and three times something called a margrave.

Yes, the Kaiser was the worst; but to most Americans—happily insulated from old-world frictions—it all seemed insane. Why would anybody fight about a murdered archduke from someone else's land? "As for the superficial contentions at issue," concluded the Washington *Post,* "a police court judge could adjust them in a week."

Searching for a deeper explanation, Americans turned to various foreign visitors. But they weren't very helpful either. Cornered in New York, the Reverend J. Stuart Holden of London could only say, "What is the trouble? I don't believe there are five people who can tell."

Unconsciously, Dr. Holden was speaking for millions of other Englishmen. With almost bitter-sweet resignation, Britain felt honor-bound to fight, but participation didn't make it any less bewildering. For days the English lived in a kind of twilight—clearly at war but still surrounded by vestiges of peace.

"The shooting season is now upon us," chirped the *Illustrated London News* on August 8, and the full irony of the passage only emerged as the reader read on: "A neat and pretty interior to the shooting box adds to the comfort and enjoyment." The same week, the *Sphere* was still advertising pleasure trips to Hamburg.

Even three weeks later the *Sphere's* lady columnist had an odd assessment of the situation: "Happily things are so far normal again that the women of this country are beginning, for the sake of those who would necessarily suffer if they did not, to take a chastened interest in fashions once more. So many of the shops have determined to retain their staffs as being their best service to the country, that everybody feels it a patriotic duty to second them as far as possible."

Then the casualty lists began to roll in. Long, frightful, endless. And everybody finally understood the full meaning of Sir Edward

Grey's wistful remark on the eve of war: "The lamps are going out all over Europe. We shall not see them lit again in our lifetime."

"If Europe insists on committing suicide, Europe must furnish the corpse for Europe's funeral," was the earthy way the New York *World* put it. And the comment not only echoed Sir Edward's feelings but expressed the universal relief that America was not involved. "Peace-loving citizens of this country," declared the Chicago *Record-Herald,* "will now rise up and tender a hearty vote of thanks to Columbus for having discovered America."

All agreed that the war would have little effect on life at home. The New Haven *Journal-Courier* worried about a possible labor shortage as European reservists hurried back, but it was hard to regard this very seriously. Economists puzzled over the business consequences but came up with nothing startling. *Current Opinion* felt that foreign sales of shoes and blankets would benefit, non-military goods would drop off. Among the latter, the magazine listed oil, automobiles, copper, and machinery. None of this seemed to affect the average person.

But strange things began happening almost right away. Less than a week after England's declaration, the small Cheyenne Milling Company sold six thousand sacks of wheat on the Denver market in one bonanza day—something the sleepy little mill never dreamed of doing before. Almost ruefully, the Cheyenne *State-Leader* reminded the management that it owed a lot to the town in other days; let it not forget the local housewife in setting its prices now. But prices were, of course, beyond any single firm's control—up, up they soared. Would they ever come back down?

Economics were only part of the story. Almost overnight, Americans lost a happy, easygoing, confident way of looking at things. Gone was the bright lilt of "When You Wore a Tulip"; already it was the sadly nostalgic, "There's a Long, Long Trail a-Winding," or the grimly suggestive, "I Didn't Raise My Boy to Be a Soldier." A mounting crescendo of screaming headlines . . . atrocity stories . . . U-boat sinkings . . . charges and counter-charges shocked the nation, jarred its faith, left a residue of doubt and dismay.

Nothing seemed simple any more. Nothing was black and white.

Nothing was "right" or "wrong," the way Theodore Roosevelt used to describe things. And as the simple problems vanished, so did the simple solutions. Trust-busting, direct primaries, arbitration treaties and all the rest. They somehow lost their glamour as exciting panaceas, and nothing took their place. But the problems grew and grew— preparedness . . . taxes . . . war . . . Bolshevism . . . disillusionment . . . depression . . . Fascism . . . Moscow . . . fallout . . . space . . . more taxes.

So the old life slipped away, never to return again, and wise men sensed it almost at once. Men like Henry White, the immensely urbane diplomat who had served the country so well. "He instinctively felt," according to his biographer Allan Nevins, "that his world—the world of constant travel, cosmopolitan intercourse, secure comfort and culture —would never be the same again." The Philadelphia *North American* felt the same way, but in blunter words: "What does this mean but that our boasted civilization has broken down?"

Perhaps it was just as well. There was much that was wrong with this old way of living—its injustices, its naïveté, its waste, its smug self-assurance. Men would come along to fix all that. New laws, controls, regulations, forms filled out in triplicate would keep anybody from getting too much or too little. And swarms of consultants, researchers, special assistants, and executive committees would make sure that great men always said and did the right thing.

There would be great gains. But after all the gains had been counted, it would turn out that something was also lost—a touch of optimism, confidence, exuberance, and hope. The spirit of an era can't be blocked out and measured, but it is there nonetheless. And in these brief, buoyant years it was a spark that somehow gave extra promise to life. By the light of this spark, men and women saw themselves as heroes shaping the world, rather than victims struggling through it.

Actually, this was nothing unique. People had seen the spark before, would surely do so again. For it can never die as long as men breathe. But sometimes it burns low, leaving men uncertain in the shadows; other times it glows bright, catching the eye with breath-taking visions of the future.

Acknowledgments

"I am grateful that I lived during this period, when in my opinion America was at its best," says Miss Mathilda Duester, recalling the pleasure of growing up at the turn of the century.

There are many like her. Whether they lived quietly in a small New England town like Miss Duester, or played a colorful role in the exciting events that unfolded—like George Schuster who won the great New York to Paris auto race in 1908—all sorts of people still draw happiness and satisfaction from having been part of the era.

Perhaps this inner satisfaction explains their easy graciousness today. In any case, so many of them have contributed so much to this book that it is impossible to thank them all. These brief acknowledgments give only a glimpse of my gratitude.

And the glimpse is necessarily kaleidoscopic, for it is difficult to imagine a more varied collection of interesting people: Dr. Carrington Goodrich of Columbia University, who dodged the Boxers' cannonballs . . . Mrs. Charles Dickey, who whirled to Nahan Franko's music at the glittering Hyde Ball . . . Judge Charles F. Koelsch, who was in the midst of the Haywood trial . . . Miss Alice Paul, who battled so hard for woman suffrage . . . Truxton Midgett, who delivered the Wright brothers' groceries . . . Chief Rudy Schubert, who fought the flames in San Francisco . . . the Honorable Howard W. Jackson and the Honorable George L. Radcliffe, who did their bit for Woodrow Wilson—to name only a few.

Some have helped not so much on any single event as on threads running through the whole period. Mrs. Kermit Roosevelt, for instance, is wonderfully wise about her illustrious family. And Mrs. Henry B. Harris is invaluable when it comes to anything about the entertainment world—after all, she was the first woman brave enough to be a theatrical producer.

Others have gone to endless trouble just to clear up some specific aspect of a larger event. Sidney Ehrman took time out from a busy law practice to help piece together Caruso's movements during the San Francisco fire. Harry Moore left a cool home on a hot Norfolk day to discuss the *Virginian-Pilot's* scoop on the Wright brothers' first flight. Miss Pauline Robinson took the pains to write a charming vignette of the actress Réjane at the famous Hyde Ball. Miss Ruth Ingram, answering a call for Boxer Rebellion survivors, found herself drafted to research a point in Boston—and did it perfectly without a murmur. Mrs. Portia Willis Fitzgerald gave up a carefully planned afternoon to explain the distinction between various suffrage groups.

Mrs. J. Borden Harriman was another who contributed to the suffrage story, and as we talked, it became evident that she could help equally on the chapters dealing with social life, travel and Wilson's nomination. I'm afraid I exploited this bonanza unmercifully. Another who helped on more than one story was Mrs. Frank R. Girard. She not only was in the San Francisco earthquake but was nearly murdered during the Western mining wars. Chatting with her today in her lovely home, it's difficult to believe that this gentle lady once received a lethal dose of strychnine in her milk.

Times have changed so much. Again, it's hard to realize that one can still talk with the very first person to greet Wilbur Wright when he arrived in Kitty Hawk. Yet Elijah Baum couldn't be more chipper —living proof that the vast strides of aviation have all taken place within an incredibly short period.

Many of these fine people contributed not only their own experiences, but rummaged through drawers and attics for pertinent letters, diaries and pictures. The Reverend M. Gardner Tewksbury, for instance, contributed beautiful photographs of the Boxer Rebellion, as well as a handwritten plea for help by Sir Claude MacDonald. Mrs. Robert Hunt Walker dug out all sorts of leads on other early suffrage workers. Mr. L. Wethered Barroll supplied the notes he kept on the 1912 Democratic Convention. It's been some time since Mrs. Raymond S. Leopold made available that bon voyage letter she received on the *Titanic*, but I'm no less grateful for the chance to use it. Mrs. Sheldon G. Kellogg looked anything but ninety, bustling about, collecting her family letters on the San Francisco fire and earthquake. Lawrence W. Harris survived not only that disaster but an endless bombardment of requests for help on various problems. He has never failed me.

But once started on San Francisco, there's no end to the people who should be thanked. To name a few: Mrs. Gustavus R. A. Browne, Mrs. Jack Dohrmann, Judge Timothy I. Fitzpatrick, Dion R. Holm, Mrs. Alfred Hurtgen, Mrs. Ben Jordan, Oscar Lewis, Mrs. L. M. McKinley, Chief William F. Murray, Mrs. Sanford Newbauer, Harry Perry, Mrs. E. B. Sutton, Miss Emily Timlow, and Mrs. John I. Walters. The late E. D. Coblentz was also immensely helpful.

In the case of some events, the actual participants are no longer alive but their families have been magnificent. On McKinley's assassination, Miss Frances Babcock supplied a fascinating eight-page letter by her father, Louis L. Babcock, who stood only a few feet from the shooting; Dean Julian Park lent me an unexpurgated manuscript by his distinguished father, Dr. Roswell Park, who attended the dying President; Mrs. Robert North provided interesting details on the defense of Leon Czolgosz by her grandfather, Judge Loran L. Lewis.

For the story of E. H. Harriman's daring raid on the Northern Pacific Railroad, I relied mainly on written material, but Mrs. Walter Rothschild gave me charming recollections of her grandfather, Jacob Schiff, and his great rival, James J. Hill. Mr. Sam Tate provided lively details handed down by his father, Dan Tate, who worked for the Wrights at Kitty Hawk.

Needless to say, these many kind people share no responsibility for my thoughts or conclusions, no blame for any errors or misinterpretations, only credit for whatever new light is thrown on this fascinating period.

Aside from those having some personal connection with the events covered, students and authorities on almost every subject have generously contributed information. The late Fred C. Kelly poured out his knowledge on the Wright brothers—his fine biography remains the definitive work on the subject. Fred J. Thibold of Louis Sherry, Inc., lovingly described the old days at Sherry's and made available the famous restaurant's order books. Dr. Merle Wells was invaluable on the Haywood murder trial—what can compare with the confidential Pinkerton reports he unearthed in the cellar of the Idaho Historical Society? Frederick B. Adams guided me through the Morgan Library and showed me that copy of *Prometheus Unbound,* so movingly inscribed after the Panic of 1907. Russell A. Langdon proved to be a gold mine of items on the Great White Fleet. John Edward Weems made the greatest sacrifice an author can make—he took time out from his own book *Race for the Pole* to help me on points about Robert E. Peary.

Those unsung heroes, the librarians, were as helpful as ever. I'm especially grateful to: The Board of Missions of the Methodist Church for unpublished material on Dr. Frank D. Gamewell; the Missionary Research Library, the Army and Navy Historical staffs, and the Marine archives for other Boxer material; Miss Ann Costakis of the Library of Congress for a fine rush job on photographs; the Buffalo Historical Association for data on McKinley's assassination—and for letting me examine Czolgosz's pistol.

I'm also indebted to the National Park Association for so much help at Kitty Hawk; the California Historical Society for letters on the San Francisco earthquake and fire (or fire and earthquake, as they have gently taught me to say); the Idaho Historical Society for mountains of material on the Haywood trial; Admiral E. M. Eller and his fine staff at the Navy Department for material on the Great White Fleet; the Maryland Historical Society for information on the 1912 Democratic Convention; and the National Child Labor Committee for priceless papers and correspondence dealing with their gallant, uphill struggle throughout the period.

Along with the unpublished data, all these libraries and associations made available many books, pamphlets and periodicals. A selected bibliography follows these pages.

Certain helpful individuals sometimes took the place of libraries. Peter Brooks assisted greatly in locating material for the first chapter. Mrs. Diana Hobby produced the cartoon of "Little 1900." Thomas G. Carney performed the heroic feat of raiding the Treasury Department for the first income-tax blank. Mrs. Roger Butterfield gave priceless help on all the illustrations. Jack Crooks did wonders on the Index.

Finally, there are a number of people closer to me personally. Some were sort of "guardian angels," who guided me in various places where research was necessary—like Robert Meech in Buffalo; Alec Brown at Kitty Hawk; William Orrick in San Francisco; Commander Herb Gimpel in Washington; Jerry Swinney in Boise; Francis F. Beirne and John E. Semmes in Baltimore. Others simply couldn't escape—like Evan Thomas, my long-suffering editor, and Florence Cassedy, who once again undertook the monumental task of deciphering my illegible handwriting.

Published Material

In addition to the interviews, diaries, notes and correspondence mentioned in the Acknowledgments, I relied on much published material. This included newspapers from some twenty-five cities—really necessary to get the full flavor of the period. It's impossible to list everything, but here—chapter by chapter—is what might be called a selected bibliography.

A New Year

All incidents are taken from newspapers dated December 31, 1899 to January 2, 1900, in the following cities: New York, St. Louis, Boston, Los Angeles, Louisville, Cheyenne, Chicago, Houston, New Orleans, Denver, Birmingham, Ala., and Portland, Ore. Predictions generally came a year later, when the new century technically began. The best of dozens: H. G. Wells, "Anticipations: an Experiment in Prophecy," *North American Review*, Vols. 172-173; "Supplement on the Twentieth Century," New York *World*, December 30, 1900; Ray Stannard Baker, "The Automobile in Common Use," *McClure's*, July, 1899; John Bates Clark, "Recollections of the Twentieth Century," *Atlantic*, January, 1902.

The Fumbling Imperialists

Top billing must go to Dr. G. E. Morrison's magnificent dispatches on the siege of Peking, London *Times*, October 13, 15, 1900. Some other stimulating first-hand accounts: Sir Robert Hart, *These from the Land of Sinim;* Arthur H. Smith, *China in Convulsion;* B. L. Putnam Weale, *Indiscreet Letters from Peking;* A. H. Tuttle, *Mary Porter Gamewell and Her Story of the Siege;* Sarah Pike Conger, *Letters from China;* Mary Hooker, *Behind the Scenes in Peking;* Ada Haven Mateer, *Siege Days;* Cecile E. Payen, *Besieged in Peking.* Two good general histories: A. H. Savage-Landor,

China and the Allies, and Peter Fleming's recent *The Siege at Peking.* Best account of the Marines' role is contained in the 1901 Report of the Secretary of the Navy, Part II, pp. 1266-1273. For marvelous atmosphere on the whole imperialist adventure, there's nothing better than C. G. Bowers, *Albert Beveridge and the Progressive Era.*

A Good Man's Death

The Buffalo papers from September 7 to September 14, 1901, contain innumerable eyewitness accounts of McKinley's assassination—many of them violently contradictory. Later and more sober recollections include: Charles G. Dawes, *A Journal of the McKinley Years;* Louis L. Babcock, "The Assassination of William McKinley," *Buffalo Historical Society,* 1947; Roswell Park, *Selected Papers.* For a marvelous study of Leon Czolgosz, see Robert J. Donovan, *The Assassins.* Glimpses of other actors in the drama can be found in Hermann H. Kohlsaat, *From McKinley to Harding;* Thomas Beer, *Hanna;* and of course, Theodore Roosevelt's *Autobiography.* The endless "memorial" biographies of McKinley (for instance, Murat Halstead's *Illustrious Life of William McKinley*) convey the national grief but give no picture of the man. Nor does Charles S. Olcott's *The Life of William McKinley.* Margaret Leech's fine *In the Days of McKinley* has at last filled the gap.

Big Stick, Big Business

All the participants in the raid on the Northern Pacific have huge, "doorstopper" biographies, containing their version of the story: George Kennan, *E. H. Harriman, a Biography;* Cyrus H. Adler, *Jacob Schiff, His Life and Letters;* Joseph Gilpin Pyle, *The Life of James J. Hill;* Anna Robeson Burr, *Portrait of a Banker: James Stillman;* Herbert L. Satterlee, *J. Pierpont Morgan, an Intimate Portrait.* For more refreshing treatment, see Frederick Lewis Allen, *Lords of Creation;* Stewart Holbrook, *Age of the Moguls.* The effect on those not "in the know" is well covered by the New York press— especially the *Tribune, Post,* and *Herald.* These papers also convey the astonishment that greeted Theodore Roosevelt's subsequent antitrust suit. For Pierpont Morgan's classic proposal, see Joseph Bucklin Bishop, *Theodore Roosevelt and His Time.* For data on the coal strike, I relied mainly on Philip C. Jessup, *Elihu Root;* E. G. Gluck, *John Mitchell;* Anthracite Coal Strike Commission, *Report,* 1903; Theodore Roosevelt, *Autobiography;* and the New York newspapers already mentioned.

349

Theodore Roosevelt runs through this and other chapters, and it's impossible to list all the stimulating books about him. Three personal favorites: Henry F. Pringle's *Theodore Roosevelt, a Biography; Theodore Roosevelt's Letters to His Children,* edited by Joseph Buklin Bishop; and Mark Sullivan's *Our Times,* which in fact gloriously covers the whole period.

"The Whopper Flying Machine"

Three fine sources: Marvin W. McFarland, *The Papers of Wilbur and Orville Wright;* Fred C. Kelly, *The Wright Brothers;* and the same author's *Miracle at Kitty Hawk.* For the thoughts of aviation skeptics, see issues of *McClure's, The Independent,* and *North American Review* mentioned in the text. The December 17, 1903, issue of the Norfolk *Virginian-Pilot* contains the historic scoop on the first flight, but in some ways the most fascinating early account is the curious item by A. I. Root in *Gleanings in Bee Culture,* March 1, 1904.

The Golden Circus

The Hyde Ball was thoroughly covered by the New York papers—especially the *Times, Tribune,* and *World.* The latter's fierce charges were answered rather meekly by the *Metropolitan Magazine,* March, 1905. Practices revealed by the subsequent insurance investigation are summarized in Burton J. Hendrick, *Story of Life Insurance.* On the general doings of Society, see Cleveland Amory, *The Last Resorts;* Frederick Lewis Allen, *The Big Change;* Lloyd Morris, *Postscript to Yesterday;* Grace Mayer, *Once upon a City.* And of course, the newspapers—not just the society section, but the front page, where everyone felt such news belonged.

The Town That Refused to Die

Most of the prominent people in San Francisco left interesting accounts: see William James, *Memories and Studies,* and also the *Letters of William James;* Frederick Funston, "How the Army Worked to Save San Francisco," *Cosmopolitan,* July, 1906; John Barrymore, *Confessions of an Actor;* Pierre Key, *Enrico Caruso;* Charmian London, *The Book of Jack London;* London's own account in *Collier's,* May 5, 1906; Franklin K. Lane, *Letters;* Mark James and Jessie James, *Biography of a Bank* (for A. P. Giannini). Perhaps the best first-hand accounts of all: James Hopper's article in *Everybody's* June, 1906, and James B. Stetson's pamphlet, *San Francisco during the Eventful Days of April, 1906.* A good contemporary book is David Starr Jordan, *The California Earthquake of 1906;* and for a fine modern treatment, see William Bronson, *The Earth Shook, the Sky Burned.*

Trial of a Union Man

Most of those involved had something to say: Clarence Darrow, *The Story of My Life;* William Haywood, *Bill Haywood's Book;* Fremont Wood, *Moyer, Haywood, Pettibone and Orchard;* Harry Orchard, *The Confessions and Autobiography of Harry Orchard.* (But my favorite glimpse of Orchard remains that contained in Ethel Barrymore's *Autobiography.*) For Darrow's summation, see Arthur Weinberg, *Attorney for the Damned;* for Borah's, see Boise *Idaho Daily Statesman* and *Evening Capital News.* The press is important throughout this story: the Caldwell *Tribune* for details on Steunenberg's murder; the Boise papers for coverage of the trial; almost any national magazine or newspaper for public acceptance of Haywood's guilt; the *Appeal to Reason* and the *Miners Magazine* for left-wing bitterness. For a lively modern treatment, see Stewart Holbrook, *The Rocky Mountain Revolution.*

The Panic

The 1907 bank runs were vividly described by every newspaper. For what went on behind the scenes, see the testimony given during the Congressional investigations of the U.S. Steel Corporation (Stanley Committee Hearings) and the so-called "money trust" (Pujo Committee Hearings). Morgan's role is also described in Herbert L. Satterlee, *J. Pierpont Morgan, an Intimate Portrait;* Bishop William Morris, *Memories of a Happy Life;* Thomas W. Lamont, *Henry P. Davison;* Frederick Lewis Allen, *The Great Pierpont Morgan;* John A. Garraty, "A Lion in the Street," *American Heritage,* June, 1957.

The Great White Fleet

For good general accounts of the Navy's world cruise, see Franklin Matthews, *With the Battle Fleet;* H. Kent Hewitt, "The Around the World Cruise," *Shipmate,* July, 1958; and dispatches that appeared almost daily throughout the voyage—especially those in the New York *Sun, Evening Mail, World* and *Herald.* A sample of Europe's forebodings can be found in the London *Daily Mail, Times,* and *Evening News* during the days just before departure. President Roosevelt's views are partly described in his

Autobiography, but his secret worries about Japan lie unpublished in National Archives' voluminous files about the voyage. Japan's actual enthusiasm can best be gauged from a glance at the *Yokahama Boyaki Shimpo,* October 17, 1908.

The Dash to the Pole

They all had a book in them: Frederick A. Cook, *My Attainment of the Pole* and *Return from the Pole;* Robert E. Peary, *The North Pole;* Robert A. Bartlett, *The Log of Bob Bartlett;* Donald B. MacMillan, *How Peary Reached the Pole;* George Borup, *A Tenderfoot with Peary;* Matthew A. Henson, *A Negro Explorer at the North Pole.* For the great controversy, it's absolutely essential to follow the pro-Cook New York *Herald* and the pro-Peary *Times* through September-November, 1909. W. T. Stead has some devastating blasts at Peary in the *Review of Reviews* during this period, and Sir Philip Gibbs offers a counter-attack against Cook in his *Adventures in Journalism.* A good standard book on the story—William H. Hobbs, *Peary;* and a fascinating recent one—John Edward Weems, *Race for the Pole.* For a little-known gem, see Peary's touching lines in memory of George Borup, Yale University, *History of the Class of 1907.*

The Cosmopolites

Edward VII's death and funeral produced some memorable accounts: Sir Philip Gibbs, *Adventures in Journalism;* Allan Nevins, *Henry White: Thirty Years of American Diplomacy;* Archie Butt, *Taft and Roosevelt; the Intimate Letters of Archie Butt;* Vol. I, pp. 426-430; "A King's Funeral as Reported by Theodore Roosevelt," *American Heritage,* December, 1954. For Roosevelt's royal progress through Europe: Lawrence Abbott, *Impressions of Theodore Roosevelt; The Letters of Theodore Roosevelt,* Vol. VII, edited by Elting E. Morison. International marriages during the period were covered meticulously by the *New York Times* and breezily by the *World.* The transatlantic social whirl has many fine observers: Consuelo Vanderbilt Balsan, *The Glitter and the Gold;* James Laver, *Edwardian Promenade;* A. Heckstall-Smith, *Sacred Cowes;* Virginia Cowles, *Gay Monarch,* to name a few.

Women Triumphant

The anti-suffrage forces boasted some heavy artillery: James M. Buckley, *The Wrong and Peril of Woman Suffrage;* Sir Almroth Wright, *The Un-*

expurgated Case against Woman Suffrage; Anti-Suffrage Essays by Massachusetts Women; almost any issue of *The Ladies' Home Journal* and the old *Life* magazine; the *New York Times* when sufficiently aroused. For a lively story of the British women's counter-attack, see Sylvia Pankhurst, *The Suffragette Movement: an Intimate Account of Persons and Ideals.* Accounts of the American movement include Harriot Stanton Blatch, *Challenging Years;* Carrie Chapman Catt and Nettie Rogers Shuler, *Woman Suffrage and Politics;* Belle Squire, *The Woman Movement in America.* The great 1912 parade was well covered by *Harper's Weekly,* the New York *Tribune, Post, World,* and the still skeptical *Times.*

Big Man Off Campus

The Baltimore *Sun* is indispensable for the day-to-day story of the 1912 convention. Most of the key figures later turned out their own versions of the battle: W. F. McCombs, *Making Woodrow Wilson President;* W. G. McAdoo, *Crowded Years;* Mary B. Bryan, *Memoirs of William Jennings Bryan;* Champ Clark, *My Quarter Century of American Politics;* Josephus Daniels, *The Wilson Era;* Mrs. J. Borden Harriman, *From Pinafores to Politics.* For the interludes at Sea Girt, see Joseph Tumulty, *Woodrow Wilson as I Knew Him;* Eleanor Wilson McAdoo, *The Woodrow Wilsons.* There's also the monumental Ray Stannard Baker, *Woodrow Wilson, Life and Letters,* plus two new interpretations: Arthur S. Link, *Wilson: The Road to the White House,* and Arthur Walworth, *Woodrow Wilson, American Prophet.*

Children at Work

Much of the contemporary literature seems too lurid to have been fully effective: John Spargo, *The Bitter Cry of the Children;* Edwin Markham, *Children in Bondage;* and Bessie Van Vorst, *The Cry of the Children,* and so forth. On the other hand, the steady flow of bulletins issued by The National Child Labor Committee are calm, factual, and thoroughly devastating. The cause was also helped by the tendency of the child labor advocates to hang themselves: to wit, Thomas R. Dawley, *The Child That Toileth Not;* F. B. Gordan's article in *Social Service Magazine,* Vol. V (1902), pp. 148-149; "Argument for Child Labor," *Literary Digest,* March 23, 1912. The struggle in Georgia is well covered by E. H. Davidson's *Child Labor Legislation in the Southern Textile States;* "Child Labor in Georgia," NCLC *Bulletin No. 194;* items appearing from time to time in the Atlanta

Journal and *Georgian* in 1913. Data on the management of certain Georgia mills has been drawn from *Davison's Textile Blue Book, 1905-06.*

The Last Summer

The assassination of Franz Ferdinand is covered by Joachim Remak, *Sarajevo;* James Cameron, *1914;* and the *New York Times,* June 29, 1914. For a picture of the lazy July that followed, I relied mainly on newspapers from a cross-section of cities: Washington, San Francisco, Philadelphia, Grand Forks, N.D., Atlanta, Cheyenne, Little Rock, New York, Muskogee, Okla., Denver, Houston, and Chicago. For the coming of war to Britain, see James Laver, *Edwardian Promenade;* Lady Diana Cooper, *The Rainbow Comes and Goes;* Viscount Edward Grey, *Twenty-five Years;* the *Sphere* and the *Illustrated London News.* America's sad awakening can be traced in any of the papers already cited; also, in such magazines as *World's Work, Literary Digest, Outlook, Current Opinion,* and *Review of Reviews* throughout that frightful autumn.

Index

355

61, 64, 65; and Morgan, 68, 79 ff.,
181, 205; and "Muckrakers," 90;
and Navy, 206 ff.; and Nobel Prize,
149; and Northern Securities case,
67-68, 80-82; and Panama Canal,
149, 222; and Peary, 226-227, 231,
255; and Progressive Party, 317;
and San Francisco fire, 148; and
suffrage, 273, 280; and "Tennis
Cabinet," 65, 223, 224, 225; and
"trust busting," 80-82; and unions,
84-86, 165; and Wall Street, 65, 180-
181, 188, 190, 194, 197-198, 200, 203-
204, 205; and Wilson, 317-318
Roosevelt, Mrs. Theodore, 259
Roosevelt, 226, 228, 229, 231-236, 242,
243, 245, 246, 247, 249, 250, 252, 255
Root, Elihu, 58, 60, 81, 86, 204, 209
Root, Robert K., 290
Rosen, Baroness, 274
Ross, E. A., 69
Rossi, opera singer, 129, 135
Rudisill, Mrs. Jessie, 146
Ruef, Abe, 130
Rullman, Fred, 129
Russell, Charles Edward, 89
Russell, L. T., 302, 303
Russell, Lillian, 278, 336
Russell, Sam, 169, 172, 173, 177
Ruth, Babe, 221, 331
Ryan, Thomas Fortune, 192, 293, 296,
303, 304, 307, 312, 313, 314
Ryter, L. E., 141

Sacramento *Union,* 211
Saint Nicholas Magazine, 329
Salome, 171
Sanad Khan Montas es Sultaneh, 261
San Francisco *Call,* 120
San Francisco *Chronicle,* 337
San Francisco earthquake and fire,
122 ff.
Santo Domingo, 223, 334
Santos-Dumont, Alberto, 98
Sarajevo, 332-333, 334

Satterlee, Herbert, 185, 192, 195, 197,
205
Saulsbury, Sen. Willard, 313
Schiff, Jacob, 71-72, 73, 74, 78
Schley, W. S., 251
Schmitz, Eugene, 123, 130, 133-134, 214
"School Days," 218, 306
Schubert, Rudy, 121, 125, 131, 133, 141,
143, 144, 145
Schuster, George, 219, 220
Schwab, Charlie, 115
Scofield, J. M., 85-86
Scott, Lt., 302
Scott, Robert F., 255
Scotti, Antonio, 121, 125, 129, 132
Seager, Henry Rogers, 284
Searight, Frank, 141
Sebern, O. V., 172
Seddon, Alfred E., 326
Seegloo, 233, 245
Seligman, Isaac, 258
Sells-Floto Circus, 355
Sembrich, Marcella, 132, 136, 137
Sentimental Journey, 168
"September Morn," 319, 329
Seymour, Sir Edward, 15, 27, 37
Sezinov, Sergei, 336
"Shame of the Cities," 89
Shamrock IV, 336
Shaw, Anna Howard, 278, 283, 287
Shaw, George Bernard, 6
Sheffield, D. Z., 8
Sheldon, Edward W., 205
Shelley, Percy B., 205
Sheppard, Eli T., 144
Sheppard, Mrs. Eli T., 144-145
Sherman Antitrust Act, 67, 68, 82, 160
Sherry, Louis, 104, 106, 182, 184
Sherry's, 104-105, 109, 118, 119, 187
Shiba, Col., 22, 35
Shively, Sen. Benjamin F., 307
Sinclair, Upton, 90
Skinner, Mrs. Otis, 282
Smith, Arthur, 19, 39
Smith, Big Jim, 290-291
Smith, Hoke, 322

INDEX

Smith, Mary (Polly), Condit, 12, 16, 30, 31, 33, 37
smoking: McKinley on, 5; by women, 218, 274
Socco, Mary, 116
Social Service, 323
Society, 104 ff., 264 ff.
"Some of These Days . . ." 283
South Pole, discovery of, 255
Spalding, Jack J., 325
Spanish-American War, 7
Spencer, Anna Garland, 287
Sperry, Charles, 212-213, 215-217
Sphere, 340
Spinks, Sen., 328
Springfield *Republican,* 179
"Square Deal," 222
Squiers, Fargo, 20
Squiers, Herbert, 13, 20, 26, 31
Squiers, Mrs. Herbert, 12, 13, 19, 26, 37
Squire, Belle, 287
Standard Oil, 77, 89, 200
Stanton, Elizabeth Cady, 275, 280
"Star-Spangled Banner," 302
Stead, W. T., 253
Steele, Charles, 68
Steel Preferred, 78
Steensby, P. H. P., 253
Steffens, Lincoln, 89
Stetson, James, 142, 143
Steunenberg, Frank, 151, 152, 158, 168, 171, 173, 175
Steunenberg, Mrs. Frank, 152, 174-175
Stevens, Ashton, 121
Stewart, Marie, 283
Stillman, James, 105, 185, 190, 192, 193, 201
stock exchange, 69, 72 ff., 180-181, 195 ff., 258
Stone, Gov. William A., 85, 313
Stone, Sen., 312
strikes, 83 ff., 151, 158, 161, 162
"Strike Up the Band," 218
Strömgren, Prof., 254
Strong, Benjamin, 193, 201, 202
Strouts, Capt., 31

submarines, 5, 6, 230
subway, 100
suffrage, 272 ff.
Sugiyama, Chancellor, 15
Sullivan, Boetius, 315
Sullivan, Dennis, 125, 134
Sullivan, John L., 65, 225
Sullivan, Mark, 222
Sullivan, Roger, 294, 315
Sullivan, Mrs. Roger, 315
Sulzer, Cong., 311, 312
Sverdrup, Otto, 227, 249, 250
Swann, Laura, 118
Swanson, Claude, 248
swimming, 274-275, 331
"Sylvia," 338
Synge, J. M., 318

Taft, Helen, 317
Taft, William Howard, 180, 221-222, 247, 295, 317
Taggert, Tom, 294, 314
Tammany, 296, 299, 308, 309, 312, 313
tango, 269, 329, 335-336
Tarbell, Ida, 89, 273, 276
tariff, 44, 300
Taylor, Anna Edna, 273
Taylor, Charlie, 91
telephone, 100, 291
Tennessee Coal & Iron Co., 199, 200, 201, 203
tennis, 221, 222, 274, 334, 337
"Tennis Cabinet," 65, 223, 224, 225
Tevis, Harry, 132, 137, 138
Thaw, Harry, 115
theater: *Captain Jinks of the Horse Marines,* 171; *Chocolate Soldier,* 255; *The Dictator,* 121; *Floradora Girl,* 5; *The Hen Pecks,* 269; *Mamzelle Champagne,* 115; *Pink Lady,* 263; *Playboy of the Western World,* 318; *Potash and Perlmutter,* 284; *Salome,* 171; *Wild Rose,* 105; *Ziegfeld Follies,* 205
"There's a Long, Long Trail . . . ," 341
"There's No Place like Home," 218

367